MAKING

GIRLS INTO WOMEN

American Women's Writing

and the Rise of Lesbian

Identity

KATHRYN R. KENT

DUKE UNIVERSITY PRESS

Durham & London

2003

© 2003 Duke University Press

All rights reserved. Printed in the United States of

America on acid-free paper. ∞ Designed by Amy Ruth Buchanan.

Typeset in Sabon by G & S Typesetters, Inc. Library of Congress

Cataloging-in-Publication Data appear on the

last printed page of this book.

In loving memory of

Ruth Hughes Kent (1903–1996)

and

Brian Selsky (1967–1997)

❧

CONTENTS

❧

ACKNOWLEDGMENTS

Writing this book would not have been possible without the support of many individuals and institutions. In graduate school, I was lucky to be surrounded by an inspiring, fierce group of colleagues, including Amanda Berry, Benjamin Weaver, Brian Selsky, Gus Stadler, Jennifer Doyle, Johannes von Moltke, John Vincent, Jonathan Flatley, José Muñoz, Kerstin Barndt, Mark Simpson, Maura Nolan, and Samira Kawash. Much of this book began in conversation with these friends, and their work continues to challenge and inspire me. I am also deeply grateful to the members of my dissertation committee for their support and critical acuity in reading this work in its early drafts. I benefited greatly from Thomas Ferraro's infectious enthusiasm and useful commentary. Cathy Davidson has been unfailingly generous with her (always excellent) advice. Janice Radway first opened my eyes to the complexities of reading and has served, as my teacher and my friend, as an exemplary model of passionate engagement. Michael Moon, in his absorption in all things queer and his sheer pleasure in teasing out the heart of the matter, showed me a whole new way to think about literature and encouraged this project from the very beginning. Eve Kosofsky Sedgwick has provided me with all the intellectual, political, and social resources available to her and more—I have learned and benefited so much from her work and her amazing presence.

Two other teachers deserve special mention here, Wendy Brown and Suzanne Graver, whose examples of scholarship and pedagogy, as well as their friendship, sustained me as an undergraduate in ways too numerous to count. More recently, as my colleague, Suzanne's perceptive and thorough readings of this manuscript have made it a better book.

Indeed, I have benefited enormously from the generosity of all my colleagues in the English Department at Williams College. I thank in particular Larry Raab and Louise Glück, who each, in different ways, have challenged me to stay close to the text, and I thank Stephen Fix, who appreciates my obsession with details. John Limon aided and abetted my absorption in Stein—his appreciation of difficulty made him an especially helpful, smart reader of this book in its many drafts. Christopher Pye brought to this project his intense, incisive scrutiny. His exhaustive and generous comments helped me to articulate what was at stake in this project. I also thank my former colleagues at Arizona State University and Sarah Lawrence College, especially Lyde Sizer, Mary LaChapelle, Mary Porter, and Bella Brodzki. My students at Sarah Lawrence College, Arizona State University, and Williams College have helped to shape my thinking on many of the issues at the heart of this book. I thank especially Laura Bush and H. Michelle Phillips for their able research assistance. I am also grateful to the staff of the Williams College Children's Center and the Colorado College Children's Center, who gave my son loving care while I completed this project. Thanks, also, to the staff at the Colorado College Library, who were patient with my numerous requests for obscure materials.

Funding from various sources supported my research and writing at various stages. For fellowships, I thank the Mellon Foundation in the Humanities and the American Council of Learned Societies. A sabbatical leave from Williams College enabled me to complete this book.

An earlier version of chapter 1 appeared in *American Literature* 69.1 (March 1997): 39–65; and a portion of chapter 3 was originally published in the *Review of Contemporary Fiction* 13.3 (fall 1993): 89–96, under the title, "'Lullaby for a Ladies' Lady': Lesbian Identity in *Ladies Almanack*."

At Duke University Press Ken Wissoker proved himself to be as generous an editor as he is a friend. He knew just when to leave me alone and when to push. A sincere thanks to Christine Habermaas, whose expert and timely editorial assistance I could not have done without. Many thanks, also, to the two anonymous readers for Duke Press, whose thoughtful, detailed comments were invaluable to me as I revised this manuscript.

I am also indebted to the many dear friends who have supported me during the completion of this book, especially Anna Bean; Beauty Bragg and Poncho McFarland; Lisa Duggan; David Eppel and Victor Paquette; Monica Escalante and Daniel Raffin; Elizabeth Feder and Mark Johnson; Elizabeth Freeman; Jonathan Goldberg; Janet Helson and Betty Lundquist; Andrea, Malcolm, Uly, and Gideon Lucard; Julie Marler; Molly Mc-Garry; Mandy Merck; Kenda Mutongi and Alan De Gooyer; Barry Sarchett; Jana Sawicki and Laurie Benjamin; Caroline Schneider, Doug Hacker, and Ethan; Hal Sedgwick; Cathy Silber; Willard Spiegelman; Kim Springer; Sasha Torres; Chris Waters; and Heather Zwicker.

My family has provided me with much-needed encouragement and assistance throughout this project. My thanks to Marvin Weaver, Jill Stearns, Jane and Scott Stearns, Ransom Weaver, and Chris and Kristi Thorndike-Kent for their good humor and support. Minnie Bruce Pratt and Leslie Feinberg continue to inspire and challenge me with their own writing and activism. My parents, John Kent and Shirley M. Kent, have always stood behind me, even when they weren't sure what I was up to. My father taught me the value of a strong argument, and my mother indulged and encouraged in me, especially by her own example, an obsession with books. Amanda Berry provided intensity, clarity, and necessary distraction. Regina Kunzel read numerous drafts of this project; her provocative insight and intelligence have made this book and my life immeasurably more rich. Simon Bruce Kent brings endless joy. And Benjamin Weaver aided in ways too numerous to list here. His patience, his care, his brilliance, and his love make everything else possible.

Brian Selsky was a dear friend, coconspirator, partner in culinary adventure, and the first reader of much of this manuscript. I miss him, always. Ruth Hughes Kent wished in 1920 to live a life of the mind. That dream thwarted, she went on to support her entire family, myself included. To these two extraordinary people this book is dedicated.

INTRODUCTION

❧

"Mothers are the *best* lovers in the whole world," declares Jo March, the heroine of Louisa May Alcott's immensely popular "girls' story," *Little Women*.[1] What are we to make of such a statement? Clearly we cannot import contemporary versions of lesbian identity into a novel written and serialized from 1868 to 1869. It would be anachronistic to take Jo's words as evidence of her lesbianism when she displays none of the characteristics that, according to Lisa Duggan, define the "new lesbian subjectivity" that was emerging in the late-nineteenth-century United States. These characteristics include "see[ing one's] self as an erotic subject—as a woman whose desire for women was felt as a fundamental component of her sense of self, marking her as erotically different from most other women," and identifying in some way with "public lesbian identities and communities."[2] Yet, at the same time, it would be wrong to read Jo's declaration as simply another example of an attempt to sentimentalize mothers and motherhood. Instead, in this volume I propose that modern lesbian identity has its roots in the United States not just or even primarily in sexology and medicalization but in white, middle-class "women's culture," distinguished in part by its central focus on the mother.[3] Foucauldian-inspired studies of the emergence of sexual identity have tended to focus on a particular set of public discourses, primarily those intended to regulate male gender and sexual behavior, in order to describe the formation of the "homosexual." In this volume I look elsewhere—to what has been termed "women's" or "sentimental" writing, and to its interlocking discourses of gender and sexuality, of racial and class embodiment, and of material production and reproduction—in order to offer one account of the emergence of "the lesbian" in the United States.

Specifically, in this book I demonstrate how the subject-forming structure of what Richard Brodhead terms "disciplinary intimacy,"[4] the intense maternal-pedagogical system that compelled young girls to internalize the mandates of bourgeois womanhood, ended up inciting in them other, less-normative desires and identifications, including ones that I call "protolesbian" and "queer." Through close readings of selected postbellum texts, including Harriet Beecher Stowe's *Oldtown Folks* (1869), the works of Alcott, and Emma Dunham Kelley's *Megda* (1891), I not only elucidate how texts represent queer erotics but also theorize how texts might produce them in readers. I then trace how queer female identities, identifications, and desires are transmitted and critiqued in the early twentieth century, by examining works by Djuna Barnes, Gertrude Stein, Marianne Moore, and Elizabeth Bishop, as well as the queer subject-forming effects of another modern invention, the Girl Scouts.

Even though it would be historically inaccurate to label women in the nineteenth century "lesbian," it would also be a mistake, as Lisa Moore points out, to assume that there are no connections between earlier forms of same-sex desire and identification and their manifestations at the present time.[5] I use the term "protolesbian" as a way to signal a historical connection to modern lesbian subjectivity while at the same time acknowledging the difference made by the shift from a sexuality organized primarily through acts to one defined *as* identity. "Protolesbian," in other words, is intended to designate a preidentity formation that nevertheless functions as a form of protoidentity. Protolesbian subjects are those for whom assumptions about their sexualities or sexual practices are connected to assumptions about their *being*.

I employ the term "queer," on the other hand, as a more encompassing and therefore more transhistoric term that may include any act or proto-identity that exists outside the realm of bourgeois, heteronormative reproduction and its correlative ideology of gender roles. "Queer" is not meant to carry the same politically radical connotations that it does when used in contemporary parlance: instead, I intend it to be understood as a term that is simultaneously oppositional and nonspecific, in a way that "proto-lesbian" is not.

My aim in using both terms is to call into question the teleology of identity that assumes that identifications and desires automatically lead to identities. As I demonstrate in this book, queer forms of identification and desire do not always produce lesbian identities. Nevertheless, I also explore the connections between preidentity forms of same-sex desire and identification and the emergence of the lesbian as an identity.

Indeed, the question of these connections is what motivates me in this project. In focusing on the discursive production of protolesbian and queer identities and identifications, I provide a way out of what I see as the often-paralyzing opposition between the search for lesbian visibility and the valorization of lesbian invisibility that has divided lesbian-affirmative scholarship: either they *are* there and we have the incontrovertible evidence to prove it, or they are not, and that is what makes them queer.[6]

Scholarship that emphasizes lesbian visibility often looks for evidence of what Marylynne Diggs, following Terry Castle, terms "libidinal self-awareness" or documented sexual contact as proof of lesbian existence.[7] Other scholars reject visibility altogether (and often, by extension, any form of historically specific argument) and focus on the unrepresentable, the invisible, and the abject as a space or trope of lesbian (im)possibility.[8] Ironically, such positions seem to have an inverse relation to the idea that there are historical connections between temporally distinct forms of female-female desire: lesbian invisibility often sets out to prove the existence of lesbians across time, whereas lesbian visibility shows how hard it is to claim that lesbians ever existed prior to the twentieth century.

Although male-male homoerotics and sexualities in the nineteenth century, through the efforts of recent scholarship,[9] have become opulently and abundantly visible, lesbian-affirmative scholarship has struggled with the apparent lack, at least in America, of visible representations of female-female homoeroticism or protolesbian identities prior to the twentieth century. Instead, for the most part, female-female sexualities have continued to languish in the rosy, undefinable "female world of love and friendship" first delineated by Carroll Smith-Rosenberg and Lillian Faderman.[10] In its similarities to Adrienne Rich's "lesbian continuum,"[11] this line of inquiry often threatens to sacrifice the specificities of historical practice for the hazy proposition that women's relationships with other women in general (within the white middle class) were loving, eroticized, and intimate, regardless of their psychosexual positioning in relation to other women and men.

Yet, although they share a kind of bland, universalizing approach to female-female interactions, the political intentions and effects of the descriptions of Smith-Rosenberg, Faderman, and Rich are almost diametrically opposed. Rich claims all female-female relationships as lesbian, whereas Smith-Rosenberg and Faderman, in describing white bourgeois women's relationships with one another in the nineteenth century, firmly imply or openly assert that none of them could have been lesbian.[12]

Of course, this refusal makes good political sense when attempting to trace the cultural and historical specificities of sexuality (and gender) in the United States and when trying, at least in Smith-Rosenberg's case, to prevent the imposition of present, normative post-Freudian notions of female sexuality onto a quite different past.[13] Obviously, it would be anachronistic to apply contemporary standards of lesbian identity to women in a period in which the term "homosexual" (as well as the term "heterosexual") did not even exist.[14] But to assert that there are no possible continuities between modern lesbian identity and the recent past is to act as if lesbianism was solely an invention of sexology or medicine and has no roots elsewhere in culture.[15]

Moreover, the fact that the women within romantic friendships seemed to feel no need to hide or defend their relationships, or to censor their frank expressions of love and what often sounds like desire, means to Smith-Rosenberg and Faderman that these desires must have been nonsexual, or at least indeterminate, because if they were sexual they could not have been expressed so openly without at least some manifestation of anxiety on the part of the writers or the communities of which they were a part. According to this theory, Jo's reference to mothers as lovers must be nonsexual because it is so openly asserted. Smith-Rosenberg and Faderman may be too quick to impose a model of the closet, to use Eve Kosofsky Sedgwick's terms, back onto the nineteenth century. They acknowledge that the relationships they analyze may be sensual, but both of their arguments are predicated on the idea that the women within them lack "libidinal self-awareness." [16]

As Moore has perceptively pointed out, this assumption stems in part from, at least in Faderman's case, a desire to see nineteenth-century romantic friendships as based in gender affiliation rather than sexual desire.[17] It may also reflect the contemporary political imperative that many lesbian-affirmative scholars and activists have felt in order to argue that being a lesbian has been less about sex than it has been about a form of protofeminist connection. Unfortunately, this stance also reiterates the stereotypes associated with white, middle-class femininity as sexless and innocent/ignorant of sexual mores; stereotypes that were used in the nineteenth century and continue to be used to argue for white women's "purity" by making a supposed contrast between white women's "innocence" and the sexual knowledge of working-class women and women of color.

Smith-Rosenberg's choice to emphasize the mother-daughter relationship as the paradigm for all the other relationships she analyzes situates the romantic friendship within the familial structure. Because Smith-Rosenberg automatically assumes that such familial relationships are, by definition, nonsexual, she views even those relationships that are in actuality nonfamilial as inherently also nonsexual.[18] I take the opposite position, however, by arguing that familial relationships between mothers and daughters, as well as nonfamilial relationships between women, are at times openly eroticized in nineteenth-century sentimental culture.[19]

Such relationships and the protolesbian identifications, identities, and desires that accompany them emerge in conjunction with the rise of what Brodhead calls the "domestic-tutelary" emphasis in U.S. culture. His thesis is that in nineteenth-century America disciplinary power is not anonymous, as it is in Michel Foucault's account of the modern prison, but is instead personalized, most immediately and intensely in the role of the mother.[20] Children internalize the mother's example and her gaze, not through fear of punishment but through the power of love. Loving guidance replaces corporal punishment as the preferred mode of character (re)formation. Brodhead argues that a set of cultural institutions come together to produce the disciplinary subject: not only is the family rewritten as the site of loving guidance provided preeminently by the mother, but schools share the philosophy of "spar[ing] the rod," and literature itself, through the processes of sentimental identification, becomes another site for the enactment of "maternal tutelage." Drawing on Brodhead's revision of the Foucauldian historical account of the subject and on queer revisions of Freud's theory of identification, I investigate the intense, erotic subject-forming effects of this overlap, and often confusion, of spaces: What happens when the distance between the family, the school, and the book, often rigorously enforced in antebellum U.S. culture, begins to break down in the second half of the nineteenth century? I will argue that the subject-forming project at the heart of disciplinary intimacy threatens to queer, even as it regulates, the female subject.

꧁ꕤ꧂

Sentimental culture maintains itself through striving to uphold a series of ideological distinctions, all of which have gendered, sexual, economic, and racial implications: distinctions between mothers and others (nonrepro-ductive women, men); private and public; domestic work and work (in-dustrial, mass productive, overtly economic) that threatens the sanctity of the domestic sphere; proper reproduction (seen as a property of *white* womanhood) and a reproductivity that is not properly controlled (often associated with women of color and/or working-class women). To be a woman in the nineteenth century *is* to be a mother—to be normatively gendered as feminine requires one to reproduce and to do the work of rais-ing children, the "labor of love" within the domestic sphere. The mother is also a sexual identity, albeit a deeroticized one: to mother, one almost always must engage in procreative sex; that is, sex defined by its ability to produce offspring as opposed to pleasure.[21] Women who do not mother risk being thought of not only as improperly gendered but also, as I will argue in chapter 1, as "queerly" sexualized, as do women, ironically, who reproduce too little or too much. Often a failure to mother or to mother properly is also conceived of as an improperly limited relation to or ex-cessive fixation with labor (a failure to preserve the domestic as a space ideologically separate from the economic), and this is mirrored by other failures of self-regulation—all of which are sexualized and sometimes racialized. Bourgeois, white heteromaternality thus gains its cultural cen-trality in part through its supposed distance from what I will establish is a form of protolesbian or queer female identity, distinguished by its failures at both reproduction and production.

Increasingly in the postbellum period, however, these distinctions be-gin to break down. As the business of forming (especially) white, female, middle-class subjects shifts from the home to the school, women's col-lege, workplace, boardinghouse, and other spaces that I term "semipublic/semiprivate" (including the imaginative space provided by novel reading), the role of the mother is augmented and sometimes replaced altogether by other women, and the boundaries between the domestic and other, more public, realms begin to dissolve. Is the classroom a public or a private space? Is the factory floor a location that is part of the economic sphere, or does this space necessarily contain within it elements of the domestic? Does a teacher or a supervisor serve as a mother-away-from-home or something else?

In the shift away from the home, a new form of what I will call "identi-ficatory erotics" emerges: in undergoing the disciplinary rigors of increas-ingly rationalized forms of subject formation, girls not only want to be but increasingly want to have the teacher, supervisor, coworker, Girl Scout leader, older poet, and perhaps even their mothers; and such desires, to be and to have, become at times indistinguishable from one another. The mother's unstable proximity to other women, as well as the proximity of domestic space to these new semipublic/semiprivate spaces, provide opportunities for the always already eroticized homosocial relations within them to emerge (at least sometimes) explicitly as such. Not only is mothering thoroughly queered but queers begin to mother.

My use of the term "identificatory erotics" brings together two narratives of subject formation often perceived to be at odds: Foucauldian-inflected historical accounts of the emergence of the modern (female) subject and queer revisions of Freudian psychoanalysis. On the New Historicist side, contemporary theorists of sentimentality, including Brodhead, use the term "identification" quite frequently, without considering its psychoanalytic connotations. Instead, it is employed as a term to describe the various ways in which characters within texts as well as readers are affiliated through forms of shared sentiment, sometimes to the degree that one subject, for better or worse, is unable to distinguish herself from another. Nonetheless, such critics' descriptions of the workings of disciplinary culture often rely on what is essentially an account of identification to describe the formation of the subject: in internalizing the gaze of the "other," the subject takes up that gaze, thereby surveying herself.[22] Regulation shifts from being an external to an internal process, and in that shift the subject is transformed. But how exactly does this happen?

Foucault has been rightly criticized for his inability to account for the formation of the individual subject:[23] in contrast, both sentimental fiction and psychoanalysis offer intricate representations of this process. That they should share this focus should not be surprising, because, as Diana Fuss has noted in her compelling history of identification, Freud himself viewed his attempts to theorize identification as a way to rationalize theories of "sympathy," the very same theories that underlie sentimental culture.[24] For Freud this included a necessary narrowing and taxonomizing of what he viewed as an ascientific, "literary" account of the subject. In this volume I restage this encounter between literature, history, and psychoanalysis, seeking instead to understand what revisions these historically specific, literary representations of and incitements to identification could offer to a psychoanalytic perspective.

Freud describes identification most simply as "an emotional tie with another person," the process by which desire and loss are converted into particular forms of subjectivity.[25] In its most normative account of the subject,

Freudian psychoanalysis insists that to be "healthy" (always at best a precarious state of being), a subject must achieve "successful" oedipalization, which includes attaining "mature" (hetero)sexuality, and involves, indeed mandates, the lining up of one's gender identifications and sexual desires with the binaries of a narrowly conceived heterosexuality.[26] For example, to become properly oedipalized, a little girl must replace what is an originary desire for her mother with an identification with her: when successful, this firmly genders the girl (as a woman) and redirects her desire toward a man.

This process of identification may not always be harmonious, Freud argues, yet "normal" oedipalization always matches up biological sex with gender and with heterosexuality: a boy identifies with a man, as a man, in order to possess a woman. Even when things go awry and subjects desire members of the "same" gender, this occurs, according to Freud, because these subjects misidentify. For example, he presents the case of a male homosexual who instead of transferring his love from his mother to another woman identifies with her and desires other men.[27] Thus, Freud's identificatory schemas always preserve gender binarisms, making it impossible for a woman to both identify as and desire another woman. According to traditional psychoanalytic accounts, desire and identification are always oppositional processes: one cannot have and be the same object.[28]

Recent work in queer theory makes clear the ways in which Freud, at his most normative, wanted to fix spatially and hierarchize temporally what is an endless process.[29] In the Freudian narrative, it is *the* mother and father within *the* family who constitute the child's sexual and social identity; anyone else is simply a mother substitute or a father figure. This preserves an ahistorical heterosexuality as *the* (re)productive process both biologically and socially, and fixes all such models in an ahistorical, oedipal time. Any identification after the "originary" ones is always just a return to or a repetition of these first ties, rather than an identification with and desire for a historically and culturally specific "other" that takes place at a particular time and place. Repeatedly, as Fuss demonstrates in tracing the trajectory of Freud's thinking, Freud seeks to narrow an almost unlimited range of identificatory possibilities into a set of rigidly gendered (and by extension heterosexualized) subject positions, which in turn reflect an originary account of the subject based in what is for Freud an ahistorical libido.[30]

Such a privileging of an ahistorical ideal of desire posits the existence of the subject (whether as pure drives or as a body) prior to the social. Theories of social transformation based on this definition of desire can often only conceive of resistance as a momentary eruption of, in Lacanian terms, the imaginary into the symbolic, or as a primary asociality that always threatens any illusory social stability or sense of identity. Such theories also tend often to reproduce, rather than undermine, an essential sexual difference, which is grounded in models of the preoedipal "feminine" and oedipal "masculine" that, even in their recasting of gender binaries, repeat an essential heterosexualization of psychic and social reality.[31] The theories offer no real possibility of imagining any social or historical transformation in the ways gender and sexuality are lived, internally and externally.

For example, most tempting for this project are the critiques of identification posed by queer critics such as Leo Bersani and Teresa de Lauretis.[32] In both cases, in response to what they see as a dangerous crossing of identity boundaries between gay or lesbian and heterosexual subjects (not to mention between lesbians and gays), a crossing produced by the instability of identification, they posit instead a separatist notion of desire (grounded in an ahistorical presocial or what Bersani often terms prepolitical or apolitical space).[33] Although it may be strategically powerful to imagine an originary (gay/lesbian/queer) desire (for the sake of counteracting the constant sociocultural attempts to erase and eradicate such desires with an essential psychic model of resistance), these accounts remain unable to describe the ways in which specific historical shifts make thinkable specific forms of desire, identification, and identity (including those idealized as outside history or the political). Moreover, these accounts also risk repeating the same old Freudian tropes of homosexuality as primitive and regressive, existing only in opposition to the social.

Other queer theorists, however, have significantly revised Freud by showing how identification (and the desire that always accompanies it) refuses an oppositional model of the (homo)sexual and the social.[34] According to this oppositional model, the existence of one is predicated on the repression of the other, as evidenced in the false distinction Freud tries to maintain between the homosexual and the homosocial, an opposition I am centrally concerned with overturning.[35] As Fuss eloquently puts it: "Identification is the point where the psychical/social distinction becomes impossibly confused and finally untenable."[36] Identification always requires an encounter with an "other" that is also an encounter with a history, a time, and a place, not only as instantiated in the "other" but also produced through the historically specific space of encounter itself (something Foucault insists on in his discussion of the importance of institutional space to the workings of power). Thus, by combining a Foucauldian model of disciplinary pedagogy with a revised psychoanalytic account of identification/desire, I offer a way to introduce the vagaries of history, of culture, and of location into what has been a narrow oedipal model.[37]

More specifically, this book will argue that relations between women within specific semipublic/semiprivate spaces in the late nineteenth century constitute a challenge not only to the opposition in Freudian psychoanalysis between the homosocial and the homosexual but also to that between identification and desire. As Judith Butler rightly declares, "It is important to consider that identification and desire can coexist, and that their formulation in terms of mutually exclusive oppositions serves a heterosexual matrix."[38] Revising Freud's account of primary narcissism, Mikkel Borch-Jacobsen emphasizes that the infant subject must first identify with an "other" in order to be able to desire at all, and that identification itself is a form of desire (the "desire to be"), which is fundamentally inseparable from the desire to have.[39] Butler puts forth a similar model: in her attempts to account more fully for a theory of the subject that does not make recourse to a "before," as well as for a theory of agency that resists falling back into either voluntarism or complete overdetermination, her theory of the iterability of the subject joins a Freudian-based theory of identification with a Foucauldian disciplinary model of self-formation and social formation. Subjectivity becomes a repeated process of identification.[40]

Nevertheless, Butler's work is also universalizing and transhistorical because, rhetorically, it seeks to insert itself into a similar tradition. Like Borch-Jacobsen's model, it risks essentializing the subject: it still relies on an originary "desire to be," which in this case is traced to Spinoza.[41] My project offers instead a particular, historically situated case study of identifications and their effects, as theorized and produced not only by a prior world represented within literary texts but by texts themselves. As I affiliate myself most closely with this genealogy of the subject, however, I also risk essentializing, especially in arguing that any particular psychoanalytic process inaugurates the subject. My aim here is not simply to reveal or to try to resolve the contradiction between the Foucauldian impulse to resist making claims about the truth of the subject, and the political, intellectual, and historical need to assert, against the overwhelming effects of silence, the presence of (homo)erotic desires and identifications, a need still served quite well by a revised psychoanalytic approach. Instead, I see this contradiction itself as a site of rich theoretical possibility. At its best, such a rethinking of the subject allows the specificities of history and culture to enter into (and thereby transform) the psychoanalytic scene. Although I attempt to imagine a psychoanalysis that is not essentialist, ultimately for me the risk of essentializing is worth taking if it makes legible what the force of heteronormativity often works so hard to obscure.

Despite its limits, psychoanalysis still provides a way to make sexual desires and identifications visible, to assert their presence through identifying the moments where discursive regimes overlap or stand in for one another. For example, the psychoanalytic concept of the symptom joins a discourse of the body to a discourse of (repressed) desire, the unconscious. Within the traditional psychoanalytic purview, however, such analyses usually (re)produce a pejorative "surface vs. depth" model of the subject (e.g., through the processes of "condensation," "displacement," and "transference"), where what appears on the surface is merely a stand-in for a deeper problem. Thus, a young woman's expressed desire for an older female acquaintance is really just a reaction to a repressed desire for her father, and homoerotic attachment is really just a displacement for a deeper, heteroerotic desire.[42]

I, however, refuse this surface-depth model; I attempt not to reveal the buried sexual secrets of the text but instead offer a reading of the surface *as* surface. I point out moments of discursive overlap; for example, where one discourse (labor) is intertwined with another (sex), so that to describe one is crucially to invoke the other without seeing either as prior or grounding. To do so is not only to challenge the conventions of psychoanalysis but also those of Foucauldian New Historicism. Whether one believes that sentimental fiction is a form of radical democratic affiliation or social normalization, it is the activity of identifying with others that distinguishes the sentimental project as an inevitable reading effect.[43] Yet few New Historical critics consider either the intricacies of this process or the (especially homo- but also hetero-) erotics produced by it. When they pay attention to erotics at all, critics either see them as furthering radical democratic possibility (although usually only male sentimental relations figure in this category) through eroticizing national union[44] or as ultimately furthering the processes of normalization. Girls may desire their mothers, but that desire is always in the service of and/or overruled by the inevitable marital closure that seals the girls' fates within the heteromater-

nal. (The majority of these examples deal only with female-female homoerotics, although recently this version of sentimentalism as normalization
has been extended somewhat to include male ones as well.)[45] Regardless
of critics' views of them, the possible erotic effects of disciplinary intimacy
are routinely subordinated to what is viewed as a more important or
"deeper" "political" argument and are rarely viewed as significant in and
of themselves.[46]

I do not dispute that queerness is inseparable from normalization, but
I argue that in internalizing the specific norms of femininity advocated by
sentimental, disciplinary culture, girls run the risk of desiring these ideals
as well. When historically specific models for identification other than the
heteromaternal become more available, rather than simply convert their
desires for "the mother" into desires to be her, girls begin to make other
erotic and identificatory attachments. In other words, protolesbian and
queer identifications and desires themselves begin to constitute a reverse
discourse to the heteromaternal.

I do not unequivocally celebrate queer identifications or desires as inherently radical or transgressive: identifying as a lesbian may also end up
having normalizing or normativizing effects. This point is obvious even
in Susan Warner's *The Wide, Wide World* (1850), a text that forms the
basis for Brodhead's understanding of what he terms "the workings of
disciplinary intimacy" and that may be considered, in Jane Tompkin's
words, "the Ur-text of the nineteenth-century United States."[47] Although
it has become commonplace to discuss the influence of the character Alice
Humphreys (the pious, Christian, older friend and mother substitute) on
Ellen Montgomery (the motherless heroine of the novel), and especially
to discuss the ways in which Alice encourages Ellen to become a self-
disciplining subject through inspiring Ellen's identificatory allegiances,
the erotic valences of this interaction have been for the most part overlooked.[48] The novel epitomizes the incitement to female-female identification at the same time that it appears to end in normalization.

Alice represents one example of the female equivalent of male patronage—that is, women's organized social and religious evangelism. Describing relationships between middle-class male patrons and the "gentle boys
from the dangerous classes" that these men "befriended," Michael Moon
has argued that "one can readily see how closely congruent a rhetoric
of seduction could be with discourses of middle-class philanthropy."[49]
Through her ministrations to the young orphan, Alice captivates Ellen—

she fervently desires to be just like Alice. In following Alice's model, Ellen gradually develops the essential values of domesticity: submission to patriarchal authority, self-control, and often silence. Her wish to be Alice is finally realized when Alice dies, and Ellen, through the processes of self-reformation, becomes as pious and submissive as Alice had been, prompting John, Alice's brother, to propose to her. Thus, when Ellen marries John, she is not only his wife but also, through internalizing Alice's model, his sister. And here the novel more than hints at the incestuous desires that motivate John's proposal and seal Ellen's fate as "true woman."

At the same time, however, Alice's fervent desire to convert and domesticate Ellen produces as a side effect homoerotic feeling. Her efforts to *be* Alice express a desire also to have her and to continue their homoerotic intimacy, forged most centrally in the text through the moments where the two young women pray and then weep in an abundance of tears, as in this passage:

> And they knelt together there on the moss beside the stone, where Ellen's head rested and her friend's folded hands were laid. It might have been two children speaking to their father, for the simplicity of that prayer; difference of age seemed to be forgotten, and what suited one suited the other. It was not without difficulty that the speaker carried it calmly through, for Ellen's sobs went nigh to check her more than once. When they rose Ellen silently sought her friend's arms again, and laying her face on her shoulder and putting both arms round her neck, she wept still,—but what different tears! It was like the gentle rain falling through sunshine, after the dark cloud and the thunder and the hurricane have passed by. And they kissed each other before either of them spoke.[50]

Here, crying and tears may stand in for sexual release and masturbation, which in *The Wide, Wide World* is definitely mutual.[51] As a textbook case of pedagogical power, these "physical intimacies" are channeled back into the greater good, toward Ellen's belief in God and her control over her unruly desires. When Alice asks after the two girls kiss, "'You will not forget your Bible and prayer again, Ellen?'"[52] the exchange illustrates the instabilities between conversion and perversion.

Although the terms of disciplinary intimacy may reinstate the heterosexual family, they may also enable other queer subject effects. Even within the space of the maternal pedagogical, such exercises of dominance, the processes by which subjects internalize regulatory systems through identification, may produce homoerotic desires, if only so as to subordinate them to obedience to God or husband.[53] At the heart of the maternal project lies the unstable erotics of identification, even if ostensibly these identifications seem to replicate the heterosexual, nuclear family.

The Wide, Wide World provides Ellen Montgomery with no other option than to stay within the confines of the bourgeois family: she may either take up a position as wife/sister to John, or remain a pseudodaughter to her Scottish relations. After the Civil War the model of female subject formation based in the primacy of the family is matched and at times replaced by a model that places an emphasis on the role played by various forms of extrafamilial cultures and locations in the production of selves. This emergence of semipublic/semiprivate spaces such as boarding schools, factories, and even mass-produced books is inseparable from the ideology of industrial capitalism in general and, in particular, from the changing ideologies of the production and reproduction of persons and things. These changing ideologies shake up and threaten to replace the old ideal that the production and reproduction of selves and things is firmly rooted in the literal and metaphorical idealization of a particular ideological vision of procreative sex, the model in which "natural" forms of production mirror "natural" forms of reproduction that is central to both bourgeois and marxist economics. This older (but by no means obsolete) model defines productive and reproductive labor through an idealization of use value that is itself based on a model of heterosexual reproduction. "Good" sex is that which produces a child, "bad" sex is that which either produces nothing and is wasted or that which produces too much and results in "excess" pleasure and desire; good labor is that which only produces use value, as opposed to the excess value—profit without work— that is generated by exchange. These definitions are challenged by new "unnatural" forms of labor and subject formation.

Although nineteenth-century texts such as Stowe's and Alcott's are alternately horrified and euphoric about the possibilities of "unnatural" (re)production—possibilities that are directly connected to "unnatural" forms of female subjectivity—modernist texts such as Gertrude Stein's *Tender Buttons* transform these possibilities into complex embodiments and theories of textual and sexual economy and value. In the process, queer female identity is rescued from its position as reviled "other" to heteromaternality, and is shown, in poems such as Moore's "An Octopus," to play a central role in the production of culture and even the nation, albeit not always with politically liberatory results.

By focusing on forms of queer reproduction, then, this volume joins other recent efforts to overturn the centrality of the heterosexual family (and by extension, a particular version of heterosexual sex) as both a metaphoric and literal model for the production and reproduction of culture.[54] I also show how efforts to limit models of cultural (re)production to the oedipal nuclear mother and father end up obscuring the rich, strange, and sometimes violent ways in which queer identities (in this case, queer female identities) are produced and transmitted.

Sedgwick has argued that the modern homo/heterosexual binary is "indicatively male" and that modern male homosociality (instantiated most often through the technologies of managerial capitalism) is predicated on the performative repression or denial of male homosexuality.[55] I assert that this break between the homosocial and the homosexual may have not been as dramatic for women; instead, it is often the tension between the homosocial and the homoerotic (and later the homosexual) that distinguishes "women's culture" as a demarcated space and thus sustains it. Moreover, I assert that this tension is intensely productive for the formation of female subjectivity in general, regardless of whether or not it leads to lesbian self-identification.[56] In some ways, then, one could see this project as an effort to specify historically the role that space itself plays in the formation of desires and sometimes identities; that it is precisely the increasingly ideological instability between the private and the public that allowed for these new formations of identification/desire to emerge.

In emphasizing the importance of space itself in the formation of identity and identification/desire, I build both on the work of theorists of the public sphere and on psychoanalytic accounts of fantasy. The term "counterpublic" connotes what are, in the words of Nancy Fraser, "parallel discursive arenas where members of subordinated social groups reinvent and circulate counterdiscourses to formulate oppositional interpretations of their identities, interests, and needs."[57] Fraser insists not only that such spaces allow for collective moments of social organization but also that they are potent spaces for the production of identity itself.[58] Such descriptions of the counterpublic sphere often define an alternative public sphere as one that is made up of collective expressions of oppositional identity, forms of *visible* publicity.[59] And indeed, much of the revisionist work on the public sphere has been based on a critique of the private sphere as an arbitrary class-specific and historically and racially specific ideology.[60]

At the same time, however, such an emphasis on "publicity" cannot account for the ways in which the alternations of public and private as the mix of ideologies of, for example, the family and the institution, have potent subject-forming effects: as Louisa May Alcott's novels query, "Are you my teacher or my mother? Are you my sister or my lover? Are you my daughter or my pupil?" (And what it means to be a daughter, because Jo is more of a "son" than a daughter to Marmee, destabilizes even these categories.) How do we account for forms of social organization that center on *less visible*, semipublic/semiprivate spaces in which the alternation of what counts as public and private itself may be highly charged both politically and erotically, such as Diana and Persis's studio; the bright, cheerful rooms of Miss Mill's boardinghouse in *An Old-Fashioned Girl*; or even the discursive arena that Alcott's novels might have offered her readers?

It is my contention that lesbianism as an identity emerges at this unstable conjunction between mothers and "others," public and private realms, and that literature and the act of reading in particular play crucial roles in this development. Thus, modern lesbian identity marks an extension, and sometimes simultaneously a critique of rather than a break from, nineteenth-century "women's culture." As I outline in chapters 1 and 2, postbellum "sentimental" texts, such as those written by Stowe, Alcott, and Kelley, illustrate, eroticize, phobically react against, and even, in their own efforts to shape girls' selves, performatively contribute to the production of queer female identifications and identities. In the remaining chapters I then explore how early-twentieth-century modernist lesbian writing continues and engages, rather than rejects, this subject-forming project.

In chapter 1 I discuss the ways in which the figure of the spinster functions as "other" to bourgeois heteromaternality and thus as a kind of protolesbian identity. As Stowe's *Oldtown Folks* illustrates, spinsters are often represented as unable to keep private and public spheres separate, and in their promiscuous mixing of the home and market are connected to the dangers of capitalism. They become emblems of impending modernization and of a demonized, "unnatural" relation to production and reproduction. Although the spinster, I demonstrate, is also a specifically white identity, because of her marginality to normative femininity she is linked to other minoritized identities.

In the second chapter I examine Alcott's writings for children and examples from her pulp fiction, as well as her novel *Work: A Story of Experience* and her unfinished novella, *Diana and Persis*. Through this analysis I reveal how, in the latter half of the nineteenth century, the distance between mother and "other" begins to disintegrate, especially as the proximity of home to school and workplace allows for new relations of identification and desire between women. At the same time, the family's increasingly unstable distance from the public sphere at moments allows for a suspension of gendered and sexual norms. Alcott's work also claims an erotics of self-making for white women who, up to this point, have for the most part been denied access to this model of self-formation.

In comparing Alcott's work, in particular *Little Women,* to one of the first novels written by an African American woman, Kelley's *Megda,* in chapter 2 I then explore the racial limits of an identificatory erotics. I also discuss the degree to which relations of disciplinary intimacy function as forms of cultural imperialism. In chapter 3 I continue this line of inquiry: the context provided by a queer reading of disciplinary intimacy makes clear the connections between modern lesbian identity (as represented in Djuna Barnes's *Ladies Almanack*) and other, less-celebrated, social identities and their correlative forms of social organization. In analyzing the formal and ideological similarities between the *Almanack* and the *Girl Scout Handbook,* I demonstrate how both modernism and mass culture utilize the metaphors of mass production for their own attempts at reproducing specific forms of female subjectivity: while the Girl Scouts use the erotics of disciplinary intimacy to make immigrants into white, middle-class citizens, Barnes imagines that modern lesbians recruit in much the same way.

Similarly, in adopting the logic of commodity culture, Gertrude Stein's *Tender Buttons* queers both the sentimental vision of the domestic and relations of female-female intimacy within it, as I discuss in chapter 4. In so doing Stein deconstructs any ideological distinction between home and market, writing and money, and "natural" and "unnatural" (re)production in order to produce a queer theory of representation. Through revaluing anti-Semitic and antiqueer cultural associations (the link between usury, punning, and sodomy), Stein reveals the reliance on narrow ideas of the "natural" that underpins both literary and economic theory, thereby creating a poetics that sharply distinguishes her from other modernists. In so doing, she makes what has been a stigmatizing figure of the unnatural spinster into a reverse discourse of modern lesbian identity.

Finally, through reading Marianne Moore and Elizabeth Bishop's relationship as an example of eroticized disciplinary relations between women rather than as another ahistorical example of an oedipal mother/daughter conflict, in chapters 5 and 6 I present a queer theory of poetic influence based in an identificatory erotics. Such a perspective enables us to see that conflicts in Moore's and Bishop's work and in their intimacy were not simply moments of maternal prohibition or prudery or filial rebellion but instead complex disagreements over the ways in which gender and sexual identities should be represented in language.

Chapter 1

"SINGLE WHITE FEMALE":

THE SEXUAL POLITICS OF SPINSTERHOOD

IN HARRIET BEECHER STOWE'S

OLDTOWN FOLKS

༒

In this regard of self-dependence, and a greater simplicity and fullness of being, we must hail as a preliminary the increase of the class contemptuously designated as old maids.—Margaret Fuller, *Woman in the Nineteenth Century*

It is one of the peculiarities of American womanhood that the body of a coquette often encloses the soul of a prude and the angular form of a spinster is possessed by a nature of the tropics.—Gertrude Stein, *Q.E.D.*

The "problem" of making girls into women preoccupies much of antebellum sentimental fiction. Richard Brodhead's readings of girls' character (re)formation in Susan Warner's *The Wide, Wide World* (1850) and Harriet Beecher Stowe's *Uncle Tom's Cabin* (1851), establishes the conventions of what he terms the "maternal-tutelary mode": the move away from a model of subject formation based in physical punishment and toward one based in the internalization of disciplinary power, centrally metaphorized in American texts as a "mother's love." [1] As discussed in my introduction, in *The Wide, Wide World* Alice replaces Mrs. Montgomery as Ellen's substitute "mother" (and "sister"), but this occurs *only after* Aunt Fortune, Ellen's spinster relative, has failed at instilling in her the ideals of self-regulation essential to an internalization of disciplinary power. Similarly, in *Uncle Tom's Cabin*, Aunt Ophelia, another spinster, is unable to reform the orphaned slave Topsy, and it is only Little Eva's loving example that inspires Topsy to "be good." As Brodhead observes, in both cases spinster characters function in the narratives as key contrasts or foils against which to measure the successes of the other mother substitutes: they represent an earlier form of regulatory power, that of brute force, and thus are unable to "love" their charges into obedience and transformation.

Stowe repeats this narrative trope almost exactly in *Oldtown Folks* (1869).[2] Miss Asphyxia, the first single woman to take in the orphan Tina, uses corporal punishment to try to regulate Tina's behavior. Such actions recall an earlier disciplinary regime—what Stowe refers to as "the literal use of the rod" (115)—and are explicitly linked to the evils of slavery. When Tina's brother, Harry, hears of her mistreatment and recalls his own abuse at the hands of Miss Asphxyia's brother, "the blood flushed into the boy's face, and he breathed short. Something stirred within him, such as makes slavery bitter" (99). For both children, this disciplinary regime fails completely. In particular, it inspires in Tina only hatred and the desire to rebel, implying that such physical exercises of brute disciplinary power do indeed inspire uprisings, not docility:

> A child's hatred and a child's revenge have an intensity of bitterness entirely unalloyed by moral considerations; and when a child is without an object of affection, and feels itself unloved, its whole vigor of being goes into the channels of hate. . . . In fact, the child considered herself and Miss Asphyxia as in a state of warfare which suspends all moral rules. (113)

Such examples confirm the connection Brodhead traces between the failure to inspire obedience through corporal punishment in the military and in education (prior to becoming self-employed, Miss Asphyxia was a schoolteacher) and the failure of the terrorizing discipline that characterizes slavery. Alternatively, although she does not wholly succeed as maternal pedagogue, Miss Mehitable, the spinster who subsequently becomes Tina's guardian, manages to soften Tina's anger through her loving example. In some ways, then, she stands in for what Brodhead argues is the substitution of "disciplinary intimacy" for physical force.

This genealogy of subject formation underlies *Oldtown Folks;* however, it cannot fully account for the intertwining of cultural anxieties regarding gender, sexuality, race, and their relationship to female subjectivity—those struggles over the "vigor [of a child's] being" and the "object of [her] affection"—that I argue constitute the central focus of the first third of the novel. Stowe does contrast one form of childrearing against another in ways that follow dominant domestic tropes, but she adds a crucial difference: instead of replacing the inept spinster with a woman who is designed to epitomize an idealized version of white femininity (so pure and good that in fact only death can preserve it), in *Oldtown Folks* one spinster's failure at mothering becomes another spinster's success (albeit limited). Neither women can ever fully succeed, in part because their efforts are measured against the standard of (hetero)maternal normalcy and normalization epitomized in the character of Grandmother Badger. Yet the novel does not pit a secure vision of heteromaternality against a (queer) sterility in a way that simply anticipates or replicates the hetero/homo binary. Instead, in its efforts to taxonomize spinsterhood, *Oldtown Folks* explores the limits of the transferability of maternal agency and power (what historians have come to refer to as the "professionalization of motherhood") from the biological family to other domestic and increasingly extradomestic spheres. In so doing, the novel simultaneously establishes such limits, illustrating why one single woman fails at the labor of love while another, at least temporarily, succeeds.

The economic and racial specificities of a postbellum context connect these successes and failures to larger social transformations unique to the post–Civil War United States. Specifically, *Oldtown Folks* engages three key historical shifts: the end of slavery and the era of Reconstruction; the massive increase in single white women who would never marry in part owing to a lack of available men; and the coming of widespread industrialization, which brought with it an intensification of the ideological pressures to keep the home separate from the "heartless world" of capitalist endeavor. Each of these shifts contributes to a figuring of the spinster, but the figure is more than an example of a gender failure or freakishness, as signaled by the spinster's failure to mother; or as Brodhead would have it, a simple, prebourgeois contrast to the triumph of the maternal pedagogical (and by extension the middle class). Indeed, the white spinster, enmeshed in the overlapping discourses of race, gender, sexuality, and labor, also comes to embody an emergent, queer, protoidentity.

In confining my discussion to white spinsters, I do not mean to imply that spinsters of color did not exist in the postbellum era. But under slavery, the married/nonmarried distinction was denied to most slaves, while in the postbellum period a woman's single status or refusal or avoidance of marriage carried very different connotations for white and African American women. As Hortense Spillers has noted, marriage itself took on racially specific political implications, as it was one of the only possible ways that African American men and women could enter into the public sphere, thereby asserting their rights as citizens.[3] Although white, middle-class women were increasingly "escaping" or being forced to exist outside of marriage and in the process finding ways to enter the public sphere, one could argue that for African American women the opposite was true: through marriage (and through a black man) African American women might attain some semblance of entitlement, including the right to exist within the "private," but their status as members of an oppressed minority also meant that marriage was always already a public, civic duty, a way to sustain the race.[4]

For example, in a novel such as Frances E. W. Harper's *Iola Leroy* (1892), Leroy's conflict centers around how best to organize her sexuality and her labor for the good of the race, and marriage signifies less a route to personal fulfillment, and more an aid to this larger political goal.[5] This may be one reason why early African American women novelists such as Mrs. A. E. Johnson make many of their single women characters widows rather than spinsters. By already having been married, such women are made respectable and are shown to be claiming their right to enjoy the legal privileges of matrimony.[6] Regardless of Johnson's motives, however, African American women in general, not just single women, were viewed by the dominant culture as sexually suspect and unnaturally reproductive; thus the specific connotations that I argue were being attached to white spinsters were also being attached to all black women.

Although the spinster might be viewed as a racially specific identity, Stowe's text allies her with other minority subjects. In *Oldtown Folks,* just as the spinster's "unnatural" relation to femininity is signaled by her simultaneous proximity to and distance from "natural," essentialized maternality, her queerness is signified or made visible in the text through the discursive links the narrative establishes between various forms of production and reproduction considered excessive or wasteful, forms of production and reproduction that are also connected to race and ethnicity. *Oldtown Folks* reveals the degree to which both the subjectivity of the white spinster and that of the racial and ethnic minorities briefly represented within the text are constituted through what Lauren Berlant has termed the processes of "stereotypic embodiment," the ways in which the individual bodies and lives of subjects are condensed and distorted to fit the meanings dictated, in this case, by the postbellum public sphere.[7]

Although it may seem misleading when discussing sentimental fiction to describe particular characters as stereotypes (which implies that others are not) when one might argue that sentimental fiction seeks to make all forms of subjectivity into legible, easily demarcated and easily replicable forms of personhood ("*the* mother," "*the* daughter"), within this characterological universe there is still what Berlant calls a "social hierarchy." In discussing the workings of stereotype in contemporary U.S. culture, Berlant distinguishes between those subjects who are allowed the "privilege of individuality" with the illusion that their subjectivities are both unique and universal, and those whose particular lived experiences are simplified and distorted into the narrow limits of "the queer" or "the person of color."[8] By contrast, in sentimental novels such as Stowe's, and in nineteenth-century U.S. culture as a whole, I would argue, such a privilege of individuality is denied for all women. Still, female identity itself exists in a hierarchy, with white, heteromaternal, "natural" femininity at the top.

In his discussion of the workings of colonial discourse, Homi Bhabha argues that the discursive effects of the stereotype are structured as ambivalence. Against an analysis that would simply identify stereotypes as "positive" or "negative," or would decide a priori their cultural power or inefficacy, he calls for "an understanding of the *processes of signification* made possible (and plausible) through stereotypical discourse."[9] As I will outline in this chapter, the representations of spinsters in *Oldtown Folks* reveal the novel's unquestioned replication of dominant nineteenth-century stereotypes of spinsterhood, as well as the old maids' own "masochistic identification" with them.[10] Yet, at the same time, because the stereotype always represents a process of signification, it also suggests ways to articulate a queer female protoidentity, one that within *Oldtown Folks* can only be a deviant form of femininity. In arguing that the figure of the spinster has a history, my aim here is to provide a starting point for interventions into this stereotype, the reverse discourse of spinsterhood that I will argue modernist queer female writers effect in the early twentieth century.

The figure of the old maid or spinster recurs throughout nineteenth-century white women's writing, from Catharine Maria Sedgwick's character Lucy Ray in "Old Maids" (1834) to the unattached, unnamed narrator of Sarah Orne Jewett's *The Country of the Pointed Firs* (1896).[11] Because bourgeois white womanhood was increasingly defined in the nineteenth century by its relation to mothering and the private domestic leisure and labor of love, the cultural work of such women is often represented as, at best, a ridiculous, excessive copy of such endeavors, or a cheapened, commodified version of it (something spinsters do for money, as opposed to love and selfless dedication).[12] Even more often, a spinster's labor and subjectivity go unrecognized as cultural work altogether both by critics and by the texts.

Some feminist critics have turned this liability into an asset, seeing the spinster as either a nineteenth-century harbinger of the liberal feminist ideal of the "autonomous woman" or the radical feminist ideal of the woman who exists outside patriarchy.[13] It is tempting to read the spinster as a self-exile from bourgeois reproductive heterosexuality, but this implies that there is an outside both to the norms of (hetero)sexuality and to the economy, a utopian space not familiar to most single white women in the United States in the mid- to late nineteenth century. White women without the physical and economic protection of a husband were often doomed to abject poverty or to the tyrannies and whims of their brothers or fathers; women who did not participate in the "natural" feminine functions of wife and mother were socially ostracized and culturally ridiculed.[14] And, after the Civil War, in part because of the war's huge death toll and in part because of western expansion, there were many more women than men in the eastern United States. As Alice Kessler-Harris notes, "*The New York Times* estimated in 1869 that about a quarter of a million young women in the eastern seaboard states could never look forward to any matrimonial alliance, because they outnumbered men by that much."[15] This trend would continue throughout the rest of the nineteenth century; government statistics from the 1880s estimated that one-third of the female population over twenty-one would never marry.[16]

Yet simply to equate spinsterhood with a deficit of eligible men does not do justice to the complexities of the position. Due partly to the changing needs of industrial capitalism, in the latter half of the nineteenth century bourgeois white women were allowed (and actively agitated for) education and access to jobs in postbellum public spaces. Schooling and the possibility of a career made it increasingly imaginable for these women to be economically independent of either marriage or the support of their families. By the late 1800s, single, middle-class, white women were often portrayed as dangerous and mannish, overinvolved in the public sphere and underinvolved in traditionally feminine pursuits.[17] But, as I will argue, even in 1869 single white women were already embodying cultural fears, not only about historical shifts both in what counted as women's work and in what constituted "proper" femininity, but also about "proper" female (hetero)sexuality.

Oldtown Folks is something of a genre hybrid: known for its representations of "local color" and set in the post-Revolutionary days of the early Republic, it constructs a regionalist historical romance of national origins. Yet the novel is also clearly a critique of Reconstruction and "northern-style capitalism,"[18] and its representations of childrearing imply that republican mothers were already adopting the pedagogics of disciplinary intimacy. In occupying both of these two historical-discursive positions, *Oldtown Folks* is able to construct a legitimating romance of origins for Stowe's political vision of American society at the same time that it explores pressing cultural concerns in the postbellum period. As the narrator informs us on the opening page:

> My object is to interpret to the world the New England life and character in that particular time of its history which may be called the seminal period. I would endeavor to show you New England in its *seed-bed,* before the hot suns of modern progress had developed its sprouting germs into the great trees of to-day.
>
> New England has been to these United States what the Dorian hive was to Greece. It has always been a capital country to emigrate from, an[d] North, South, East, and West have been populated largely from New England, so that the seed-bed of New England was the seed-bed of this great American Republic, and of all that is likely to come of it. (3)

Oldtown Folks addresses a number of issues: it illustrates the problems of Calvinism, it debates the question of what should constitute a utopian society, and it focuses in large part on reproduction and mothering. Indeed, the emphasis in the above passage on "seed" and on imperial procreation—New England populating (and as a consequence, conquering) the entire United States—illustrates the degree to which one of the central projects of the novel is to describe how this reproduction takes place. But more important than seeds are the "seed-beds," metaphorically both the land and the women in which the seeds were planted. *Oldtown Folks* illuminates Stowe's vision of the possibilities of public mothering, and it makes "good mothering" the key to national subject formation because mothering is in every way responsible for the birth of the nation.

Mothering as a role and a duty was one of Stowe's central concerns throughout her literary career and it formed the basis of her politics, as evidenced by the domestic handbook she and her sister, Catharine E. Beecher, coauthored, *The American Woman's Home or, Principles of Domestic Science; Being A Guide to the Formation and Maintenance of Economical, Healthful[,] Beautiful and Christian Homes* (1869).[19] With chapter headings that include "The Christian Family," "The Management of Young Children," and "Care of the Homeless, the Helpless, and the Vicious," this volume is a revision of Beecher's enormously popular earlier work, *Treatise on Domestic Economy for the Use of Young Ladies at Home and at School* (1841).[20] In *The American Woman's Home*, Beecher and Stowe describe the family as a productive, loving, culturally central unit. They elevate the domestic sphere above, and as an alternative to, the public world of politics, which enables them to claim power both inside and outside the private sphere for women.

In particular, the book preserves the ideology that motherhood is based in biology while at the same time presenting the maternal role as an occupation; motherhood and its inevitable accompaniment, domesticity, become simultaneously woman's "natural" role and something for which she needs an education. This argument thus allows Beecher and Stowe to claim that education for women is necessary to train them for their most important duty, reproduction. As part of their discussion of motherhood, the authors describe what might be the fate of those women who cannot or do not marry and become "real" mothers:

> The blessed privileges of the family state are not confined to those who rear children of their own. Any woman who can earn a livelihood, as every woman should be trained to do, can take a properly qualified female associate, and institute a family of her own, receiving to its heavenly influences the orphan, the sick, the homeless, and the sinful, and by motherly devotion train them to follow the self-denying example of Christ, in educating his earthly children for true happiness in this life and for his eternal home.[21]

In extending their discussion of motherhood beyond the confines of the traditional family, Beecher and Stowe achieve a political sleight of hand. By emphasizing the occupation of motherhood over its actual biological details, not to mention its supposed male-female social context, the authors are able to extend their pleas for education to all women, regardless of their marital status (although for Beecher and Stowe it must be noted that "woman" connotes white, middle class, and American born). By making motherhood a profession, they are also able to carve out a space for women to pursue careers outside of the realm of bourgeois marriage, but only by making the domestic sphere a model for the public space of mothering.[22] Thus, they are also able to distance mothering from heterosexuality but not from the ideology of domesticity.

Published in the same year as *The American Woman's Home,* the first third of *Oldtown Folks* also concentrates on childrearing, specifically on the proper way to raise a little girl. Set shortly after the American Revolution, the novel opens with the death of a young woman who is passing through the town of "Needmore" on her way to Boston to find her errant British husband. She leaves two children, Harry and Tina, who are placed at the mercy of Old Crab Smith, whose abused wife tries to shelter them from his anger and violence. Because Smith is unable to view the children in any terms other than their capacity for labor, he sees in Harry a worthwhile investment but decides he has no use for Tina, observing, "'There won't be no great profit in this 'ere these ten year'" (78). Instead, Smith turns Tina over to his spinster sister, Miss Asphyxia. The narrative then describes in graphic detail Miss Asphyxia's abuse of Tina and Tina's subsequent rebellion.

Finally, when Harry can bear the thought of his sister's unhappiness no more, the children run away from Needmore. After a series of adventures in the liminal space between Needmore and the nearby proto–middle-class bastion of post-Revolutionary family values, "Oldtown," the children are rescued by the grandmother of Horace Holyoke, the narrator, and the charge of mothering Tina is turned over to another spinster, Miss Mehitable. She proves more suited for the job, although her mothering is also not without faults.

Miss Asphyxia's character and her body, as well as her spectacular failure to produce children, are the objects of much of the narrative scrutiny of the first part of *Oldtown Folks.* The scandal of her adoption of Tina occupies many an afternoon conversation around the hearth or washtub, as the central women and many of the male characters debate the ethics of allowing Miss Asphyxia to "keep" Tina. In many ways, Miss Asphyxia resembles the stock "eccentric" old maid characters of numerous nineteenth-century novels, a figure whose actions are viewed as somehow outside the implied standards of the small-town community in which she lives.[23] Miss Asphyxia's name itself invokes this eccentricity, yet it is also not without other kinds of narrative significance. According to *Webster's New Collegiate Dictionary,* Asphyxia literally means "a lack of oxygen or excess of carbon dioxide in the body that is usually caused by interruption of breathing and that causes unconsciousness." Not only does Miss Asphyxia stifle Tina, as well as others, but she also smothers herself. Her subjectivity is out of equilibrium; she is lacking, especially in agency, to the point of unconsciousness, in part because of her excessive attachment to work: "Now all Miss Asphyxia's ideas of the purpose and aim of human existence were comprised in one word,—work. She was herself a working machine, always wound up and going,—up at early cock-crowing, and busy till bedtime, with a rampant and fatiguing industry that never paused for a moment" (87).

The narrative insists on the connection between Miss Asphyxia's body and a machine, as in another passage: "We have before described her as a working machine, forever wound up to high-pressure working-point; and this being her nature, she trod down and crushed w[h]atever stood in the way of her work, with as little compunction as if she had been a steam-engine or a power-loom"(93).[24] Miss Asphyxia's body, and by implication her subjectivity, become indistinguishable from the machines that were revolutionizing methods of material production: the power looms that enabled the rise of the textile industry and the steam engines that, among other things, powered printing presses and locomotives (to which Miss Asphyxia is also compared in Stowe's text).

These analogies pose a temporal problem: they render the narrative anachronistic in that these modern inventions were not yet in existence within the historical frame of the story. Miss Asphyxia becomes in this context, then, a portent of things to come, a warning of the dangers of industrialization and, in particular, of the effects of the capitalist reorganization of production on the body and on subjectivity. The text implies that these new technological innovations will turn humans into machines and women into monsters. More specifically, it invokes the specter of the single woman who is incapable of fulfilling what for Stowe was still her most important duty, childrearing, and along with it the dangers of mixing the domestic and the market.

At the same time that Miss Asphyxia represents the threat of an unbridled industrial capitalism, however, her location in a lineage of childrearing (or, to put it more accurately, child abuse) signals that her household occupies a historical space before the separation of production and reproduction. Just like the figure of Ellen's aunt "Miss Fortune" in *The Wide, Wide World*, who views the inside of the house and its duties as coterminous and inseparable from the outside and its labors,[25] Miss Asphyxia cannot even imagine the middle-class ideal of the home as center of either emotional intimacy or leisure, because for her it is inseparable from the burdens of subsistence production. Similar to Miss Fortune, she is constitutionally unable to mother her charge into obedience. Instead, character is formed solely through hard work; children are whipped into obedience in the same way they are whipped into learning how to sew or read. It is as if industrial capitalism itself threatens to bring back this older disciplinary regime with a vengeance; Miss Asphyxia stands in as both its memory and its future.

Crucial to these regimes is the blurring of the economic and the domestic. With the formation of the middle class comes the fantasy of a new separation of labor and reproduction—the domestic sphere is sharply demarcated ideologically from the public sphere. According to Brodhead, "[the space of the home] is affectionate, so much so that the cultivation of close relations might be said to be its productive activity." [26] Stowe and Beecher's writings on motherhood participate in this ideology. At a time when household labor was being reconceived in the face of machine production, women, especially those of the middle class, needed something to dignify and describe their leisure.[27] Bourgeois women's work in the home thus became increasingly defined as the labor of love of raising children, while conspicuous manual labor was to be performed by someone else (a white, working-class servant, an Irish immigrant woman, or an African American woman). White, American-born, middle-class women were thus to do the mental labor of forming, through their loving example, their children's characters.

In opposition to the dominant ideology of domesticity, Miss Asphyxia's view of children is explicitly connected to internecine capitalist economics. Like her brother, she can only view Tina in terms of the value of her labor; when faced with Tina's beauty, which the narrative insists over and over again is Tina's greatest asset, her physical capital—guarantor of her class, race, and gender position and source of her (later dangerous and at times manipulative) power—Miss Asphyxia cannot even begin to comprehend it: "Apparently she was somewhat puzzled, and rather scandalized, that Nature should evidently have expended so much in a merely ornamental way on an article which ought to have been made simply for service" (88). Here, Tina becomes "an article" not a human being:[28] "'She's tol'able strong and well-limbed for her age,' added that lady, feeling of the child's arms and limbs, 'her flesh is solid. I think she'll make a strong woman, only put her to work early and keep her at it. I could rub out clothes at the wash-tub afore I was at her age'" (88). Not only does this passage express a view of the subject as solely defined by her labor power, but it also explicitly connects Miss Asphyxia to the discourse of slavery.

In her discussion of Stowe's understanding of the workings of property under the slave system, Gillian Brown asserts that Stowe is most horrified by slavery because it brings the workings of the market into the home: "Slavery disregards this opposition between the family at home and the exterior workplace. The distinction between work and family is eradicated in the slave, for whom there is no separation between economic and private status."[29] Lora Romero has termed this the "miscegenation" of home and market, the unnatural mixing of the domestic and the economic which, according to Stowe, reaches its epitome under slavery.[30] Miss Asphyxia herself, I would propose, embodies this "miscegenation"; she is both a propagator and a product of its ills. In *Oldtown Folks* Stowe transfers her critique from slavery to the effects of burgeoning market capitalism: in other words, she links as she condemns "white slavery" and the bondage of wage labor.[31]

Comparing Miss Asphyxia's reproductive and productive labor to mechanical (re)production, the narrative portrays the threat posed to the liberal subject by machines, which in their reproductive power deny the fantasy of liberal agency.[32] This fear is explicitly connected not only to the (self-)control of domestic labor but also to the workings of heterosexual reproduction itself. Miss Asphyxia threatens to replace the intimate drama of maternal pedagogy with the violence of (mass) production. She stands in for the impersonality of capitalism and in the process replaces a system of sentimental property relations with one that dramatizes the brutality of the market. Thus, it is imperative that Miss Asphyxia fail as a mother: through her example we see the violence of machine culture, which threatens to destroy the white, bourgeois family and replace it with sterile, single, working women.

By Stowe's (il)logical extension, this terror of machine production finds its parallel in the novel's representations of racist stereotypes of the overproduction and overreproduction of African Americans.[33] Just as the text, through the process of stereotypic embodiment, represents Miss Asphyxia's exaggerated propensity for work as written on her body, so too are labor and sexuality written on the bodies of the people of color within the text.

Consider, for example, the grotesque, racist images of the most "industrious" members of the Native American and African American communities. The character Lem Sudock is described as "a great, coarse, heavy-moulded [sic] Indian, with gigantic limbs and a savage face, but much in request for laying stone walls, digging wells, and other tasks for which mere physical strength was the chief requisite" (45). Similarly, Primus King is "a gigantic, retired whaleman, black as a coal, with enormous hands and feet, universally in demand in all the region about as assistant in butchering operations" (46). The propensity for work is what distinguishes these men of color, what redeems them from the undifferentiated "Indian" or "Negro" categories that Stowe employs to signify a Native or African American presence. Yet it is also as though these men's bodies were made for work, their "gigantic" size a physical sign of their "natural" and unmediated connection to unremitting labor.[34]

Miss Asphyxia bears on her body the marks of this discipline in the same way that the people of color in the book embody the effects of their own naturalized reduction to "animality" or brute force: Miss Asphyxia, too, is a laboring machine/animal, and she has always seen herself this way. Her views of children, and presumably of herself, participate in this racialized economy of work. As she observes: " 'Yes,' said Miss Asphyxia; 'there can be a good deal got out of a child if you keep at 'em, hold 'em in tight, and never let 'em have their head a minute; push right hard on behind 'em, and you get considerable. That's the way I was raised' " (89). Miss Asphyxia here recognizes the workings of a particular form of disciplinary power: not only will she continue to pass this power along, in terms that compare childrearing to the breaking of a mule, but she also states unequivocally that this is how she herself was produced.

Stowe poses, against this threat to maternality, the idea of a "different ethic of possession," what Brown terms elsewhere as "sentimental possession."[35] It is not necessarily evil for children to work; in fact, it builds character. Nor is it wrong for children to be disciplined and influenced by their parents. But children are a particular kind of property. Brown describes the workings of sentimental fiction:

> If . . . sentimentalism has operated as a representational tactic for extending human rights to the disenfranchised, it nevertheless retains the slave or woman or child within the inventory of human proprietorship. That is, the case for shared humanity and human rights is made, not in terms of equality, but in terms of the humanity vested in a subject by virtue of its possession, through an intimacy and identification developed in the history of a proprietorship.[36]

Miss Asphyxia's crime, at least in part, is that she refuses to sentimental-ize her possession of Tina. Nor does she encourage Tina to develop a re-lationship of sentimentalized, liberal self-possession. And indeed, Miss As-phyxia's own self-understanding reflects her sense that she could never share in such a proposition: "Miss Asphyxia was tall and spare. Nature had made her, as she often remarked of herself, entirely for use" (93). Throughout the text, Miss Asphyxia is represented and represents herself as entirely without sentiment, as existing only for use and to be used up. Seemingly unable to control her compulsion to work, she spends herself tirelessly, never to be completely "spent."

Miss Asphyxia expresses bewilderment when confronted with the in-adequacies of her approach to childrearing because she herself is a prod-uct of the same system. Her failures, including her inability to separate home and market, also ally Miss Asphyxia with Aunt Nancy Prime, an Af-rican American woman whose name itself relegates her to the margins of both family and the white community. Prime has literally bought herself an African American husband, and in the process she has allowed the mar-ket to pollute her most intimate domestic relationship.[37] As the narrator observes,

> The only thing she gained by this matrimonial speculation was an abun-dant crop of noisy children. . . . I remember once, when I was on a visit to her cottage . . . Nancy lifted the trap-door which went down into the cellar below. Forthwith the whole skirmishing tribe of little darkies, who had been rolling about the floor, seemed suddenly to unite in one coil, and, with a final flop, disappeared in the hole. (47)

When business invades the domestic, the narrative implies, it corrupts all the relationships within it. Moreover, here we see Stowe's representa-tion of African American reproduction as excessive but, paradoxically, as worthless. These children do not have the privilege of individuality af-forded the white children in the book; these children are simply "skir-mishing . . . little darkies." Here the danger of machine production is im-plicitly connected to the dangers of the reproducing ethnic and racial "others" who lack, it is imagined, any individuality but are simply a col-lection of exaggerated, racist types. Miss Asphyxia's mothering is danger-ous because it threatens to deny Tina's individualized (read white, female, middle class) identity and turn her into an undifferentiated (and thereby raced, ethnicized, and/or classed) mass subject/slave.

After the Civil War, as historians have noted, the white middle class was solidified through its fear of the "take over" of America by immigration and African American migration. Carroll Smith-Rosenberg links these concerns to a male-dominated medical establishment, which sets out to criminalize abortion amid white supremacist panic that white, middle-class women were not reproducing enough or were refusing to reproduce altogether. During this period arose the image of the "unnatural" bourgeois matron, to use Smith-Rosenberg's terms, an image of a woman who refused to bear children. Smith-Rosenberg argues that this stereotype, first attributed to nonprocreative women, was then transferred onto women's sexualities:

> Male asylum directors, doctors, academics, psychiatrists, and psychologists (all members of the new bourgeois professions and bureaucracies) shifted the definition of female deviance from the New Woman's rejection of motherhood to their rejection of men. From being "unnaturally" barren, the autonomous woman, outside of heterosexual marriage, emerged as "unnaturally" sexual.[38]

Although Smith-Rosenberg locates this shift in the 1890s, her description of the move from "unnatural mothering" to "unnatural sexuality" matches Miss Asphyxia's narrative trajectory. Miss Asphyxia embodies this symbolic construction as she continually crosses back and forth between these unnatural positions. In fact, the two positions are not ideologically or historically distinct. Queer sexual practices have long been considered unnatural because they do not produce children: Foucault asserts that sexuality in the nineteenth century was primarily organized around reproductive married sexual acts versus nonreproductive sexual acts.[39] In *Oldtown Folks* the inability to mother renders a woman unnatural; at the same time it is Miss Asphyxia's unnatural and sexualized relationship to production that makes it impossible for her to mother "naturally." Not only does her overcathected relationship to labor mark her as outside the domestic economy, it also marks her as somehow unfeminine and as "queer" because for Stowe womanhood and mothering are inseparable—mothering is the model for women's labor; women are essentially mothers. Both the fact that Miss Asphyxia cannot mother—or as Grandmother Badger proclaims, "'You'd no business to take a child at all; you haven't got a grain of motherliness in you . . . it's *broodin'* that young creatures wants; and you hain't got a bit of broodin' in you" (202)—and the fact that Miss Asphyxia was born without the ability to brood/breed, makes her somehow not female, unnatural.[40]

As Sol Peters, an Oldtown elder, exclaims: "'Lordy massy, an old gal like her ain't nobody to bring up a child. It takes a woman that's got juice in her to do that. Why, that 'ere crittur's drier 'n a two-year-old mullenstalk. There ain't no sap ris in her these 'ere thirty years'" (123). A dried-up, old plant cannot reproduce, just as a spinster like Miss Asphyxia is constitutionally incapable of mothering. "Sap" alludes to heterosexual attractiveness or appeal; it signifies Miss Asphyxia's lack of desire, which can be understood not in terms of an overt sexual desire for men but rather secondarily as a "natural" desire to rear sentimentally the children such a heterosexual, culturally sanctioned encounter would provide.[41]

Instead, Miss Asphyxia's connection to work itself, her conviction that she exists entirely for "use," recalls sexual discourses dominant in the nineteenth century, the elaborate set of prohibitions against "self-abuse," or masturbation. Use of self and abuse of self—in Stowe these two categories seem implicitly related. As Romero has perceptively discussed, Stowe's theory of subjectivity includes an economic theory of the equilibrium of the self:

> [Stowe] speaks of overwork as an "overdraft on the nervous energy, which helps us to use up in one hour the strength of whole days". . . . Artificial brightness, produced under the stimulus of excessive labor or narcotic indulgence, destabilizes subjectivity. To be artificially stimulated is to surrender self-determination and willpower and to make the body work independently of the mind.[42]

Romero speaks specifically of Stowe's analysis of the hysterical housewife who gets too caught up in housework and therefore loses the delicate balance between mind and body, a description that matches Miss Asphyxia's obsessive relationship to work. Stowe's analysis also resembles other economic theories of the subject in nineteenth-century writings on sex: as G. J. Barker-Benfield explains, men were thought to have a limited reserve of sperm that could be emptied too quickly, with adverse physiological and psychological results. Wives and husbands were called on to regulate this "spermatic economy" and not make excessive demands on its coffers.[43] Just as excessive laboring drained one's energy, both heterosexual intercourse for the sole purpose of pleasure and, above all, masturbation were seen as unnecessary and unnatural expenditures of sexual energy that destroyed the subject's natural equilibrium. (Notice here again the emphasis on the regulation of the subject implicit in the name Asphyxia.)

In other words, to use Eve Kosofsky Sedgwick's terms, these sexual practices were regarded as "crises of the will"; that is, failures of self-possession that pose as their ideal a self-regulating subject. In her discussion of female masturbation in the late eighteenth and nineteenth century, Sedgwick elucidates how representations of female masturbators highlight such "crises," which are supposedly inherent in their struggles to "control themselves."[44] Masturbation becomes a compulsion and an addiction, but it is always seen as something one should be able to regulate. Miss Asphyxia's addictive, perhaps even onanistic, relationship to work places her outside these bourgeois norms of propriety, which are literalized in the saying, "waste not, want not." She thus embodies the term "surplus," used to describe a spinster's relation to the heterosexual reproductive and productive economy. She represents excess and extraness, an impulse to work that should be properly channeled elsewhere in the same way that the impulse to masturbate should be channeled into the impulse to reproduce. This excess, at once economic and sexual, becomes condensed into a stereotype or protoidentity in the figure of the spinster.

Sedgwick argues that the invention of the "masturbator" presages modern sexual identities or is perhaps itself a sexual identity. Similarly, Miss Asphyxia's surplus, her unnatural relationship to work and childrearing mark her as "queer" and as outside a regime of bourgeois heterosexuality that reflects a particular version of bourgeois economics. In so doing, the figure of the white spinster stands in for, and sometimes exchanges with, other forms of pathologized and racialized production and reproduction in postbellum U.S. culture.

Thus, the central fantasy of at least the first third of *Oldtown Folks* is that Miss Asphyxia, as representative of the evils both of slavery and of mechanical reproduction, through her "unnatural" influence will make Tina, the emblem of white, middle-class femininity, into a black, nonfemale (and by proxy, nonheterosexually reproductive) slave. In perhaps the most peculiar scene in the book, Miss Asphyxia cuts Tina's hair:

> When well scrubbed and wiped, Miss Asphyxia put on a coarse homespun nightgown, and, pinning a cloth round the child's neck, began with her scissors the work of cutting off her hair. Snip, snip, went the fatal shears, and down into the towel fell bright curls, once the pride of a mother's heart, till finally the small head was despoiled completely. (95)

By cutting off Tina's curls, Miss Asphyxia metaphorically ruins her. In effect, she threatens Tina's sexual purity; she despoils Tina's head. Not only is Miss Asphyxia physically abusive but she also commits what might be termed "gender abuse" as well.

This is in part because Miss Asphyxia fails to view Tina and her gender sentimentally, as a mother would view a daughter. Instead, she wants to make Tina over in her own queer image. By extension, she refuses to recognize the place of Tina's hair, and by proxy her gender, within what Brown has termed the "extra-market domestic economy," which is "[a] rather remarkable resistance to commodity fetishism which . . . takes the form of an objection not to fetishism but to commodities." [45] In other words, one may fetishize an object as long as one does not commodify it. The narrator participates in this economy, with remarkably fetishistic results:

> [Miss Asphyxia] then proceeded to the kitchen, raked open the fire, and shook the golden curls into the bed of embers, and stood grimly over them while they seethed and twisted and writhed, as if they had been living things suffering a fiery torture. . . .
>
> "I wonder now," she said to herself, "if any of this will rise and get into the next pudding?" She spoke with a spice of bitterness, poor woman, as if it would be just the way things usually went on, if it did. (95–96)

While Tina's hair takes on a life of its own, Miss Asphyxia's fear that it may pollute the food signals her inability to view it as anything but interference with utility. Miss Asphyxia, then, becomes a portent of the dangers of machine production and wage labor, which may, in emphasizing only use, destroy the particularly feminine influences and identities that Stowe holds most dear and that are central to her domestic politics.[46] Foremost among these identities is the role of the mother to produce and reproduce racial and gender (and concomitantly, compulsory heterosexual) identity in her children: the curls, after all, are "the pride of a mother's heart." According to Stowe, Miss Asphyxia's connection to racial "others" and to the working class makes it impossible for her to fulfill the proper maternal function, just as it renders her improperly or incompletely gendered.

It is precisely this failure that marks Miss Asphyxia as queer. Such a failure is not just that of a universal disciplinary intimacy, as Brodhead would have it, but instead is one that is shot through with the valences of race, class, gender, and sexuality. Miss Asphyxia stands as a protolesbian figure, a figure marked by a certain form of self-sufficiency, not the abstract, vacuous "autonomy" of liberal feminist rhetoric but an eroticized form of (over)productivity that, at great cost, removes her from the legitimating realm of Stowe's maternal (hetero)sexuality. This identity does not signify the utopian "free" space of an unbridled "independence" but rather represents the coalescing in Stowe's narrative of some of the most damning accounts of "unnatural" femininity while it also provides the possibility of what Foucault might term a "reverse discourse" of female perverse identity.

Significantly, it is not a married "birth" mother who forms the sole ideological opposition to Miss Asphyxia's queer disciplinarity. After Harry and Tina escape the clutches of Miss Asphyxia and Old Crab Smith, Tina is given to Miss Mehitable, *another* old maid in Oldtown. Miss Mehitable is the other spinster on whom the narrative gaze affixes itself, and her differences from Miss Asphyxia help to establish the taxonomy of spinsterhood that characterizes the first third of *Oldtown Folks*. Thus, Stowe's text does not simply replicate a prototype of what we now term the homo/hetero divide in relation to childrearing; instead, through her conversion from queer spinster to devoted mother, the figure of Miss Mehitable illuminates how queer female identity in the nineteenth century may be made "visible" only through its contrast to dominant narratives of what counts as "proper" female productivity/reproductivity and its relation to race and class.

The Labor of Leisure: Miss Mehitable's Maternal Transformation

Within the historical frame of the narrative, Miss Mehitable Rossiter represents the last gasp of the pre-Revolutionary Tory aristocracy, which presumably is dying out in the democratic atmosphere of the new Republic. This decline in actual influence and pecuniary power is declared in the novel by the deterioration of Miss Mehitable's clothes: "Still, as everybody knew that it was Miss Mehitable Rossiter, and no meaner person, her queer bonnets and dyed gowns were accepted as part of those inexplicable dispensations of the Providence that watches over the higher classes, which are to be received by faith alone" (49). Miss Mehitable, like her clothes, has surely seen better days. Moreover, she simultaneously stands in for the newly leisured, middle-to-upper class, postbellum white woman of the Gilded Age, whose status in regard to labor was the cause of much anxiety after the Civil War. Unlike another elderly female character in the novel, Grandmother Badger, Miss Mehitable does not spend her hours organizing a bustling household and supervising numerous children and grandchildren. Instead, it is implied that the only "work" she performs consists of the dubious intellectual labor of scholarship; her capital is not the product of her father's industrial accumulation but is instead the cultural capital of an education.

Such intellectual labor has two effects: it masculinizes Miss Mehitable (although the narrative is careful to preserve the hidden possibility of her femininity), and it removes her from the provinces of heterosexual attraction. Because she speaks like a man to other men, she is only able to view them as "comrades," and they, in turn, simply "admire" but do not desire her:

> But in her quaint, uncomely body was lodged, not only a most active and even masculine mind, but a heart capable of those passionate extremes of devotion which belong to the purely feminine side of women. . . . Men always admired her as they admired other men, and talked to her as they talked with each other. Many, during the course of her life, had formed friendships with her, which were mere relations of comradeship, but which never touched the inner sphere of the heart. (197)

Miss Mehitable has at best an unmined relationship to femininity. Like Miss Asphyxia, she also bears a queer relationship to production: her failure to labor properly as a woman, her unstable class position, and her devotion to literary pursuits render her "unfeminine" and therefore undesirable to men.[47]

The inversion of power between Miss Mehitable and her servant, Polly, provides a clear indicator of Miss Mehitable's failure at "proper" white, middle-class feminine labor. In both *The American Woman's Home* and *House and Home Papers* Beecher and Stowe argue that a good housekeeper must be able to manage her servants: if one is not careful the servants will instead end up managing the lady of the house. In Miss Mehitable's household, "Polly considered Miss Mehitable as a sort of child under her wardship, and conducted the whole business of life for her with a sovereign and unanswerable authority" (64). In much the same way that Miss Mehitable reuses her clothes by turning them inside out, the language of this passage turns inside out what were for Beecher and Stowe the conventions of mistress-servant relations: the mistress should treat the servant like a child who needs supervision and a proper upbringing. But in the Rossiter household it is the servant who treats the mistress like a child. Polly rules the house with an iron grip; when Miss Mehitable adopts Tina, she worries lest Polly will disapprove.

Miss Mehitable, then, poses a problem to the narrative, that of her improper relationship to both production and gender/sexuality. As might be expected, it is her adoption of Tina that solves (albeit partially) these issues. When Miss Mehitable first meets Tina, "there was a sudden, almost convulsive pressure of the little one to the kind old breast, and Miss Mehitable's face wore a strange expression, that looked like the smothered pang of some great anguish blended with a peculiar tenderness" (170). Immediately this "silent inner act of adoption" (170) forms a sharp contrast to Miss Asphyxia's perceptions of Tina. In Miss Mehitable, Stowe creates a representation of the effects of "natural" embodied motherhood. Miss Mehitable remarks,

> "You never know what you may find in the odd corners of an old maid's heart, when you fairly look into them. There are often unused hoards of maternal affection enough to set-up an orphan-asylum; but it's like iron filings and a magnet,—you must try them with a live child, and if there is anything in 'em you find it out." (171–72)

Miss Mehitable is instantly transformed from an old maid into a mother, in an almost mystical process. Her class position makes it possible for her to view Tina as a mother *should* naturally view a child: unlike Miss Asphyxia, Miss Mehitable understands that a child must be a sentimentalized possession, in part because she herself possesses what becomes a class-marked form of capital, those heretofore "unused hoards of maternal affection." And indeed, Miss Mehitable gets great pleasure from the thought that Tina is hers: "*My* little one! Miss Mehitable's heart gave a great throb at this possessive pronoun" (175). It is this relationship of possession that "makes" Miss Mehitable into a "real" mother: "Suddenly she awoke as from a dark dream, and found herself sole possessor of beauty, youth, and love, in a glowing little form, all her own, with no moral to dispute it. She had a mother's right in a child. She might have a daughter's love. The whole house seemed changed" (176). As a "real" mother, Miss Mehitable sets out to raise Tina properly, to set a good example for her and to love her into submission. Tina immediately responds to this model; as she declares, "'When I lived with Miss Asphyxia, I wanted to be bad, I tried to be bad; but now I am changed. I mean to be good, because you are good to me'" (175). By implication, Stowe asserts that only a middle-class (white) woman could achieve such a result: Miss Asphyxia's failures at self-regulation, her obsession with work, as well as her inability to "love," make it impossible for her to replicate this process.

Although Miss Mehitable has the best intentions, ultimately we are led to believe that she fails at raising Tina. Because she loves Tina so much, she indulges her, spoils her, and fails to regulate her activity and her consumption, and even Tina's later experience of coeducation cannot prevent her from at first making wrong choices in marriage. Yet, at least for the time being, Miss Mehitable manages to preserve all that Miss Asphyxia threatens to deny or destroy: Tina's body, her physical capital, her gender and sexual identity. In so doing, Miss Mehitable's existence is legitimated and redeemed: she, too, earns "the blessed privileges of the family state."

To return to the earlier description of Miss Mehitable as masculine—a man among men, interestingly enough—it is mother love and not heterosexual attraction that converts Miss Mehitable from "masculine" to "feminine" by bringing out "a heart capable of those passionate extremes of devotion which belong to the purely feminine side of women." The language in which the text chooses to describe Miss Mehitable's relationship with Tina indicates that while relationships with men have "never touched the inner sphere of [her] heart," just the mention of Tina as her possession causes Miss Mehitable's heart to give a "great throb." Here, through the echoes of the term "heart throb," maternality is contrasted with yet simultaneously implicated in the language of romance; already, then, there are hints that this maternal affection contains a homoerotic charge.

Romero, describing Tina's erotic attractiveness, writes that "Stowe suggests that women's power over men depends upon their ability to please. Her character Tina's spectacular beauty, far from being a source of temptation for Stowe's male characters, is instead presented as, potentially, an agent of their regeneration. The narrator speaks of romantic 'LOVE' as the 'greatest and holiest of all the natural sacraments and means of grace.'"[48] Ironically, it is this same irresistible attractiveness of Tina's that makes it impossible for Miss Mehitable to discipline her properly, and instead leads her to give into Tina's demands. As love for Tina will later lead male characters to repentance, here Miss Mehitable's love for the girl is almost immediately translated in the novel into a relationship with God. Hearing Tina recite an old hymn, Miss Mehitable is flooded with a new sense of

God's presence, as shown when she narrates her experience in a letter to her brother: "When I laid my little Tina down to sleep tonight, I came down here to think over this strange, new thought,—that I, even I, in my joyless old age, my poverty, my perplexities, my loneliness, am no longer alone! I am beloved. There is One who does love me,—the One Friend, whose love, like the sunshine, can be the portion of each individual of the human race, without exhaustion" (184). Realistically speaking, Miss Mehitable is "no longer alone" because she has adopted Tina, but the narrative immediately converts this adoption into a religious reawakening. Homoerotic "love" becomes sanctified affiliation. Such a shift from a love between a (surrogate) mother and daughter to one that emphasizes a "higher" love also distinguishes many other pedagogic scenes of postbellum disciplinary intimacy, as I will explain in my next chapter. Yet there may still remain a trace of this other love, even as the narrative tries to replace it with something more "pure."

⸻

In being "useless" because of her marginal relation to domestic labor, and "unnatural" because she does not have children, the spinster may represent the site of queer or protolesbian possibilities in nineteenth-century U.S. culture. In signifying the boundaries of what counts both as acceptable forms of female "work" and as "natural" forms of maternality, she mediates between the public and private, the market and domestic sphere, the middle and working class, and in some cases the lines of racist division between white subjectivities and those marked as racially or ethnically "other." Thus, we may see the spinster as categorized with and therefore allied with people of color.

But while stereotyping may link her with other "iconic minority subjects," to use Berlant's term, the old maid is simultaneously a racially marked or specific identity category and represents a specific form of white femininity. Thus, she reminds us that twentieth-century conceptions of lesbian identity, which engage, repeat, and revalue even as they revise tropes of the spinster's discursive position, may originate in a particular racial context.

It is only in retrospect, in reinscribing and simultaneously reclaiming the spinster that, as I will demonstrate below, modernist lesbian writers are able to create a reverse discourse for themselves of the "old maid." It seems unlikely that white women who did not marry in the latter half of the nineteenth century would have been able unambivalently, or at all, to claim spinsterhood as an empowering identity category or to celebrate its unnatural ties to modernization or the mobility it signified for women. Nevertheless, it may be the case that the spinster offered an alternative to sexology for imagining and representing a modern lesbian identity.

Chapter 2

"TRYING ALL KINDS":

LOUISA MAY ALCOTT'S

PEDAGOGIC EROTICS

❦

"'Mothers are the *best* lovers in the whole world,'" Jo March declares in *Little Women;* however, she doesn't end her sentence there, she continues, "'but I don't mind whispering to Marmee, that I'd like to try all kinds'" (537). At the same time that this statement maintains the centrality of the mother's influence—Jo confesses her hope to "try all kinds" *to* her mother—and the desire it inspires, it extends the structure of disciplinary intimacy beyond the realm of the mother. Although in Stowe's *Oldtown Folks* (1869) the political and erotic imaginary of the novel ostensibly maintains a distance between (hetero)maternality and queerness, Alcott's writing breaks down this (false) opposition as it interrogates the erotic possibilities of mothering itself, as well as those of the various semipublic/semiprivate spaces arising for women in the mid- to late nineteenth century. In so doing, Alcott's novels deconstruct the opposition between the domestic and the public and the family and the institution. At the same time that the production of white, middle-class female identity begins to take place outside the family, a proliferation of identifications and desires within the family undermines even as it reinstates heteronormative masculinity and femininity. Indeed, as I will illustrate in this chapter, Alcott's texts endlessly detail how individuals are made and remade through the loving example and discipline not only of mothers but of fathers, brothers, sisters, teachers, mentors, writers, and readers.

The fact that so many different possibilities for protopedagogic encounters populate Alcott's texts points to the historical context of her writing: after the Civil War, in part because of the needs of capitalist reorganization, white, middle-class women began to trade the subject-forming powers of the home and the maternal for other institutionalized arenas in which they found competing models for identity formation.[1] Alcott's novels and stories continually traverse these supposedly distinct spaces: in *Little Men: Life at Plumfield with Jo's Boys* (1871) and *Jo's Boys, and How They Turned Out* (1886), Jo's school, Plumfield, mixes the ideals of the family with the workings of the institution, while in *An Old-Fashioned Girl* (1870), the heroine, Polly, moves between her own home, that of the overly leisured Shaw family, and the idealized boardinghouse in which she has "a room of her own."[2] Similarly, *Diana and Persis* (1879), Alcott's unfinished novella, dramatizes the semipublic/semiprivate rewards of the artist's studio (especially when contrasted with the sacrifices of marriage and motherhood), whereas Christie, the main character of *Work: A Story of Experience* (1873),[3] leaves what has never really been "home" to occupy a variety of public and private spaces as she changes jobs, only to end up in what is a utopian counterpublic sphere of women that conflates both the domestic and the public.[4]

In traversing these spaces *Little Women*, as well as Alcott's oeuvre as a whole, illustrates, as it simultaneously produces, a slippage between an identificatory erotics located inside (and confined to) the family; a slippage that finds new models for identification and desire outside its bounds. Such an extension of the sentimental scene of maternal tutelage to new semipublic/semiprivate spaces, in turn, I will argue, challenges the normative effects of disciplinary intimacy even as it reinstates them. Alcott's novels, in their charting of a proliferation of (proto)pedagogic, (proto) maternal disciplinary encounters, do more than just reinforce oppressive and repressive norms of gender and sexuality. Although they at times inevitably reproduce the discursive structures that enclose their subjects, they also interrogate and deconstruct these structures, sometimes producing through them new sites of resistance. Specifically, in this chapter I will illustrate how, in the shift in U.S. culture in the mid- to late nineteenth century from an emphasis on the mother to other models for identification, emulation, and concomitantly, desire, new organizations of erotic expression and subjectivity begin to emerge for white, middle-class women, ones that are inexorably tied to the workings of disciplinary culture, ideologies of possessive individualism, and the exigencies of the market.

To argue that the effects of maternal tutelage might be multiple is to challenge the conventions of much of the criticism of Alcott's work. Through their didacticism and their emphasis on the inculcation of "family values," especially the imperatives of domesticity for women, Alcott's novels, or at least those written for children, most obviously extend and popularize the disciplinary structure of identification at the heart of much of antebellum domestic fiction.[5] As I will discuss in detail below, many of Alcott's works, especially *Little Women,* delineate quite extensively the workings of disciplinary intimacy, as Richard Brodhead and others writing after him have demonstrated. This has led many critics to condemn Alcott's project, albeit often reluctantly, as ultimately one of gender and sexual normalization. For instance, Elizabeth Barnes, in her attempt to revise Brodhead's model in order to bring out what she argues is the violence at the heart of disciplinary intimacy—the violence of turning one's anger at the world inward and against one's self—writes that, "In contrast to Brodhead's reading, . . . the internalization of parental discipline in Alcott's writing becomes an internalization of aggression, of attempts to master the self through various forms of self-abuse. At its most successful, the child might even *seek out* punishment in order to be assured of the parent's love."[6]

In their efforts to create "union" through a "love" that Barnes reads as always a form of (self-)abuse, Alcott's novels try to force readers into a repressive form of community modeled on what Barnes views as a relentlessly patriarchal family. A longing for a truly autonomous (female) self, freed from the oppressive norms of this vision of family, as well as from the inevitable (but seemingly transcendable) splitting of the self produced by disciplinary culture, underlies such critiques. Even Elizabeth Young, whose provocative discussion of Alcott's Civil War fiction charts its (and, she argues, Alcott's) fascination with homoerotic desire and cross-gender identification (what Young terms "the permeable boundary between masculinity and femininity"), ends up concluding that the emphasis on the carnivalesque in Alcott is ultimately overcome by her reassertion of a feminine disciplinarity as the model for female *and* male subject formation. Young describes this as the moment when white, middle-class "feminization becomes feminism," and as Alcott's representation of an attempt to reform the nation along the principles of domestic self-regulation, yet she also views it as ultimately a "marked victory of civility over conflict," the success of which is predicated on the repression of "topsy-turvy" gender and sexual instability, as well as racial difference.[7]

Such readings epitomize the tendency that I have argued in my introduction characterizes much criticism of sentimentality, that of viewing it as either essentially normative (antifeminist, a symptom rather than a critique of capitalism and/or patriarchy) or radically democratic (anti-patriarchal, antimarket). Sexuality within these criticisms becomes either an agent of repression or a utopian (and often unsustainable) form of inter-subjective affiliation. In Alcott's case, these judgments are based on what are taken within her texts to be stable forms of opposition between a fe-male subjectivity formed through the market and one formed outside of it, between repressive mothering/domesticity and liberating masculinity/publicity (in Young), and (in Barnes) between a subjectivity formed inside and one formed outside the norms of a patriarchal family/nation (i.e., be-tween a split subjectivity constructed through a structure of disciplinary identification that is inherently violent, abusive, and self-alienating and an unrepresented yet always already underlying vision of an escape from in-tersubjective, psychic relations of power, which would in turn presumably produce a unified female self). In particular, these critics overlook the pleasures of disciplinary identification, as well as the sites of resistance or subjective reformulation that such pleasure might produce.[8]

Examining the possibly resistive aspects of pleasure, centrally conceived here as relations of identification/desire, is not, however, to imagine plea-sure as always already liberatory or as capable of transcending the dis-cursive structures that produce the subject. Instead, in this chapter I seek to understand the ways in which subjects "make do" within overarching structures of domination by renegotiating, reinhabiting, or to use Judith Butler's terms, "performing" with a difference what are often limiting forms of identification.[9]

Although subject formation in general always involves a self-relation, I describe in this chapter the effect of the more particular and historically specific ideology of autonomous individualism ("self-making" in the his-torically limited sense) on white female subjects. Alcott's oeuvre as a whole is centrally concerned with the tensions, differences, and increasing overlaps between a disciplinary individualism instantiated within senti-mentalism as a (quintessentially "feminine") form of self-loss and a pos-sessive individualism represented as a (normatively "masculine") form of self-making.[10] Disciplinary intimacy purports to replace an unruly self with another's superior example (producing continual self-loss, a repeated giving up of self for all others, as epitomized in the mother) whereas pos-sessive individualism views the self as one's own property, in which one in-vests and in which one "improves" through the ideologies of self-making.[11] These two accounts of self-formation are often opposed: disciplinary sub-jection cancels out and repudiates agency whereas possessive individualism epitomizes it. Rather than reiterate this opposition, however, I am interested in the ways in which in Alcott's novels the distinctions between the oppositions break down. For example, the assumption behind Marmee's efforts to reform Jo is that in fact selves can be (re)made: self-making is at the heart of the disciplinary.

Furthermore, in examining the intersubjective relations between texts and readers, I not only investigate the ways in which texts might reproduce relations of disciplinary intimacy (with readers identifying *as* Jo, submitting to Marmee's authority), but I explore to what degree Jo's continual (self-)discipline and continual self-making may become an eroticized model for readerly emulation/desire. Although the *Little Women* series may illustrate the limits placed on Jo's identifications/desires by the heterosexual family, these books simultaneously allow their *readers,* through the processes of fantasy, to "try all kinds." Commodity culture becomes, then, not just a symptom of cultural decline, but an avenue for new forms of queer identity.

Finally, in this chapter I examine the workings of disciplinary intimacy in an interracial context, as well as in post-Reconstruction texts authored by African American women. Focusing on Topsy's self-(re)formation in *Uncle Tom's Cabin* (1851) and on Emma Dunham Kelley's *Megda* (1891),[12] which, as Claudia Tate has argued, may be viewed as an explicit response to *Little Women,*[13] I argue that the political and social limits placed on African American women mean that self-making is not necessarily the same celebrated or eroticized practice that it is for white women. Because disciplinary intimacy is used to control and sometimes eradicate minority subjects or at least signs of racial or cultural difference, assuming in advance an identificatory erotics may be difficult and even problematic. On the other hand, texts such as *Megda* do employ these same structures of subject production and do contain examples of eroticized relations between women.

Like Mother, Like Daughter

Any examination of the workings of identification in Alcott must begin with thoughts of Marmee. Her entire identity is consumed by mothering— this leads Beth, when making Marmee's Christmas present, to embroider "Mother" on a set of handkerchiefs. "'Bless the child, she's gone and put "Mother" on the handkerchiefs instead of "M. March"; how funny!'" (22), Jo teases, but Beth's choice of appellations makes perfect sense because Marmee *embodies* motherhood, something that Beth, who represents the familiar nineteenth-century stereotype of the dying, pure daughter, intuitively understands. "Mother" is Marmee's true name.

It is Marmee's duty to encourage in her girls "the sweetness of self-denial and self-control" (104). Restraint includes managing anger: as Marmee famously confides to Jo, "'I am angry nearly every day of my life . . . but I have learned not to show it, though it may take me another forty years to do so'" (101). The novel includes numerous examples of Mrs. March's maternal tutelage. For instance, she instructs Jo on how to handle her temper; she sets up a week without work to demonstrate to the four sisters the importance of selfless domestic labor; and she steps in to save Meg's relationship with her husband, John, and thus rescues and restores her daughter's relation to the domestic sphere. In almost every case, Marmee's teachings replicate the most stereotypical and confining ideas of women's role within the home, the "cult of true womanhood." She provides the maternal basis for disciplinary intimacy: through playing on the girls' sympathies and devotion she encourages them to become self-regulating, and she is so successful that they readily and regularly confess their sins and vow to do better.[14]

Marmee's influence so pervades the lives of her daughters that, having fully internalized her surveillance, they leave home each day looking over their shoulders for her, as this somewhat ambivalent, sentimentalized description narrates:

> They always looked back before turning the corner, for their mother was always at the window, to nod, and smile, and wave her hand to them. Somehow it seemed as if they couldn't have got through the day without that, for whatever their mood might be, the last glimpse of that motherly face was sure to affect them like sunshine. (48)

In general, Marmee reflects the values of domesticity: she defers to her ineffectual husband, often crediting him for her own disciplinary transformation; she takes John's side against Meg's when evaluating the failures of the marriage; and she worries when Jo goes off into her "vortex" of writing, as though this activity were somehow dangerous to Jo's sense of self (and indeed it is).

There are some exceptions to this control, however. Marmee encourages each girl to find her vocation, and she does not advocate marriage at all costs: "'Better happy old maids than unhappy wives, or unmaidenly girls, running about to find husbands'" (123). And the effects of her loving example have caused decades of critics and readers great anxiety. As Ann Murphy sums up the critical history of *Little Women:* "Is *Little Women* adolescent, sentimental, and repressive, an instrument for teaching girls how to become little, domesticated, and silent? Is the novel subversive, matriarchal, and implicitly revolutionary, fostering discontent with the very model of female domesticity it purports to admire?"[15] Although not always explicitly acknowledged, this debate centers on the effects of Marmee's influence on the March girls, in particular on Jo.

Jo is Marmee's problem child. She needs special attention—Marmee takes her aside more often than the other girls to praise or indict her antics. Although Marmee inspires in Jo the desire to "be good" and, in imitating her example, to submit to the dictates of bourgeois femininity, she also inspires in Jo other desires. Through Marmee's intense pedagogy and her efforts to mold Jo and her sisters in her own image, she produces homoerotic (and openly incestuous) longings that are naturalized, although not without some amount of narrative discomfort, within *Little Women:* "It wasn't quite the thing, I'm afraid, but the minute [Meg] was fairly married, [she] cried, 'The first kiss for Marmee!' and turning, gave it to her with her heart on her lips" (311). The narrator excuses Meg's actions as "not quite the thing," as somewhat out of fashion or favor. But what the scene describes is Meg kissing her mother instead of her husband. "Turning" away from her husband, she seals her marriage to mother(hood) over her marriage to a man.

Feminist critics have tended to read such moments in Alcott as simply reinscribing Carroll Smith-Rosenberg's "female world of love and ritual."[16] As Judith Fetterley notes:

> Despite Marmee's dictum about being loved by men, what we see and feel in reading *Little Women* is the love that exists between women: Marmee and her daughters; Jo and Beth. Thus while the events of Jo's life are determined by the book's overt message, her wish to resist the imperative to be a little woman and to instead marry her sister and remain forever with her mother is endorsed by the book's covert message.[17]

In her use of the terms "overt" and "covert," Fetterley reinscribes the idea of surface versus depth in Alcott, the hidden rebellion that finds its alibi in domestic sentimentality.[18] She views homoerotics as the secret "message" of the text. Certainly Alcott, in representing Marmee's character-building influence, relies on and replicates the conventions of the nineteenth-century domestic novel. Yet she *explicitly* queers this process; the homoerotics are there in full view, not hidden away as Fetterley implies.

On the other hand, because they are so visible it would be wrong to read these expressions of erotic devotion between white women in the nineteenth century as having no social or political currency but simply existing within the landscape of bourgeois culture. Such a reading has allowed critics to dismiss any such intensities between women as "passionate friendships," as though this term summed up the complexities of these interactions. This argument in fact creates a border behind which critics feel justified to remain, and in which the imprecision of the "female world" is used as a catch-all for any erotic or nonerotic relationship or practice. Instead, *Little Women,* and Alcott's oeuvre as a whole, constitutes a commentary on the workings of maternal discipline: it represents a historically specific form of "mother loving," one that is inseparable from the molding of subjectivity expected by nineteenth-century ideals of (self-) formation.[19] Moreover, it is the proximity of the works to other female-female spaces that makes explicit the homoerotics at the heart of this relationship.

That the phenomenon of the queering of disciplinary intimacy was common *outside* the confines of the family has been documented by historians of women's education. Helen Lefkowitz Horowitz, in outlining the educational philosophy of Mary Lyon (the founder of Mt. Holyoke College) describes how Lyon tried to reproduce the mother/daughter relationship within the school for "larger" ends:

> A daughter's most intimate tie was to her mother; in seeking to imitate her, a daughter normally reproduced her mother's life. In the seminary Lyon re-created the mother-daughter relationship in the link between teacher and student. However, unlike the mother, the teacher offered an alternative way of life: rationality, rather than tradition; the order of the clock, rather than the rhythms of nature. To win the love of one's teacher, one imitated her.[20]

Educational establishments drew on the mother/daughter relationship and its proven moral benefits as the model for teacher/student intimacy, although with some important differences. As Horowitz notes, the space of the institution organized and rationed what might have been in the intimacy of the bourgeois home an excess of affection or of time spent together, one on one. Martha Vicinus, in her analysis of the effects of boarding school life on white, bourgeois girls, credits precisely this semipublic/

semiprivate space of the school, which is not the cozy domestic nest, with nurturing homoerotic female-female relationships.[21] She highlights the ways in which the meaning of the "private," the special meeting of student and teacher to discuss the student's salvation or progress in Latin, was heightened through its tension with the overwhelming emphasis on publicness. To get special attention was every girl's dream, and this motivated her to work harder (or in some cases to draw attention to herself through less publicly affirmed displays of behavior). This in itself, Vicinus argues, created erotic tensions, intense feelings of identification/desire that were channeled into the educational mission of the institution. It is these sorts of movements from distance (achieved through what Horowitz calls the "rationality" of time and space in the "public" sphere of the school) and proximity (the stolen smile from a special teacher, the shameful dressing-down for one's inadequacies at deportment) that produce the most powerful identificatory effects.[22]

When read against these descriptions of the mimetic imperative in the semipublic/semiprivate sphere of the school, the erotic valences of Marmee's instructional intent become even more obvious. By inspiring in Jo the desire to *be* her, Marmee invokes the desire to *have* her as well. Being thus becomes a form of having and is inseparable from it. As Mikkel Borch-Jacobsen puts it, "Identification is not a means for the fulfillment of desire, it is that 'fulfillment' itself."[23] And it is because Jo wants to have Marmee that she works so hard to "become" a good little woman: unlike the first generation of college graduates, who might fight their way into newly organized professions for women, Jo has few socially recognized identificatory options available to her other than that of mother and, secondarily, of wife, although she does struggle with the identity of "writer." Thus, it may seem that identificatory desire here is simply an agent of normalization, the force that makes Jo into her mother, as represented most clearly through Jo's marriage to what critics often see as a father substitute, Professor Bhaer.[24]

Furthermore, Jo also uses the space of the school to inspire in her young charges the same values that Marmee has inculcated at home, what Karen Haltunnen has termed the "key virtues in the 'moral management of the calculated life' that were becoming the Victorian ideal of conduct as the American middle classes rose to cultural dominance in the 'age of capital'"; that is, "self-knowledge, self-help, and self-control."[25] In so doing, Jo becomes (just like) Marmee. Alcott's narrative makes this explicit in *Jo's Boys,* when Jo repeats to Dan, her favorite problem pupil/son, what her mother had once said to her. When Dan is confiding his failures at self-control, "Mrs. Jo" replies: "'I can sympathize with you; for I've been trying to govern my own temper all my life, and haven't learned yet'" (96).

This moment of repetition is often interpreted by feminist critics as signaling Jo's total reformation, the triumph of the maternal-tutelary and the inevitability of its reproduction.[26] Such a reading, however, misses the other identificatory possibilities open to Jo before and after her marriage, as well as its significance or nonsignificance: ever since Alcott published *Good Wives,* the eagerly awaited sequel to *Little Women,* Jo's marriage has constituted a seemingly insurmountable problem for readers and critics. Dismayed when Jo refused Laurie's proposal, readers were even more dissatisfied with her ultimate choice of male partners; critics share this disappointment, often reading Jo's union with Professor Bhaer as signifying her final submission to patriarchal authority.[27] As I discuss in more detail below, that Jo married at all was viewed by Alcott herself as a concession to her readers, what one might call "a marriage of (narrative) convenience." Against those critics who would read Alcott as simply submitting to the dictates of bourgeois compulsory heterosexuality, Donna Campbell argues compellingly that Alcott manipulates sentimental conventions: while ostensibly fulfilling the expectations of the genre (Jo marries the older, well-established male who plays a disciplinary role himself in her education, just as Ellen marries John in Warner's *The Wide, Wide World*), Alcott reveals the limits of heterosexual romance, the distasteful allegiances that are disguised in the ideology of sentiment.[28]

In marrying a man like her father, and in disciplining her own children as well as her pupils, Jo has become Marmee, yet this is repetition with a difference.[29] Without question Jo identifies as a mother; however, she rarely identifies as a *woman,* except when allying herself with the position of the "old maid." Thus, as I discuss in the next section of this chapter, Jo's eroticized relation to maternal tutelage is of a somewhat different type than Marmee's; indeed, so different that it cannot easily be subsumed within accounts of Jo's inevitable "fall" into domesticity and of her as simply an agent of normalization. Therefore, instead I will demonstrate how Alcott's novels are engaged in "trying all kinds," taxonomizing and elaborating a multiplicity of identificatory erotics that traverse what seem at first within the texts to be paired binary oppositions such as "married" versus "unmarried," mother versus "other," as well as those of women versus men, girls versus boys, and little versus big.

Alongside Marmee's disciplinary influence, *Little Women* provides other models for Jo's subject formation, as signaled most notably by the fact that Jo, for most of the novel, asserts that she will remain "a literary spinster," while in *Little Men* and in *Jo's Boys* she remains a writer and becomes, most importantly, a teacher. As something of a "literary spinster" herself, Aunt March, the (quasi) old maid of the family, constitutes one important identificatory alternative for Jo.[30] In her will, Aunt March leaves to Jo her large, well-furnished home, Plumfield, which enables Jo to fulfill her long-time fantasy:

> "Before my Fritz came, I used to think how, when I'd made my fortune, and no one needed me at home, I'd hire a big house, and pick up some poor, forlorn little lads, who hadn't any mothers, and take care of them, and make life jolly for them before it was too late. . . . I've always longed for lots of boys, and never had enough; now I can fill the house full, and revel in the little dears to my heart's content. Think what luxury; Plumfield my own, and a wilderness of boys to enjoy it with me!" (592–93)

Here Jo indicates that her plans to run a home/school for boys predate her relationship with her husband. Not only has her aunt given her the material means by which to achieve this goal but Aunt March herself has at least attempted to exert her influence over Jo, even though for much of the novel Jo has resisted and regretted their interactions. She finds her job as Aunt March's companion interminably boring yet it also offers her access to books, which are crucial to Jo's development as a writer. And both she and Amy undergo Aunt March's version of domestic instruction.[31]

Even though Aunt March and Jo often appear to be at loggerheads, the text indicates that Jo has internalized her example. Like Aunt March, she always speaks her mind: when news reaches the March family that their aunt has died, the narrator describes their reaction: "They loved the old lady in spite of her sharp tongue" (591); and it is this same sharp tongue that always gets Jo into trouble. In addition, Jo herself explicitly identifies as a spinster: when Laurie, Jo's boyhood companion, cautiously drops the subject of marriage, Jo replies, "There should always be one old maid in a family" (306). For much of the novel Jo intends to take up Aunt March's place, and the fact that she inherits the spinster's home and turns it into a school indicates that, despite her marriage, in some ways Jo has become her aunt.

Yet, although an old maid may provide the material and identificatory possibilities for Jo to imagine herself existing outside the family, through pursuing a profession in teaching, it is her persistent masculine identification throughout all of the books in the series that constitutes the most obvious challenge to any reading of her as submitting in full to the limits of domesticity. When *Little Women* begins, Jo is fifteen years old; the book details lovingly her appearance: "Jo in maroon, with a stiff, gentlemanly linen collar, and a white chrysanthemum or two for her only ornament" (36); and "Laurie's bashfulness soon wore off, for Jo's gentlemanly demeanor amused and set him at his ease" (40). Jo often refers to herself as a boy; when discussing what Christmas presents each sister should give to Marmee, she proclaims, "'I'm the man of the family now papa is away, and *I* shall provide the slippers, for he told me to take special care of mother while he was gone'" (12). Similarly, when getting to know Laurie, Jo states, "'Don't go to school; I'm a business man—girl, I mean'" (66). Over and over she wishes that she were "born" a boy: when Meg's marriage threatens the tightly knit homoerotic atmosphere of the family, Jo intones: "'Oh, deary me! why weren't we all boys? then there wouldn't be any bother'" (250). Furthermore, Jo wants to steal off with Laurie and have adventures: "'If I was a boy, we'd run away together, and have a capital time; but as I'm a miserable girl, I must be proper, and stop at home'" (262). It is especially around Laurie that these cross-gender identifications occur: under the pressure of her mother's pedagogical intensity Jo often confesses herself to be an inadequate girl or woman, but with Laurie she prefers to be called "my dear fellow."[32]

Such details are often read as demonstrating that the relationship between Laurie and Jo is one of sameness and therefore not "romantic." For example, Madelon Bedell argues, "[Laurie and Jo] are not romantic at all, more like two boys together."[33] It seems that Marmee shares this view as well; when Jo confesses that she fears Laurie's marital intentions, Marmee responds, "'You are too much alike, and too fond of freedom, not to mention hot tempers and strong wills, to get on happily together, in a relation which needs infinite patience and forbearance, as well as love'" (407). But these two definitions of sameness differ: in the first, Bedell assumes that gender symmetry automatically rules out desire; in the second, Marmee recognizes that Jo and Laurie's relationship would not hold up under the strictures of socially circumscribed marriage, at the same time that she hints that their samenesses may nonetheless produce passions, "love," or at the very least, "hot tempers."

Jo identifies *as* a boy, thus marriage is not the appropriate frame for her relationship with another boy. Marriage challenges both of their positions as boys: Jo must become a woman and Laurie must be transformed into a man. Even the scene of the refused proposal begins to change him: "And when [Laurie] left [Jo], without a look behind him, she knew that the boy Laurie would never come again" (455). No more can they be boys together when the norms of compulsory marriage come between them.

Alcott taxonomizes the social meaning of boyhood, girlhood, woman-hood, and manhood in *Little Women*. Being a girl may mean being a boy, but being a woman does not. Similarly, being a boy may mean being a girl (the gender confusion inspired by both Jo and Laurie's names undermines any stable gender assignation), and while they both are boys together, Laurie longs to be a sister and a part of the family.[34] After the excitement of his entrance to the sisters' Pickwick Club, an "all-male" establishment, has died down, the narrator remarks: "A long discussion followed, and every one came out surprising, for everyone did her best" (133). At the same time that he has become a man among men, Laurie has also become a girl among girls.[35]

On the other hand, Laurie prefers his own name to "Dora," the nick-name his classmates called him, as though "Laurie" were more masculine. Gender itself remains variable in *Little Women;* what matters is that one remains part of the family, which is why Jo is so threatened by Meg's mar-riage: " 'I just wish I could marry Meg myself, and keep her safe in the fam-ily' "; " 'Meg will be absorbed, and no good to me any more; Brooke will scratch up a fortune somehow,—carry her off and make a hole in the fam-ily; and I shall break my heart, and everything will be abominably un-comfortable' " (250). It is also why Laurie seems so determined to marry Amy even though he remains in love with Jo.[36]

But for a boy to marry he must become a "man," as Amy discovers. When she first encounters Laurie after Jo has rejected his proposal, Amy is disturbed to see the changes that disappointment has wrought in him: " 'If that's the way he's going to grow up, I wish he'd stay a boy' " (466). Yet this is also what makes him available to her as an erotic object: "She had seen her old friend in a new light,—not as 'our boy,' but as a hand-some and agreeable man, and she was conscious of a very natural desire to find favor in his sight" (468–69). Laurie must no longer be just "a boy" to Amy; his manhood attracts her—losing "boyness" makes Laurie an acceptable object for heterosexual married "romance." But he still must be a brother:

> If all brothers were treated as well as Laurie was at this period, they would be a much happier race of beings than they are. . . . As few brothers are complimented by having their letters carried about in their sisters' pockets, read and re-read diligently, cried over when short, kissed when long, and treasured carefully, we will not hint that Amy did any of these fond and foolish things. (522)

Here the novel eroticizes sibling relationships, hinting that the sexual charge in Amy and Laurie's romance is that it verges on incest. If one can keep one's relationship within the family, then its erotic intricacies may be sustained, not forbidden.[37] After marrying Amy and returning with her to the Orchards, when Laurie addresses the two sisters as " 'sister Jo and wife Amy,' " all the conventional significance of both terms has been thoroughly obliterated in a somewhat dizzying identificatory slippage from sister to wife, brother to husband, girl to boy. Gendered and familial markers of identity are unmoored in this queer notion of family.

Critics, when they notice these desires, insist that within the family they are limited to heterosexual (usually epitomized by father-daughter) incest and that any other forms of desire are ruled out by this structure.[38] But such interpretations overlook the many instances in Alcott's writing of same-sex desire that flourish within the sphere of the family/semipublic: certainly same-sex desire flows between sisters, or cross-generationally between mothers and daughters (the scene of Meg's wedding being just one example), as well as mothers and sons. Indeed, such desires often seal the bonds of familial affiliation in Alcott's novels. It would be a mistake, however, to read Alcott as using such illicit desires simply to reiterate the sentimental belief in the private sphere, metaphorized here by a *queer* family, as the heart of society, the family as emblem for national union.[39] Alcott's writing explores the connections between relationships of power and intimacy outside the nuclear family and those within it; therefore, she can reinvest these domestic interactions with erotic intensity. In other words, such a proliferation of homoerotic incestuous attractions can survive because the family's distance from the institution, like the mother's distance from the role of teacher and the sister's distance from the role of fellow artist, is so unstable. Alcott's work is premised on the understanding that not only may an institution resemble a family but a family may resemble an institution.[40] Her novels illustrate what happens when the pedagogics of maternal intimacy become the project of other spheres, and when mothers become teachers and teachers mimic mothers. Her writing reflects a promiscuous mixing of public and private and familial and nonfamilial space, and in so doing undermines the family's centrality even as it reasserts its potency.[41]

This slippage between mother and "other" may also help to explain how and why Jo forges her own relationship to her role within the family. Almost from the start of their acquaintance when she manages to put aside her masculinity, or perhaps at least at first in an effort to do so, Jo maternalizes her relationship with Laurie. She identifies with her mother's pedagogical impulse, as when she exclaims, in *Jo's Boys,* "'I have great hopes of my boy'" (223) or addresses him as "Teddy [her nickname for him], my son" (267). Her language here mimics almost exactly that of Marmee's hopes for Jo and her sisters, as in this passage in *Little Women:*

> "I want *my daughters* to be beautiful, accomplished, and good; to be admired, loved, and respected, to have a happy youth, to be well and wisely married, and to lead useful, pleasant lives, with as little care and sorrow to try them as God sees fit to send. To be loved and chosen by a good man is the best and sweetest thing which can happen to a woman; and I sincerely hope *my girls* may know this beautiful experience." (123; emphasis mine)

It is this emphasis on possession that Jo imitates, "*my* boy," "Teddy, *my* dear." At the same time, she eroticizes it. If she cannot have Marmee, she will be her. If she cannot be a boy, she will mother one.

This is not, however, the oedipal trajectory hypothesized by Freud in which women who desire to *have* the phallus acquire it through having a baby boy; rather, this is a masculine maternal in which having and being are indistinguishable. Jo never relinquishes her cross-gender identifications: even as a middle-aged matron she identifies *as* a boy, or at least as having been one.[42] Her understanding of her two "biological" children reflects this, as described in *Jo's Boys:*

> Rob and Teddy were called the "Lion and the Lamb"; for the latter was as rampant as the king of beasts, and the former as gentle as any sheep that ever baaed. Mrs. Jo called him "my daughter", and found him the most dutiful of children, with plenty of manliness underlying the quiet

manners and tender nature. But in Ted she seemed to see all the faults, whims, aspirations, and fun of her own youth in a new shape. With his tawny locks always in wild confusion, his long legs and arms, loud voice, and continual activity, Ted was a prominent figure at Plumfield. . . . He was [Jo's] pride and joy as well as torment, being a very bright lad for his age, and so full of all sorts of budding talent, that her maternal mind was much exercised as to what this remarkable boy would become. (9)

Rob is a girl like his/her father, whereas Ted is a boy like his mother. Jo identifies with/as Ted, at the same time that the narrative reiterates the maternal-pedagogical imperative, as Jo wonders what lies in Ted's future. Similarly, Jo feels such a strong bond to Dan, the untamed orphan, because, as she explains to her husband in *Little Men*, "He won't bear sternness nor much restraint, but a soft word and infinite patience will lead him as it used to lead me." Her identification with Dan seems to threaten Professor Bhaer, as he responds, "laughing, yet half angry at the idea": "'As if you were ever like this little rascal!'" To this Jo answers, "'I was in spirit, though I showed it in a different way. I seem to know by instinct how he feels, to understand what will win and touch him, and to sympathize with his temptations and faults'" (142). In spirit, Jo feels herself a boy, and a bad boy at that, and this leads her to confuse herself with her pupils, to identify with them at the same time that she compels through her seductive example their identifications with her.

Elsewhere, we are led to understand that Jo prefers boys to girls because, as she puts it in *Jo's Boys*, "'Boys don't gush, so I can stand it. The last time I let in a party of girls one fell into my arms and said, "Darling, love me!" I wanted to shake her'" (46). Here Jo's desire for/identification with boys is contrasted with female-female homoeroticism. Just as it would be wrong to read Jo as some prototype of what Kate Chopin, following Walt Whitman, will later call a "mother-woman," it would also be a mistake to read her as a "male-identified lesbian." Not only is this label historically inaccurate but, as the passage above explains, Jo prefers her own kind, boys, to girls. Rather than the adoration of women (or men), Jo longs for and cultivates the love of boys.[43] Alcott makes sentimental maternity itself into a cross-gendered, homoerotic practice. This understanding of Jo's development from boy to mother contrasts with most feminist interpretations, which either read Jo as submitting to the dictates of domesticity or, at best, as eternally ambivalent, oscillating between desire for her mother and an imperfect heterosexuality.[44] Instead, through a masculine form of maternality, Jo preserves her (his?) own erotic relation to maleness, including her (his) own.

Nevertheless, it would be wrong to romanticize Jo's position as "Mother Bhaer" as some kind of precursor to the equally romanticized twenty-first-century "queer subject" and as totally liberated from the bounds of gender and sexuality, thereby crossing and demolishing lines between masculine and feminine, homosexual and heterosexual, at will. Even the masculine maternal still functions through the structures of disciplinary intimacy, which although they allow for gender ambiguity, at least for Jo, simultaneously limit and normativize other aspects of subjectivity (most notably class and race). As Young points out, Alcott's vision of a reformed nation can only accommodate specific forms of difference: Dan's racialized body must be exiled to the West.[45] Yet Jo's continued cross-gender identifications and her privileging of a male-male pedagogic erotics within which she includes herself indicate the texts' attempt to articulate a queer relation to subjection. To read Jo as an example of a masculine maternal also thwarts and historicizes a narrow psychoanalytic model that must always see such figures as either male/father or female/mother and must pathologize any mixing of categories of gender, sexuality, and desire.

That Jo's history of queer identifications occurs within what are so obviously circumscribed limits—the limits of a domesticity interpenetrated by the proximity of the institution, the limits of her own trajectory, which stop short at a rejection of the identity categories "wife" and "mother"—may indicate that they are designed to draw readerly attention to the restrictions they place on their female and male subjects. Alcott's *Little Women* series, and her entire oeuvre, dramatizes the need for women (and men) to find other identity categories and social spaces besides those offered by the nuclear family, even as her novels appropriate, revise, and queer the familial. In the next section of this chapter, I will demonstrate the ways in which much of Alcott's oeuvre explores such spaces, as well as the queer subject-forming effects these semipublic/semiprivate locations have on the women within them.

The Erotics of Semipublicity

Writing in 1898, Robert Stein penned his vision of the ideal community for single women:

If one thousand unmarried women, instead of living scattered over a large city, could be made to combine their incomes and live together in one house, they could obtain a thousand conveniences of which they are deprived while living apart. They would be in far greater financial security, for only a few of them would at any time be out of work, and the expenses of these could be borne by the rest, till, finding employment, they could pay arrears. Above all, since the essential pleasures of life arise out of our relations with one another, these cooperators, having the amplest opportunity to enter (or avoid entering) into the most varied relations with others, would have the best chance of happiness.[46]

In other words, such an arrangement would prevent unhappy marriages and instead provide "the most varied relations" because women would have a way to maintain their economic independence even through times of temporary hardship, and they would not be forced to marry for money nor to assume even more unspeakable occupations. Stein imagines all social classes of women living together in harmony, with class divisions carefully maintained. The more genteel women would, by their example, inspire the uplift of the poorer women, and all would live without fear of financial ruin. The pedagogical impulse of this vision is so strong that Stein advocates calling such boardinghouses "colleges" in order to highlight their subject-forming possibilities.[47]

While such pedagogical dynamics, as I have illustrated above, flourish in *Little Men* at the "coeducational" Plumfield and later, in *Jo's Boys,* at Laurence College, within Alcott's other children's novels the space of the boardinghouse also resembles a women's college or, alternatively, a settlement house, as *An Old-Fashioned Girl* illustrates. In one scene, the character Polly has been asked by the generous Miss Mills to move into Mills's house. Elated, Polly describes her new "home":

Two old widow ladies live below me, several students overhead, poor Mrs. Kean and her lame boy have the back parlor, and Jenny the little bedroom next Miss Mills. Each pays what they can; that's independent, and makes us feel better: but that dear woman [Miss Mills] does a thousand things that money can't pay for, and we feel her influence all through the house. (224)

Miss Mills, like Jane Addams, runs her own mini settlement house, where she may make her influence felt through her benevolent supervision. Not only do a variety of women who are down on their luck live in the establishment, but so, too, does a group of young, "independent" girls: "Through Miss Mills, who was the counselor and comforter of several, Polly came to know a little sisterhood of busy, happy, independent girls, who each had a purpose to execute, a talent to develop, an ambition to achieve, and brought to the work patience and perseverance, hope and courage" (197). Included in this democratic vision is Jane, a working-class girl who is rescued by Miss Mills and who becomes a "daughter" to her. At the same time that she mothers Jane, Miss Mills refers to Polly as her "head teacher" (219), reinforcing the links between the space of the boardinghouse, the school, and the family. Miss Mills charges her daughters/pupils with the same philanthropic mission that Marmee represents:

> "*I'm* not a 'rampant woman's rights reformer,'" added Miss Mills, with a smile at Polly's sober face; "but I think that women can do a great deal for each other, if they will only stop fearing what 'people will think,' and take a hearty interest in whatever is going to fit their sisters and themselves to deserve and enjoy the rights God gave them. . . . I don't ask you to go and make speeches, only a few have the gift for that, but I do want every girl and woman to feel this duty, and make any little sacrifice of time or feeling that may be asked of them, because there is so much to do, and no one can do it as well as ourselves, if we only think so." (183)

Boardinghouses did not originate in the postbellum period—women had been supporting their families by taking in boarders since at least the beginning of the nineteenth century. However, after the Civil War many more single white women lived in them, leaving behind their family of origin. Although many boardinghouses catered to the working poor (the type of establishment Christie, the protagonist of *Work*, lives in intermittently for the first half of the novel), by mid-century the "problem" of "genteel" single white women living outside of their nuclear families had begun to receive widespread public attention. Yet, as historians Kessler-Harris and Joann Meyerowitz note, most women living on their own were working-class "women adrift," as they were termed.[48] "Women adrift" is also the term used in *Work* to describe a woman's utter destitution, without home or friends; for example, at one point Christie cannot allow herself to believe that she has found security and support at the Sterling's: "The old sadness crept over her, as she remembered how often she had thought this before, and how soon the dream ended, the ties were broken, and she *adrift* again" (242; emphasis mine). Nonetheless, Christie's struggles, as well as Polly's or Jo's, do not represent the lot of most working-class women, and these characters are always signified as embodying an instinctive gentility that places them above the working masses.[49] Thus, Christie represents Alcott's concern with the lot of white, middle-class women in particular.

Many boardinghouses, as well as the workplace itself, offered single men and women the opportunity to intermingle without the watchful eyes of parents. Thus, production of young women's and men's "character" shifted from being the sole responsibility of the family of origin, in particular the mother, to the institutions themselves. For example, in *An Old-Fashioned Girl* Miss Mills takes on the responsibility of managing the women under her roof, and she recruits Polly as her assistant. Moreover, in such boardinghouses young men and women encountered one another without many of the restraints and models of their own family structure (although sometimes the boardinghouses were organized so as to *reflect* the order of the family). In addition to facilitating intragender encounters, these semipublic spaces offered new forms of intimacy and interaction between women *and* between men, ones that may themselves have helped codify and sustain alternative forms of desire.[50]

Alcott's novels, specifically *Work,* put the dramas of the burgeoning market economy to their own use: because of the harsh realities of the workplace, home becomes even more overvalued. At the same time, the fact that "home" becomes a space distanced from the nuclear family—a space in which women enact domesticity with other women—changes these dynamics. In his essay on Horatio Alger, Michael Moon asserts that "Alger's reformulation of domestic fiction as a particular brand of male homoerotic romance functions as the support for capitalism."[51] Moon indicates that it is the rapidly expanding industrial capitalist public sphere and its concomitant demands that in part allow for such male-male intimacies in the first place. Unlike Alger's bootblacks and newspaper boys-turned-petit-bourgeoisie, there was little room for women within the male homoerotics of capitalist management. Instead, white, middle-class women forged their own homosocial spaces (settlement houses, women's clubs such as Sorosis, women's political organizations) within which such dramas of female homoerotic uplift could occur.[52]

For example, in *Work,* Christie meets Rachel in a precursor of the modern sweatshop, a needlework establishment where they both are employed as seamstresses. Their friendship resembles a courtship; it begins with them flirting with one another, an activity increasingly enabled by the proximity such flourishing spaces provided:

> Among the girls was one quiet, skillful creature, whose black dress, peculiar face, and silent ways attracted Christie. Her evident desire to be let alone amused the new comer at first, and she made no effort to know her. But presently she became aware that Rachel watched her with covert interest, stealing quick, shy glances at her as she sat musing over her work. Christie smiled at her when she caught these glances, as if to reassure the looker of her good-will. But Rachel only colored, kept her eyes fixed on her work, and was more reserved than ever. (130)

Although Rachel appears to ignore Christie's ministrations, her eyes give away her longings: "Her eyes belied her words, and those fugitive glances betrayed the longing of a lonely heart that dared not yield itself to the genial companionship so freely offered it" (130–31). It is this private exchange of glances in the midst of public labor that makes the exchange so highly charged. Likewise, Christie finds in Rachel a challenge for her sentimental impulses: "She wooed this shy, cold girl as patiently and as gently as a lover might, determined to win her confidence, because all the others had failed to do it" (131). Here the narrative imports the ideology of disciplinary pedagogy into the workplace; Christie is determined to "win [Rachel's] confidence" just as Marmee compels Jo's confessions.

As part of this philanthropic relationship, Christie wants to give Rachel all that she has: "There was nothing in her possession that she did not offer Rachel, from the whole of her heart to the larger half of her little room" (132). In other words, Christie offers her the private rewards of domesticity, which are contrasted with the deprivations offered by the public sphere of the needlework shop:

> "I'm tired of thinking only of myself . . . I must love somebody, and 'love them hard,' as children say; so why can't you come and stay with me? There's room enough, and we could be so cosy evenings with our books and work. I know you need some one to look after you, and I love dearly to take care of people. Do come," [Christie] would say, with most persuasive hospitality. (133)

It may be impossible to be certain what the "truth" of this scenario might be; yet it is made a potent moment of protolesbian pedagogy by the fact that its mission replicates the structures of female homoerotic intimacies and that it may be this homoerotic "undercurrent" that motivates Rachel's transformation from fallen woman to good Christian. Christie offers her "home," and in the process her *self*, to Rachel through the conventions of Christian charity.

Predictably, Alcott's narrative subsumes such moments into the rhetoric of the family. When Rachel's past is revealed, "Christie, remembering only that they were two loving women, alone in a world of sin and sorrow, took Rachel in her arms, kissed and cried over her with *sisterly* affection, and watched her prayerfully" (142; emphasis mine). *Work* instantiates an erotics of identificatory substitution that shifts continually, as Rachel is described as Christie's "friend," her "sister," her fantasized rival in love (for awhile), and even her "mother." When Rachel arrives back from her mission, she finds that Christie has sunk to the depths of despair, having failed to find new employment, and has fallen ill with overwork, to the point that she has contemplated suicide:

> "Home! ah, Rachel, I've got no home, and for want of one I shall be lost!"
>
> The lament that broke from her was more pathetic than the tears that streamed down, hot and heavy, melting from her heart the frost of her despair. Her friend let her weep, knowing well the worth of tears, and while Christie sobbed herself quiet, Rachel took thought for her as tenderly as any mother. (162)

Intersubjective substitution takes on a new form here; while Rachel has been busy "becoming" (worthy of) Christie, Christie has become Rachel, to the point that she has lost the "home" she previously offered and, along with it, her sense of self. Rachel then replaces Christie as the "mother" in the relationship.

In effect Rachel and Christie have switched places. Unlike the philanthropic scene, in which a middle-class patron always maintains his/her class position above those whom he/she "rescues," *Work* narrates this substitution or trading of identities: Rachel becomes Christie; Christie becomes Rachel, and goes to stay with the same woman, Mrs. Wilkins, with whom Rachel had once lived. But the substitutions do not stop there. Just as in *Little Women*, where the relationships of family are exchanged and reformed continuously (e.g., Laurie goes from sister/brother to husband), in a whirlwind tour through the kinship structure Christie ends up in Rachel's place, as sister to David, Rachel's long-lost brother. When Christie and David are then married, Christie then becomes Rachel's "real" sister;

when David dies soon after the marriage (but not until after Christie conceives, so that she can be a mother to a daughter), Rachel and Christie are legitimately part of the "same" family. As Christie describes it, "'She was my friend when I had no other: she is my dear sister now, and nothing can ever change the love between us'" (353). It is tempting to read this event as another version of the Alcottian "marriage of convenience": through marrying David, Christie gets what she most wants, Rachel (and a daughter for good measure).[53]

They and the rest of the women gathered in what Jean Fagan Yellin terms *Work*'s "feminist commune" as Alcott's "utopian vision" are bound at the end of the novel by their dedication to their vocation, working on behalf of women:[54] "Christie stretched her hands to the friends about her, and with one accord they laid theirs on hers, a loving league of sisters, old and young, black and white, rich and poor, each ready to do her part to hasten the coming of the happy end" (442).[55] Together, these women have found a purpose in life or vocation beyond that of wife and mother, yet in naming this group "a loving league of sisters," the text still mobilizes the terms of affiliation offered by a remade family while simultaneously linking these terms to new forms of female-female association.

In blurring the lines between devotion to one's family and to a "league," the novel also highlights the ambiguities inherent in the term "vocation," which occupies a special place in Alcott's lexicon. As Jo speculates in *Jo's Boys,* "'I sometimes feel as if I'd missed my vocation and ought to have remained single'" (19). Vocation held ambiguous meaning for white, middle-class women in the nineteenth century, as Lee Chambers-Schiller explains:

> Despite the value placed on vocation for the upper and middle classes, it was, in the popular mind, a sex-linked concept. . . . Having a wide variety of possible choices before him, a young man searched for and reverenced his calling as part of the process of social and personal maturation. No such act was deemed necessary on the part of a young woman. She had only to assume the inherent, biologically rooted vocation in which all of her sex were expected to serve their race, God, and country.[56]

Of course, motherhood is the "inherent, biologically rooted vocation." After the Civil War, as I argue in chapter 1, the rhetoric of maternalism offered white, middle-class women a legitimating rhetoric for their extra-maternal aspirations. "Vocation" connotes a religious calling, the ultimate form of self-erasure and a totally selfless dedication to others mirrored on earth in the mother's relation to her children, yet increasingly in the nineteenth century it was also a term used by women to describe their choice of careers outside of the home. By describing such choices as one's "vocation," one could legitimate such pursuits as inside the rhetoric of self-loss even as they became forms of self-making. Through the concept of vocation, the mandate of self-loss in mothering in earlier sentimental fiction is remade into the absorption the woman feels in service to the greater social good (mothering the world), one's career, or simply one's aspirations. At the same time, vocation as a synonym for *career* also increasingly connoted choice and offered a certain measure of social mobility. It thereby confuses an ideology of feminine self-abnegation with an ideology of self-making. Furthermore, through the language of vocation a woman could justify her participation in the public sphere; this was her calling, her preordained destiny, over which she had little volition. Alcott's texts explore, in other words, women's efforts to gain access to the capitalist ideology of self-production, efforts that are legitimated through the discourse of female "vocation."

It is this idea of vocation that binds together the women at the close of *Work*. The ending represents a fantasy of counterpublicity, in which these women, through their collective efforts, may redefine their political and social identities alongside, even in place of, their supposed callings as wife and mother.[57] In Alcott's unfinished late novella *Diana and Persis,* the ideology of vocation as it is nurtured in the semipublic/semiprivate space of the artist's studio not only facilitates this form of collectivity but also provides a way to describe and mediate homoerotic desire between women. In particular, it allows Alcott to rewrite self-loss into an erotics of aesthetic (self-)absorption and (self-)production and, by proxy, absorption in one's female "colleagues"/"sisters."

In *Diana and Persis,* the young, white, middle-class women whose names form the coupled title have devoted themselves to art. Although this has been a singular pursuit for Diana, for Persis (nicknamed Percy) it has been much harder to turn away from the distractions of heterosexual flirtation. Only her sense of vocation keeps her from succumbing to conventional, bourgeois female destiny:

> Percy could no more help having lovers than a clover can forbid the bees
> and butterflies from coming for its honey, and but for her dreams of art,
> she might soon have found her fate as many a young girl does, believing

that women were born to be wives only, and finding out too late that every soul has its own life to live and cannot hastily ignore its duties to itself without bitter suffering and loss. (393)

That the self "has duties to itself" harnesses the language of domestic femininity to the service of nondomestic vocation. And alongside Percy's apparent commitment to herself, and thus to art, lies her commitment to Diana. Here Alcott's text draws on the discourse of artistic apprenticeship to represent another eroticized pedagogical relationship. Diana mentors Persis; she monitors her devotion to her chosen career:

Diana, devoutly believing that "Success is impossible, unless the passion for art overcomes all desultory passions," held Percy to her ideal with stern vigor, always hoping that the time would come when her friend would give all to art and let love go, as she herself had done. Therefore she trembled at every temptation, rejoiced at every fresh denial, and now although her heart sank at the thought of its great loneliness in losing Percy, she bade her go, sure that in work alone her salvation as an artist lay. (393)

But is it really devotion to art or is it a devotion to each other that Diana desires, and "trembles" at the thought of losing? That the two are inseparable, that in fact Diana and art are continuously confused with one another within the narrative, is demonstrated in the scene that inaugurates the tale. After dismissing yet another heterosexual flirtation, Percy returns to the studio that she and Diana share. Renouncing her dalliances with men, she declares, " 'Art is a jealous mistress and now I give myself to her entirely.' . . . Percy threw herself into the arms of her friend with a dramatic gesture, as if she personified the austere goddess henceforth to be served with perfect devotion" (388). This deliberate instability between single-minded pursuit of art and of Diana continues throughout the unfinished narrative, even though the two artists are separated as Persis goes off to Paris to study painting, leaving Diana with the promise that they shall meet up again in Rome. After a chapter of Persis's letters, which detail her single, unencumbered life, the scene suddenly shifts and Diana is on her way to make a surprise visit to Persis, her husband, and their new baby. In the ellipsis between chapters 2 and 3 it seems that Persis has finally given in to her penchant for men and has married, which in turn implies that she has abandoned her artistic aspirations and, by extension, Diana.

The narrative expresses Diana's feelings of sadness and longing at being left behind; she has "a certain proud yet sad conviction that she was no longer first and dearest" (410). Or is it art that Persis has left behind? Although she insists that she has accomplished much on her work since her marriage, when Persis shows Diana her studio there is dust on every surface.

Moving with Jamesian acuity between extremes of revelation and denial, the narrative alternately describes Diana's destitution at being deserted by Persis and the jealousy and sense of endangerment that August, Persis's husband, feels at the arrival of this rival, while at the same time asserting that this is simply a reunion of old friends. These narrative ambivalencies are mediated by the commonplaces of sentimental fiction, as this passage illustrates:

> So they ate and drank gaily together, with all the loveliness of spring outside, and the greater loveliness of love itself inside, touching everything with its peculiar charm. The sense of having stepped into a romance grew upon Diana every moment, and she kept saying to herself, "I shall wake presently in the old studio at home." But she had no wish to wake, for she heartily enjoyed this glimpse of the sweet old story forever being told the wide world over, and forever full of enchantment for those who read as for those who write it. (419)

At one moment in this excerpt, Diana thinks of her intrusion into domestic heterosexuality as a nightmare from which she longs to awake, wishing that she might find herself in the studio, which signifies throughout the narrative as a homoerotic location. At the next moment, these expressions of discomfort are smothered under layers of conventional sentimentality.

Similarly, the narrative account of August's reaction to Diana is tinged by disavowal:

> With feminine tact the women ignored a past in which he had no part and discussed topics of general interest; but allusions and reminiscences, old hopes and projects insensibly slipped into their conversation, enlightening him as to many things he had never known or vaguely guessed before. Presently he fell silent and sat watching Percy while she listened to Diana's plans with a growing ardor in her face, an unconscious tone of regret now and then in her eager voice, an entire absorption in the subject which for the first time in her married life made her forgetful of his presence. . . . He scrutinized [Diana] with intense but covert interest

as if trying to read the character of this friend whose influence he already saw was much stronger than he had imagined. (419)

August fears the sway of Diana's "influence," which may make Persis forget him. Although Diana ostensibly represents the attractions of a single-minded devotion to art, she also represents the (erotic) rewards of female-female relations. Persis threatens to become absorbed in her vocation just as she threatens to become absorbed in Diana. Both pursuits leave no room for her husband.

As if to reassure the readers that no such undercurrent exists, the narrator interjects,

> No jealousy mingled with the very natural anxiety which grew upon him, lest the new element should disturb the peace of home, very precious to a man so long homeless. The generous desire that Percy should have all the happiness life could give her, even if he were not the donor, struggled with a fear that, by this rousing the old ambitions, something of the old unrest and discontent might mar the beautiful repose which had possessed her for a year. He knew by sad experience how hard the effort is to bind a passionate desire and hold it captive at the feet of duty, yet he also knew what rich compensations such sacrifices sometimes bring, since mastery of self is nobler than mastery of the world. He was more ambitious for this young wife of his, both as woman and artist, than she was for herself, but manlike he loved the woman best, and yearned to keep her for a little longer all his own. . . . A shadow crept into the eyes that watched Diana, as if she were the fair serpent who was beguiling his impetuous Eve to taste the ruddy apple she had nibbled at already. (419–20)

Although this passage begins by asserting that August felt "no jealousy," by the end of his ruminations on the danger of a devotion to art over a devotion to being a "woman," August compares Diana to the serpent in the Garden of Eden. It is sexual temptation, as well as the wiles of vocation, that Diana represents here, whereas August's selfish expectations of Persis, his need to hold her "captive at the feet of duty," are revealed.

Already the bonds of this captivity are loosening: Persis is transformed, so much so that she neglects August. She turns her intensity of devotion away from meeting his needs and toward Diana and her art: "He drank the last drops in his neglected coffee cup, finishing them both cold and bitter since Percy had forgotten to replenish it" (420). When he returns from a long walk (presumably taken in order to "cool off"), he finds Diana and Persis painting portraits of the baby daughter, lost in their absorption in their art and, by proxy, each other:

> Both women were intent upon this task [painting the nude baby], working as rapidly as they talked, with frequent bursts of laughter at the impossibility of catching the pretty poses of their lively model. There was a brilliant color in Percy's cheeks, her eyes shone with unusual fire, and she wore what her husband called her "painting frenzy" look, an excited, absorbed expression which he had not seen since she used to come in after a successful day at the Gallery in London. (421)

Percy flushes with the pleasure of the homoerotic space that Diana's reminder of her vocation has offered her and that the studio she had shared with Diana once made possible. That this is an explicitly sexual moment is made even more obvious by the words that August, supposedly in jest, utters at seeing "his" daughter, naked, on the floor. He queries, "'Unnatural mother! Would you sacrifice your child at the altar of your insatiable art?'" (421); the term "unnatural" hints at the awareness that devotion to art might also equal an "unnatural" or queer "insatiable" devotion to another woman, and perhaps even an "unnatural" form of reproductivity.[58]

The chapter ends with a confrontation between Persis, Diana, and August, precipitated by Diana's somewhat spiteful yet irresistible query, "'Do you ever regret the old life, Percy?'" Persis replies with a resounding denial, at the same time attempting to link the two rivals with her body, by taking each one in arm. This action does not ameliorate the situation: "Both [Diana and August] were already conscious of the affectionate jealousy, the spirit of rivalry with which they could not help regarding the richly endowed woman who stood between them, since they represented the two strong passions which divided her heart and ruled her life" (423). Are these "two strong passions" marriage versus art, or are they August versus Diana? This question is impossible to answer because the passions are indistinguishable from one another.

Diana and Persis is Alcott's most elaborated vision of both the homoerotic possibilities of women's semipublic/semiprivate spheres, in this case the studio, and of the ideology of vocation. Looking back again at one of the other instances of female counterpublicity in Alcott, the boarding-house scenes in *An Old-Fashioned Girl* or the vision of female alliance that ends *Work,* the connection between vocation and eroticism seems even more queer. But often the idea of finding one's vocation, like finding one's self, is a solitary endeavor, not as obviously mediated through another woman.

The Erotics of Self-Making

How does one approach the question of the erotics of autonomy, independence, or spinsterhood, its social marker in much of Alcott's work? I have in this chapter explored the ways in which subjects, through the processes of "protolesbian" or queer pedagogy that occur within these spaces, in seeking to "be" or "become" an ideal subject, also seek to have that subject. But at the heart of this process lies a relationship to one's subjectivity itself: when identifying with an "other," one seeks to become an idealized version of one's self, as mirrored in the "other." In encouraging Jo to become self-disciplining, Marmee, at the same time that she inspires Jo to mimic her, also reflects an ideal "little woman," Jo herself. At the heart of disciplinary intimacy lies the erotics of self-production, an eroticized relationship not only to the "other" with whom one identifies but to one's self.

Freud insists that homosexuality is either a problem of identification (as I outlined earlier) or of self-love or "secondary narcissism," taking one's self as one's love object. Expanding on this assertion even as he reformulates it, Michael Warner, in his essay "Homo-Narcissism; or, Heterosexuality," notes that this is in fact *the* model for subject formation in modern culture. As he aptly reminds us, even though Lacan's theory of the subject posits an essential narcissism (the subject is always looking for the "other" who will reflect back to him an image of himself), both Lacan and Freud insist that the "other" is always gendered oppositely. At the heart of their project, as in Hegel's, is the assumption of gender alterity, which then is translated and naturalized into the dialectic of heterosexuality. In these theorizations of subjectivity, only homosexuals look for their self-image in those of the same gender, which both Lacan and Freud read as the root of their "perversion." Following Luce Irigaray, Warner argues that (at least) male sexuality is always a desire for the same (reminiscent of Irigaray's *hommosexualité*), yet Warner insists that this relation to sameness has a historical context, modernity—in particular, ideas of agency and self-possession.[59] What Warner postulates is simply that homosexuality revels in this truism, that it queers the liberal fantasy of agency, of self-making. As he describes it:

The homosexual who makes a choice of "what he himself would like to be" expresses the utopian erotics of modern subjectivity. This utopian self-relation, far from being the pathology of the homosexual, could instead be seen as a historical condition and, in the perverse and unrecuperated mode of homosexual subjectivity, the source of a critical potential.[60]

In Warner's reading of Freud, modernity and, in particular, liberalism produces autoerotic desire, an idealization of self as self-made. (Male) homosexuality becomes the utopian performance of what really underlies *all* subject formation. Yet these ideals of the erotics and politics of queer self-production may often lead to a simple instantiation of the logics and ideology of market capitalism, the idea of free agency. Moreover, such a celebratory vision of utopian self-making has historically been unavailable to women, as well as to people of color.

Building on this fact, feminist accounts of subject formation take one of two positions. Either they follow a psychoanalytic, Lacanian-influenced line of argument such as Irigaray's, which contends that because women occupy the empty space of the "other," they have no subject position from which to desire at all (at least within the symbolic) (and Irigaray posits extrasymbolic fantasies of subjectless female intimacy as an alternative to this positioning)[61] or they take up a New Historicist position such as Glenn Hendler's, which argues that Alcott's novels dramatize a dichotomy between absolute self-loss, what he sees as the "feminine" subjectivity, and self-possession, the fantasy of liberal agency. Seeing Alcott's novels as unable to resolve what for him are the contradictions between these two positions, Hendler postulates that the novels' solution to them is to pose a "feminine—even feminist—collectivity" that enables both the self-loss of identification and collective self-possession.[62] This vision of feminist collectivity resembles closely Irigaray's preoedipal, especially in that it still asserts that individual self-possession is impossible for women (and thereby continues the tradition of seeing them as unable to exercise *individual* agency within the symbolic).

I would argue instead, modifying Hendler's position, that the construction of self in Alcott rewrites self-loss into an erotics of *vocation,* an erotics of self-absorption in one's career and, by proxy, one's female colleagues. At the same time, Alcott's writing illustrates the dilemmas that white, middle-class women face when trying to co-opt possessive individualism for themselves. In attempting to "make" themselves, they end up imitating another's example; in identifying with an "other," they end up "making" themselves. As Mark Seltzer describes this paradox, "The uncertain individuality of the individual, in consumer culture, keeps steadily visible the tension between self-possession and self-discipline, between the particular (one's standard) and the generic (standard ones)."[63]

Throughout Alcott's oeuvre an emphasis on self-production appears again and again, but it is tempered by an engagement with the compulsions of disciplinary culture. As *Diana and Persis* illustrates, it is art itself that epitomizes this engagement: "Diana hid herself in her little studio, consecrating even her beauty to her art, and being her own model, since a better it would be hard to find" (392). Here the workings of disciplinary pedagogy as a self-reforming process are theorized through the conceit of art. "Being her own model" means using her own image as an inspiration, taking herself as her own ideal object, a kind of self-love and self-production that cannot help but inspire Persis to do the same: "Percy staunchly tried to follow her example in spite of many obstacles, her winsome self included" (392).

Although through her idealization of the aesthetic Alcott seems to be trying to imagine a space for self-formation outside the market (although not the marriage market, as Persis's dilemma illustrates), Alcott's *Work* explores the dialectics of subjectivity under capitalism; at the same time that it co-opts the fantasy of liberal agency through self-production for a feminist project it also dramatizes the ways in which Christie's identity is determined and controlled by the realm of production she occupies. Although the novel begins with her "Declaration of Independence," a metaphor that illustrates Alcott's desire to claim the benefits of democracy for American white women, here citizenship equals the ability to participate in the labor market and to experience the mobility (and constriction) of self such an entrance produces.

Each chapter heading of *Work* details the ways in which Christie's identity shifts as she changes jobs. She goes from "Christie" to "Servant" to "Actress" to "Governess" to "Seamstress," as though each movement changed her name and, by proxy, her sense of self.[64] By the time we reach Christie's marriage to David, we expect to see "Wife" listed as just another employment; her tenure as a married woman does not even last as long as some of her other jobs. In so doing, *Work* undoes the "naturalized" relation between femininity and heterosexuality. Marriage becomes one profession among many.[65] Simultaneously, Alcott demonstrates the ways in which the disciplinary regime of production determines one's identity: as working-class servant, Christie may not protest when the mistress of the house decides to rename her "Jane" because that is what she calls all the servants.

In *Behind a Mask,* Alcott's thriller of 1866, femininity and the "romance" of heterosexuality are further denaturalized.[66] Jean Muir, an impoverished, unmarried woman who is thirty years old and thus beyond the acceptable age of marriage uses her skills as an actress to trick an entire family of men into falling in love with her by impersonating a much younger maiden. After toying with the younger male members, her gaze finally sets on the older and most materially secure man in the family, and she convinces him to steal off with her and get married just before her secret is revealed. Paradoxically, she performs her uniqueness as a sexually winsome beauty, but it is her ability to "pass" as a bourgeois, accomplished gentlewoman that legitimizes her power.[67]

Behind a Mask exposes the workings of gender; gender becomes simply a theatrical performance and, as in *Work,* marriage another economic employment like any profession.[68] Yet marriage, like "work" itself, is not a voluntary activity: women are still tied to the mandates of necessity. It is almost banal to talk of gender as performative when speaking of Alcott: one does not need Judith Butler to see that Alcott was clearly aware of the ways in which femininity itself is constructed through the differing demands of family, work in the public sphere, and through commodity consumption itself. One's job determines one's self, as does one's dress, as this passage from *An Old-Fashioned Girl* indicates:

> It is a well-known fact, that dress plays a very important part in the lives of most women; and even the most sensible cannot help owning, sometimes, how much happiness they owe to a becoming gown, gracefully arranged hair, or a bonnet which brings out the best points in their faces, and puts them in a good humor. A great man was once heard to say, that what first attracted him to his well-beloved wife, was seeing her in a white muslin dress, with a blue shawl on the chair behind her. The dress caught his eye, and, stopping to admire that, the wearer's intelligent conversation interested his mind, and, in time, the woman's sweetness won his heart. (206)

Although many of Alcott's novels criticize the excesses of commodity consumption (e.g., Meg's experience of being transformed into a scandalous sexual object through her succumbing to the seduction of luxurious, fashionable, low-cut dresses and fancy accessories in *Little Women,* and

Fanny's commodity-obsessed contrast to Polly's frugality in *An Old-Fashioned Girl*), here there is an acknowledgment, however tongue-in-cheek, that consumption may enable one to alter one's identity or that "clothes make the woman" (or the man, if we remember the loving detail in which Jo's cross-dressing is described). At the same time, such fashion choices continually threaten to deny one's individuality, or, in the case of Polly or Meg, their moral superiority to a bourgeois, flirtatious femininity that is figured as wasteful and/or frivolous.

Thus, although Alcott's novels at times try to delineate forms of self-production less related to commodity culture and female display (art, virtuous femininity vs. femininity as spectacle), this distinction breaks down, as Hendler has illustrated.[69] In demonstrating the increasing overlap of the ideals of self-possession and the norms of disciplinary subject formation, Alcott's texts claim the privilege of self-making for white, middle-class women, even as they eroticize and reveal the limits of this process. The ideals of vocation blur a discourse of self-loss and devotion with a discourse of female autonomy, allowing for new organizations of individual and collective female identity. Often it is the new spaces opened up by capitalism that provide homoerotic possibilities: single women are able to enter into protopedagogic relations with other single women outside the realm of the family, even as they remake domesticity into something between women who are *not* mothers and daughters. Moreover, commodity consumption itself offers limited social mobility for some women through the effects of "trying [on] all kinds."

"Generations of Girls Were Looking On"

Up to this point I have confined my discussion of the erotics of identification and its relationship to various semipublic spaces in the late-nineteenth-century United States to their representations *within* Alcott's texts. But what if one were to examine the counterpublic space that reading itself provided to white, middle-class women after the Civil War? G. K. Chesterton cleverly alludes to such a location in this description of Alcott's readers:

> I have never known, or hardly ever known, a really admirable woman who did not confess to having read these books. Haughty ladies confessed (under torture) that they liked them still. Stately Suffragettes rose rustling from the sofa and dropped *Little Women* on the floor, covering

them with public shame. At learned ladies' colleges, it is, I firmly believe, handed about secretly, like a dangerous drug.[70]

This passage, excerpted from a tongue-in-cheek assessment of Alcott's literary accomplishments, links the scene of reading to white, middle-class women's semipublic spaces. Within such realms, reading, and in particular reading *Little Women,* constitutes a private activity, a secret practice in which one must "confess" one has indulged. It is similar to an addiction, something that might inspire "public shame" (and again, here one might notice echoes of the shame of masturbation). This description underscores the value of the private, eroticized space within the adamant publicity of the institution, the effects of secrecy within publicity. Chesterton implies that *Little Women* itself becomes a catalyst, that the act of reading connects it, however shamefully or privately, to other secret (and perhaps sexual) occurrences at "ladies' colleges," and perhaps even leads to the suffragettes' very public agitation for the vote, a form of feminist collective political action.

That generations of reviewers have viewed with suspicion the influence of *Little Women,* and in particular of Jo, on its readers should come as no surprise. As Elizabeth Janeway defensively asserts, "Jo is a tomboy, but never [a] masculinized or Lesbian figure."[71] In making such a statement, Janeway assumes that Jo served (and continues to serve) as a "role model" for young women. More broadly, critics of sentimental literature often assume that texts affect their readers, although they disagree as to *how.* In most cases, critics simply extend their understandings of intertextual dynamics to those outside the texts: subjects are abused within texts, therefore readers must suffer the same abuses.[72] Sympathy overcomes barriers of race, class, and gender to join characters within texts in democratic union; through reading such texts readers are able to imagine themselves part of the same utopian community.[73] Another version or view of the effects of reading simply inverts the text-reader relation: although texts appear to represent voluntary forms of democratic affiliation between the characters within them, reading them actually enacts a violent form of subjection. While subjects inside texts undergo violent forms of subjection, readers, through vicariously experiencing this subjection, are able either to shore up their own difference from these subjects (as opposed to erase it)[74] or are able to access a realm of the body beyond its own subjection.[75] Assuming in advance the effects of the disciplinary, few if any critics explore the psychological processes involved in reading as producing multiple forms of identification. On the other hand, historians who attempt to document the reading experiences of actual, individual readers often are reluctant to make *any* assumptions about reading's effects, especially in regard to sexuality.

Rather than interpret the reading subject as in a one-to-one relation to the text, by drawing on queer theory's critique of such strategies I explore in the rest of this section the ways in which reading decenters the subject, not in a fashion that allows the subject to escape the social but within a scene always already circumscribed by the social (including, significantly, the requirements and pleasures of literary form itself). Building on historians' attempts to access and analyze the reading experiences of turn-of-the-century girls/women who avidly consumed Alcott's texts, I theorize readerly identifications/desires in order to argue that readers may experience what I have termed the erotics of disciplinarity with similar identificatory intensity to Jo, and with similarly unpredictable effects.[76] Placing reading within the particular context of late-nineteenth-century (white) women's culture, I will contend that the space of reading provides readers with another semipublic/semiprivate space in which the intensity of the mother/daughter dyad is mediated or replaced by other forms of subject production.

Recently, historians have begun to try to document female readers' experiences: most notably, Barbara Sicherman has examined the effects of reading on white, middle-class girls and women in the United States at the turn of the century. Through closely examining journals, letters, and other documents in which women confided their reading habits and likes and dislikes, Sicherman argues convincingly that reading did not just reinforce domesticity but that in fact it encouraged such dutiful daughters to imagine themselves as active members of public culture, as "heroines" of their own lives.[77] Most significant to this project is Sicherman's survey of the ways in which *Little Women,* and especially Jo March, served as a model for the fantasies of young, bourgeois girls who would go on to become some of the most successful "public" women in U.S. history. Not only, however, did young girls identify with successful women, Sicherman implies that they also identified with male heroes of adventure and historical fame, which then inspired these women to take on roles and responsibilities formerly reserved for men.[78] Furthermore, through examining the specific reading habits of M. Carey Thomas, future president of Bryn Mawr

College and pioneer in women's education, Sicherman demonstrates that reading was not always an isolated, individual activity but often a social one: Thomas and a group of women friends shared their reading experiences and evaluated and argued about their literary tastes. This often-collective experience, Sicherman asserts, gave these women a chance to "try on" selves, to "perform" identities.[79] Simultaneously, she alludes to the other institutional spaces of subject formation in which such young women were ensconced: "Whether stimulated by families, boarding-school and college life, an older tradition of homosocial bonding, or all three, young women often found in reading space to imagine themselves in new ways and to 'talk back' to even the most acclaimed authors."[80] In much the same ways that Alcott's fantasies of female semipublic/semi-private space within her novels enabled different performances of female identity, so, too, argues Sicherman, did these gatherings based on common reading experiences.

Such work is invaluable to any project that attempts to understand the effects of print culture on subjectivity. It is especially important in light of the many feminist readings of Alcott that view her as simply reinforcing sentimental, disempowering ideals of "true womanhood," encouraging young girls to become obedient, self-denying wives and mothers.[81] These histories of women's reading confine their speculations to female ambition, however: while Sicherman hints that Thomas may have found, at the very least, in books a nurturing space for her desires for women, and a space to express and debate these desires with other women through her "Friday Night Club," she shies away from making any claims about the effects of reading on sexuality/sexual identities. She does not suggest, for example, that reading *generated* desires for heroism or for anything else. As she puts it, "Reading was thus not so much a 'cause' of female ambition as a vehicle for articulating and, consequently, intensifying desires."[82] It enabled these young women to redefine white bourgeois femininity—it "authorized" individualism.[83] But is this the limit of reading's effects on girls and women?

Alcott's journals and her representation of Jo's struggles with fandom in *Jo's Boys* describe the overwhelming response her children's books generated. Not only do young girls throw themselves at her with openly erotic adoration but even "grown women" respond to her presence with outpourings of emotion, as in this account from Alcott's journal of her experiences at the Women's Congress in Syracuse in 1875:

Funny time with the girls.

Write loads of autographs, dodge at the theatre, and am kissed to death by gushing damsels. One energetic lady grasped my hand in the crowd, exclaiming, "If you ever come to Oshkosh, your feet will not be allowed to touch the ground: you will be borne in the arms of the people! Will you come?" "Never," responded Miss A., trying to look affable, and dying to laugh . . . and from the gallery generations of girls were looking on. "This, this is fame!" [84]

Alcott represents herself here as bemused and somewhat distanced from the rewards of fame, so distanced that she writes of herself in the third person, a technique she rarely employs in her journals. Is this a false modesty because the metaphor "generations of girls" implies that she comprehends her influence on her readership and she expects to inspire generations to come? Or is this an effort to extricate herself metaphorically from the "particular attentions" of her avid fans? [85]

Not only did the *Little Women* series move Alcott's readers to action but it became for them a vocational guide. For example, in Alcott's journal for 1873, she records the arrival of a new servant: "It was curious how she came to us. She had taught and sewed, and was tired, and wanted something else; decided to try for a housekeeper's place, but happened to read *Work,* and thought she'd do as Christie did—take anything that came." [86] For this young woman, *Work* became a handbook of sorts, a guide to female identity formation within the rapidly consolidating industrial capitalist economy. [87] It inspired her to mimic Christie's example, to become a specific kind of worker who will "take anything that [comes along]."

Here, as Sicherman points out, Alcott's writing has direct effects. But how exactly does reading influence or produce identity? Sicherman draws on recent work in cultural studies and psychology, most notably analyses of fantasy and identification, in order to assert that reading reinforced, and perhaps even motivated, female action and activism. [88] In particular, she makes reference to the work of cultural theorists Janice Radway, Alison Light, and Cora Kaplan to make her case. All three theorists explore the ways in which women's reading of romance novels, while often dismissed as pure "escapism," may in fact allow women possibilities for erotic and political agency. Against those who would view romance reading as simply reenacting and sugar-coating the rigid strictures of compulsory heterosexuality, and concomitantly of oppressive gender roles, these critics argue that the "stock" or repetitive features of these novels may in fact provide a space for the relaxation of dominant sexual and gender ideologies. In fact it may be that, as Kaplan postulates, the fixed closure of the genre enables romance readers to fantasize themselves into a multiplicity of positions within the confines of the narrative, as at least *both* the hero and the heroine: because the reader is assured of marriage as the outcome of the genre, all kinds of fantasmatic identifications may occur between the beginning and the end of the text.[89]

To make this assertion is to argue at the level of form, as well as content, that Alcott's texts do more than simply advocate submission to nineteenth-century confining ideals of feminine domesticity. Feminist critics of the novels often fault their use of form, in particular, for reinforcing culturally determined reactionary narratives of the inevitability of heterosexual marriage. Yet Alcott carefully intervenes in these conventions through her representation of Jo's "choice" of Bhaer over Laurie.[90] Alcott understood the requirements of her genre: she notes in her journal that her readers want to know whom Jo will marry in the second part of *Little Women:* "Girls write to ask who the little women marry, as if that was the only end and aim of a woman's life. I *won't* marry Jo to Laurie to please any one."[91] Despite Alcott's passionate denunciation of marrying Jo to Laurie, Jo does marry, indicating that Alcott *did* respond in part to her readers' demands and to the demands of the genre.

Yet at the same time, as I have demonstrated, Alcott's novels are rife with instabilities of identification/desire. In Radway's new introduction to her study of romance readers she admits that she assumed that readers identified solely with the heroines of the romances. Her assumption resembles Laura Mulvey's argument about the position of the woman viewer in classic film: both take for granted the gender rigidities of fantasmatic identification that women identify unproblematically with the female heroine and reenact through her the rewards of heterosexual romance often denied them in "real life."[92] In opposition to this, Kaplan and Light argue that it is precisely the instability of identification that makes such novels so erotically powerful. For example, Kaplan, in analyzing Colleen McCullough's *The Thorn Birds,* writes:

> These long blockbuster romances do not solicit the reader to identify with a single female protagonist. Rather they evoke powerful overlapping scenarios in which the relation of reader to character is often deli-

ciously blurred. They invite, I would argue, the female reader to identify across sexual difference and to engage with narrative fantasy from a variety of subject positions and at various levels.[93]

Jo and Laurie offer these identificatory indeterminacies to readers. Who identifies "with"/"as" which gender, as well as who might end up desiring whom, becomes difficult to determine and even more difficult to control, at least within the narrative of Jo and Laurie's ambiguous adolescence. This might enable the reader herself to "try all kinds of lovers" within the narrative frame of compulsory heterosexuality.

Kaplan's discussion of fantasy allows for this reading of Alcott, but only in spite of itself. As is obvious in the passage cited above, Kaplan *confuses* sexuality and gender: when she writes "sexual difference" she means to say "gender difference." These cross-gender or plural-gender assignations may indeed enable homoerotic alliances, as I have argued above, but they do not guarantee them. At the same time that Kaplan hints at the possibilities that fantasy opens up for male-male homoeroticism and articulates its occurrences within McCullough's novel, she never once mentions female homoeroticism. On the other hand, although Light in her reading of Daphne du Maurier's *Rebecca* implies that Rebecca and Mrs. Danvers's relationship may have been sexual, and that female readers "can have the pleasure of finding Rebecca desirable *and* of condemning her in advance," she cannot posit female-female sexuality as a real alternative to the bourgeois heterosexuality she so thoroughly examines. Instead, Rebecca becomes a signifier of "deviant femininities" and a repository for a vague utopian vision of female empowerment. In a peculiarly ahistorical move, especially considering that Light takes great pains to locate her analysis in the context of post–World War I British class relations, she cannot read Rebecca as anything more than an amorphous "other" to heterosexuality, regardless of the fact that by the 1930s, the time of the novel's writing, "lesbian" was an available identity category.[94]

This is the problem with many such analyses that maintain heterosexuality, metaphorized through the dialectical poles of "male" and "female," as their epistemological frame—even as they try to dethrone it. It is also one of the weakness of those analyses that substitute various (liberal) visions of a "freed" femininity as their nadir.[95] Perhaps this weakness occurs so frequently in feminist criticism (within which interpretations of Alcott become paradigmatic) because making any assertion about something like lesbianism, which has remained adamantly invisible and insistently denied and disavowed in the face of the absolute visibility of compulsory marriage and romanticized heterosexuality, is almost always empirically impossible. It may also be due to the reality that although it is very politically expedient to declare heterosexuality culturally constructed and maintained, a product of a certain kind of breeding, so to speak, it is much more politically dangerous to declare protolesbian desire itself an effect of a text. Or alternatively, these critical omissions are simply the legacy of a particular discourse of sexuality, psychoanalysis, which consistently subsumes the historical vicissitudes of gender and sexuality into the oedipal model, in which female-female homoeroticism is almost always figured as presymbolic, preconscious, and pre- or ahistorical.[96]

On the other hand, most queer understandings of fantasy, while they emphasize the multiple effects of identification/desire, often cannot account for the effects of history or culture, either. Butler, in her analysis of the overlaps between feminist and adamantly nonfeminist critiques of pornography, employs a psychoanalytically inflected notion of fantasy against those who would argue that representations produce specific forms of harm. Butler exposes how this argument relies on a limited conception of the workings of fantasy and identification (it assumes that women always identify with the victim in the pornographic scene, and men with the victimizer). Like Kaplan, she follows J. Laplanche and J.-B. Pontalis's suggestion that fantasy is precisely the scene of multiple identifications, not only with the dominated and the dominatrix, for example, but with the details of the scene of domination itself.[97]

Butler concedes that "a feminist critic like [Andrea] Dworkin has shown us the importance of pornographic material in its status as *social text* which facilitates certain kinds of readings of domination. And yet, the pornographic fantasy does not restrict identification to any one position."[98] Embedded in this admission is an implicit separation between the social and the fantasmatic. Butler's seemingly casual remark reinstates the division/omission at the heart of psychoanalysis, that the subject can be *divorced* from the social and that the workings of psychic formation happen transhistorically.

This same inability to answer to the social leaves Butler virtually speechless when confronting the racism of Mapplethorpe's images. Her arguments for the euphoric instability of identification cannot address issues of race, except (rightly) to accuse Jesse Helms of an underlying fear of miscegenation. Yet Butler then forms an uneasy rhetorical alliance with Dworkin by arguing that representations *do* "violate" if they attempt to censor. Thus, the only representations that have harmful effects, in Butler's opinion, are those that try to restrict other representations. In answer to Helms's and Dworkin's call for censorship, she makes a passionate cry for proliferation: "If prohibitions invariably *produce* and *proliferate* the representations that they seek to control, then the political task is to promote a proliferation of representations, sites of discursive production, which might then contest the authoritative production produced by the prohibitive law." [99]

On the one hand, Butler's pronouncement (à la Foucault) sounds very much like Kaplan's understanding of the workings of closure in romance fiction: the fact that the law is always already in place is in itself what produces unlawful desires. On the other hand, Butler's political pronouncement, her faith in the powers of "proliferation" itself, which she repeats in similar terms in *Gender Trouble,* sounds suspiciously similar to late capitalism's relationship to commodification. [100]

How might we understand the ways in which fantasy and identification are themselves enabled or foiled by a cultural or historical context? Take the rise of commodity culture in the United States, for example. [101] Laplanche and Pontalis's description of the workings of fantasy dwells lovingly on the *accoutrements* of the scene itself; its "habitus," to use Pierre Bourdieu's terms. [102] Taking psychoanalysis itself as a historical development concurrent with and in a constitutive relationship to modernization and, in particular, market capitalism (the bourgeois family, the domestic, private sphere), I would argue that new forms of the social might enable (or organize differently) new identificatory possibilities. Without reinstating the vulgar, deterministic logics of antiporn advocates who read representation as having a one-to-one relationship to violence, or of a particular brand of deterministic Marxism, which sees homosexual identity as a direct result of capitalism, I would argue that representations do have certain kinds of effects, ones inevitably tied to changes in production. [103]

Alcott's novels invest the domestic space itself, as it is newly filled with the benefits of commodity capitalism, albeit carefully and with great frugality, with new, eroticized, identificatory possibilities that are not located solely in the subject but in the semipublic/semiprivate locations themselves. Numerous descriptions of rooms and domestic furnishings and feasts reveal the commodification of everyday life occurring during the period. [104] This may have had an effect on the reader not explicitly intended within the text: as Nina Auerbach points out, "Despite the girls' mechanical grumbling [in *Little Women*], it is difficult for the reader to believe in what they have given up when she finds herself surrounded with what they have."[105] These scenes of domestic bliss eroticize a fantasy of female agency based in "autonomy," as well as the relationships between the "independent" women who inhabited these spaces together. Take, for example, the description of Polly's chamber in Miss Mills's boardinghouse in *An Old-Fashioned Girl*:

> There was a bright drugget over the faded carpet, the little rocking-chair and sewing-table stood at one window, the ivy ran all over the other, and hid the banqueting performances which went on in that corner. Bookshelves hung over the sofa, a picture or two on the walls, and a great vase of autumn leaves and grasses beautified the low chimney-piece. It was a very humble little room, but Polly had done her best to make it pleasant, and it already had a home-like look, with the cheery fire, and the household pets chirping and purring confidingly on the rug. (140)

Crucial to the "making" and "self-making" of American women was "home-making"; unlike men, who find in the work world a variety of male-male intimacies, as well as what Warner terms the possibilities of "homo-narcissism," the erotics of self-production may be for women—for the most part denied access to capitalist bureaucracy—the erotics of domesticity itself.[106] But this domesticity is not just any kind, rather it is the making of a home with other young "independent women."[107] Young girls might read themselves into such domestic, yet semipublic scenes, perhaps identifying with Fanny's position as she contemplates Polly's "single" existence and shares a meal with the other self-sufficient girls in the boardinghouse: Kate King, "the authoress"; Rebecca Jeffrey and Lizzy Shaw, the artists (who are earlier prototypes for Diana and Persis); and Polly, herself a teacher. They dine on jam and oranges and Fanny finds herself transported:

> Fanny had been to many elegant lunches, but never enjoyed one more than that droll picnic in the studio; for there was a freedom about it that was charming, an artistic flavor to everything, and such a spirit of goodwill and gayety, that she felt at home at once . . . finding it as interesting as any romance to hear these young women discuss their plans, ambitions, successes, and defeats. It was a new world to her, and they seemed a different race of creatures from the girls whose lives were spent in dress, gossip, pleasure, or *ennui*. They were girls still, full of spirits, fun, and youth; but below the light-heartedness each cherished a purpose,

which seemed to ennoble her womanhood, to give her a certain power, a sustaining satisfaction, a daily stimulus, that led her on to daily effort, and in time to some success in circumstance or character, which was worth all the patience, hope, and labor of her life. (230)

Ostensibly, this foray into the delights of independent living has a pedagogical effect on Fanny, influencing her to abandon her life of conspicuous leisure for more edifying employment. But the passage promises more than moral uplift to its readers: it implies that if one takes on a profession, other homosocial and, increasingly, homosexual rewards lie ahead.[108]

Although there is no way to make a verifiable statement about actual reading experiences (even when one has "informants" available, absolute empirical "truth" is never possible, as Radway admits in reassessing her ethnography of romance readers),[109] I would argue, nevertheless, that specific reading experiences, widely available to white, middle-class women as books became increasingly a mass-market item, paved the way for new organizations of sexual, as well as gender, identities. The intense pedagogical scenes of reading, as well as the passionate identifications many readers made with such heroines as Jo, may have enabled them to imagine having, as well as being, such women (and such men). Moreover, at the level of form, the ways in which the *Little Women* series, as well as many of Alcott's other novels, deployed generic conventions while at the same time suspending and critiquing them may have opened up a space for readers to inhabit multiply a variety of desiring subject positions. The serial form of the novels themselves, which encouraged repeated, passionate identifications with characters and spaces, replicates the seriality of (self-) production: at the level of form as well as content, these novels imagine subject formation to be a process of repeated identifications.

The Limits of Self-Making: Topsy and Megda

For the most part, in this chapter I have been exploring the ways in which modernity's reliance on disciplinary subjectivity may itself, within particular social relations, have produced erotic effects; what I have termed protolesbian or queer pedagogy. It would be easy to idealize these moments, yet to do so would be to overlook their interconnection with other forms of imperial conquest and to ignore their simultaneous implication in what Laura Wexler has termed the "tender violence" of sentimentalized attempts at subject formation.[110] Wexler equates sentimental forms of subject production with other more obviously violent attempts to control minority populations, attempts that seek either to wipe out any signs of cultural difference or literally to eradicate these populations. Following her lead, one might argue that Eva's power over Topsy in *Uncle Tom's Cabin*, her ability to succeed where the spinster, Aunt Ophelia, has failed, rests on Eva's irresistible "love" for Topsy, a love that seeks to convert Topsy to a form of Christianity that is synonymous with self-regulation and an internalization of norms associated with white womanhood. In this way female-female homoerotics become inseparable from a normalizing project that has at its center the control of a difference represented in Stowe as racialized. Given this context, it may be easier to understand the power that *Little Women* had over readers other than white, middle-class girls. For example, as Sicherman notes, Jewish immigrants read *Little Women*, in its detailing of Jo's meticulous process of self-(re)formation, not as the story of her coming of age as a woman, but as a quintessential story of Americanization. They found in the novel a representation, in other words, of the ways ethnic and racial subjects are forced to remake themselves to fit larger white, bourgeois norms.[111] We cannot ignore the fact that at the same time that it may represent homoerotic identities and identifications, Alcott's oeuvre also follows the basic patterns of benevolent philanthropy, and of a specifically class and race-marked set of mores and assumptions.[112]

Moreover, the idealized family/semipublic in Alcott's novels is often also an all-white space. Racial and ethnic difference is rarely included within the remade school/family/semipublic sphere: although *Work*'s ending includes the African American character Hepsey, in its vision of female homoerotic counterpublicity, in the *Little Women* series, as Young has argued, bodies that are too racialized cannot be readmitted to Plumfield. Young writes convincingly that Alcott's vision of a remade family and, by extension, the nation after the Civil War is at root a white one.[113] For African American and other minority subjects inclusion and full participation in such a family/nation was not often allowed. Although Jewish male immigrants might assimilate, however painfully and incompletely, into what was becoming the more capacious category of "white ethnic," for black men and women in post-Reconstruction America, Jim Crow laws and the rigid policing of the color line meant that an individual could only "rise" so far within the majoritarian public sphere.[114]

Similarly, antebellum sentimental texts, when they portray interracial examples of disciplinary intimacy, always stop short of portraying them as unproblematically familial. For instance, Topsy's emigration at the end of *Uncle Tom's Cabin* signals the inevitable limits of a disciplinary intimacy structured by racial inequality: because she is always already black, Topsy cannot within the United States fully "become" another Eva, or even another Miss Ophelia (one of "our folks," as the narrative puts it), so Topsy must be relocated to another continent:

> So thoroughly efficient was Miss Ophelia in her conscientious endeavor to do her duty by her elève, that [Topsy] rapidly grew in grace and in favor with the family and the neighborhood. At the age of womanhood, she was, by her own request, baptized, and became a member of the Christian church in the place: and showed so much intelligence, activity and zeal, and desire to do good in the world, that she was at last recommended, and approved, as a missionary to one of the stations in Africa; and we have heard that the same activity and ingenuity which, when a child, made her so multiform and restless in her developments, is now employed, in a safer and wholesomer manner, in teaching the children of her own country. (377)

Critics have commented extensively on the implications of the ending of *Uncle Tom's Cabin*, which denies to African Americans real citizenship in the United States, as signaled here by the curious reference to an unnamed African nation as Topsy's "own" country, even though presumably she was born in the United States.[115] Stowe's narrative is unable or unwilling to imagine a racially integrated American family, yet it fantasizes that properly trained black subjects will in turn colonize Africa using the same disciplinary techniques that were so successfully utilized on them. Topsy continues the disciplinary project, although one safely contained within only her "own" race (and, by extension, nation).

The underlying implication of eroticized interracial disciplinary intimacy that such relations might constitute or at least lead to metaphoric and literal miscegenation (or expose the degree to which many American families had already crossed the color line) is something Stowe's novel resists.[116] In her text as well as in Alcott's, the utopian promise of self-making, of one's ability to "become" the "other," seems to be predicated on an assumption of underlying racial/ethnic sameness, signified and in Alcott often literalized through the familial metaphor.

Within the African American literary tradition, passing narratives explore these limits from the other side, so to speak, often dramatizing the impossibility of or the great loss involved in crossing or passing over into individual white families. Whereas such texts represent individual mixed-race characters' abilities to pass "as white," most of them also advocate abandoning what are seen as dangerous extremes of self-making for an identification instead "with the race." Thus, in a narrative such as Frances E. W. Harper's *Iola Leroy* (1892), the title character rejects an offer of marriage from a white doctor, even though it seems she desires him, in favor of her commitment to her African American family and, by extension, her race. As such, these novels constitute a critique of the American fantasy of individual autonomy that Alcott is trying to claim for white women.

Nevertheless, post-Reconstruction texts authored by African American women that focus on relations between characters of the "same" race often detail the same structures of disciplinary intimacy as do white women's texts; in particular, the ways in which one young women remakes herself in another's image.[117] Many of these novels appear to be adapting the literary conventions of an earlier moment, those of the antebellum sentimental novel of spiritual conversion and idealized female domesticity (as epitomized in *The Wide, Wide World*). As critics such as Ann duCille and Claudia Tate have convincingly argued, however, these African American novels are not simply aesthetic throwbacks or second-rate efforts to copy an outdated genre. Instead, their use of sentimental conventions reflects their most obvious goal—to demonstrate how completely African Americans have internalized the gendered norms of disciplinary self-regulation and thereby gain social recognition and respect, while at the same time shifting to some degree gendered relations of power.[118] Their political purpose is to inspire, presumably, a black readership and contribute to their "uplift," but also to provide counterimages of African Americans to those circulating in the majoritarian public sphere.

As I noted in my first chapter, in the nineteenth century African American women in particular were viewed as sexually unself-regulating. These novels, through their deployment of sentimental ideology, represent black women claiming agency through exercising the right to marriage, to reside in the private sphere, and to a self-possession that includes literal possession of reproduction and sexuality. Because for African Americans marriage was a civil right and signified control over one's sexuality and reproduction, it was not understood as a limit or end to a woman's freedom but as an exercise of freedom. By creating narratives of young women's spiritual transformations and their achievement of domestic reproductive heterosexuality, these novels claim these rights for black women while simultaneously demonstrating that black women not only longed for but already embodied the norms of bourgeois respectability. As duCille and Siobhan Somerville assert, this vision of black womanhood and marriage does not always include sexual passion: duCille thus refers to the obligatory marriage plot as the "coupling convention," emphasizing that marriage is often represented in these novels as a routinized bond rather than a source of romantic fulfillment.[119] Somerville outlines how such an absence of heterosexual passion served a political objective as well—it claimed for black women the same "passionless" image that white women already possessed. But as she further provocatively asserts, it also leaves open the question of other kinds of passion, such as homosexual ones, that may or may not have been represented in black women's texts.[120]

Given these historical differences, in the remainder of this chapter I explore the degree to which we may find the same sorts of eroticized disciplinary relations between women, as well as the same importance of the semipublic/semiprivate sphere, in *Megda* (1891), a text authored by an African American woman, Emma Dunham Kelley. This novel describes the title character's reformation from a proud, independent, outspoken young woman to a submissive and Christian wife and mother. Tate argues convincingly that it would be inappropriate to judge this text using the same criteria that white feminists have applied to its contemporary, *Little Women*, despite the intriguing connection that Tate herself draws between the title character's name and Alcott's novel—namely that "Megda," as Tate puts it, "seems to be a conflation of two names: Magda, which is a condensed form of the biblical Magadalene, and Meg (March), Jo March's sister." [121] Although she seems to agree that *Little Women* represents a critique of patriarchy's demands on white women, as symbolized by the disappointment readers feel at Jo's marriage, Tate argues that *Megda,* despite its ending in matrimony, should be read as an attempt to articulate what appears to be an African American version of a domestic feminism, which valorizes the role of the (black) woman within the family and celebrates her unique, gendered power as mother, homemaker, and Christian.[122] As Tate puts it, "*Little Women* resigns itself to female subordination to patriarchal culture, whereas *Megda* celebrates female piety as an effective mediator of patriarchal proscription." [123] In this way Tate's claims for *Megda* resemble most closely Tompkins's assertions regarding earlier texts such as *The Wide, Wide World.*

Following Tate's lead, we might ask whether it is appropriate also to judge *Megda*'s representations of female-female homoerotics using criteria that emerge from queer readings of "white" texts. Certainly the fact that marriage was a political imperative for African Americans, and that any open expression of sexual desire was more dangerous for a group viewed by the majoritarian public sphere as analogous with uncontrolled sexuality, means that, as I noted above, such texts might be expected to be less eager to cast aside reproductive heterosexuality, especially given the emphasis in these novels on the restoration of the family. Yet in overemphasizing the import of the marriage plot, some of the queer possibilities these texts preserve and/or foreclose might also be missed.

For example, while Tate, in her most recent, groundbreaking reading of *Megda,* explores the homoerotic intensity of the title character's relationships with other women within the novel, her readings are limited by an oedipal model that overdetermines rather than illuminates the account of subject formation within the text. The novel's historical investment in the restoration of the (oedipal) family becomes in Tate's reading simply another repetition of Freudian psychoanalytic norms. She makes married, reproductive heterosexuality the inevitable outcome of the narrative, not for historical or political reasons but for seemingly immutable psychological ones. Relations of homoerotic identification and desire thus become equally dehistoricized, and Megda's intimacies with the text's other central female character, Ethel, become inevitably less central to the narrative (because they are simply echoes of the preoedipal mother/daughter dyad, which is always in Freudian terms just a warm-up for the "real thing," uniting with the father) than Megda's relationship with her future husband, the young minister, Mr. Stanley (the "father" figure). If the novel is instead read as an example of the identificatory erotics enabled by particular historical circumstances—namely, in this case, the political imperative for African American women to display their own successful attempts at internalizing the norms of disciplinary culture, coupled with their increasing access to the same semipublic/semiprivate spheres that white women were already inhabiting—it may be easier to recognize the competing homoerotic and heteroerotic claims on Megda that structure the narrative.[124]

Megda centers on the title character's transformation from magnetic young girl to Christian mother and minister's wife. It begins in the last year of her schooling and portrays a close-knit group of schoolchums similar to the March family or to the girls who gather in the boardinghouse in Al-cott's *An Old-Fashioned Girl*.[125] Among this group of friends are Ethel, whose submissive, pious, self-denying character is the "angel" that con-stitutes the ideal for womanhood in the novel; Laurie, Megda's submissive yet devoted friend; Maude, Megda's nemesis; and Ruth, the charity stu-dent who despite her poverty displays a constancy of moral character and, consequently, through her eventual marriage is able to class ascend. The novel follows what might be viewed as a revival within this community, as girl after girl "heeds the call" and makes a public profession of faith. Re-sponsibility for this revival lies both with the young minister, Arthur Stan-ley, and with Ethel, whose pious example the novel credits with drawing others to the cause. Although Megda and the minister have a flirtatious first meeting early in the novel, what Tate convincingly argues is an ex-plicitly eroticized encounter, as the narrative progresses Megda comes to realize that Mr. Stanley in fact desires to marry Ethel.[126] In the account of the narrative that favors the heterosexual romance, Megda must put aside her desire for Mr. Stanley and focus on her own self-reformation in order to become the model Christian woman, at which time she will be ready for marriage. After Ethel dies on the day she is to wed the minister, Megda carries on, teaching for awhile in the same school in which she was en-rolled as a student, until eventually she and Mr. Stanley marry and have several children. Meanwhile, Maude, who marries for money, dies in pov-erty, leaving her own daughter to Megda to raise.

The novel is structured by a set of ambivalences that are linked to com-peting identifications/desires and spaces. Although on the one hand the trajectory of the novel matches many other stories of conversion in which the main character undergoes a process of self-reformation that culminates in her new relationship to God and her success as an idealized Christian woman, the intensity of the narrator's descriptions of Megda's allure and strength of character prior to her conversion call into question the novel's rote repetition of and submission to these conventions.[127] For example, this passage appears divided in its attempt to temper its descriptions of Megda's attractiveness with that of her "lack":

> This girl with the laughing face and light, merry heart, who thought her-self sufficient for her own perfect happiness, and who was beloved by man, woman and child for her own lovable, wayward, charming self—this girl, lacking only the one thing to make her one of God's most per-

fect creations, not because of her beautiful face, for it was not beautiful, only fair and sweet and girlish—but because of her great capability of loving and of making all people love her—this girl, I say, opened the door and went into her home with this feeling filling her heart. (26)

On one hand, Megda's problem is the classic Christian dilemma: she "[thinks] herself sufficient for her own perfect happiness" and fails to realize her need to submit to God's authority; on the other hand, her self-assurance also puts her outside the bounds of respectable feminine behavior. She is too self-reliant, too outspoken, and too attractive to others. Even the narrator seems irresistibly drawn to Megda's spirit:

> When I write this, it seems as if I must stop and rest, with my pen in my hand, while my thoughts travel back and dwell upon this part of that night's proceedings. Can anyone imagine—it seems as if everyone must—that crowd of bright-haired girls hovering around the heroine of the hour—their pride and queen? Oh, how the girlish hearts beat, as their eager, loving fingers smoothed a fold here, and fastened a clasp there! If Meg shared their nervousness, she never showed it, except it was a brighter sparkle in the dark eyes, and a firmer setting of the full lips. (156–57)

The narrator here ostensibly describes Megda's costuming for the role of Lady MacBeth, but the details also reveal Medga's homoerotic attractiveness, which even the narrator cannot resist. Molly Hite, who wrote the introduction to the 1988 edition of the novel, is right to note the degree to which the narrative expresses ambivalence at Megda's supposedly necessary renunciation of what is represented here as regal power. Yet she identifies this passage as a moment of "maternal[ity]" on the part of the narrator, a moment where the trajectory of the novel toward Megda's "Christian self-abasement" is challenged.[128] Instead of maternality, I would argue that this passage demonstrates the narrator's own attraction to Megda's excess, as well as her nostalgia for the female-female homoerotic relations, signaled here as a group of adoring girls caressing their "queen," that the marriage plot ostensibly replaces.[129]

The narrator's own ambivalence toward Megda's allure *is* echoed, however, in the ways in which Megda's mother is represented. On the one hand, the novel presents a sentimentalized vision of the mother's influence, as in this declaration by Megda's mother and the description of her daughters' reactions:

"My girls know what I wish of them; they know that the desire of their mother's heart is that they shall grow to be good, pure, noble-minded women, respecting themselves and thus commanding respect from all with whom they come in contact. I trust you both, fully, and am more thankful than I can tell, that I am able to do so."

The laugh had faded from Meg's eyes and given place to a serious look, while Elsie's [Megda's sister] filled with tears as she said earnestly:

"And I think, mother, that that very trust which you place in us, does more toward making us try to become what you would like to have us be than almost anything else would." Elsie wanted to say "except your prayers," but she was afraid Meg would laugh at her. (55–56)

"Trust" here signifies the internalization of self-regulating norms. In describing Elsie's moment of self-censorship, however, the passage belies the degree to which Megda has failed her mother (and perhaps also the degree to which her mother has failed to instill in her the proper responses), by laughing when she should be moved to tears (there are several instances in the novel where Megda in fact does laugh at moments when the proper sentimental response would be to cry, signaling again her failure to regulate her emotional responses).

No one in Medga's family can bring themselves to challenge her self-image. They are all bewitched and "confused" (31) by Megda's allure: "[Elsie] had tried so many times before to talk seriously to Meg about religion, and every time she had found herself unable to get only just so far. Meg would turn that laughing face of hers, with the little scornful curve of the red lips, toward her, and she would stop confused, ashamed, and almost ready to beg Meg's pardon for presuming to preach to her" (31). Consequently, almost everyone around Megda cannot successfully help her to internalize the mandates of Christian self-regulation. As the narrator puts it, even though Megda's mother recognizes her faults, "her love for her darling was so deep that she could not bear to trouble or displease [Megda]" (26). Although within Alcott's or Stowe's model of maternal tutelage this attitude indicates simply a failure on the mother's part, we might ask what difference here an African American context might make. Is this excessive love a result of the fact that under slavery mothers and daughters were violently separated, so that after the Civil War maternal indulgence could perhaps be excused or at least understood?[130]

Regardless of the answer, the majority of Megda's disciplining occurs not within the family but through her relationships with two other figures.[131] One is the educated, middle-class Mr. Stanley, who seeks to uplift the community through spiritual renewal. Signifying perhaps Megda's unregulated publicity, their first encounter takes place outside the domestic sphere, literally in the street. That such a location provides an opportunity for a heteroerotic intimacy to develop may signal the narrative's ambivalence about such spaces, although such spaces are also a continuing source of both heteroerotic and homoerotic pleasure, as in the scene in which Megda's theatrical performance of her elocutionary talents produces strong emotions in all who witness it. That Megda may be too public, that such forms of publicity pose a specific risk to African American young women, is a possibility with which the narrator struggles. And although Mr. Stanley ostensibly objects to theater on religious grounds, his displeasure at Megda's self-display as Lady MacBeth is the strongest voice of disapproval in the text. Ethel also, after she becomes a true Christian, foregoes the theater.

In fact, even before Megda meets Mr. Stanley, she is subjected by Ethel to what will be the first of many judgments of Megda's character. The novel begins not with Megda's first, eroticized encounter with Mr. Stanley but instead with Ethel's assessment of Megda's character, which the rest of the novel will then illustrate. Ethel offers to read Megda's palm, but instead of offering the expected "fortune" of detailing who Megda will marry, Ethel uses the occasion to imagine Megda's conversion. In light of Ethel's scrutiny Megda repeatedly confesses herself unworthy, and as the novel progresses she begins to feel this unworthiness as a moral flaw or lack. Megda begins the novel proud of her independence, professing her belief in the "equality of the sexes," but increasingly comes to doubt these values. The novel signals this transformation through its play on the word "spirit," as well as on the distinctions it draws between regal, earthly power and the power of the real king. Megda must exchange a belief in "spirit" as defined by assertiveness, personal integrity, honesty, and charisma, with a Christian relinquishing of self-reliance to a larger "Spirit." She must exchange her "queenly" power and allure for the "robe of whiteness and a crown of beauty that fadeth not away" in heaven (143). And significantly, she must trade her own desire to be an elocutionist for a desire to be married to one.

Tate argues convincingly that Megda's increasing sense of restlessness and unfulfillment mixes erotic and spiritual longing in ways that would have been easily recognizable to late-nineteenth-century readers.[132] Yet she confines this longing to heterosexual fulfillment: through becoming a good

Christian, Megda not only receives spiritual fulfillment through her relationship with God, but eventually she achieves sexual fulfillment through her relationship with the minister. But conversion brings another kind of intimacy as well, that between Megda and Ethel. That Megda is attracted to both characters is signaled in the fact that the novel uses similar tropes to describe Megda's reaction to both Ethel and Mr. Stanley. Not only does Megda blush, for instance, when her brother teases her about her encounter with the minister, but she also flushes when he asks her opinion of Ethel. After brutally demolishing the personality of all of her other friends, in ways that reveal Megda to be an acute, ruthless judge of character, Megda instead praises Ethel:

> For the first time Meg's eyes fell, and a burning blush suffused her face. Hal was almost startled at the effect his words had upon her. He did not know what a feeling of shame filled the girlish heart at his innocent thrust. But Meg was honor itself; she would not sully her lips with a lie. What she thought, she would say.
>
> "I honor and respect Ethel Lawton above all my acquaintances. I am proud to think she has called me her friend." (66–67)

As it becomes increasingly obvious that Ethel and Mr. Stanley are falling in love, it is hard to tell why Megda is troubled by this turn of events: she seems as or more upset at losing Ethel than she is at losing the minister. In fact, the only time that Megda experiences feelings of rivalry, the time when "Meg felt a jealous pang shoot through her heart—the first she had ever known" (196), is when she witnesses Ethel's increased intimacy with another girl, Laurie, after Laurie becomes a Christian. Tate argues that the novel "overstates" this jealousy, and that it uses what appears to be Megda's "covetous" feelings for Ethel, her feelings of "sibling [!] rivalry" as a cover for her real "sexual jealousy" toward her.[133] In so doing, she activates the familiar surface-versus-depth model, in which any homoerotic attachments are merely covers for deeper heteroerotic ones, and in which the daughter's desire for the mother is merely a stand-in for her deeper desire for the father. Although Tate quite brilliantly illustrates the ways in which Megda increasingly comes to identify with Ethel, she continuously imposes the norms of the oedipal family model onto their relationship. Thus, Tate credits "unrequited love" for Mr. Stanley rather than for Ethel as ultimately producing Megda's conversion (Megda wants to become like Ethel in order to be desired by Mr. Stanley).[134]

This reading overlooks the degree to which having Ethel is equated in the text with being (like) her. Ethel pays more attention to Maude, Megda's nemesis, and to Laurie because of their conversions. Moreover, conversion in the text is represented as a moment of protolesbian pedagogy, as in this highly erotic moment of evangelical exchange:

[Ethel's] low, solemn voice drove the mocking light out of Meg's eyes, and the laughter from her face. She forgot Maude and everything else, in looking at the pale, lovely face before her—lovely, with the sweet, solemn light upon it.

Meg drew nearer and nestled her head against Ethel's shoulder in the old, caressing way, and Ethel's arms quickly encircled her and held her close and sure. (141)

Unlike anyone else, just a glimpse of Ethel's face is enough to lead Megda to control her emotional reactions, to stifle her urge to "laugh" or "mock." Ethel uses this moment of intensity to entreat Megda to be saved, and in gazing at Ethel Megda feels a new sort of emotion: "As she looked a feeling crept into her heart—a strange, happy, peaceful feeling. It seemed to Meg that her heart must be drawing this feeling from Ethel's face. She had never felt like this before" (142–43). This "strange, happy, peaceful feeling," not an unrequited love for Stanley, is what Megda will then continue to search for and experience as missing until she becomes saved.

Furthermore, although it is clear that Megda suffers (and thus develops more depth as a character) as she watches the intimacy between Ethel and Arthur deepen, it is unclear as to whose loss as an object of desire Megda mourns more. For example, late in the narrative, Megda's gaze once again fixes on Ethel:

All the evening Meg could not keep her eyes off Ethel. She had never seen such an expression on any face in her life. So tender, so happy, so full of glad delight, yet withal so peaceful and trusting. In all the years that followed Meg only remembered Ethel's face as she saw it that night. When Mr. Stanley spoke to Ethel, or stood near where he could watch her, Meg turned her eyes away; she could not trust herself to watch the proud, tender light in the dark-blue eyes. (310)

On the one hand, Megda "turn[s] her eyes away" from the two lovers because ostensibly she wishes that Mr. Stanley regarded her in the same light as he does Ethel. On the other hand, there are hints here that she also despairs because Mr. Stanley is "proud" in his possession of Ethel, which emphasizes how much Megda will lose when he marries her. Marriage for Megda often constitutes a loss: when her brother, Hal, announces his engagement to her close friend, Laurie, Megda accuses him of "selfishness" (352) and "oppose[s]" the marriage "because she could not bear the thought of having Laurie go from them" (353).[135]

The narrator seems to share Megda's views. The majority of Megda's encounters with Ethel occur in the semipublic/semiprivate, single-sex space of the school. And unlike church or meetings for Bible study, this location is represented in the novel as temporally limited. The nostalgic, almost funereal descriptions of this space as fleeting signify the narrative ambivalence over the exchange of the realm of the school, and the homoerotic connections between the girls within it, for the realm of marriage and its concomitant domesticity, as in this description:

> It was, indeed, a beautiful picture. . . . May was curled up in the other window-seat, with her head leaning against the dark wood. Meg lay at full length on one sofa, one arm thrown up over her head, the other lying in her lap where the nougattines would be handy. Lill and Lulu occupied the other sofa together, their arms around each other; when one wanted a nougat the other would feed her with one. Dell was buried in the depths of an easy chair, Ruth in another, while Laurie sat on an ottoman and leaned her head against Meg's sofa. Ethel's easy-chair was drawn up beside the fire-place. That had always been, in Summer and Winter, Ethel's acknowledged place. The dark, gaping mouth of the fire-place was filled with ferns and potted plants, until it looked like a little, cool, green glen. . . . It was a dear, dear room. . . . Dear it was at all times and at all hours but more especially at the "hour of all hours" to our girls—the twilight hour. And this was the last time they would ever sit here as pupils. Never again would it be the same to them as it was now. (245)

Not only will graduation end their time in this room, but so will marriage: describing Maude's wedding, which takes place soon after commencement, the narrator claims that "the first link was broken in the golden chain" (301).[136] It is Ethel who enjoins the girls to reaffirm the importance of this chain. At the end of their last day in the schoolroom, she asks the girls to "gather close together, and clasp hands in a circle, and promise to love and remember each other all our lives long. No matter how far we may stray apart in the years to come, our *hearts* will always be united; and if we never meet again on earth, we will try to meet each other in Heaven, where the wicked cease from troubling, and the weary are at rest" (248).

Although Tate argues that in identifying with Ethel and thus trying to internalize her example Megda wants, as an act of aggression, to replace her, and therefore Ethel's death (as mother) is necessary to fulfill the oedipal plot, I view this relationship as much more ambivalent, just as I see the text's attitude toward marriage as much more double-edged than Tate acknowledges.[137] Through Megda's taking up Ethel's place (and ultimately through marrying Arthur), it might also be argued that this event is a way for Megda's heart to "remain united" with Ethel even after death/marriage; and that death and marriage are analogous is signaled by the fact that when Ethel dies in lieu of marriage, the narrator writes that "the second link in the golden chain was broken" (340).[138]

Tate draws on feminist theories of the preoedipal mother-daughter relationship to argue that Megda in fact does never fully relinquish her attachments to Ethel. In so doing, though, she contrasts a regressive, asocial pleasure with a politically central and socially sanctioned one. In other words, the novel's political imperative that Megda marry becomes a psychosexual imperative that in order to mature, the daughter must give up her love for her mother. This trajectory obscures the specific reasons that, especially for black women in the post-Reconstruction era, homoerotic intimacies may not have been compatible with the demands of black bourgeois femininity, given that the latter required that women marry. Furthermore, it overlooks the fact that for some of the same reasons, while white, middle-class women might increasingly be able to remain in such semipublic/semiprivate spheres as the school, African American women's relationship to them was always already more precarious, given that they were trying to reassert a right to domesticity.

It may be problematic, however, to assume that texts such as *Megda* reflect (as opposed to intervene in) a uniquely African American reality, because it is never clear in *Megda* or in Kelley's other novel (as well as in those of her contemporary, Mrs. A. E. Johnson) whether the characters and milieu being described are white or black. As critics have noted, there are conflicting cultural cues provided: although references are made in both of Kelley's novels to "Cottage City," the precursor to the predominantly African American resort area of Martha's Vineyard, which might subtly indicate, at least to African American readers, that the characters in her novels were black, all of these novels (including Johnson's and those of Pauline Hopkins) use, however unevenly, metaphors that connect color with moral and spiritual hierarchies of value.[139] Whiteness in these texts often signifies purity and goodness, whereas blackness often signifies corruption. Whether one views this as an attempt on the author's part to assert the universality of both Christian salvation and the possibility of bourgeois (self-)reformation (by making it impossible to tell for sure what race these characters are),[140] or to write in ways that would appease and hail a white audience, or to imagine a utopian world beyond the socially proscribed color line (where colors signify only moral and spiritual values and are not connected to race),[141] one point seems clear: female-female homoerotics in these texts are still based on relations of power, in which distinctions of character are often signified through hierarchies of color (Ethel's purity is consistently metaphorized by the text in her extreme "whiteness").

Moreover, as is true in texts authored by white women that portray the spiritual transformation of young girls into pious, Christian wives, such a transformation also assures that the women conform to bourgeois norms of femininity. Tate sees political significance in the fact that Kelley's and Johnson's texts echo these same norms: these novels prove that black women are capable of the same kinds of idealized, "feminine" self-loss.[142] Furthermore, although spiritual transformation might offer equality under God, given the structural inequalities of American society, a focus on the capitalist logic of self-making would not only put an African American woman outside the norms of her gender but also would be doubly futile given her race. Thus, it would be wrong to dismiss these narratives as simply conservative accounts of normalization. It is only in the early twentieth century, I would argue, that black women writers are able to begin to critique more fully the limits of disciplinary intimacy: we might consider Nella Larsen's novel *Passing* (1929) in this context as an exploration of the possibilities as well as the limits of an identificatory erotics based on the ambiguities between Clare's desire to be or have Irene (and with that, black bourgeois respectability).[143]

When they occur in an interracial context, however, such relations of disciplinary intimacy are less apt to seem erotic and more apt to seem simply coercive and sadomasochistic. In other words, because texts such as Kelley's adapt the structure of disciplinary intimacy for a (possibly) black context, they may also inevitably replicate a structure of subject formation that in an interracial context has been and continues to be deployed not just to reform but to eradicate the racialized subject (and indeed, even in Kelley, the most idealized female character is always the "whitest"). That such erotics are inseparable from the exercise of power may also explain why some African American women—for example, Audre Lorde—have often tried to look elsewhere to find an outside to power rooted in an essentialized notion of the female and to identify a uniquely African American women's (lesbian) sexuality.[144]

While these efforts are extremely important, such a view may overestimate the ability to get outside what has become the dominant structure of subject formation, and it may also discount the productive aspects of power. Just as it would be wrong simply to celebrate the workings of power within disciplinary intimacy, it would also be wrong to assume that the minority subjects who read such texts as Stowe's and Alcott's or who internalized the structures of disciplinary intimacy did not find in them at least moments for what José Muñoz has termed the processes of "disidentification." Describing his own conflicted relation to the racist and homophobic images promulgated by the contemporary public sphere, Muñoz writes,

> The price of the ticket is this: to find self within the dominant public sphere, we need to deny self. The contradictory subjectivity one is left with is not just the fragmentary subjectivity of some unspecified postmodern condition; it is instead the story of the minoritarian subject within the majoritarian public sphere. Fortunately, this story does not end at this difficult point, this juncture of painful contradiction. Sometimes misrecognition can be *tactical*. Identification itself can also be manipulated and worked in ways that promise narratives of self that surpass the limits prescribed by the dominant culture.[145]

Muñoz's focus on disidentification is significant in that he rejects the idea of a minoritarian subject who could, even if she/he wanted to, exist completely outside the reach of the majoritarian public sphere. He implicitly addresses accusations of "selling out" that accompany any minoritarian subject who claims a desire for or an identification with it. Instead, Muñoz goes on to discuss examples, in a contemporary U.S. context, of the ways in which minority subjects, through identifying only partially and in complex ways with majority subjects, do not simply try to assimilate themselves into majority norms or gain access to them vicariously through, for example, taking white lovers. Nor do they simply replace them with what he calls "counteridentifications," which simply invert the relations of power rather than redeploy them.[146]

Muñoz's work focuses primarily on radical contemporary performance artists and visual artists of color. Given the different historical and political context that produced *Megda,* in which we should not expect such radical forms of intervention into the majoritarian public sphere, I would still argue that Muñoz's idea of disidentification provides us with a way to theorize *Megda*'s relationship to a disciplinary power that is designed to control or eliminate racial difference. The text, as Tate notes, is careful to point out not the ways in which Medga seamlessly has become Ethel but rather the subtle and not so subtle ways in which Medga also still differs from her. In particular, Ethel's extreme whiteness has been replaced by Megda's more colorful and less controlled subjectivity. As the narrator describes Megda, five years after her marriage: "[She] is far from being perfect. Yet her husband loves every little fault in her—the little flashes of temper, the spirit of pride that shows itself now and then, the natural willfulness of her disposition—he loves them all" (376). Tate views this as the novel's subversive attempt to replace a white, idealized image with a blacker one.[147] As she argues, in psychoanalytic terms, the darker daughter kills the idealized white mother. To me this either/or view reflects the limits of the oedipal trajectory, which cannot view identification and desire as compatible. What Tate views as Megda's counteridentification with Ethel, I would argue, following Muñoz, is a more ambivalent negotiation of identity. This is especially true given the fact that not only must Ethel, the "whitest" character in the novel, die, but the novel closes with another death, that of Maude, who has been consistently identified as the "blackest."[148]

In describing the act of passing, Muñoz writes: "Passing is often not about bold-faced opposition to a dominant paradigm or a wholesale selling out to that form. Like disidentification itself, passing can be a third modality where a dominant structure is co-opted, worked on and against. The subject who passes can be simultaneously disidentifying with and rejecting a dominant form." [149] In this context we might ask whether Kelley's whole novel is trying to "pass" as an example of sentimental fiction while "work[ing] on and against" its disciplinary exercises of power. Viewed in this way, Megda's imperfect, partial, and tactical disidentification with Ethel, what I have termed elsewhere her imitation with a difference of the norms Ethel represents, might more successfully preserve the ambivalence that characterizes their relationship, and in particular the traces of the desire to have that remain within the desire to be.

Conclusion

In psychoanalytic terms, one might say that Alcott describes and historicizes the slippage between what Freud would term the superego and the ego ideal, which echoes what in Foucauldian-inspired New Historicism has become the difference between disciplinary and possessive individualism. Although Alcott's novels illuminate the ways in which Freud's model is a historically specific form of subjectivity, psychoanalytic theory brings out its erotics: in desiring (to be) the "other," one also desires (to be) an idealized version of one's self. In Alcott's texts, scenes of eroticized identification between women become interchangeable with scenes of eroticized self-making, most notably through the discourses of "art" and/as "work." In so doing, Alcott is able to co-opt the discourse of self-making for white women, but only through adopting the emerging logics of the market. Thus, instead of condemning disciplinary intimacy as providing white women no access to power, or alternatively condemning the effects of the market on the self, I describe the ways in which an eroticized female autonomy emerges from Alcott's novels' explicit combination of disciplinary and possessive forms of subject formation.

Focusing specifically on *Megda*'s differences from *Little Women,* we might argue that Kelley tips her hand when she implicitly compares the title character of her own novel to Meg, rather than to Jo. After all, although Jo hopes to be a writer, one version of self-making, Meg (March) aspires to be a wife and mother, as epitomized through self-loss. In allying Megda with Meg, Kelley signals her submission to the ideological requirement that African American women in the late nineteenth century, despite the fact that they were participating in their own women's organizations and through them entering the public sphere, as well as working to support their families, should be represented as desiring domesticity over any other career "outside the home." It emphasizes also the degree to which the utopian fantasies of Alcott's female (inter)independence rely on the material privileges of whiteness.

Interestingly, however, unlike Jo, whose eventual marriage to Professor Bhaer is viewed by many readers as passionless, Megda's alliance with Arthur, as Tate brilliantly argues, is an erotic one. No wonder, then, that

Megda turns down an offer of marriage from Professor Weir, a teacher at her school with whom she is working; once again, Kelley seems to be signaling Megda's difference from Jo (who marries her own "Professor Bhaer"). In other words, unlike Alcott, Kelley struggles to represent a marriage that was founded in part on passion (while remaining within the bounds of propriety), because for African American women marriage was such a political necessity.

Despite these key differences, however, my discussion of the erotics of both disciplinary intimacy and the semipublic/semiprivate in texts authored by African American women has demonstrated that middle-class black women in the late nineteenth century were liable to encounter at least some of the same possibilities for an identificatory erotics as white women did. Although this form of female homoerotics seems particularly enabled by the "female space" of white, bourgeois culture in the United States, it is by no means confined to it: in addition to the schoolroom in *Megda*, Kelley's descriptions of the holiday lodgings, midnight feasts, and intimacies of a group of young, middle-class, African American women in her second book, *Four Girls at Cottage City* (1898), and Hopkins's representation of the boardinghouse in her magazine-serialized novel of 1899–1900, *Contending Forces*, invoke the same sorts of eroticized representations of autonomy through their investment in commodities themselves (carpets, snacks, "hot chocolate," etc.).[150] At times marriage is similarly "marginalized," as duCille puts it, or even subtly criticized, if only in the context of the possible loss of homoerotic intimacy it entails.[151] At times marriage and heteroerotics form a counterpart to, but not necessarily a replacement for, homoerotic attractions. In these novels, however, because of the specificities of African American women's historical situation at the turn of the century, semipublic/semiprivate female-female spaces are represented as much more transitory and fragile, and the young women within them are not striving to continue to exist "on their own" or in all-female communities such as the ones Alcott's works sometimes represent, nor are they as openly transgressing gendered norms. Instead, at least by the end of these novels, the majority of these characters are ensconced in heterosexual reproductive domesticity.[152] Nonetheless, as happens in Alcott's novels, often friends marry family members in ways that keep homosocial relations intact: for example, in *Four Girls at Cottage City* one of the four main female characters, Vera, marries the cousin of two of the others while Megda's brother marries Laurie, in both cases insuring that these young women will remain within an enlarged family. Most significantly, perhaps, both *Megda* and *Little Women* represent the subject's struggles to negotiate disciplinary power's regulatory effects. Despite the fact that Jo and Megda's strategies for identifying with a difference are quite distinct, in part because of the structural disparities in their subject positions, in both cases desire "to have" becomes a way to negotiate, not just fulfill, the demand "to be."

Chapter 3

Scouting for Girls (1920), the second edition of the official handbook of the Girl Scouts, includes Louisa May Alcott in a list of what one might term "proto-Scouts," those women who embodied the ideals of Scouting before the movement ever existed.[1] In addition to "the first Girl Scout," Magdelaine de Verchères, a young French Canadian girl who defended from the Iroquois a fort in Quebec for eight days, the handbook also contains profiles of "the explorer," Sacajawea; "the pioneer," Anna Shaw; and "the homemaker," none other than Louisa May herself.[2] As the handbook explains,

> With all our modern inventions nobody has yet invented a substitute for a good, all-round woman, in a family, and until somebody can invent one, we must continue to take off our hats to girls like Louisa Alcott. Imagine what her feelings would have been if someone had told her that she had earned half a dozen merit badges by her knowledge of home economics and her clever writing!
>
> And let every Scout who finds housework dull, and feels that she is capable of bigger things, remember this: the woman whose books for girls are more widely known than any such books ever written in America, had to drop the pen, often and often, for the needle, the dishcloth and the broom.[3]

In describing Alcott as not only a writer but also a woman who is willing to "drop the pen, often and often, for the needle, the dishcloth and the broom," this passage locates her firmly within the ideology of domesticity.

Alcott may have been a best-selling author, this excerpt asserts, but she was also and primarily a "housekeeper." Here the Girl Scouts claim Alcott and, by association, her novels as precursor to their own project, a project that, as I will demonstrate in this chapter, mass markets domestic ideology while simultaneously claiming young women's right of access to the public sphere. The Girl Scouts turn the disciplinary project of sentimental literature into a mass movement for the formation of girls' "character."

In chapter 2 I argue that although Alcott's novels ostensibly seek to reproduce gender (and correlatively heterosexual) normativity in both their main characters and their readers, they simultaneously allow both characters and readers to "try all kinds." Moreover, many of Alcott's texts coopt the ideology of self-making for women, even as they extend the disciplinary project of maternal tutelage to new semipublic/semiprivate spaces. They combine an emphasis on sentimentalized pedagogic relations between women with a homoerotics of female autonomy and interindependence. In this way, Alcott's texts become "handbooks" for female (and perhaps queer) identities, desires, and identifications. As I will illustrate, the early Girl Scout movement intensifies and standardizes this process. Girl Scouting markets itself to girls not only through a literal handbook but also through other forms of print and material culture, including Girl Scout series books and Girl Scout uniforms. The movement intends explicitly to instruct girls in how to make themselves through imitating highly scripted and regimented ideals of female identity, and its model of "character building" assumes that reading has subject-forming effects. Like Alcott's ideology of vocation, Scouting uses the language of "duty" both as another marker of the need for female self-sacrifice and as a way for girls to claim the privileges of self-possession, publicity, and citizenship formerly reserved for boys. For example, early Girl Scout handbooks assert that girls, like boys, have a duty to help their country, a duty that then allows girls to don uniforms and practice military-style marching and formations.

Through consolidating what was in the nineteenth century a more local, haphazard project of regulating identification into a systematic form of subject production, Girl Scouting also, I will argue, continues to draw on the power of this system's identificatory erotics. The movement aims explicitly to regulate girls' sexuality through a theory of imitation: girls imitate "good" role models and shun "bad" ones—yet such a theory of (self-)reformation, as I will demonstrate below, reveals the instabilities of imitation, identification, and desire.

By comparing the workings of the *Girl Scout Handbook* (and its accompanying movement) to Djuna Barnes's experimental, modernist novella *Ladies Almanack* (1928),[4] I will illustrate how both volumes transform the intimate queer pedagogy of the domestic novel into a disciplinary erotics of mass production, through which the protolesbian moments I have described above become organized and standardized into a named identity category or "type." As a "how-to" manual for (re)producing lesbian identity, Barnes's *Almanack* parodies the genre of the handbook, celebrating even as it critiques a fantasy of lesbian recruitment that, in its efforts at "making girls," imitates the subject-forming conventions of such organizations as the Girl Scouts. The *Almanack* revels in the erotic transformational power of such seductive attempts at (sexual) reformation, but it also reveals these attempts' connection with other forms of imperial conquest. Similarly, the Girl Scouts make no effort to disguise the connections between their movement and other forms of colonizing power. Although the Scouts at times espouse what appears to be a progressive version of liberal pluralism, they continue the imperial project of disciplinary intimacy by seeking to homogenize all girls into a particular ideal of white, middle-class womanhood. That Alcott shares the spotlight as role model with the young girl who defended a fort from the Iroquois is no coincidence: imperial transformation ("national defense") begins at home, the Girl Scout handbook implies.

Indeed, both Barnes's novella and the Girl Scout Handbook implicitly invoke a theory of reading as itself formative of the subject. Both assume that through reading such handbooks and joining such movements, "little women" can now remake themselves into "Girl Scouts" and . . . or . . . "lesbians." In so doing, however, they may be forced to relinquish other forms of racial, ethnic, class, national, or religious affiliation. In other words, in this chapter I explore the uneasy connection between identifying as a lesbian and other forms of (self-)regulation that are based on a denial of racial, ethnic, class, and other differences.

Early Girl Scouting

Most accounts of the emergence of the category "lesbian" have tended to concentrate on the at times moralistic and pathologizing pseudomedical taxonomies of sexual behaviors recorded in and produced by sexology and the criminal records of "deviants." Many historians and theorists of sexual identity have sought to understand how queer individuals and com-

munities forged reverse discourses of identity and identification in relationship to these narratives, in the process remaking what were often
viewed as pathologizing impulses into powerful discourses of erotic subjectivity.[5] My genealogy of the formation of lesbian identity from within
white, middle-class women's culture is intended to supplement and complicate, rather than supersede, these accounts: what many of these historians miss is the degree to which identity *in general* was at the turn of the
century becoming codified and represented in American culture. In other
words, the norms of disciplinary culture during this period demanded that
one "make" one's self by conforming to the image of a "type." As Martha
Banta elucidates,

> Reactionaries, who longed to arrange the heterogeneous American pop-
> ulation into tidy, dogmatic batches, leagued with liberals, who willingly
> risked living in the midst of social pluralism. Reactionaries classified out
> of desperation as they tried to box off enemies from friends. Liberals
> classified in the hope of detecting a fundamentally democratic unity in
> multiplicity. Divergent in their motives, both groups relied on the view-
> ing and interpretation of objects, peoples, and events held to the lowest
> common denominator, *the type.*[6]

In her provocative study of representations of American women during this period, Banta explains how criminology, the newly emerging field
of psychology, advertising, and high- and middlebrow art all sought to
identify standard "types" of people. She concentrates specifically on the
dominant characterizations of (mostly white, middle-class) women, which
were widely represented in popular and what was rapidly becoming
"middlebrow," as well as "highbrow" American culture,[7] what she identifies as versions of the "American Girl." Banta argues that three subtypes
of the American Girl are combined to make up a "new" feminine figure:
"The particular mark of the times becomes apparent when the images of
the Beautiful Charmer, the New England Woman, and the Outdoors Girl
evolve into yet another type—the New Woman."[8] All of these types are
promulgated in emergent commodity culture, with the concomitant expectation that they reflected "real" girls and that "real" girls could reproduce these images through styles of dress, leisure, education, and so forth.
Related to this emergent identity comes another commodified type newly
available to young women, one that also combines the three subtypes: the
Girl Scout.

Founded in 1912 by Juliette Gordon Low, an upper-middle-class, white widow from Georgia who was inspired by the examples she witnessed of both the Boy Scouts and Girl Guides in England, the early Girl Scout movement exploited the ambiguity that Mark Seltzer has argued lies at the heart of turn-of-the-century culture: the continued emphasis on individual self-making combined with the increasing awareness of the relay between bodies and machines that implied that subjects could be mass produced.[9] As Seltzer has established in reference to the early Boy Scout organization, such a technology of power underlines the tension between ideals of self-making as a form of proprietary individualism and the sometimes utopian, sometimes dystopian fantasy of the self as an easily reproducible "type."

In his book on the machine-body complex, Seltzer notes that at the turn of the century the future of (white male) masculinity and, by extension, of America seemed far from secure. The closing of the frontier "indicated a three-fold relocation of the making of Americans: a relocation of the topography of masculinity to the surrogate frontier of the natural body, to the newly invented national parks or 'nature museums,' and to the imperialist frontier."[10] In the process, Seltzer asserts, a discourse of the "natural" and the "national" body developed in which the "natural" individual body became interchangeable with the "national" collective one and in which both were opposed to an idea of the rapidly developing machine culture of consumption. As Seltzer illustrates, Earnest Thompson Seton, one of the founders of the Boy Scouts, links this sort of consumption with the wasting effects on the body of the illness called consumption. In order to combat this weakening of the body, as well as of the nation, boys must be "made into men" by removing them from the feminizing domestic sphere of the home and taking them out into "nature."[11]

While positioning itself in contrast to commodity culture, however, the Boy Scouts, as Seltzer illustrates, adapted the ideologies of mass production for their own subject-forming purposes. Through absorbing the pedagogical examples of the male leaders and through meeting the requirements for awards and advancement contained within the Boy Scout handbook, boys could and would become "men" in a standardized, nationalized fashion. The emphasis on uniforms and uniformity enhanced this fantasy of mass production, what Mark Rosenthal terms the "character factory" of Scouting.[12]

That boys could be mass (re)produced outside the home and that it took the stringent requirements of the "wilderness" to (re)form their character were concepts also repeated in the founding of the Girl Scouts. The idea of the body in "nature," the "making" of character, and the self's relation to nation building are transposed right into the early Girl Scout handbooks in sections often written by Lord Robert Baden-Powell or Seton themselves.[13] Yet Juliette Gordon Low and the early proponents of the Girl Scouts faced another set of problems, for "the topography of masculinity" was just that—masculine. Hence, although the Girl Scouts were able to use to their advantage the language of production that Seltzer identifies as characteristic of both the natural body and the machine culture, at the same time they were forced to mobilize other discourses to legitimate their existence. Low had to balance her desire to employ the "masculine" character-building techniques of "wilderness" living regimented by the Boy Scouts with a nationalized and standardized endorsement of domesticity, heterosexuality, and motherhood.[14] In many ways reminiscent of Alcott, the Girl Scouts thus mixed the capitalist ideology of the "self-made" man with the maternal/pedagogic project initiated by sentimental ideology in order to produce a "character factory" of their own. They needed to find ideological justification for an organization that could easily be viewed as trying to make girls into men instead of into women.

In the first few years after its inception, fears ran high that the Girl Scouts were trying to turn girls into men, so much so that the head of the Boy Scouts of America attempted to force the Girl Scouts to merge with the more "home-oriented" Camp Fire Girls and to change the Girl Scouts' name back to "Girl Guides," an appellation that seemed to connote more clearly the role of woman as guide to husband and child.[15] To use the term "scout" was to imply that girls wanted to be just like boys, as this letter from Baden-Powell makes clear:

> The term "to Guide" seems to sum up in one word the high mission of woman, whether as a mother, a wife or a citizen. The title of "Guide," therefore is the best applicable to the girl as an inspiring reminder to her of the ideas to which she is training herself.
>
> But the whole value were missed and the aim debased if one used the term "Scout."
>
> This would mean nothing more than an imitation of the boys' Movement without ulterior aim or idea, and invites girlhood merely to follow a lead rather than to take a line of its own.[16]

This treatise reflects what Seltzer has identified as a central tenet of turn-of-the-century anxieties around subject formation: if subjectivity, no matter how "naturalized," was something that could be made, then what was to prevent this process of (re)production from having "unnatural" effects? If subjects were constituted through a process of standardized identification, then logically girls could, by "imitating" boys, become them. Dr. Luther Gulick, the founder of the Camp Fire Girls, expressed moral abhorrence of this idea: "For girls to copy the Boy Scout movement would be 'utterly and fundamentally evil.'" [17] His panic at this possibility, which resembles the moral panic inspired by the New Woman, points to what both George Chauncey and Carroll Smith-Rosenberg have argued is a larger cultural discourse about the masculinizing effects of the public sphere on white, middle-class women.[18] At the same time, the vehemence of Gulick's utterance alludes to a deeper fear of the evils of imitation, one that Havelock Ellis echoes in his writings about the dangerous effects of all-female environments:

> I do not say that these unquestionable influences of modern movements can directly cause sexual inversion, though they may indirectly, in so far as they promote hereditary neurosis; but they develop the germs of it, and they probably cause spurious imitation. This spurious imitation is due to the fact that the congenital anomaly occurs with special frequency in women of high intelligence who, voluntarily or involuntarily, influence others.[19]

The "modern movement" to which Ellis, writing in 1897, most obviously refers is feminism, as Nancy Sahli notes in her citation of him. Yet his warnings continue throughout the early twentieth century, as "lesbianism," albeit unevenly, gains publicity as an "identity." Although Ellis believed that some women were "born" inverts, he also believed that women could be "recruited" into the practice, in much the same way that they could be recruited into a political or social movement. Implicitly Low, along with the administrators of the women's colleges and boarding schools, was increasingly battling the widespread cultural suspicion that her new movement could turn girls into lesbians. According to the logic of "inversion," masculinity in women was a "sign" of lesbianism. If Low masculinized women by allowing them to "copy men" and by giving them through Scouting forms of access to the activities and ideologies, even the forms of dress formerly reserved for men, then she might risk producing as well "masculine" desires for women in women themselves.[20] *How Girls Can Help Their Country: Handbook for Girl Scouts,* the first edition of the Girl Scout handbook, anxiously addresses the issue of masculinization.

The chapter titled "Duties" has as its first heading the command, "Be Womanly":

> No one wants women to be soldiers. None of us like women who ape men.
>
> An imitation diamond is not as good as a real diamond. An imitation fur coat is not as good as real fur. Girls will do not good by trying to imitate boys. You will only be a poor imitation. It is better to be a real girl such as no boy can possibly be. Everybody loves a girl who is sweet and tender and who can gently soothe those who are weary or in pain. Some girls like to do scouting, but scouting for girls is not the same kind of scouting as for boys. The Chief difference is in the courses of instruction. For the boys it teaches MANLINESS, but for the girls it all tends to WOMANLINESS and enables girls the better to help in the great battle of life.[21]

Here the handbook asserts that the courses of instruction differ along the lines of gender, despite the fact that much of the early Girl Scout program *was* simply copied verbatim from the boys' program. Moreover, the injunctions against "imitating" boys echo exactly Ellis's language. But when Ellis warns of the dangers of imitation, he alludes to a theory of the production of sexual identity that goes beyond crude equations between gender expression and sexual identity and between gender difference and desire. Instead, he describes relations of similarity, of a desire to "imitate" through "influence." Such terms recall almost exactly the terms used to describe the maternal-pedagogical scene: through her benevolent influence the (m)other will inspire in her children/pupils/wards/boarders a desire to imitate her example. The Girl Scouts epitomize this form of disciplinary power as I have outlined it above: they draw on the gaze of the mother as an impetus for self-surveillance and regulation. Increasingly, however, the Scouts replace the mother with other "mother substitutes," as well as the supervisory power of the "troop" itself. As this bit of instruction from *How Girls Can Help Their Country* addressed to "Captains" (the name for the troop leader, usually a young woman of twenty-one or so) demonstrates, girls form their characters by imitation rather than by "didactic teaching":

> The Captain should remember that simple living in the spirit of [the Girl Scout] law is more important than being able to state the law and talk glibly about it. Children learn more from imitation and from the right

ordering of their experiences than they do from any amount of didactic teaching.

A Captain should avoid preaching and formalism. She should live with her girls in a happy, helpful, wholesome, honorable spirit and so promote the same spirit in the patrol. The finer girls in the patrol will do the rest, and youth will be led by the formative and compelling power of example.[22]

Girls should not imitate boys but imitate instead other girls. Imitation itself is not the problem, it is whom and what one imitates. But how does one put a limit on imitation? If subjectivity is formed through imitation, then there is no "natural" self that grounds the subject: imitations lead to other imitations. As I will illustrate in greater detail below, the Scouts' discussion of sexuality itself reveals the instabilities of imitation even as it tries to provide girls with "morally and spiritually edifying" models for emulation. It becomes difficult to determine how to distinguish between forms of "good" imitation and those that lead to other, possibly corrupting, subject-forming effects.

To imitate does not necessarily mean the same thing as to identify with, however. As Homi Bhabha has shown, subaltern subjects may mimic their colonizers without identifying with them. Instead, they subversively repeat as a Foucauldian tactic, a reversal of power.[23] Similarly, I would argue, even as Scouting tries to perfect a system of subject formation based in imitation as identification, it also reveals how easily such attempts can go awry through the processes of what I will term "mimetic reversibility" and of disidentification. Mimetic reversibility signals those moments where the current of power is reversed—where the subject to be imitated becomes instead the imitator. In addition, Scouting, in setting up an intensely pedagogic structure, risks that a girl may desire, rather than or along with wanting to *be,* her beloved "Captain" or another idealized Scout, which might lead her to disidentify as Scout and identify instead as "lesbian." Furthermore, in its anxious effort to demarcate "good" forms of imitation from "bad" ones, the movement underlines the instability and temporality of all identifications, including, and perhaps most significantly for my argument, those of gender and sexual identity. As the debate over the early Girl Scout movement indicates, because of this instability "good" identities must continually be shored up through repeated forms of "imitation." Otherwise, through the process of mimetic reversibility, "good" girls may end up imitating "bad" ones.

No wonder then that being a Girl Scout requires repeatedly identifying with an explicit set of norms. As is evident from the examples cited above, the language of the early handbooks either addresses a "you" explicitly, allowing the reader to insert herself into the text, or, as in the case of the instructions for earning merit badges, is written in the imperative. Such a rhetorical stance assumes an audience willing and eager to "obey orders." The early handbooks spell out the path to becoming a successful, loyal, honorable Scout, most obviously in the "Girl Scout's Promise," the oath each girl repeatedly affirms, earliest versions of which read:

I. To do my duty to God and my country
II. To help other people at all times
III. To obey the Laws of the Scouts.[24]

As *Scouting for Girls* explains, this is not a compulsory form of self-regulation: "It is a promise each girl *voluntarily* makes; it is not a rule of her home nor a command from her school nor a custom of her church. She is not forced to make it—she deliberately chooses to do so."[25] The law implies that such a movement echoes the supposedly voluntary forms of association inherent in being part of a democratic state, and it tries to soften its association with colonization and militarism. Yet this emphasis on individual, voluntary, self-regulation is immediately contradicted by the emphasis on conformity, servitude, and economy of the Girl Scout laws that each girl promises to "obey":

I. A Girl Scout's Honor is to be Trusted
II. A Girl Scout is Loyal
III. A Girl Scout's Duty is to be Useful and to Help Others
IV. A Girl Scout is a Friend to All and a Sister to every other Girl Scout [no Matter to what Social Class she May Belong][26]
V. A Girl Scout is Courteous
VI. A Girl Scout is a Friend to Animals
VII. A Girl Scout obeys Orders
VIII. A Girl Scout is Cheerful
IX. A Girl Scout is Thrifty
X. A Girl Scout is Clean in Thought, Word and Deed.[27]

These statements are performative: although they appear ostensibly to be descriptions of the ideal Scout, they also command that to be a Scout one must repeatedly fulfill or enact these standards.

These norms and the ways in which one may fulfill them are carefully laid out in the Girl Scout handbooks, most obviously in both the step-by-step instructions for advancing through the ranks of Scouting from Tenderfoot to Second Class and then First Class Scout, and in the requirements for earning various merit badges. Each "class" in Scouting involves passing a series of tests, and by the second edition of the handbook these tasks were organized under the categories "Head," "Hands," and "Helpfulness." The requirements of each rank combine, to a greater or lesser degree, instructions that ask girls to demonstrate the skills of traditional domestic accomplishment with those that expect girls to develop expertise in areas formerly less accessible to them, namely civic and economic participation (as signaled through one's knowledge of local and national government and through one's ability to accumulate money) and practical/outdoor skills. For example, to become a Tenderfoot, a girl was required to demonstrate her familiarity with the promise, laws, salute, slogan, and motto of the Scouts; prove that she understood how to respect the flag; and recite the Pledge of Allegiance, as well as the first and last stanza of the *Star-Spangled Banner.* She was required to give the name of the U.S. president, the governor of her state, and the "highest city, town, or village official" in her vicinity. She also had to "make or draw an American Flag," a requirement that ingenuously combines traditionally feminine accomplishments—sewing or drawing—with civic knowledge; tie a series of knots; and show that "[she] had saved or earned enough money to buy some part of the Scout uniform or insignia." [28]

These requirements become progressively more difficult in moving up through the ranks, so much so that to be a Second Class Scout one must "present samples of seaming, hemming, darning, and either knitting or crocheting, and press out a Scout uniform, as sample of ironing." [29] Requirements for earning the rank of First Class Scout included that one "earn or save one dollar and start a savings account in a bank or Postal Savings, or buy Thrift Stamps" and, as one option of several, "take an overnight hike carrying all necessary equipment and rations." [30]

Similarly, although in *How Girls Can Help Their Country,* as Elizabeth Israels Perry notes, Low follows fairly closely the dominant prescriptions of domesticity, in *Scouting for Girls* Low mixes badges that emphasize homemaking with those that encourage work and even careers outside the home. The badges range from "Child Nurse" and "Home Maker" to "Telegrapher," "Zoologist," and "Business Woman." [31] Each badge attempts to standardize and organize the acquisition of knowledge and skills; for example, to earn the "Electrician" badge, a girl must among other requirements, "explain the use of magnets for attraction and repulsion"; "describe fuses and their use, and how to replace a burnt-out fuse"; and "know how electricity is used as motive power for street cars, trains, and automobiles."[32]

These examples demonstrate the degree to which the function of the Girl Scouts was explicitly pedagogical and served to make girls into good citizens, mothers, housekeepers, consumers, producers and (re)producers, and perhaps even career women, at least in the second and third decades of the twentieth century. Its steps and guidelines, admonishments and examples, all work together to eliminate any debate as to the proper way to be(come) a Scout. In so doing, Girl Scouting imagines that it can mass produce a particular type of girl. Such a fantasy of subject production already transgresses the ideology of domesticity, which imagined the formation of the girl as the job of her family, in particular her mother. By encouraging girls' patriotism and national responsibility (for example, even the earliest handbook implied that girls had as much entitlement to the rights of citizens as did any boy, and at a time when women in the United States did not yet have the right to vote) Scouting also asserted girls' right to enter and participate in the public sphere.[33] It also co-opted for girls and women the "freedoms" of outdoor adventure, rigorous physical exercise, and public leadership (at least within Scouting), as well as the "right" to pursue a career, arenas formerly reserved at least ideologically for boys and men.

The theory of subject formation underlying such a system is that by applying themselves to the requirements of each badge and rank, girls would internalize the norms these accomplishments represented. When designing the Boy Scout program, in an effort to make this process less overtly didactic and thus more attractive to boys, Baden-Powell developed a whole theory of reading (and thus of writing) the handbook; he did not want to overwhelm boys with moral instruction, so he mixed explicitly pedagogic passages with other narratives describing the adventures of Scouting.[34] To some degree, *Scouting for Girls* follows this model, although its structure seems designed more to portray the rewards of obedience than to provide consistent, pleasurable "breaks" from didactic instruction. For example, in the "Self-Discipline" section of the chapter entitled "Patriotism," the heading "When in Doubt" is followed by sections on "Humility," "Self-Improvement," "Modesty," "Reading," "Waste," "Thrift," "Employment," and "Careers," which includes descriptions of famous women such as Madame Curie and a woman doctor named Mrs. Garrett Anderson, and then, last but not least, a breathless celebration of "Flying Women." Such seemingly haphazard organization actually constitutes a sophisticated harnessing of reading effects. Its logic implies that by submitting to the dictates of self-discipline, a Scout can in fact become anything or anyone, including Amelia Earhart.

Paradoxically, through absolute conformity to the norms and models provided by Scouting, a girl can become a truly great, even famous, *individual,* a woman distinguished by her unique accomplishments. Here the contradictions inherent in this model of subject formation become apparent: through a process of self-making that entails internalization of a standard (mass producing the self), the self ideally becomes supremely self-possessing and uniquely individual. The standardized self is simultaneously then the most individualized self.

Girl Scout series novels, which as cheap, widely available commodities epitomize mass production, capitalize on the popularity of the early movement and invert this ratio of readerly instruction and pleasure. These books mix the plot conventions of girls' formula fiction—a mystery to be solved, travel to another locale—with pages copied right out of the Girl Scout handbook, in order both to create an aura of authenticity and to recruit new members. Like the handbooks themselves, these novels outline the steps one must take to become a Scout, and they openly seek to recruit girls (almost every novel contains as a central function of its plot the introduction of a new girl into the movement). Through consuming such a text, a girl could imagine herself part of what might be termed, following Benedict Anderson, the "imaginary regulatory community" of Scouting.[35]

Scouting's ability to utilize girls' series fiction as an ideological arm of the movement is perhaps the most notable example of how it was from the start completely integrated into the logic of commodity culture. Not only did Scouting use reading as a way to entice girls into the organization, however; it also mobilized other, even more acquisitive, forms of commodity consumption—even the uniform itself could inspire the desire "to join on." With its similarities to male military regalia and its specifications for where one's badges, pins, and awards should be placed, the uniform also enabled women and girls to take on the roles and responsibilities usually reserved for men, without the explicit social sanctions and violence that sometimes accompanied such "cross-gendered" activities outside the organization. Paradoxically, uniformity thus may have allowed social transgression even as it reinforced norms. Imitation here does not just intensify the workings of disciplinary power but also redirects them to less socially acceptable ends.

Uniforms also point out the central ambiguity of Scouting ideology, its mixing of democratic and imperialist impulses. From its inception Scouting was unusually concerned with managing class, ethnic, cultural, and religious differences. In describing the political effects of Boy Scouting, critics debate the degree to which such a system seeks to overcome distinctions of class, through joining ideologically boys of all classes into an "imaginary community" of Boy Scouts. Uniforms become a way of blurring class distinctions and, in the process, mirroring the ideals of democracy. On the other hand, the Boy Scouts represent another arm of imperialist ideology, which both at home and abroad tries to homogenize and thereby control boys of different classes, cultures, ethnicities, and religions.[36] As a substitute for colonizing politically, economically, or through brute force other classes and countries, Scouting works on the "heart" of the boy to turn him from unruly savage to proto–middle-class Scout. In establishing the Boy Scouts along the lines of the British army, Baden-Powell wanted to produce imperial male subjects in the absence of the colonial frontier. He hoped to contain class conflict through appeals to a "universal boyhood," appeals designed to disguise the emphasis on rigid, hierarchical training and respect for traditional, class-based authority. He also wanted to ready boys for military service, a goal that was chillingly realized with the outbreak of World War I.[37]

Scouting for Girls espouses its own feminized version of liberal pluralism: "The world looks to great organizations like the Girl Scouts to break down their petty barriers of race and class and make our sex a great power for democracy in the days to come."[38] In *How Girls Can Help Their Country*, law 4 reads: "A Girl Scout Is a Friend to All, and a Sister to every Other Girl Scout [no Matter to what Social Class she May Belong]."[39] Elsewhere in this edition this command is qualified:

> Among girls there are wide class distinctions—much wider than among boys. The character training of the Scouts seems to bring these classes if not actually closer together at least much more in sympathy. It is unnecessary and perhaps injurious to obliterate them altogether. All being Scouts brings about a kindly sympathy and unity of aims.[40]

Although the skills and accomplishments required to "become" a Girl Scout are the same skills required to become a middle-class (white) American woman, Girl Scout fiction demonstrates that even when a troop befriends a working-class girl she is never fully assimilated into their peer group. In Edith Lavell's *The Girl Scouts at Camp* (1922), the girls of Pansy Troop, while on a camping trip, "rescue" Freida Hammer, the daughter of a hired hand, from her mother's corrupting influence (her mother sees nothing wrong with Freida stealing from, in her mother's words, the "rich" Scouts enjoying their leisured summer vacation). The troop plans to invite Freida to live in their suburban town in order to allow her to get an education (and thus be able to class ascend), yet as described in *The Girl Scouts' Good Turn* (1922), when she arrives Freida does not live with one of the Scouts. Rather, she boards with another, presumably working-class, family. She does not attend the exclusive Miss Allen's School in which the rest of the Scouts are enrolled, but instead goes to the public high school.[41] In later volumes, she is always significantly marked as "ward" rather than as a full member of the troop. In one novel, instead of participating fully in the troop's canoe trip, she serves as "cook."[42] In another, she attends a regional Scouting competition as the member of another troop made up of public school girls from a more urban town.[43] Presumably, Freida could join the Pansy Troop if they so desired her to, but instead Freida remains with girls from a lower class. Thus, although Scouting helps lift a girl up from the working class it does not challenge other forms of class hierarchy and self-segregation. Like Alcott's vision of the family/semipublic, only specific kinds of girls are fully integrated into the idealized "troop."

Whereas Freida needs little reform, Lilian Garis's novel *The Girl Scout Pioneers* (1920) presents a much more penetrating example of the imperial impetus at the heart of Scouting's recruiting impulse.[44] In the book a group of earnest Scouts sets out to introduce a working-class immigrant girl, Dagmar, to Scouting and, by proxy, make her over into a "Girl Scout." In the beginning of the novel, Dagmar runs away from the mill town where she works, and she is caught out after curfew by a police officer. Instead of arresting her he takes her home, where Dagmar forms a "special friendship" with his daughter, Molly: "Molly thought she had never seen a prettier girl, while in turn Dagmar decided Molly Cosgrove was the very biggest, dearest, noblest girl she had ever seen."[45] Molly, it turns out, is a "welfare worker" at the mill in addition to being the lieutenant of her troop, and she decides to combine both projects and start a troop among the mill girls. After convincing Dagmar to leave her family and her job, Molly perfunctorily changes Dagmar's name from the ethnically marked, "Dagmar Rosika Brodix" (her mother speaks a "conglomeration of Polish and Yiddish") to the Americanized "Rose Dixon." The newly christened "Rose" submits willingly to this plan. As she settles down to her first night in the Cosgrove's home, she surmises, " 'The girl scouts [sic] are better than the police,' . . . not quite understanding how both could work so intimately, along different lines, yet each reaching the same result to assist wayward girls. . . . This was, surely, a queer sort of arrest, a lovely kind of cell, and a most friendly pair of jailers, the little runaway had fallen among."[46] The Girl Scouts take over the role formerly provided by "Rose's" mother, and through their loving influence Rose is reformed from working-class immigrant to patriotic American girl. In its reiteration of self-transformation through the love and example of another girl, such a plot recalls the dramas of pedagogic transformation that marked Warner's *The Wide, Wide World* or the relationship between Christie and Rachel in Alcott's *Work*. But here those dramas have become standardized, mass-produced narratives of "scouting for girls," ones whose overlaps with domestic and international imperialism are explicit.[47]

Freida's reformation from "thief" to trusted "cook," or Dagmar's transformation into Rose, necessitates exchanging a mother's influence for that of other Scouts and echoes the historical shift that, as I have argued above, marks Alcott's fiction. Although Freida and Dagmar represent more extreme and violent examples of this shift from mother to "other," this shift is subtly represented within the early Girl Scout handbooks as the norm for *all* girls.

The first edition of the Girl Scout handbook employs the mother's gaze as the ultimate judge of behavior. As Perry writes, "One phrase summed up its caveats concerning proper female behavior: do not do anything you would not do in front of your mother."[48] By the second edition, however, this emphasis on the maternal is replaced by an emphasis on the patrol (the basic organizational unit of each larger troop, made up of eight girls) and ultimately on the authority of the "captain" or "councillor":

It is a pretty safe rule for a Girl Scout not to read things nor discuss things nor do things that could not be read nor discussed nor done by a Patrol all together. If you will think about this, you will see that it does not cut out anything that is really necessary, interesting or amusing. Nor does it mean that Scouts *should* never do anything except in Patrols; that would be ridiculous. But if they find they *could* not do so, they had better ask themselves why. When there is any doubt about this higher kind of cleanliness Captains and Councillors may always be asked for advice and explanation.[49]

Once again, as in Alcott's novels, the mother is replaced by other older women who reinforce the norms of disciplinary self-regulation within the semipublic sphere of "Scouting." Instead of submitting to the norms of the family, the Girl Scout submits to the norms of her "troop." Here the individualizing sentimental project of self-regulation, as well as the evangelical, reforming impulse of nineteenth-century bourgeois women's associations, becomes part of a national, routinized movement. Thus, law 1 is able to assure the reader that a Girl Scout effectively self-regulates: "You can go away and leave her by herself at any time; she does not require any guard but her own sense of honor, which is always to be trusted."[50] She has thoroughly internalized the idea of morality as surveillance, as it is mirrored first by the mother and then by a series of mother substitutes, as well as by peers. Most notably, this is a way to wrest the making of girls away from unsuitable families and turn the process over to a social movement, which becomes a move also toward emphasizing collectivity. Notably, the mother, especially when attempting to regulate sexuality, is gradually replaced in later editions of the Girl Scout handbook by the strictures of the Girl Scout movement and its collective representatives, the troop and its captain.

Both Boy and Girl Scouting saw as part of their mission the regulation of children's sexualities. Baden-Powell intended that Boy Scouting should serve as an edifying substitute for the solitary male habit of masturbation. The first edition of the Boy Scout handbook contains explicit antimasturbatory injunctions, although apparently nowhere near as explicit as Powell would have liked, as recent historians of the Boy Scouts have demonstrated.[51] In contrast, *How Girls Can Help Their Country* contains much less pointed guidelines; in a section titled "When In Doubt, Don't," it admonishes girls to

> Keep clear of girls who tell you nasty stories or talk to you of indecent things. If they see you don't want to join in such bad talk they will soon leave you alone; and each time you refuse to join in nasty talk even the bad girls will in their hearts respect you, and perhaps leave it off themselves, so you will do them good too. And don't read trashy books; keep your mind pure and you will keep happy and healthy.

All secret and bad habits are evil and dangerous, lead to hysteria and lunatic asylums, and serious illness is the result; so if you have any sense and courage in you throw off such temptation at once. Resisting temptation will make you more noble. Evil practices dare not face an honest person; they lead you on to blindness, paralysis, and loss of memory.

Your captains and your mother will help you, so if you feel you are not right, just go and talk it over with them. Keep your thoughts as clear as a crystal stream. Thinking evil thoughts blackens the soul.[52]

This passage preserves the gendered distinction between what was considered the appropriate level of sexual explicitness for boys versus girls. At the same time, however, as opposed to presenting the girl as always already "innocent," here she is always already susceptible, even eagerly awaiting corruption. The handbook represents girlhood as site of struggle over sexual knowledge and practice.

The language of the text sets up a mimetic imperative: "Keep clear of girls who tell you nasty stories." Once again, this theory of subject formation begins in repetition, "each time you refuse to join in nasty talk." It is also a process that is assumed to be precarious or unstable, unless repeated. One must refuse to join in multiple times. Even more curiously, the text implies that such processes of identification are endlessly reversible. If the girl holds her ground and "resists temptation," then the bad girls may in the end be won over by her example and "perhaps leave off [nasty talk] themselves." The text reflects a theory of mimetic reversibility: good girls must, instead of imitating other girls, inspire these other girls to imitate them.

The move from "nasty talk" to "trashy books" goes from group encounters to solitary ones, and from talk to reading. By equating reading with talking in a group, or succumbing to the influence of "bad girls," the text assumes that reading is as productive of action as speech. In both cases, representation incites desire. Perhaps this accounts for the deliberate vagueness of "secret and bad habits"; besides its echoing of the customary rule of not speaking "explicitly" of sexuality in front of genteel girls and women, the handbook seems aware of its status as inciting as opposed to prohibiting these evil thoughts and actions.

At this moment the handbook betrays its legacy to late-nineteenth-century theories of female instruction, which, as I described in chapter 2, were highly self-conscious about using the erotics of female-female pedagogy to inspire girls to "higher" ideals of religiosity, work, and sexual purity. The Girl Scout handbook performs as it mobilizes this slippage from mother to "other." That such scenes of confession might produce their own highly eroticized forms of "nasty talk," especially, but not solely, between girls and young women who are not their mothers, was an idea that late-nineteenth-century female educators and advocates of social reform found obvious and crucial to their theories of how to mold character. They encouraged teachers to turn obsessive identification and desire into a devotion to higher ideals: in this case captains should encourage girls to become good Scouts, wives, and citizens. Clearly, the handbook is designed also to be a mother substitute: reading and the instantiated rewards of disciplinary intimacy a girl found in a private audience with her troop leader were thought to be interchangeable.

This emphasis on "character building" standardized the potent mix of homoerotics and discipline that I have argued characterized much of nineteenth-century sentimental, educational, and other semipublic spaces into a formula for citizen production. Take, for example, this passage from *The Girl Scouts at Camp,* written in the early 1920s:

> Marjorie opened her suitcase and took out her bugle. Swinging its cord over her shoulder, she remarked: "I suppose I really ought to be learning new calls instead of looking for trails."
>
> "Nonsense; you don't get points for blowing the bugle."
>
> "No, but you get smiles and maybe something better from Captain Phillips!"
>
> "What do you mean, Marj?"
>
> "Don't ever repeat this, Lily." Marjorie lowered her voice. "When I succeeded in blowing Reveille correctly, Miss Phillips kissed me!"[53]

Gone are the haphazard days of Alice and Ellen's wilderness encounters in *The Wide, Wide World;* interactions between girls and women within the Girl Scouts become highly scripted exchanges, ones whose erotic charge may lie in the differences between public proficiency and private recognition (performing well in public leads to a private kiss).

In writing about the notion of the "crush" in girls' college fiction of the same period Sherrie Inness argues that such expressions of homoerotic desire ultimately end up "ensur[ing] that women's homoaffectionate relationships will be confined to a location where they can be closely scrutinized by institutional and state authorities."[54] They become simply a way of passing on the "community values" of the larger institution.[55] While Inness does grant that such descriptions of "smashes" (crushes between girls) "temporarily resist the discourse that identifies schoolgirl crushes as abnormal," her emphasis, nonetheless, is on the notion of temporariness.[56] Because all of the college series stories end with characters preparing to marry or actually marrying, Inness contends that the female-female homoerotic relationships detailed within the novels can mean nothing more than a way to transmit the norms of female identity more successfully. In other words, homoerotic desire is never more than an arm of disciplinary culture. What Inness fails adequately to address, however, is the degree to which such novels are an attempt to satisfy the ideological demands of the larger culture, which necessitated that the trajectory of girlhood end in marriage; ideological demands that are mirrored in the genre conventions—the marriage plot—of the novel, as well as the commercial demands of formula fiction. Presumably a book or series that withheld the expected marriage (open lesbianism seems unthinkable, as well as ahistoric, in this context) would not even be accepted for publication. If homoerotic desire between women was to be represented at all, it would have to be portrayed as fleeting and also, not surprisingly, edifying for both involved.

Taking Edith Lavell's Girl Scout series as one example within formula fiction of the generic limits placed on representations of female-female homoerotics (and representations of female subjectivity in general), I would argue one must examine what these limits also might make possible. Instead of holding these books up to an (anachronistic and) impossible standard, one in which openly lesbian young women could continue to live independently outside of marriage, what might such rigid narrative conventions actually allow to occur inside their overarching frame? For example, in Lavell's series the main character, Marjorie, manages not to marry for seven full volumes. These books follow her experiences in Scouting first in high school, then in college, then after college as a Girl Scout "director."[57] Because the form of serial fiction leads readers to assume marriage will eventually happen, it creates a space within the marriage plot for other kinds of homoerotic encounters, as well as for female characters to pursue activities usually reserved for men (e.g., summers on the ranch or motor car trips across the country).[58] Like Jo's trajectory in the *Little Women* series, then, the disciplinary frame itself allows for a degree of "wiggle room," not only for characters such as Marjorie but perhaps even more importantly for the readers of serial fiction.

Nevertheless, Marjorie must marry, as must Jo, and in the last novel in

Lavell's series marriage is contrasted with what the text represents as the dreary demands of a career. Marjorie's intimacies with her fiancé, John, are played out against a background consisting of petty, mean, lazy, mostly single, society women, whose interactions with one another, while certainly not identifiably lesbian, encourage the reader to equate spinsterhood with defects in character.

When read against the grain, such portrayals may suggest that claiming the identity of Girl Scout may itself suspend the pressure that girls in the early twentieth century increasingly may have felt to claim a heterosexual identity through marriage. As Eve Kosofsky Sedgwick has demonstrated, white, middle-class men at the turn of the century increasingly felt compelled to take up a position on either side of the emerging hetero/homo binary, albeit often incompletely and with varying degrees of incoherence.[59] For young women, naming themselves as Girl Scouts and existing within the homosocial semiprivate/semipublic spheres it provided might have been a way, albeit temporarily, to claim a "type" that resisted this binary. For white, middle-class women who turned to Scouting as a career, it may have provided this sort of shelter for a lifetime, albeit not without some stigma, as Lavell's portrayal of such women indicates. Paradoxically, then, Scouting may open up a potentially freeing temporal, spatial, or identificatory interim, a suspension of one identification, yet it does so only by means of the use of other kinds of "types."

On the other hand, the intensity of the organization's efforts to mold subjectivity, to make selfhood a matter of repeatedly identifying with a type, might also have prepared some girls to identify with other identity categories. Might a girl, having identified throughout her girlhood as "Girl Scout," have an easier time recognizing herself as "lesbian" as the latter became an increasingly available category? Might the intensities of influence, of the erotic rewards of "good behavior," have led to a mimetic reversal, in which girls were recruited out of or through Scouting into sapphism?[60]

Although such questions about the influence of the Girl Scouts must necessarily remain speculative, another "handbook" of the same period explicitly connects a fantasy of mass subject production with lesbianism. Barnes's self-published little volume of 1928, *Ladies Almanack*, engages and fancifully ruminates on the question of the multiple origins of desires, mannerisms, costumes, and identities that make up modern lesbian sexuality, the customs of what Barnes calls "Ladies of Fashion." In so doing, it actively seeks to constitute itself and its readers as lesbian at the same time that it struggles with the uneasy relationship between lesbian seduction and other, perhaps less pleasurable, forms of subject production.

"Lullaby for a Lady's Lady":
Lesbian Identity in Ladies Almanack

The frontispiece to *Ladies Almanack* contains the following inscription:

> Now as a wonder worker, Dame Musset was perhaps at her very best when, carrying a pole and muff, and sporting an endearing tippet, she stepped out upon that exce[e]ding[ly] thin ice to which it has pleased God, more and more, to call frail woman, there so conducting herself that none were put to the chagrin of sinking for the third time!

These words and their accompanying imagery (see figure 1) pose several interpretive problems, and various critics have debated the meaning of the images: Does the crude masculinization of Dame Musset, though the phallic pole she extends to the drowning women, replicate dangerous stereotypes of lesbians promulgated by a male psychoanalytic establishment?[61] Or does the alternation of "pole" and "muff," top hat, and petticoat serve as visual proof of the undecidability of the text, the "feminine" writing?[62] Few of these critical stances discuss the significance for lesbian sexuality of the cultural context within which this set of images is located, the "thin ice" on which Dame Musset appears to be balancing, while others fall through.[63] I will argue that the *Almanack* appropriates, parodies, and transforms the cultural debates and anxieties I have identified above, those that surrounded the newly solidified identity or set of identities marked "lesbian." In ways analogous to the Girl Scouts, the *Almanack* explicitly connects theories of mass production with the production of sexual subjectivity and also sees reading itself as a form of erotic recruitment.

The rise of print culture has long been linked to the rise of national identity. It is in part print culture, Benedict Anderson argues, that enables "imagined communities" of disparate peoples, who could never actually all meet face to face, to conceive of themselves as sharing a common "nationality."[64] Likewise, Michael Warner, in his discussion of the function of print culture in the republican-era American colonies, includes Benjamin Franklin's *Poor Richard's Almanack* as one example of a text that, in part through its construction of an abstract "public," helped to solidify the

Figure 1. Frontispiece to *Ladies Almanack* by Djuna Barnes, 1928.

new America.[65] The function of the *Almanack* was to standardize holidays, measures, planting times, and so forth, and like its less formally humble counterpart, the Constitution, it helped to define the bounds of the national and, in the process, to produce abstract, "American" citizens. But, as Warner and others, such as Cathy Davidson, have pointed out, the "imagined community" of abstracted individuals posited by such founding texts excluded all women, as well as men of color and men without property.[66]

As I have noted, the Girl Scout handbook co-opts the rituals and responsibilities of citizenship for (white, middle-class) women. It also attempts to "standardize" the production of femininity in the United States through its regimentation of merit badges and other awards. At first glance, *Ladies Almanack,* with its unstable narration, its mixture of prose, poetry, and drawings, and its playful opacity, seems to differ greatly from the straightforward, deliberately simple diction of the Girl Scout handbook. Yet the *Almanack* also locates itself within a tradition of "domestic manuals." Its diction is reminiscent of medieval ladies' devotional books, which themselves are part of a larger attempt to impose both religious discipline and a standardized system of time on the peasantry.[67] Moreover, its visual style recalls the woodcuts of eighteenth-century inexpensive books, which were themselves early prototypes of mass-produced fiction. As a parody of the almanac form, Barnes's *Ladies Almanack* has the following long precis after its title: "Showing their Signs and their tides; their Moons and their Changes; the Season as it is with them; their Eclipses and Equinoxes; as well as a full Record of diurnal and nocturnal Distempers." This use of the narrative frame of the calendar (the pamphlet is divided into twelve chapters, one for each month of the year, and there are numerous references to the zodiac, as well as to the seasons, the moons, and the tides) signals to the reader that this is also a handbook of sorts, although as Catharine Stimpson points out, "No one would mistake it . . . for a handbook about the joys of heterosexuality."[68] As the *Almanack* declares, "Thus begins this Almanack, which all Ladies should carry about with them, as the Priest his Breviary, as the Cook his Recipes, as the Doctor his Physic, as the Bride her Fears, and as the Lion his Roar!" (9).

The *Almanack* is full of allusions to the semipublic spaces with which Alcott's work is in dialogue: the boarding school and the college as well as their early-twentieth-century equivalents—most notably, the heretofore unheard of employment and civic opportunities offered to women during

World War I and the transnational modernist community of the Paris salon. For example, the use of slang terms for women throughout the *Almanack*—such as the nickname "Old Girl" in the phrase, "My Love she is an Old Girl, out of fashion" (15)—plays off the vernacular of both the women's boarding schools and the women's colleges, even as it parodies and reappropriates the "old boy network," implying that lesbian allegiances have replaced this former bastion of male power.[69] Similarly, Dame Musset's first or "Christian" name, "Evangeline," itself hints at her higher purpose—she constitutes a parody of the religious women who formed independent sisterhoods in the nineteenth century.[70] Her designation as "the Grand Red Cross" (6), obviously a reference to Spenser's hero in *The Faerie Queene,* also invokes another, more recent cultural register, the "wonder worker" women ambulance drivers of World War I, who exchanged the restrictions of the domestic sphere for the thrill of the war effort and of the many other women with whom they worked.[71]

In its witty encoding of such allusions, *Ladies Almanack* intervenes in the debates surrounding the effects of semipublic/semiprivate spheres on women's sexuality. It exploits widespread fears implicit in the cautionary writings of the time and made explicit in sexology and psychoanalysis, in order to reclaim what the heterosexist culture at large considered and still considers to be "unnatural" relations between women, which produce unexpected and often disruptive effects. In so doing, the text asserts that through instruction and seduction, queers reproduce other queers.

Perhaps the most obvious example of this phenomenon is the fantasy of the creation of the "woman with a difference" who springs out of an egg. The narrative confides, "This is the part about Heaven that has never been told" (24), and goes on to describe how the angels and the signs from the zodiac join forces to reproduce a lesbian: "And not nine Months later, there was heard under the Dome of Heaven a great Crowing, and from the Midst, an Egg, as incredible as a thing forgotten, fell to Earth, and striking, split and hatched, and from out of it stepped one saying 'Pardon me, I must be going!'" (26). In order to achieve such a feat of collective procreation, "all [the angels] gathered together, so close that they were not recognizable, one from the other"(26), in what appears to be a representation of literal mass (re)production. And the accompanying drawing, with its confusion of wings, reinforces this imagery (see figure 2). This "Heaven," itself a witty reflection on the various women's semipublics of turn-of-the-century U.S. and European culture, allows for new, queer

Figure 2. Illustration from *Ladies Almanack* by Djuna Barnes, 1928.

forms of reproduction.[72] As Seltzer notes, dystopic fantasies of machine production carried with them nightmarish visions of female reproductivity gone out of control, machines as mothers and mothers as machines.[73] Barnes's witty vision of "Heaven" responds to these fears.[74]

The account of the "woman with a difference" ends with this description: "After this the Angels parted, and on the Face of each was the Mother look. Why was that?" (26). Smith-Rosenberg, in her discussion of the settlement house movement and of anxieties about white, middle-class women's "autonomy" at the turn of the century, asserts that Jane Addams and others like her "assumed the role of public mothers" and, in the process, extended Beecher and Stowe's fantasy of professional mothering and claimed legitimacy for their public aspirations.[75] Certainly all of these angels follow this pattern. And the term "angel" itself might be considered a parodic reinscription of the familiar domestic stereotype, "the angel in the house," which Barnes's fantasy of collective birth makes explicit at the same time that it celebrates the fears that lie behind Juliette Gordon Low's careful negotiation of domesticity and publicity. Both Barnes and Low make subject formation the product of a "mass movement"; heading up the fight in *Ladies Almanack* is Dame Musset herself.

As part of a larger discussion in the novel about "what makes a woman a lesbian," Dame Musset represents the "invert," the lesbian who was "born that way."[76] She stands as a contrast to the other women in the text who claim that they are only occasionally seduced into lesbian pleasures. One such character, Patience Scalpel, voices another cultural assumption about lesbians, proclaiming:

> "In my time . . . Women came to enough trouble by lying abed with the Father of their Children. What then in this good Year of our Lord has paired them like to like, with never a Beard between them, layer for layer, were one to unpack them to the very Ticking. . . . Are good Mothers to supply them with Luxuries in the next Generation; for they themselves will have no Shes, unless some Her puts them forth! . . . They well have to pluck where they may. My Daughters shall go amarrying!" (12–13)

Ostensibly, Patience Scalpel enunciates precisely the stereotype of queer sexuality that homosexuality is not regenerative but requires the labor of heterosexuality, in part because it is based on sameness, "layer for layer," "like to like," thus lacking "the difference" that produces children. The division of Scalpel's last few sentences by the crude, phallic drawing of a doll-like young Dame Musset, however, calls into question the legitimacy of Scalpel's words.[77] A heavily outlined picture of blunt, stodgy Evangeline penetrates Scalpel's text. If we were not already taken in by the parody, this dildoesque figure, with its caption, "Thus Evangeline began her career," implies that in fact another kind of reproduction will take place, one based on recruitment and seduction. Evangeline is a woman "with a difference," as she embodies and redefines the cultural stereotype of the masculinized lesbian.[78] Not only will more Evangelines be born to unsuspecting "good mothers," but Musset's prowess at providing pleasure for women, signified in the phallicism of her body, also disrupts this heterosexist fantasy and disputes the idea that only fathers can lie with women and make children. Musset's body, like the pole she extends in the image in the book's frontispiece, offers alternatives to women, other kinds of eroticized differences, in order to insure that such damsels in distress will not be "put to the chagrin of sinking for the third time."

The use of the word "career" also alludes to contemporary anxieties about women's place outside the sphere of the heterosexual family. Barnes revalues the effects of modernization and the modern on women, effects bemoaned by someone like D. H. Lawrence, who in his famous representation of lesbian love makes "modern" a euphemism for lesbian. He writes in 1915 in *The Rainbow:* "Suddenly Ursula found a queer awareness existed between herself and her class-mistress, Miss Inger. The latter was a rather beautiful woman of twenty-eight, a fearless-seeming clean type of modern girl whose very independence betrays her sorrow. She was clever, and expert in what she did, accurate, quick, commanding."[79] Lawrence decries these traits, making them just another symptom, as Ursula is, of the ravages of modernization. In another context, however, such as the Girl Scouts, Ursula's attributes—her "independence," "cleverness," and her skill and decisiveness—would be an asset. The use of the term "modern girl" reappears in *Ladies Almanack,* in a passage that responds to Lawrence's representations of the predatory lesbian. But although Lawrence makes explicit the connection between the ravages of industrial capitalism and female sexual "deviance," it is less obvious here. Like the mass production of objects, the production of modern individuals itself becomes something that is removed from the confines of the heterosexual family, a particularly "modern" phenomenon.

To make this point Barnes uses Masie Tuck-and-Frill, who is simultaneously represented as both a prophet (and I cannot help but note that "Tuck-and-Frill" rhymes with "apocryphal") and a prurient midwife.

Masie gets pleasure from peeking up other women's skirts and seeking them in their beds, ostensibly in her search for signs of life,

> though she found nothing ever requiring Attention, nor any small Voice saying "Where am I?" she still cherished a fond Delusion that in one Way or another, the Pretties would yet whelp a little Sweet. . . . "For," she said, "Creation has ever been too Marvellous for us to doubt of it now, and though the Medieval way is still thought good enough, what is to prevent some modern Girl from rising from the Couch of a Girl as modern, with something new in her Mind?" (22)

This passage spells out a fantasy/prophecy of queer reproduction. Modern girls spring from other modern girls (through the differently (re)productive pleasures of lesbian sex) or are led astray by Musset's persuasive powers.

Up to this point my discussion has focused on the potentially liberatory effects of this co-optation of the rhetoric, imagery, and practice of conversion and recruitment for the purpose of establishing lesbian identities. One word I have not employed but deserves mention here, however, is "conquest." Numerous references to Dame Musset's imperial adventures, including those that repeat racial and ethnic stereotypes, recur throughout *Ladies Almanack*. For example,

> "In my day," said Dame Musset, and at once the look of the Pope, which she carried about with her as a Habit, waned a little, and there was seen to shine forth the Cunning of a Monk in Holy Orders, in some Country too old for Tradition, "in my day I was a Pioneer and a Menace, it was not then as it is now, *chic* and pointless to a degree, but as daring as a Crusade, for where now it leaves a woman talkative, so that we have not a Secret among us, then it left her in Tears and Trepidation. Then one had to lure them to the Breast, and now," she said, "You have to smack them, back and front to ween them at all! What joy has the missionary," she added, her Eyes narrowing and her long Ears moving with Disappointment, "when all the Heathen greet her with Glory Halleluja! before she opens her Mouth and with an Amen! before she shuts it!" (34)

Elsewhere she comments on the "types" of women she has seduced:

> "I know that the Orientals are cold to the Waist, and from there flame with a mighty and quick crackling Fire. I have learned that Anglo Saxons thaw slowly but that they thaw from Head to Heel, and so it is with their Minds. The Asiatic is warm and willing, and goes out like a Fire-

cracker; the Northerner is cool and cautious, but burns and burns, un-til," she said reminiscently, "you see that Candle lit by you in youth, burning about your Bier in Death." (35–36)

The original cover of the *Almanack* showed Musset, astride a horse, dressed in what appears to be Napoleonic-era military garb, leading a column of women carrying a banner, on which the title of the book is spelled out (see figure 3). Here Barnes's narrative questions, even as it cele-brates, lesbian reproduction. It points out the historical and epistemolog-ical parallels between "scouting for girls" and subject-forming attempts that are designed to preserve and spread particular, racial, classed and na-tional conceptions of feminine identity. Even in the early twenty-first cen-tury, "coming out" can feel as though one is joining a culture, and cer-tainly early "out" lesbian radicals like Jill Johnston did not hesitate to co-opt such overlaps for their own political projects.[80] And not only do many lesbian communities function this way but the structure of identity one adopts, the idea of finding the truth about one's self, also echoes the self-regulating structures of nineteenth-century disciplinary intimacy. As Barnes's text indicates, the structure of lesbian identity may also resemble a conversion.

Not only are there striking formal commonalities between the Girl Scout handbook and Barnes's *Almanack,* but there are ways in which the Girl Scouts organization can be read for its transgressive possibilities (the ways in which it may inadvertently teach girls to identify/desire queerly) and the *Almanack* can be read for its relation to imperial control. In es-tablishing a model of female selfhood as "type," Scouting encourages girls to form themselves through repeated forms of identification: in so doing, Scouting may also prepare girls to identify with other, more "deviant" types of identities (such as lesbian) that also require the same process of self-making. In connecting lesbianism to other forms of imperial recruit-ment, Barnes's text calls into question any utopian idealization of lesbian identity as automatically, in José Muñoz's words, "[a] narrative . . . of self that surpass[es] the limits prescribed by the dominant culture."[81]

Speaking from a postmodern perspective, we may be tempted simply to assert that any *identity* category is by its very nature repressive in that it automatically rules out other possibilities, and leave it at that. Yet, by sit-uating Barnes and Girl Scouting as contemporaneous, we may be able to see the historical connections between both of these forms of recruitment. If the formation of modern lesbian identity (at least insofar as it resembles

Figure 3. Original cover for *Ladies Almanack* by Djuna Barnes, 1928.

being recruited into an organization) has its roots in an explicitly imperial/ evangelical project that requires the reformation of the self to fit larger, homogenizing norms, then we may have a historical rather than simply a theoretical reason why minority queer subjects have often found that membership in the lesbian community requires that they give up racial, ethnic, and other forms of cultural difference.

But Musset's ironic forms of conquest are not the only ways lesbians are "made" in *Ladies Almanack*. Barnes's text also connects unnatural reproduction to writing. Like Barnes's pseudonym, a "lady of fashion," the character Masie Tuck-and-Frill is a "lady of fashion" herself,[82] as well as a prophet of self-fashioning, and she explicitly connects the production of lesbians with aesthetic/performative endeavor: "'A Feather,' she said, 'might accomplish it, or a Song rightly sung, or an Exclamation said in the right Place, or a Trifle done in the right Spirit, and then you would have need of me indeed!' and here she began to sing the first Lullaby ever cast for a Girl's Girl should she one day become a Mother" (22). Fashion, writing, and lesbian (re)production are explicitly linked: a feather may be the perfect trimming for a hat, one that changes one's appearance, or it may be a pen, which invokes the act of writing. A song may be the perfect catalyst for a girl to become a Girl's Girl or a Lady's Lady—that is, a lesbian, in which case the song writer becomes either a lesbian midwife, who helps nurture the effects of the song, or a mother; not a mother ensconced within the heterosexual family but a new queer mother whose writing is her form of queer reproduction.

The lighthearted tone of the passage above, echoed in the lightness of the feather, emphasizes that queer relations to aesthetic objects, as to identities, are always to some degree difficult to overdetermine. As Muñoz notes:

> Sedgwick has defined the term *queer* as a *practice* that develops for queer children as "the ability to attach intently to a few cultural objects, objects of high or popular culture or both, objects whose meaning seemed mysterious, excessive or oblique in relation to the codes most readily available to us, [which] became a prime resource for survival. We need for there to be sites where meanings didn't line up tidily with each other, and we learn to invest these sites with a fascination and love." Thus, to perform queerness is to constantly disidentify, to constantly find oneself thriving on sites where meaning does not properly "line up."[83]

It is important to note here that Muñoz is speaking specifically of queer minoritarian subjects, for whom the disparities between meanings may be immense. Yet he draws on what I have been claiming in regard to the history of "identificatory erotics" is the central paradox or "mystery" of identity as identification. If identity is constructed through repeated forms of identification, and if identification is always partial, negotiated, and shot through with desire, then even through subjection new forms of resistance are possible.

Chapter 4

"EXCREATE A NO SINCE":

THE EROTIC CURRENCY

OF GERTRUDE STEIN'S

TENDER BUTTONS

~✿~

Opaque yet resonant statements and injunctions recur throughout Gertrude Stein's prose poem of 1914, *Tender Buttons:*

> Bargaining for a little, bargain for a touch, a liberty, an estrangement, a characteristic turkey.

> Please spice, please no name, place a whole weight, sink into a standard rising, raise a circle, choose a right around, make the resonance accounted and gather green any collar.

> To bury a slender chicken, to raise an old feather, to surround a garland and to bake a pole splinter, to suggest a repose and to settle simply, to surrender one another, to succeed saving simpler, to satisfy a singularity and not be blinder, to sugar nothing darker and to read redder, to have the color better, to sort out dinner, to remain together, to surprise no sinner, to curve nothing sweeter, to continue thinner, to increase in resting recreation to design string not dimmer.[1]

Stein's words imitate and exaggerate the often seemingly random jumble of advice, narrative, instruction, and command that distinguish the early Girl Scout handbooks—compare, for example, the instructions for the economist badge in *Scouting for Girls:*

> 1. Offer record of ten per cent, savings from earnings or allowance for three months. Show card for Postal Savings, or a Savings Bank Account.

2. Show record from parent or guardian that she has:
   a. Darned stockings.
   b. Kept shoes shined and repaired.
   c. Not used safety pins or other makeshift for buttons, hooks, hems of skirts, belts, etc.
   d. Keep clothes mended and cleansed from small spots.
3. For girls who have the spending of their money, either in allowance or earnings, show by character of shoes, stockings and gloves, hair-ribbons, handkerchiefs and other accessories that they know how to select them for wearing qualities and how to keep them in repair.
4. Show record of one week's buying and menus with plans for using food economically, such as left-overs, cheap but nourishing cuts of meat, butter substitutes, thrifty use of milk such as sour, skimmed or powdered milk, and so forth.[2]

Even earlier, the genre of the almanac or domestic handbook[3] echoes obliquely the maxims, advice, and admonitions of a housewife, reflected in Stein's writing. More specifically, Stein's words may be echoes of the voice of Alice B. Toklas, Stein's domestic partner from 1910 until Stein's death in 1946, who wrote her own book of domestic advice, memoir, and recipes, *The Alice B. Toklas Cookbook* (1954).[4]

In *Lectures in America*, Stein writes, in reference to *Tender Buttons*, "I called them by their names with passion and that made poetry."[5] Written at a critical juncture in Stein's personal life, at the time when Toklas was replacing Leo, Stein's brother, as Stein's housemate and closest companion, *Tender Buttons*, as many have argued, is in part a celebration of this transformation.[6] As a voice in the poem explains, "The sister was not a mister. Was this a surprise. It was" (65). And at some basic level it was these events, as Stein herself acknowledges—the arrival of the woman who would be her lover for the rest of her life, and the consequent departure of her bullying, unsympathetic brother—that sparked *Tender Buttons*.[7]

If one reads the work as a love poem, one may interpret the housewifely voices of instruction as simply a celebration of Alice, but such a biographical reading ignores the complexity of the text. In what, if anything, does this prose poem seek to instruct the reader? Unlike the novels, handbooks, and movements discussed above, the seeming refusal of *Tender Buttons* of the disciplinary pedagogical stance that all of the rest assume may make it seem out of place in the lineage I have thus far outlined in this volume. Nonetheless, I would argue that Stein's prose poem intervenes into this tradition. As in Stowe's *Oldtown Folks, Tender Buttons* associates the spinster with a mixing of the domestic and the public (figured as the economic). Moreover, the prose poem rewrites completely the domestic sphere itself. As I will elucidate below, the poem thoroughly queers domesticity and in so doing it remakes the nineteenth-century "romantic friendship" between bourgeois women into a playful, sexual intimacy, "a perfectly unprecedented arrangement between old ladies" (24). Not only is this relationship between women revealed to be, at its root, an erotic one, but Stein's text also eroticizes the space and activities of the household itself. The poem takes on the economic values of bourgeois culture, in particular the emphasis placed on thrift (often a central theme in nineteenth-century domestic handbooks and, as I have noted, one that is carried over into the early-twentieth-century Girl Scout handbook), as well as conservation and cleanliness. *Tender Buttons* thus deconstructs these values' distance from their supposed opposites (profligacy, waste, and dirt), and, similarly, domestic forms of exchange and intimacy assumed to be outside the workings of the market are revealed to be implicated in them.

In so doing, Stein's text undermines the ideological distinction between the private/domestic and the public/economic. *Tender Buttons* challenges the cultural meanings associated with spinsterhood and labor I have outlined in earlier chapters, and thus it redefines what counts as productive, reproductive, and "unnatural" forms of work and female identity. It presents, then, a complex theory of textuality and sexuality, one that reclaims what have been labeled "unnatural" sexual practices, and links it explicitly with a queer economy of writing and signification, Stein's unique brand of modern poetics.

To make such an argument is to transgress the boundaries of interpretation of Stein's work. Many critics of her experimental writing argue that Stein's texts lack content, that they seek only, self-reflexively, to instruct readers in the problems of interpretation itself. This has led at best to sophisticated analyses of the ways in which any reader must become implicated in the making of meaning in Stein's text: her works, in other words, make it obvious that there is no truth inherent in the text, but that interpretation is a collaborative effort between the text and the reader's particular critical, historical, and personal urgencies.[8] At worst, the sheer difficulty of Stein's writing has led some critics to declare it uninterpretable, and to view such impenetrability as, most positively, a sign of Stein's language's ability to resist the corruption of modernization,[9] or most negatively, as an indication that Stein's texts are just gimmicks or "thousands of pages of disconnected trivia."[10]

Refusals to grant the interpretability of Stein's work are often also refusals to recognize its import for a queer, and specifically lesbian, tradition. Such refusals represent a variation on the theme of what Eve Kosofsky Sedgwick has termed "willed ignorance."[11] Rather than say "I just don't see it," when faced with a queer reading, these criticisms instead argue that "it just isn't possible to say anything at all about this text, except that it refuses interpretation." Ironically, many queer critics of Stein often argue something similar, that Stein turns to textual difficulty as a way to escape censorship. In other words, in these critics' view Stein creates a private language that only she and perhaps Toklas may interpret, and thus protects the sanctity of their relationship in a closet of her own creation; that is, they argue that at a moment when lesbianism had begun to gain publicity as a stigmatized "identity" Stein responds by creating a text that creates a kind of absolute privacy for her relationship with Toklas.[12]

Even such well-meaning efforts to rescue Stein's texts from charges that they have no meaning and thus no aesthetic or cultural value mystify and obscure the celebration of female-female homoerotics that *Tender Buttons* enacts. These efforts invoke the secret, unsymbolized depths of the text and ignore what is (only) surface. By locating lesbian sexuality in the unrepresentable, they perpetuate the problem I discussed in my introduction to this volume, one of relegating female-female homoerotics to silence, that which is beyond language and representation and thus beyond history. Instead, in this chapter I will argue that *Tender Buttons* engages centrally with the historical emergence of "the lesbian," not through a simple retreat into difficulty but through constructing its own sexual/textual theory of the links between words, queer sex, and money.

Similar to Barnes's *Ladies Almanack,* Stein's prose poem explores the connection between lesbianism and modernization. In the process, it makes both queer sex and queer writing analogous to, and inseparable from, other forms of "unnatural" production and reproduction. Through its representation of what Mark Seltzer terms the "*relays* articulated between the life process and the machine process," it seeks to revalue what in Stowe's *Oldtown Folks* is always a ridiculed and stigmatized connection between queer female (proto)identities and modernization.[13]

Feminist and African American scholars in the United States have revised the traditional idea of modernization as a fall from a coherent, stable, "organic" society to one that is fragmented, alienated, and depersonalized. They argue that this view overlooks the more progressive effects of modernization on the lives, cultures, and political power of women and African Americans in the United States. Houston Baker, for example, asserts that the migration of African Americans from the South to northern and midwestern cities (in particular to Harlem) in a search for work in the expanding capitalist economy created the conditions necessary for the cultural blossoming of the Harlem Renaissance. It also led to greater cultural and political awareness among African Americans in urban areas.[14] For many women, especially whites of the middle class, the shift from an economy that required the constant productive labor of the housewife to one that afforded more leisure resulted in more time for activities besides housework. Yet, at the same time, commodity culture imposed new housewifely duties. It required that the domestic sphere become the center of consumption as well as a haven from the evils of the market.[15] For many other women, as I have described in earlier chapters, the need for new kinds of bourgeois workers in industrial capitalism aided their efforts to obtain education and employment outside the home.

The emergence of industrial capitalism also affected the organization of sexuality; in particular, forms of sexuality that were not included under heterosexual reproductive norms. As I have discussed, the shift in the production of individuals from the home to the public sphere (including, but not limited to, schools, various social reform movements, and the media itself), in part through what Seltzer terms "the radical and intimate *coupling* of bodies and machines," made possible new ideas of production and reproduction, especially the production and reproduction of subjectivity, that were distanced from traditional stereotypes of labor and procreation.[16] As Seltzer explains,

> What is gradually elaborated [in late-nineteenth-century discourse] is a . . . system of transformations and relays between "opposed" and contradictory registers—between public and private spaces; between social norms and private values; between work and world on the one side, and home and family on the other; between, more generally, "the economic" and "the sexual." . . . These new, or rather, newly inflected, strategies of regulation advertise the differences between public and private, and be-

tween economic and sexual domains, even as they reinforce and extend the lines of communication between them.[17]

Seltzer's description of these "double discourses" establishes a historical and ideological context, as well as a set of (false) dichotomies, within which to locate Stein: the body and the machine, the economic and the sexual.[18]

In the rest of this chapter I examine the relationship between the changes in American society that Seltzer chronicles and a specific construction of queer labor and production: Gertrude Stein's (and Alice B. Toklas's) theory of production, consumption, and reproduction. Historians of sexuality continually debate what caused the formation of gay and lesbian public identities at the turn of the century in the United States. Aside from the familiar argument that it was through the cataloguing of sexuality (another cataloguing to which Stein's writing most obviously responds) that these identities were first articulated, there is little else to go on. When historians attempt to discuss capitalism's effects on the formation of gay and lesbian identities, they can only come up with blunt economisms: more jobs equaled more independence from family equaled new identities.[19] Instead, as I demonstrate, new cultural ideologies regarding the production and reproduction of goods and individuals may have helped to enable the formation of new sexual subjectivities. In particular, I elucidate how Stein's theories of writing, representation, and (re)production and their relation to a queer sexual practice challenge dominant theories that, in their nostalgia for a utopian vision of precapitalist society, decry the rise of commodity capitalism as the beginning of the end of "authentic" (which, as I will argue below, is always already heterosexual) society. In making the spinster the author of this new sexual/textual practice, Stein's text takes what has been a damning discourse of deviance and turns it into a culturally powerful, celebratory sexual identity. In so doing, Stein positions herself as a lesbian modernist who engages, eroticizes, and celebrates modernization itself.

Thrift

In her now legendary cookbook Alice B. Toklas describes a series of "murders" she has committed for the sake of the culinary, including one that, in its representations of work, is particularly intriguing:

> One day passing the *concierge's loge* he called me and said he had something someone had left for us. He said he would bring it to me, which

he did and which I wished he hadn't when I saw what it was, a crate of six white pigeons and a note from a friend saying she had nothing better to offer us from her home in the country, ending with But as Alice is clever she will make something delicious of them. It is certainly a mistake to allow a reputation for cleverness to be born and spread by loving friends. It is so cheaply acquired and so dearly paid for. Six white pigeons to be smothered, to be plucked, to be cleaned and all this to be accomplished before Gertrude Stein returned *for she didn't like to see work being done.*[20]

A current of eroticism underlies this passage. Toklas lovingly insists on referring to Stein by her full name,[21] because titles or names were important to Stein and Toklas—as Toklas describes their courtship in her memoir, *What Is Remembered,* the moment when Stein referred to Tolkas as "Alice" and the moment when she asked her to call her "Gertrude" stand out as highly eroticized markers of a kind of crossing over from one form of relationship to another.[22] "I called them by their names with passion," Stein writes.[23] Similarly, in the way only lovers do, Alice plays with the connotations of the formal address, savoring the roll of the name off of her tongue. By so doing, she creates a false or parodic sense of her distance from Stein. But Toklas also indicates that by virtue of its repetition the appellation really connotes the opposite, an unsurpassed familiarity.

Toklas's breathless, laissez-faire narrative also transmits beautifully the vocation to which she belongs, and of which she is perhaps the expert of experts, that of the eminently capable housewife. Yet it is difficult to categorize her career: she is not exactly a leisured bourgeoise who would have turned over the fowl to the cook, nor is she the middle-class woman without a servant who would pretend that she herself had never entered the kitchen.[24] In this passage Toklas confides and almost brags about her labor. Why, then, does she wish to conceal it from Stein?

Toklas's reasons seem to lie not in the realm of maintaining bourgeois norms of propriety but somewhere else. She refers to her "reputation for cleverness" as being "cheaply acquired." The connotations of "cheap" are double-edged here: "cheap" as in easy to possess, as well as not really earned through hard work. Toklas's language suggests that Stein desires her always to appear "easy," and that appearance has something to do with an air of effortlessness, at least in regard to what Toklas herself portrays as her "art," cooking. The sexual connotations of "cheap" (as sexually available) should also not be overlooked. What other aspects of their life together did Stein want to be easy?

Toklas's playful regretfulness about the gift of the fowl is only equaled in its oddity by her mock terror that her labor will be exposed. Disrupting traditional notions of gift giving and gratitude, in particular the idea that gifts are gains that do not require a return (and therefore are somehow outside the realm of the economic), Toklas views the six white pigeons in terms of obligation. This gift constitutes a burden, but not that of a return directed at the unnamed friend. Instead, it is the burden of work, work that must be hidden from Stein, concealed behind an appearance of effortlessness.

Besides its role in some kind of representational erotics, the economic transaction that Toklas describes appears oddly outdated. She and Stein lived in Paris during the first five decades of the twentieth century, at a time when the economies of Europe and, in particular, the United States, were undergoing drastic changes—in large part because of the burgeoning market economy and the rapid industrialization of American manufacturing. The fact that Toklas was given live pigeons that she had to slaughter and pluck herself, as opposed to buying them ready to roast, signals that Toklas was not enjoying (at least in this instance) the supposed benefits of "the culture of consumption."[25] The gift of the fowl thus represents a precapitalist mode of exchange and a premodernized form of labor, a gift that Toklas must transform into a meal without revealing the work required, as though it were instead a ready-made commodity.[26]

Increasingly viewed as the private space of consumption rather than of production, the household and the housewife were undergoing rapid redefinition at the turn of the century. As Alan Trachtenberg describes this shift:

> With the rise of food and clothing industries, domestic labor came to consist chiefly of budgeting and shopping rather than making. From the place of labor for self-support, the home had become the place of consumption. How to be a "lady who does her own work" came very quickly after the Civil War to mean how to be a lady who shops; indeed, who sustains herself as "lady" by wise and efficient shopping.[27]

Already we may recognize a context for Toklas's mock fear that Stein might see her performing work: the new role of the housewife was one of consumption not traditional forms of productive labor, and it also presented new responsibilities. According to Richard Ohmann,

For women, consumption was at the center of their new role. They could show new skills as purchasers and users of commodities; they could show care for their families with products; they could give the home social standing by placing the right things in it. They could make it a secure and loving place where those who went out to work returned to a sphere of dignity and autonomy, a place where alienated products were brought under psychic control.[28]

Certainly this was Alice's duty as Gertrude's "wife." Toklas was more than an inspiration to Stein: not only, for example, did she take care of Stein's basic material needs by doing all the cooking, cleaning, shopping, as well as sending out the laundry and managing the servants, but she also typed and edited Stein's work (a daunting task, given its unique experiments with language, syntax, grammar) and, in the process, added her own corrections, amendments, and revisions. Moreover, Stein's most famous work, *The Autobiography of Alice B. Toklas,* purports to be written by Toklas. In taking on her lover's voice, Stein signals not a simple appropriation of her subjectivity but, as Leigh Gilmore has asserted most convincingly, an emblem of their intermingling and of the complexity of their interactions, calling into question who speaks for whom, who cares for whom, and what constitutes authorship when both women seem to have collaborated on many of their texts.[29]

Tender Buttons, as I have noted above, also includes lines or fragments that resemble Toklas's voice. It also repeatedly invokes her name as it puns on it; for example, in lines such as "Eel us, eel us," the poem connects the name "Alice" to a culinary delicacy. By starting with Toklas, then, I want to underline the inseparability of Toklas and Stein's work: just as their life was a partnership, so, to a great degree, was all their art, and the celebration of *Tender Buttons* of the activities of the housewife makes such quotidian duties equivalent to other forms of aesthetic production.[30] I also want to highlight the continuities between Toklas's relatively more traditional form of narrative and Stein's more experimental prose poem. *Tender Buttons,* as well as Toklas's text, is focused on a set of intertwined concerns: the distinction or nondistinction between gifts and other kinds of (economic) exchange; the distance between the private/domestic and the public/economic, as sustained or broken down by the commodity/gift; and the possibilities within language for signifying multiply as demonstrated through both Toklas and Stein's use of puns, puns that play in particular with words that carry both sexual and economic connotations. *Tender*

Buttons also continually considers questions of use and value, but just like Stein herself, who hated to see (Toklas performing) work, her poem concerns itself with relations of production and reproduction that challenge traditional conceptions of what counts as economy, desire, need, and labor.

Ostensibly, the text seems designed simply to describe or name fragments of the bourgeois domestic sphere, as signaled most centrally by its organization. Split into three parts, the third part, titled "Rooms," is one long section, whereas within the first two parts, "Objects" and "Food," there are numerous smaller divisions. Each has a title, all in capital letters, which is followed by a period. Many of these titles bear the names of household items, especially in the section "Objects" ("A CLOTH." [20], "EYE GLASSES." [21]), or of food ("CRANBERRIES." [46]), or of words describing the action of eating ("DINING." [56]), but there are also numerous titles that do not follow this arrangement ("MORE." [20], "THIS IS THE DRESS, AIDER." [29]). After these headings, there may be one sentence, one paragraph, or several pages. The poem thus painstakingly elaborates the trappings of a middle-class, late-Victorian home, its rooms, meals, and everyday objects.

By comparing this home to other forms of commodity display, *Tender Buttons* immediately calls into question any separation between the domestic and the market. In the section titled "A RED STAMP," the poem reads "if they do this and it is not necessary it is not at all necessary if they do this they need a catalogue" (14). Just as a red stamp has its place in a stamp collector's album, so the whole entry fits into the larger poem, mimicking the action of collecting—of the bringing together and identifying of moments and pleasures, rhymes and similarities that characterize Stein's creative project. For Stein's poem creates a set of "arrangement[s] in a system. . . . All this and not ordinary, not unordered in not resembling" (9).

Stein's desire to create a "catalogue" recalls the shift from the production of goods within the domestic sphere to the production of goods in the factory and their sale to the bourgeois housewife through the spectacle of the newly developed department store. Cultural historians Neil Harris and Trachtenberg describe affinities between this location and other centers of public display. Harris links the department store with the many fairs and expositions that became popular around the turn of the century, as well as with the rise of the museum. He reads all of these spaces as places where goods were displayed and where what he terms "dramas of consumer desire" could be produced and enacted.[31] For Trachtenberg, the department store most closely resembles the mail-order catalogue. Each was designed, "as much as the school, and much like the factory," as "an educational institution" designed to teach consumer relations. He explains:

> The departments taught the social location of goods: trousers as "men's clothing," silks as "women's wear," reclining chairs as "parlor furniture." It systematized, conveniently, the world of goods into discrete names, each with its niche, and in visible spatial relation to all others. Like the mail-order catalogue, the department store organized the world as consumable objects, each serving a household role. The store *represented* the world, and represented it chiefly in the form of an ideal home inhabited by ideal role-playing characters.[32]

What Trachtenberg does not note, but what seems to be of central importance, is the way in which the department store (and presumably the mail-order catalogue) organizes or teaches consumers a specific kind of consumption. The goods he describes delineate the commodification of gender and sexuality. Not only do store and catalogue specify what constitutes clothing ("silks"), but they also dictate which gender wears it ("men's trousers," "women's wear"). These examples demonstrate that another kind of codification of gender and sexuality occurred at the turn of the century: there are newly gendered "needs" and "desires" that are supposed to reflect the binary gender oppositions of compulsory heterosexuality.[33] The domestic sphere serves within this system as a site for the production and reproduction, through consumption and display, of these norms.

By making her own catalogue of what is "not necessary," Stein both replicates and challenges these new cultural norms of consumption and display. Her emphasis on what does *not* traditionally constitute need places her outside conventional bourgeois ideals of domestic economy. Stein rewrites the pedagogy of consumer desire: the attempt to instill through advertising new needs, formerly thought of as luxuries, in consumers. She works against those who criticize these new needs as excesses and those who try to construct these desires as *the needs* (gendered and sexual). Both of these positions still divide the world into needs and wants, legitimate and illegitimate desires, male and female, heterosexual and homosexual. In sharp contrast to this, Stein poses her own system of needs and desires. Furthermore, by turning the space of the home, which was being reinforced as the private, isolated domestic refuge, into the obverse (the equivalent of the department store), Stein refutes the idea of home as private and somehow isolated from the forces of the market.

Spending

In her biography of Stein and Toklas, Diane Souhami recounts the media descriptions that accompanied the couple's return in 1934 to the United States:

> Gertrude's hat was called a jockey's cap, a deerstalker's cap, tweedy and mannish, with a visor in front and an upcurl at the back. . . . She was reported to be wearing big men's shoes, her stockings were thick and woolly, she had a masculine haircut and sturdy legs, she was stocky, she was plump . . . she was a hearty irreverent old lady, a literary eccentric, a grand old expatriate and she was altogether charming.
>
> Alice was described as the Girl Friday, enigmatic bodyguard, typist and constant companion. She was wearing a Cossack hat and black fur coat. She was tiny, thin, mouselike, nervous, dark and small. She was Gertrude's queer, birdlike shadow and twittered when persuaded to speak at all.[34]

As Souhami indicates, the American "public" was fascinated with Stein and Toklas's appearance, not only at this moment but throughout and long after their lives. Photographs of Stein and Toklas show Stein in long, flowing gowns which, legend has it, misled some into thinking she was a religious figure, perhaps "a bishop, or a cardinal."[35] She also wears her own version of the waistcoat over loose blouses and comfortable skirts, many of which were designed by her friend, Pierre Balmain.[36] Toklas wears tailored suits, dresses with half-waists, hats, and gloves. In many of the photos what strikes one is the attention to detail, the brooch at Stein's collar, the glass necklace around Toklas's neck. And one such detail forms the basis for Stein's poem: buttons.

As many critics have argued, "tender buttons" is most obviously a reference to the female body, especially to the clitoris and nipples.[37] However, critics usually read buttons only as sites, as demarcated spaces that resemble buttons on a blouse. By thinking of them as switches, a term that originates with the move into machine culture, the metaphor's resonances increase. "Buttons" signal the way the body responds when touched as if a switch were flipped, implying that the body is somehow like or equivalent to a machine. Such equivalences between the body and the machine both preserve and deconstruct ideas of the "natural" versus the "unnatural." Gay men, lesbians, and queers, considered unnatural because their sexual practices do not produce children, have long been represented as existing outside of or in opposition to ideas of the "natural."[38] By equating the lover's body with a machine, Stein overturns these oppositions at the same time that she claims the machine-as-body for her queer project.[39] Thus, the threat posed by Miss Asphyxia's machinelike self that I explored in chapter 1 is here celebrated as a metaphor for lesbian subjectivity.

As small, distinct objects, buttons also refer to the words of the poem themselves.[40] We can almost imagine the poem as a kind of button box, the words—of many hues, shapes, designs, fabrics, metals, stones, and eras—dumped out and arranged into provocative patterns, discordances, and details. Alternatively they are a button board, a display of switches to be lovingly flipped. In either scenario, the fact that they are "tender" indicates that the writing process itself is highly sexualized. Stein creates an erotics of writing where her (at times) seemingly nonsensical combinations of words, her rhythmic sentences and paragraphs are, by metaphoric connection, also sexual/textual manipulations of the female body. Writing becomes an explicitly sexual act, a way of giving pleasure to the "her" of "tend her." As readers, we are called to participate in this desiring experience, to "tend her buttons" along with the poet, who perhaps uses this command as her motivating theme. Not only, when read aloud, does the poem's assonance and alliteration exercise the tongue, but as readers we are enjoined to enter into this lesbian hermeneutics and to give ourselves pleasure through our own constructions of meaning.[41] As a handbook, then, *Tender Buttons* seeks to instruct the reader in various forms of lesbian textual/sexual gratification.

Buttons are also, of course, the stuff of the household and the housewife. In the world of domestic fantasy, Mother always has a tin of odd buttons waiting to be matched with shirts and pants and vests. By making buttons a central metaphor for writing, Stein emphasizes that the home is a place of abundant creativity, not, as many cultural critics would have it, a sterile space of passive consumption.[42]

Like coins, buttons operate along several axes of value: they serve a utilitarian purpose (as fasteners of clothing), as well as in many cases having a separate aesthetic, "inherent" value. Buttons to coins, coins to words, "legal tender."[43] That Stein would foreground equivalencies between words and coins and meaning and value in part signals her position within a modernist aesthetic. Yet unlike Pound or Eliot, for example, who attempt to inject transcendental value back into a language irreparably soiled by the vagaries of capitalism, immigration and migration, sexual "degeneracy," mass culture, and women, Stein pursues a different project.[44] Because she identified, however complexly, as female, a lesbian, and a Jew, Stein's relation to questions of economic and literary value and meaning are much more complicated. She could not easily shed those affiliations to which she had at least a tenuous connection—those affiliations often equated with the supposed corruption of modern society. And why would she want to? Stein's writing is not simply trying to escape, deny, or ameliorate the effects of modernization; instead, it forges an aesthetic practice within and in dialogue with them. For example, Maria Damon, in her chapter on what she terms Stein's "doggerel Yiddish," links Stein's use of Yiddishisms to her status as a woman and as gay and views all of these positionalities as embodiments of marginalization.[45]

But Stein goes beyond simply incorporating signifiers of Jewishness into her text at the level of content: although Damon argues that despite a cultural climate of intense anti-Semitism, Stein used Yiddish to create a space for herself within modernist critiques and revaluations of language, I would claim that Stein also revalued an economic practice associated explicitly with an anti-Semitic stereotype, usury, and found in it a central metaphor for her theory of signification. In so doing, Stein's modernism brings together the economic and the sexual.

Getting Something for Nothing

Tender Buttons, in its working out of a theory of language, locates itself within a history of aesthetic and economic debates about mimesis, value, and signification. The metaphor between buttons and coins inaugurates this discussion. Beginning with Aristotle's aesthetics, as Marc Shell demonstrates, works of art are supposed to possess inherent, transcendent value outside of a cultural and economic assessment of them. Thus, art should be mimetic, in that it reflects the natural value of the objects represented. Shell, among others, traces this assumption back to Aristotle's Poetics and economic theory, and the relation between mimesis and meaning. As Shell explains:

> The aesthetic theory of *mimesis* . . . is informed by theories of economic and biological production. . . . In the *Politics* for example, Aristotle

makes a crucial distinction between nature and convention, or between good and bad production, on which his esthetics depend. He distinguishes between a supposedly natural economics (whose end is just distribution . . .) and a supposedly unnatural chremtistics (whose end is profit).[46]

Coins trouble this theory because, like buttons, they are simultaneously aesthetic objects—miniature sculptures that almost anyone can possess— and signifiers of value, whose only worth (or utility) is dependent on their place within a larger economic system. It should come as no surprise, then, that within this dichotomy between a so-called natural economics and one considered unnatural, coins play an integral part. As Shell describes it: "Such symbols, like spoken or written words and unlike affections and works of art, bear no natural relationship to things signified. Thus, coins are both natural (as stamped art) and unnatural (as monetary tokens)."[47] Aristotle's distinction between "good" and "bad" production, between a natural and unnatural economics, in many ways resembles Marx's idea of use versus exchange value. In Marx's theory of use value, commodities are supposed to have a "natural" value that reflects the "natural" need they fulfill and the "naturally" productive labor they require to be produced. Instead of seeing definitions of need as socially constructed, then, Marxist ideas of what constitutes need and what constitutes productive labor are both based on naturalized, universalized assumptions about human nature. Jean Baudrillard is perhaps the most forceful critic of this theory. He argues:

The mystery of exchange value and the commodity can be unmasked, relatively—it has been since Marx—and raised to consciousness as a social relation. But value in the case of use value is enveloped in total mystery, for it is grounded anthropologically in the (self)-"evidence" of a naturalness, in an unsurpassable original reference. This is where we discover the real "theology" of value—in the order of finalities: in the "ideal" relation of equivalence, harmony, economy and equilibrium that the concept of utility implies. It operates at all levels: Between man and nature, man and objects, man and his body, the self and others. Value becomes absolutely self-evident, *la chose la plus simple*.[48]

Martyn Lee glosses Baudrillard's reading of Marx's theory of use value: "For Marx use value represents nothing but the expression of a natural relationship between an object and a person, so that to each object corresponds to a predetermined or unique use based upon a natural and stable need."[49]

Following Baudrillard's critique, I would argue that there is a meta-phoric link between the "natural," the "original," and the heterosexual that characterizes Aristotelian mimesis and marxist theories of use value (and one could extend the use of these economies of representation to Walter Benjamin and most recently to Fredric Jameson).[50] In particular marxist theory bases its idea of what counts as "productive" labor on the model of heterosexual reproduction. To quote from Marx himself, writing in *The German Ideology:* "Men, who daily remake their own life, begin to make other men, to propagate their kind: the relation between man and woman, parents and children, the *family.*"[51] The "original" laboring relation is a reflection of the "original" heterosexual pair, whose "natural" product is a baby.

Furthermore, Marx's theories of value embody bourgeois notions of conservation and thrift. In both bourgeois and marxist fantasies of pro-duction, there is nothing left over, no excess, no waste. As Georges Bataille notes, "humanity recognizes the right to acquire, to conserve, and to con-sume rationally, but it excludes in principle nonreproductive expendi-ture."[52] And indeed, Marx, in identifying what counts as "productive" la-bor, writes that "nothing can have value, without being an object of utility. If the thing is useless, so is the labour contained in it; the labour does not count as labour, and therefore creates no value."[53] Through his disdain for that which is wasteful, Marx reveals himself as a capitalist thinker, a product, himself, of capitalism.

Under this regime, homosexual sex, along with many other sexual acts that lie outside the sphere of heterosexual procreation, is regarded as use-less labor, for it does not reproduce biological offspring. Like the lumpen proletariat (whose labor, as Marx represents it, is considered wasteful, ex-pendable, and worthless, as Andrew Parker has shown), queers are outside of the "waste not, want not" theories of value that characterize both bour-geois and marxist thought. Parker calls on Hannah Arendt to make ex-plicit the links in marxism between biological reproduction and notions of what counts as production:

> If Marx remains both horrified and attracted by this tropology [that the lumpen proletariat embody blood, excrement, and money mixed to-gether], this may be because he finds that it parodies the central cat-egories of his thought. The question of where values come from ani-

mates the whole of his evolving critique of political economy, and his dependable answer is labor defined as "life-activity, productive life itself," where production has been modeled on procreation. In Hannah Arendt's words: Marx's work "rests on the equation of productivity with fertility"; "he based his whole theory [of production] on the understanding of laboring and the begetting as two modes of the same fertile life process." The heterosexism of this formulation is not to be dismissed as merely figural, for Marx views labor invariably as the "life of the species," as "life-engendering-life"; "productive labor" is a fact "imposed by Nature"; labor is the "father" and the earth the "mother" of value.[54]

Stein's theory of language, crucially based on her own theory of *use,* undermines these paradigms: there are natural forms of representation that correspond to original forms; there are natural uses for things; and there are natural forms of labor and value that satisfy exactly natural universal forms of need. In order to create a textual/sexual space for her body, her desire, and her creativity, Stein must radically challenge cultural, religious, and literary taboos. A voice in *Tender Buttons* queries, "If the persecution is so outrageous that nothing is solemn is there any occasion for persuasion" (42). Elsewhere a voice asserts, "[These] are no dark custom[s]" (18). Through linking what I will argue are, for Stein, two specific "dark customs"—usury and sodomy—Stein's poetics join a form of queer sex with a form of stigmatized economic activity.

In the *Politics,* Aristotle writes:

> Usury is most reasonably hated, because its gain comes from money itself and not from that for the sake of which money was invented. For money was brought into existence for the purpose of exchange, but interest increases the amount of money itself (and this is the actual origin of the Greek word *tokos:* offspring resembles parent . . . and interest is money born of money); consequently this form of the business of getting wealth is of all forms the most contrary to nature.[55]

Aristotle condemns usury as unnatural because it produces money from money. What about a poetics that produces meaning from meaning, or more meaning than it is supposed to? What about a writing practice that "borrows" meaning as opposed to creating it? If words, like coins, are simply transmitters or signifiers of value, without "natural" worth in themselves, then there is no way of controlling what they will produce or what "unnatural" excesses or surplus value of meaning they will accumulate. A line in the section "BREAKFAST" reads, "An imitation, more imitation, imitation succeed imitations" (41). Words may not be simply mimetic of prior objects but instead they imitate imitations and unleash (or borrow) unpredictable torrents of meaning.[56]

The section titled "GLAZED GLITTER" includes a discussion or revelation of "change." Because of its double meaning as both a collection of coins (what is left over, excess from a transaction) and a transformation in the state of things, Stein's poem puns "The change has come" (9). Change—an excess of coins and an excess of meaning—abounds in *Tender Buttons*. Through the "coining" of phrases Stein's project is to create "change." Money and meaning go hand in hand in an "unnatural" accumulation of signification.[57] As Stein writes elsewhere, "Money is what words are. Words are what money is."[58] *Tender Buttons* imagines a situation where (political/social) change can only come through a surplus, what is left over. And the change comes, moreover, when "the sister is not a mister," when two women form a sexual relationship, a measure for which does not exist in terms of social or sexual utility.

As with this playful rhyme, Stein puns throughout her writings. Punning itself has a long critical history, beginning again with Aristotle, as Shell explains: "Aristotle argues that of all forms of generation usury is the most unnatural, and theorists since the medieval era have argued that punning is its linguistic counterpart, since punning makes an unnatural, even a diabolical, supplement of meaning from a sound that is properly attached to only one (if any) meaning."[59] Such "unnatural" word play is key to Stein's project in *Tender Buttons*. There are crude Freudianesque images such as the titles of several of the sections—"A MOUNTED UMBRELLA" (20)—as well as strange parodies of chapter headings or cartoon captions—"A FRIGHTFUL RELEASE" (19)—that eroticize objects and moments at the same time that they satirize them. There are words within and between words: "ORANGE IN" (58) (arranging/origin); "SALMON" (57) (after "sam in"), and there are many more examples.

Through these puns, *Tender Buttons* challenges the idea that there are "natural" uses and needs. In the section "A SELTZER BOTTLE" we learn that "the use of this is manifold" (16). Stein's poem sexualizes the bottle, mocking its phallic proportions and its habit of spraying. The bottle's status as everyday object is disturbed and the reader's view of it is changed. We begin to imagine other erotic "uses" for the bottle besides its utilitarian value as receptacle of liquid, and we may get so caught up in this pleasurable imagining that we forget what the "original" use was. We are forming a catalogue of "uses" that are "not necessary . . . not at all necessary" but instead takes these objects beyond their assigned roles in both the domestic and sexual economy.

"Using" sexual difference—for example, the question "is there any difference?" (70) recurs in various forms throughout the poem—is crucial to this exploration. As the "use" of a seltzer bottle is manifold, so, too, is the "use" of heterosexual appellations and situations to describe the lesbian relationship: the "man" within "manifold" hints that a (female) lover could be a "man" through its use. By borrowing markers of heterosexual union, such as "husband," "wife," and "wedding," the poem "uses" these identities to parody their claims to naturalness, forming a complex erotic code.[60] Rather than fault Stein for her "male-identification,"[61] I would argue that this practice is analogous to what Judith Butler describes as "gender parody." Butler refuses what she terms a kind of "lesbian modernism" that strives for the (impossible) lesbian space outside of heterosexual norms as epitomized in the various theories of *écriture feminine*. As she puts it, "there are structures of psychic homosexuality within heterosexual relations, and structures of psychic heterosexuality within gay and lesbian sexuality and relationships."[62] The last sentence in "A CARAFE, THAT IS A BLIND GLASS" alludes to this possibility, declaring "the difference is spreading" (9).[63] Besides connoting female genitalia, a marker of gender difference that is revealed when the legs are spread, "difference" is also that which is left over (in financial transactions, "change") when one thing is subtracted from another. And this remainder is gathering force or "spreading" out. Similarly, the title "MILDRED'S UMBRELLA" (13) parodies phallic power in its choice of an umbrella as phallic object (this happens in a "MOUNTED UMBRELLA" as well) and co-opts it by the addition of Mildred as owner. Gender identity, like an umbrella, can be "borrowed" or "used."[64]

Stein makes "use" of sexual difference in a way that vexes the instrumental notion of use. In the slippage between use and usury, we find a breakdown between any idea of "natural" use value and unnatural "exchange" or surplus value: objects have many uses, uses beyond their "natural" purpose, which produce a multiplicity of values. Instead of being used as an anti-Semitic stereotype, then, in *Tender Buttons* usury is thus revalued as a linguistic strategy. "GLAZED GLITTER," after interrogating the identity of (a) nickel, continues: "It was chosen yesterday, that showed spitting and perhaps washing and polishing. It certainly showed no obligation and perhaps *if borrowing is not natural there is some use in giving"* (9; emphasis mine). Here the poem employs almost exactly the same language as does Aristotle to discuss the practice of lending: "not natural." Through the multiple meanings of "use," however, the poem destroys the difference between loans and gifts, lending and giving. To make use of language, as Stein's poem describes when it asserts "the use of this is manifold," is to produce more than the "utilitarian" meaning of a word, to "get something from nothing," to accrue a kind of metaphorical interest. It is to make use into usury.

Many forms of giving traditionally have been viewed as economic transactions that occur outside of obligation, as "pure" forms of exchange.[65] If we read the clause quoted above as "there is some use [usury] [even] in giving,"[66] we see that *Tender Buttons* challenges any romanticized notion of giving that places it outside relations of return and responsibility.[67] This sets up an erotics of exchange that is all about expenditure, giving and receiving and accumulating pleasure. Yet this expenditure also requires returns, in much the same way that the gift of the six white pigeons requires that Toklas work.[68]

Stein's poem refuses any idealized notion of gift giving, destroying any hierarchy between natural and unnatural increase and production. An act of giving incurs obligation, not exactly in the same way that a loan accrues interest but still incurring some form of debt. Both require payment and both produce "money from money," something from nothing, income supposedly without labor. "Natural expenditure" (gift giving) produces income, as does "unnatural expenditure" (usury)—the difference breaks down. Instead of resorting to traditional stereotypes of female labor—utility, thriftiness, and conservation—*Tender Buttons* revels in expenditure and waste. More specifically, the poem theorizes the relation between sexuality and economic and linguistic excess through its focus on an anal poetics. In so doing, as I will demonstrate below, the prose poem gains "value" for a queer sexual and textual practice.[69]

Steinian Sodomy: "A Violent Kind of Delightfulness"

A voice in "A SUBSTANCE IN A CUSHION" queries, "What is the use of a violent kind of delightfulness if there is no pleasure in not getting tired of it" (10). This question can be rephrased to read, "What is the use, [usury, value] of a violent kind of delightfulness?" But what exactly *is* this pleasure? As Bataille notes:

The goal of [material utility] is, theoretically pleasure—but only in a moderate form, since violent pleasure is seen as *pathological*. On the one hand, this material utility is limited to acquisition (in practice, to production) and to the conservation of goods; on the other, it is limited to reproduction and to the conservation of human life.[70]

Tender Buttons describes a specific kind of "violent pleasure": sodomy. The definition of sodomy I am employing here includes both oral and anal sex between members of the "same" or "opposite" genders.[71] Its violence lies in its break with the regime of heterosexual procreative sexuality. Its violence does not lie necessarily in its expressions of power, although it would be naive to argue that any sexual practice does not sometimes carry with it dangerous and/or exciting and/or eroticized power relations. Within the Christian legal tradition, sodomy (otherwise known as "unnatural sexual practices") and usury are linked.[72] Usury produces money from money, and sodomy produces sexual pleasure without biological reproduction.

In the passage from "GLAZED GLITTER" quoted above ("It was chosen yesterday, that showed spitting and perhaps washing and polishing"), the sexualized language of "spitting," "washing," and "polishing" also invokes oral sex, "tending her buttons," one form of sodomy or unnatural production, which explicitly couples Stein's text's verbal usury and its recuperation of queer sexuality. Furthermore, the "that" that showed "spitting and perhaps washing and polishing" alludes to the traditionally feminine task of keeping the household items sparkling.[73] Cunnilingus becomes, like polishing the silver, the job of the housewife.[74]

Elsewhere the noonday meal is described in highly suggestive terms: "A little lunch is a break in skate a little lunch so slimy, a west end of a board line is that which shows a little beneath so that necessity is a silk under wear. That is best wet. It is so natural" (48–49). In this passage, by defining (sexual) necessity as a "silk under wear," the poem makes necessity itself into a luxury and luxury into a necessity, thereby breaking down the distinction between desire and need. The gendered connotations of "silk under wear. That is best wet" lead the reader to assume that "lunch" is the female genitalia. In this transformed household, this activity or meal "is so natural." Earlier in the poem, a voice states, "The one way to use custom is to use soap and silk for cleaning" (12). Traditional female household activities, "custom" and "cleaning," are radically eroticized, emphasizing Stein's text's appropriation and subversion of domestic economy.

The bourgeois ideology of rational consumption and production, "waste not, want not," disintegrates under this pressure.

By placing *Tender Buttons* within the domestic sphere, Stein utterly disrupts what little is left of the Victorian notion of women in the home. Good housekeepers control and regulate consumption and (re)production within the home. This includes preparing food and managing waste and keeping rooms and bodies clean. Good housekeepers are good mothers. They are thrifty, resourceful, and strictly follow their budgets. Stein's text invokes as it deconstructs this idealized image:

> In between a place and candy is a narrow footpath that shows more mounting than anything, so much really that a calling meaning a bolster measured a whole thing with that. A virgin a whole virgin is judged made and so between curves and outlines and real seasons and more out glasses and a perfectly unprecedented arrangement between old ladies and mild colds there is no satin wood shining. (24)

The juxtaposition of the "virgin" and the "old ladies" hints at the sexual connotations of this passage. Its use of the term "mounting," the description of the "narrow footpath that shows more mounting than anything," suggests that it is a reference to the vagina. The vagina is "in between" the clitoris and the anus, although the ambiguity of "a place and candy" makes it impossible to pin down to which "place" these terms refer (is the clitoris "candy" and the anus "a place" or vice versa?). From the well-traveled "foot-path" of femininity and traditional notions of reproduction, Stein's poem leads us to other pleasurable (and often forgotten or ignored) spaces of the female anatomy. It remaps the erogenous zones of the female body, just as it changes the landscape of the parlor and the bedroom. In the chambers of *Tender Buttons* the piano legs are sexualized, and purses "show . . . that it was open, that is all it showed" (19), the many connotations of purse—as vagina, as place of savings, as source of change—hinting at an overflow of wealth and satisfaction. The "perfectly unprecedented arrangement [verbal, sexual, economic] between old ladies" takes over the power to "judge" and "ma[k]e" distinctions as to who is a virgin and on what terms.

That *Tender Buttons* would reclaim sodomy and usury, these anti-Semitic and homophobic mainstays, may give some pause: in so doing some might contend that Stein reinforces or expresses a kind of self-hatred.[75] I would argue instead that by insisting on these two practices as metaphors for her literary and sexual practice, Stein takes up the most damaging and damning cultural scripts used against Jews and homosexuals and turns them into a joyful, sly, sexy poetics.

Alice, A Lass, All Ass

In "A SUBSTANCE IN A CUSHION," Stein writes: "Callous is something hardening leaves behind what will be soft if there is a genuine interest in there being present as many girls as men. Does this change. It shows that dirt is clean when there is a volume" (10). "Callous" carries sexual connotations: it rhymes with phallus, it feels hard.[76] The last part of the quote evokes against this phallic allusion the power of softness, if there are "as many girls as men." Is this a balancing act of difference, girls against the men? Or is it girls masquerading *as* men?

The lack of punctuation in this excerpt obscures the syntax, which in turn blurs clear lines of demarcation between soft and hard, girls and men. If girls borrow masculine clothing and play up the male role, does anything happen? The last sentence indicates that something indeed occurs: "It shows that dirt is clean when there is a volume" (10). Definitions are turned inside out.[77] Dirt becomes clean, that which is forbidden is redeemed, when there is a volume, an accumulation of differences, a book or poem. Here the poem tries to reform the sexual connotations of what counts as "dirty": it may also allude to as it revalues the anti-Semitic epithet, "dirty Jew."

In the echo of "Alice" in "callous" Toklas is also invoked as part of these erotics.[78] In particular, her labor is metaphorized through the image of callused hands, hands that both maintain the household and make exuberant love to Gertrude.[79] The voice of domestic knowledge often speaks within the poem, uttering such platitudes as "sugar is not a vegetable" (9), and "the settling of stationing cleaning is one way not to shatter scatter and scattering" (12). As noted above, this voice resembles the asides and directives of Toklas's cookbook. Even more important, *Tender Buttons* calls Alice by her "name . . . with passion and that ma[kes] poetry"—it puns on Alice's name throughout the poem.[80] In the section titled "COOKING," a reference to Alice's art, Stein's writing lovingly croons, "Alas, alas the pull alas the bell alas the coach in china, alas the little put in leaf alas the wedding butter meat, alas the receptacle, alas the back shape of mussle, mussle and soda" (53).[81] Alice, "alas," may also be read as "a lass" or "all ass." The poem again invokes the anus when it describes Alice as "alas the receptacle, alas the back shape of mussle." It increases its emphasis on transgression by comparing Alice to "mussle" (mussel), a shell-fish whose consumption is forbidden in Jewish law. Society regulates female-female sexuality and diet in much the same way, through the construction and enforcement of cultural and religious laws and taboos.

By transforming Alice into "all ass," Stein makes her into a model or muse for her writing practice. Two sections later *Tender Buttons* revels in this notion, writing: "Alas a dirty word, alas a dirty third alas a dirty third, alas a dirty bird" (54). When we remember the three spaces of female sexual pleasure, "a narrow foot-path that shows much more mounting than anything," "candy," and "a place," Alice, as "all ass," as "dirty third," becomes another marker of a new eroticism, the third term in a definition of female sexuality that usually only includes two, if that, genitally focused centers of female pleasure.[82]

At one point, the poem, in the middle of a long paragraph describing Alice and Gertrude's life together, confides:

> A line in life, a single line and a stairway, a rigid cook, no cook and no equator, all the same there is higher than that another evasion. Did that mean shame, it meant memory. Looking into a place that was hanging and was visible looking into this place and seeing a chair did that mean relief, it did, it certainly did not cause constipation. (71–72)

Instead of succumbing to the shame associated with the sexual/textual practices that *Tender Buttons* so lovingly describes, this passage indicates that Stein's "line in life" with Alice, "a rigid cook," produces abundant inspiration, and "certainly did not cause constipation." Confirming our sense that words and excrement are linked, thereby inscribing an anal erotic and queer sexuality as reproductive, the poem asserts that, together, Gertrude and Alice make poetry.[83] Elsewhere it lauds Alice's giving in another inscription, in which Alice becomes "a sign of extra, a sac a small sac and an established color and cunning, a slender grey and no ribbon, this means a loss a great loss a restitution" (13). Not only does Alice as housekeeper feed Gertrude sexually and actually, which allows her to excrete meaning, but Alice's identity is constituted here in utter self-loss, Alice as "a loss." An economy of giving, in love and in writing, develops.

"Giving it away, not giving it away, is there any difference. Giving it away. Not giving it away" (70), queries a voice in the poem. Alice gives herself to Gertrude and gets herself back, restated and secured; and Gertrude, through her writing, "gives it away," inviting the reader into the bedroom and kitchen where she and Alice make love and write. These relations of giving and receiving, loss and restitution, set up a complicated system of erotic, economic, and epistemologic circulation. Crucial to this economy is an accumulation of writing, a "volume" that includes the revaluing of waste, where "dirt is clean." The erotics of the anus, as a non-reproductive, nongenitally focused locus of textual production, are made explicit in the exhortation of *Tender Buttons* to "excreate a no since" (58). The meanings of this are manifold: the act of writing is transformed into "excreation," a condensation of signifiers that makes writing into both excretion and procreation. "Excreation" thus becomes an alternative form of both production and reproduction.[84]

And what does one (re)produce? "A no since" contains within in it the defiant statement, "no sin," as well as the pun for "nonsense." Words that are thought to have no meaning in the system of value eschewed by both bourgeois and marxist economies, those that are "nonsense" and equal "no cents" or that have no currency, become priceless in this queer poetic economy. In so doing, Stein revises notions of reproduction to include all that the bourgeois family would like to exclude. Every household becomes a scene of a profusion of pleasure, and the anus becomes a central, visible site of productive and pleasurable activity. From a poetics of luxurious plenitude, signified through verbal usury, we move to a space of excess, where the mouth-oral connection, eating (perhaps as prototype of consumption), produces writing/excretion, formerly thought of as waste, through the processes of digestion in the belly. Stein replaces traditional means of reproduction, the injection of semen and gestation, by reclaiming sodomy, lesbian desire, and the customary duties of the housewife. The exhortation of *Tender Buttons* to the reader (which is also the writer's statement of purpose) thus gains even more force when we realize that it also commands us to "tend her butt."

In this reinscription of consumption as (re)productive and of use as abundance, does Stein rewrite the domestic sphere or does she simply reiterate its structure within commodity capitalism? To view (and dismiss) Stein's texts as simply mirroring the logic of the market, in which new uses are invented through advertising and in which "natural" production is challenged by the advent of mass production in machine culture, is to subsume the queer project within a critique of capitalism that, as I have demonstrated above, reinscribes (heterosexist) notions of what counts as production, useful labor, and natural or original use. Stein's theory of writing does not assume the impossible, that one *can* step outside of commodity culture; that one can claim a position above the fray.

Recent writing in cultural studies has emphasized that consumption it-self constitutes labor, especially for women, people of color, and all those denied access to traditional forms of "productive labor."[85] For those de-nied access to the means of production, whether it be cultural, economic, or other forms of labor, consumption has proved a way to take back or re-claim one's ownership. Michel de Certeau's model of textual poaching, in its choice of metaphor, emphasizes this challenge.[86] It also links consump-tion to the renegotiation of space, which Stein's writing clearly achieves as it moves from "objects" to "food" to "rooms." Certainly Gertrude and Alice's production and consumption do cultural work: they claim the do-mestic sphere for lesbian sex and lesbian creativity.[87]

Yet many of these rewritings of consumption, if they discuss sexuality at all, do so only using vague terms such as "pleasure" and "desire." Al-though they allow for the productive effects of (sexual) fantasy, they con-sistently present an idea of the sexual that is not historicized and very of-ten completely unspecified.[88] If it is marked at all, it is as heterosexual or as simply deconstructive. These critiques invert, even as their terms reflect, the more traditional marxist-based dismissals of consumption and com-modity capitalism as sexualized and as using sexuality (and by implica-tion, destroying some natural sexual ideal that only exists prior to capi-talism) only to sell goods.[89] In its most extreme version, this view dismisses homosexuality as just another symptom of advanced capitalism.

Instead, as I demonstrate in this chapter, new cultural ideologies re-garding the production and reproduction of goods and individuals may have helped to enable the formation of new sexual subjectivities. These ideologies, however, are no less shot through with contradictions: for ex-ample, within commodity culture gender stereotypes were reinvented in ways that were particularly confining for women. Instead of reinscribing these rigidities, however, Stein's writing employs the logic of commodity capitalism for its own erotic and quixotic project. At the same time, *Ten-der Buttons* wrestles with dominant conceptions of *what counts* as sex and the sexual. In this way, we can see how Stein's writing responds to a "de-sexualization" of the domestic or private sphere that prevailed in the white bourgeois culture of nineteenth-century America, a culture that read bour-geois white women as increasingly unproductive and asexual.[90] The poem also acts as an antidote to some contemporary investigations of nine-teenth-century female-female domestic(ated) relationships that can only read "sex" or the sexual as documented genital contact. In listing and obliquely describing or signifying on the domestic sphere, Stein is generating an alternative taxonomy of libidinal and cultural possibilities, a catalogue of pleasures and perversions, one that is "not necessary . . . not at all necessary"; that is, a catalogue that is not about dominant definitions of the necessities of the domestic household but about a pleasure that transforms the traditional nexus of production and reproduction. In the process, Stein rewrites the nineteenth-century stereotype of the sterile spinster into an empowering lesbian identity, and she makes her relationship with Alice B. Toklas into a model of a new kind of domestic (re)productivity.

Chapter 5

THE M MULTIPLYING:

MARIANNE MOORE, ELIZABETH BISHOP, AND

THE PLEASURES OF INFLUENCE,

PART I

The following two letters, one from seventeen-year-old "BISHOP" to her good friend, Frani Blough; the other addressed to Elizabeth Bishop from "Miss Talbot," a teacher at her boarding school, Walnut Hill, inaugurate the collected volume of Bishop's correspondence, *One Art:*

> Great Village, Nova Scotia
> December 31, 1928

> Thank you for the helpful little card. Of course I realize that you could never quite realize the full significance of all this [the "love letter" from their teacher] but isn't it too sweet for words, anyway? Auntie [Grace] read it and said our friend had an "aching void." Alas, all she needed was a little snow. And *what* do you suppose she didn't dare say? Oh, Miss Talbot told me a mystery that will appeal to your romantic soul. I'll tell you when I get back, if I ever do—

> and *my* love
> BISHOP

Teacher's note: "Elizabeth my dear, Come up the path through the fir trees and white birches to my little cottage by the sea and there by the fireside, where nothing is "developed" save friendliness and poems and contentment, I would tell you that this was meant to be a wee book to slip into your pocket and to say "Merrie Christmas" for me . . .

There are fairy colors in the driftwood blaze in my fire. I picked up the stick down in the rock cave at low tide; and now it is dry it flames a tale in emerald and turquoise and copper-red. *I think you would understand it* [underlined by EB in wavy lines]. Outside there is a Christmas moon of clear silver beauty. Shall I tell you things that can only be told here—ah well, someday when you come . . .

Meanwhile Christmas joys, and the star-shine of a poem, and my love."[1]

These letters appear without comment, but they stand out, perhaps ironically, as some of the most erotically charged writings of Bishop's entire letter collection.[2] What is particularly potent about these exchanges is the way that the teacher expresses love and desire for Bishop, a desire that Bishop can then share with her classmate through writing. Writing functions in these letters as both the means of erotic expression and the border beyond which words no longer suffice. Bishop wonders to Frani, "And *what* do you suppose she didn't dare say? Oh, Miss Talbot told me a mystery." Echoing uncannily the commonplace expression for homosexuality, "the love that dare not speak its name," Bishop's confidences reveal that the power of this letter, and its protolesbian, if not lesbian, erotics, lie precisely in what cannot be said: "Isn't it too sweet for words?" It is these silences that speak most loudly. By including Elizabeth in some sort of unspecified "understand[ing]," Miss Talbot interpellates her as special, as knowing, as also sharing a secret. Bishop, in turn, seems reluctant to allow Frani full access to this world: "Of course I realize that you could never quite realize the full significance of all this." With these words, Bishop preserves this realm of knowing as private, as just between her and her teacher.[3]

Similarly, Miss Talbot thinks of her note as a book to slip into Bishop's pocket, a way for her to get close to Bishop's body.[4] At this moment the letter stands in for the teacher's desire itself; the images it contains—the "blaze" of the fire, the stick that "flames a tale"—connote, almost crudely, the heat of passion. And desires do tell tales: Miss Talbot's love becomes linked, as well, to poetry: "The star-shine of a poem, and my love." Poetry and epistolary writings both become erotic markers of a relationship between two women, one older and one younger.

Bishop may not just want to be *with* Miss Talbot—she also indicates that she may also want to "be" her. As Robert Giroux explains in his notes to the text, "E[lizabeth] B[ishop] drew a line from her teacher's three final words to her own closing."[5] She copies her teacher's salutation, "and my love," while adding her own unique emphasis, "*my* love." This impulse to copy is reminiscent of the many schoolgirl moments detailed in the mass-produced "girl's literature" of the same period, the endless attempts at reproducing a beloved teacher's signature, or voice, or clothing; the specificities of the identificatory erotics I have outlined above. Bishop aspires to imitate Miss Talbot, yet at the same time she adds her own emphasis to the salutation. A complex transfer of "love" is occurring here: Bishop finds in Miss Talbot's expressions of desire a way to express her own love for Frani. As in the eroticized pedagogic relationships Alcott's writing repeatedly describes, here desire for the loved one is indistinguishable from and serves as a model for how to *be* the loved one for another.

Miss Talbot is just one in a long list of influential older women in Bishop's life. Critics typically view Bishop's relationships with such figures as prototypes of the mother/daughter dyad, the older woman serving as mother substitute to an orphaned Bishop, as well as an oedipalizing model for her personal and poetic development.[6] Auntie Gracie's opinion of Miss Talbot also participates in this reading; her observation that the teacher has an "aching void" alludes to the belief, still dominant today, that unmarried, childless women are somehow inherently empty and lacking. Bishop thus becomes a child substitute for Miss Talbot, whose "barren" womb is literally aching.

Yet one could also read this image in an entirely different way; that is, as a metaphor for sexual desire, a yearning that centers around Bishop. She herself alludes to this possibility when she remarks, "Alas, all she needed was a little snow," meaning something that would cool the teacher's passion or dampen her fire, so to speak. In this chapter and the next I address the identifications and, concomitantly, the desires that circulated between Bishop and perhaps the most influential of her mentors, Marianne Moore. Drawing on the models of female-female identificatory erotics and queer reproduction offered in the rest of this book, in these last two chapters I will explore how both Bishop *and* Moore's subjectivities were formed and reformed in part out of their intense, sometimes tense, sometimes erotic, relationship of power and nurture. Through examining their literary and personal exchanges, including the intertextualities of their poems, the richness of their letters, and, in Bishop's case, her memoir of her relationship with Moore, I will argue that their interactions pose a challenge to the use by feminist literary critics of the mother/daughter relationship as the dominant model for female-female "literary influence" and for understandings of the emergence of female gender and sexual identity. Through this challenge, I will illustrate how Moore and Bishop's relationship offers another, prominent example of the ways in which queer subjects reproduce or transmit queer identifications and desires, as well as in some cases refuse them.

Not only do I show that the relationship between Moore and Bishop is better viewed within the purview of what I have been calling lesbian pedagogy than within traditional understandings of mother/daughter forms of intimacy, but also I use their relationship as exemplary of a different conception of poetic influence. Limiting Moore and Bishop's relationship to the oedipal model forecloses the possibility that "influence" could go both ways. It ignores the tripling of influence that, as I will illustrate below, Moore's own mother added to the Moore-Bishop relation, as well as the playful, tripling relation to linguistic negation or denial that I will argue Marianne Moore often performs in her letters and responses to Bishop.[7]

In tracing the complexities of influence as it occurs within Moore and Bishop's relationship, this chapter also examines the similarities and differences between the two writers' gender and sexual identities, differences that the dominant oedipal model of a daughter's rebellion toward or acceptance of a mother's inevitable heterosexual reproductivity obscures or overlooks altogether. In so doing, I hope to overturn any urge to find the biographical truth of Moore or Bishop's identity, lying behind or at the root of their poems or personal exchanges. Rather, I will demonstrate how subjectivity for them was fundamentally performative—in other words, how all of their (self-)representations are ongoing, (in)voluntary efforts to produce and inhabit a particularly gendered, raced, and sexualized subject within and through the discursive limits of their different historical situations.[8] Although the two poets share an understanding of both the pains and the pleasures of identifications as identity, or should I say, identity as (a series of) identifications,[9] they ultimately perform two quite different versions of queer female identity.

Not Mother/Not Daughter

In an often-cited passage from the end of "Efforts of Affection" (1969), Bishop's unfinished memoir of her relationship with Moore, Bishop leaves the reader with a set of images designed to sum up their history:

> I find it impossible to draw conclusions or even to summarize. When I try to, I become foolishly bemused: I have a sort of subliminal glimpse of the capital letter M multiplying. I am turning the pages of an illumi-

nated manuscript and seeing that initial letter again and again: Marianne's monogram; mother; manners; morals; and I catch myself murmuring, "Manners and morals; manners *as* morals? Or is it morals *as* manners?" Since like Alice, "in a dreamy sort of way," I can't answer either question, it doesn't much matter which way I put it; it *seems* to be making sense.[10]

Literary critics view this passage, more often than any other, as evidence of Bishop's feelings toward Moore: they interpret Moore as "mother" to an orphaned Bishop (Bishop's father died when she was less than a year old and her mother was institutionalized for the rest of her life for mental illness when Bishop was five), with Marianne as censoring arbiter of "manners" and, more important, "morals" to closeted lesbian Elizabeth. As one critic asserts:

> Moore . . . can be told only a partial truth because the whole truth of her daughter's identity would shock her into alienation. The imperative to be the good daughter is the burden Bishop assumes in her friendship with Moore, whereas in her work Bishop could sufficiently define herself against [Moore's] controlling, censorious, domineering presence.[11]

In this reading of their relationship, Moore is portrayed as transparently and unambivalently "the mother," and as the epitome of a form of maternality characterized only by repressiveness. Marianne becomes simply the prudish, asexual, censoring mom to an alternatively dutiful and rebellious daughter. Such positionings are so ubiquitous within literary criticism as to be almost completely naturalized: let me briefly trace, then, their critical history.

This mother/daughter model emerges as a feminist response to Harold Bloom's theory of influence. Bloom's model takes the form of an oedipal drama, a struggle between father and son; the son poet must both kill off and incorporate his literary forefather in order to create his own poetry, and consequently the son's work always misreads but includes the father's. Feminist literary critics such as Sandra Gilbert and Susan Gubar have criticized the masculinist bias in Bloom's model at the same time that they rewrite it for women. They argue that women writers suffer not so much from an "anxiety of influence" as "anxiety of authorship."[12] In order to combat a patriarchal literary system that denies that women can be authors, women writers must find their literary mothers.

Gilbert and Gubar are just one example of a trend in feminist literary criticism that is noted especially for its revisions of psychoanalysis; a trend that Teresa de Lauretis has labeled "the maternal imaginary." [13] These critics apply universalizing, ahistorical notions of mothers and daughters to a variety of intertextual relationships between women. At best, lesbianism becomes in these theories simply a substitute for a lost mother/daughter primal unity, a romantic, preoedipal utopia, and, in the process, female-female erotic relationships are drained of their historical and political significance. At worst, lesbianism is represented through homophobic replications of stereotypes about domineering or absent mothers and the ways they "make" daughters into lesbians. (And implicit in many critical readings of Bishop's sexuality is the assumption that her lesbianism— and by extension, all lesbianism—is really just a search for a lost mother.) All of these accounts take as their bases the Freudian myth of the oedipal family, a model for the development of the subject that, as I have noted above, is grounded in heterosexual reproduction and a rigid division of gender differences. Even when lesbianism is revalued within this system, it can always be traced back to a heterosexual origin: the child's relationship with a woman who is centrally defined by her place within heterosexual reproduction.

When I locate mother/daughter relationships within a heterosexual, reproductive model, I do not mean to deny the fact that lesbians (as well as gay men) biologically reproduce, or that lesbians (as well as gay men) in fact *do* mother. But in employing this universalizing metaphor of poetic influence and transmission, feminist critics do not complicate or specify their mother/daughter models enough to begin to even entertain these possibilities, let alone take them on as complications to their theories of poetic lineage. Instead, in both their idealization or its inverse, demonization—and concomitant desexualization—of the mother/daughter bond, they invoke traditional ideas about nurture, discipline, and exchange between women that preclude any sexuality other than reproductive heterosexuality; make mothering solely a (sexually) repressive function; and are structurally unable to imagine the ways in which influence may travel backward, from "daughter" to "mother." Assuming that both Moore and Bishop actively resisted not only heterosexuality but a gender system in the early twentieth century that continued to define "true women" through heteromaternality (an assumption I will explain in detail below), aside from sheer willed ignorance, why is it that even the most nuanced readers of Moore and Bishop's relationship engage in an almost compulsory re-production of a maternal/filial version of it?[14] One reason is that most crit-ics cannot resist romanticizing Bishop's orphanhood. In addition to the universal "loss" of the mother that all must suffer in the oedipal model, Bishop literally lost her mother because after her mother's institutional-ization she never saw her again. Adding even more evidentiary weight to this assumption is the coincidence of Moore and Bishop's first meet-ing: they began their lifelong association in the same year that Bishop's mother died. Many critics read this timing as evidence that Bishop needed a mother substitute, and that Moore came along at exactly the right moment.[15]

Coincidence aside, perhaps the most obvious reason this model has per-sisted is, first, because of the way Bishop was undeniably haunted by a sense of "homelessness" throughout her life, a lack defined centrally by the lack of *either* parent;[16] and, second, because of the way in which critics read Bishop's own descriptions of her relationship with Moore, as well as biographical accounts of their interactions. The image of Moore as censo-rious mother is based specifically on Bishop's report in "Efforts of Affec-tion" of their exchanges concerning homosexuality, in which Bishop re-lates a conversation in which Moore brought up the subject: "I remember her worrying about the fate of a mutual friend whose sexual tastes had al-ways seemed quite obvious to me: 'What are we going to do about X . . . ? Why, sometimes I think he may even be in the clutches of a *sodom-ite* . . . !'" (130). Commentators regularly couple this singular statement with Moore's apparent rejection of Walt Whitman:

> But on one occasion, when we were walking in Brooklyn on our way to a favored tea shop, I noticed we were on a street associated with the *Brooklyn Eagle,* and I said fatuously, "Marianne, isn't it odd to think of you and Walt Whitman walking this same street over and over?" She exclaimed in her mock-ferocious tone, "*Elizabeth,* don't speak to me about that man!" So I never did again. (143)

Together, these two statements are mobilized repeatedly by critics to "prove" that Moore could never have accepted Bishop's sexuality, and in fact acted as a kind of regulatory figure, preventing Bishop from express-ing her "true" self, not only to Moore but in her poetry as well. As Betsy Erkkila explains: "The fact that Bishop remembered this particular inci-dent with its accompanying moral weight of brimstone and damnation suggests the early and potentially repressive role Moore played in encouraging her to mask and mute, particularly in her writing, her own wicked and *sodomite* desire as a woman who sexually loved other women."[17]

Setting aside, for a moment, the most obvious distinction one could make about Moore's statement, that she is distancing herself from homosexual relationships between *men* (and not necessarily between women), and in particular from the flamboyant male homoerotic (and heteroerotic) poetry and persona of Whitman, in a larger sense readings such as Erkkila's are founded on a set of limiting ideas about what is said and unsaid, revealed and concealed, not only in Bishop's memoir but also in her poetry. These readings rely on a narrow definition of what counts as a visible representation of the sexual, but overvalue *what* is said without examining *how* it is said, something Bishop herself carefully represents in her memoir of Moore.

Moore's feigned, "mock-ferocious" responses to Bishop enact what I would term eroticized, performative versions of knowing and unknowing. As I will illustrate in greater detail below, there is an element of playfulness to Moore and Bishop's interactions, even at their most tense, which signals that these unknowing moments are usually more about the pleasures of a kind of flirtation based on hyperbolic performances of (Moore's) shock and (Bishop's) provocation/submission than on a will to exert or experience a censoring, maternal power.[18] Can we imagine Moore and Bishop walking through Brooklyn in the late afternoon engrossed in conversation, hands flashing in the air, Moore flushed pink, as she was often known to do, with excitement and enjoyment, while Bishop teases her with the comparison to Whitman and all it might imply?

In "Efforts of Affection" Bishop also provides other examples of Moore's relationship to gay male authors, which would contradict any such reading of Moore as simple censor. After citing the Walt Whitman incident, Bishop goes on in the same paragraph to detail Moore's own accounts of her reactions to other writers. Is it no coincidence that two out of the three, Crane and Auden, were openly homosexual? And Moore's relation to Auden, Bishop tells us, was one of admiration and friendship: Moore was "devoted to [him]."[19] Indeed, throughout her life Moore maintained intimate friendships with both gay men and lesbians, whose same-sex relationships she seems both aware of and comfortable with.[20]

"Evidence" of, at the very least, Moore's "tolerance" aside, I would argue that Bishop's retelling of the "how" of these events leaves room for imagining Moore as something other than repressive and disapproving, as do her key juxtapositions of Whitman with Auden. Although it may be impossible to "prove" definitively this claim, I want nevertheless to make a case here for preserving a space within which to articulate the erotics of silence, and even playful prohibition—an erotics often associated in the twentieth century with the more productive aspects of the closet, with the power and poignancy and even sexiness of what *cannot* be acknowledged yet is so palpably *there*. In their determination to make Moore fit the stereotype of the censoring mother, critics wipe out completely this possibility. In fact they become themselves censors of the text, instantiating the same repressiveness they claim to find in Moore.[21]

This is not to deny that Moore and Bishop disagreed on a number of issues, nor is it to say that Moore was not in any way occupying the place of the maternal in relation to Bishop: as I have argued in detail above, it is precisely the slippage between the mother and "others" that is so powerfully productive of the new identificatory erotics between women in the late nineteenth and, in this case, the early twentieth century. In some ways Moore *may have* mothered Bishop, or at least viewed their relationship in this light, but to restrict readings of their relationship to this easy appellation denies the complexities *and* the power of the fact that it was precisely because Moore was not a mother and Bishop was not her daughter that so much of the productive, queer, and wonderfully powerful valences of their relationship could exist at all.

With this in mind, let me now return to the famous passage of the "*M* multiplying" that began this section. What if we were to read it differently? The passage itself suggests that we should: the reference to Alice is from *Through the Looking-Glass,* where the mirror, instead of mirroring and reflecting back Alice's image, leads her into other fantastical spaces. The "*M* multiplying," a spontaneous reproduction of an image, recurs elsewhere in Bishop's writing, usually demarcating a process of subject formation, a decentering of self that happens when that self encounters images that multiply and will not stay stable.

Lee Edelman, in his remarkable piece on Bishop's late poem "In the Waiting Room" (1976), delineates the ways in which the child in the poem is inducted into womanhood through a process of reluctant, almost forced identifications with the images of racially and nationally marked femininity she sees around her, in particular with her aunt's cry of pain and with the hanging breasts of an African woman.[22] These identifications, which are produced by an overwhelming amount of sensation, resemble in number and effect the image of the *M* multiplying. The child resists this moment of self-construction, for she recognizes that femininity and pain are in some ways linked, but she also realizes that her own entrance into language, symbolized by her name, "But I felt: you are an *I*, / you are an *Elizabeth*, / you are one of *them*,"[23] makes it impossible for her to escape this incorporation. Significantly, it is not a mother that produces this realization but a combination of women, each occupying a different historical, racial, and national subject position.

Bishop's oeuvre includes numerous representations of such constitutive moments of subject formation, so many so that one might argue that this process itself constitutes a central "theme" of her work as a whole. In particular, much of her writing is fascinated with precisely the question of influence, especially the influence exerted by single women, or women who are decidedly *not* mothers, at least as they have been traditionally defined. For example, although critics often use "In the Village" (1965),[24] Bishop's fictionalized account of a child witnessing her mother's descent into mental illness, to validate their readings of Bishop as centrally concerned with motherlessness,[25] the majority of these critics ignore the fact that the story is equally obsessed with the strange single women who populate the village, in particular the dressmaker who comes to fit the child's mother for a new dress.[26]

The text's descriptions of the dressmaker are notably ambivalent: she is portrayed as "crawling around and around on her knees eating pins as Nebuchadnezzar had crawled eating grass" (252). Most obviously this is because she represents danger to the child, who thinks it is this woman's fault when her mother screams (when actually it is mental illness that causes her outburst). In other words, her status as single and outside the realm of the family is (mis)interpreted by the child as a threat. This status is repeatedly symbolized within the narrative: for example, the dressmaker's name, "Miss Gurley" recalls the name "girlie" assigned randomly to any unmarried woman, regardless of age. One is a girl until one marries, and sometimes even after then, especially if one is African American and/or working class; that is, one remains a "girl" in the eyes of the dominant culture.[27] Miss Gurley is described in precisely the terms that, as I outlined in chapter 1, portray single, working-class women:

> Her house is littered with scraps of cloth and tissue-paper patterns, yellow, pinked, with holes in the shapes of *A*, *B*, *C*, and *D* in them, and numbers; and threads everywhere like a fine vegetation. She has a bosom full of needles with threads ready to pull out and make nests with. She

sleeps in her thimble. A gray kitten once lay on the treadle of her sewing machine, where she rocked it as she sewed, like a baby in a cradle, but it got hanged on the belt. Or did she make that up? But another gray-and-white one lies now by the arm of the machine, in imminent danger of being sewn into a turban. (258)

Miss Gurley cannot (or chooses not to) mother successfully. Her bosom is full of pins and her work causes her to risk killing kittens. In other words, her labor itself causes death.[28] In ways reminiscent of Miss Asphyxia, Harriet Beecher Stowe's representation of the single woman whose overcathected, "unnatural," and class-marked relationship to labor replaces her "natural" role as biological mother, Miss Gurley's overproduction, her industry at work, renders her incapable of procreation. When she tries to "rock" the kitten "like a baby in a cradle," her efforts lead only to murder. She is constitutionally unable to mother, a failure that forms not so much a contrast to the child's mother but instead a parallel, because her mother also is unable successfully to perform the expectations of her role due to her increasing mental instability.

But unlike the child's mother, whose inability to mother is only a poignant failure, the dressmaker is also portrayed as an artist. Dressmaking as Bishop describes it above requires patterns marked with the alphabet, an allusion to rhyme scheme, the pattern of the way form functions in poetry. And the dressmaker's effect on Bishop is long lasting: as the child leaves, Miss Gurley gives her a coin with King George on it, a coin that, as Bishop notes, would have been, because of Miss Gurley's poverty, quite a sacrifice to give up. The child puts it in her mouth for safekeeping and accidentally swallows it. The episode ends with an image of the coin inside her: "Months later, as far as I know, it is still in me, transmuting all its precious metal into my growing teeth and hair" (259). Like her memory of Miss Gurley, the coin literally enters the child's body, helping to produce the developing poet.[29]

Thus, the story offers a countermodel, or companionate model, of female identification and incorporation for the model of the mother.[30] The mother's loss or unavailability, and the fear her instability produces in the child, forces Bishop to look elsewhere for models of subjectivity. Almost accidentally or involuntarily, what starts out as a taste of difference becomes a literal ingestion and incorporation of the dressmaker's model.

Looking back to the letters at the opening of this chapter we can see, in Bishop's appropriation of Miss Talbot's salutation ("all my love" becomes "all *my* love"), a model of the identificatory erotics that I have argued characterizes queer female subject formation. Through becoming like (but not completely identical to) Miss Talbot, Bishop finds a way to express her own lesbian desires. These examples (and there are more) from Bishop's oeuvre are not simply "mother substitutes" or generic stand-ins for or deficient copies of an originary model that has been, literally in this case, lost. Instead they are identificatory models for negotiating a world outside the family, the specific milieu of the single woman in the early twentieth century, and through her representations of such models Bishop imagines subject formation not as an endless regressive process of returning back to the mother but as a series of mimetic incorporations of different "others."

Thus, as a metaphor for Moore and Bishop's relationship, the *M* multiplying does not just connote the dyadic opposition of mother versus "me." Instead, it can be read to signify abundance, the many identificatory possibilities that Moore offers Bishop and that (through the processes of what I have termed above as "mimetic reversibility") perhaps Bishop also provides for Moore. Furthermore, the reference to "mother" may not even refer to Marianne at all, but to Marianne's own mother, and to the central role Mrs. Moore played not only in Marianne's life but also in Bishop's. In the rest of this chapter I will chart some of the ways in which Bishop and Moore represent this abundance, as well as the moments of painful disjunction and disaffiliation at which efforts of affection and of identification failed.

"Efforts of Affection"

Bishop and Moore's first meeting took place on a Saturday afternoon in 1934 at the bench to "the right of the door leading to the reading room of the New York Public Library" (123) (Bishop's rendering of Moore's exact instructions)—yet another ambiguously public yet simultaneously private space.[31] Descriptions of this first meeting, including Bishop's, indicate that it bears all the markers of a momentous encounter, a sizing up or looking over, in this case, of the younger, apprentice poet by an older, more established (if of debatable reputation) master. Bishop does not simply accede to this clichéd rendering of such a meeting in her memoir, however. Instead, she subtly responds to this scene of judgment by including in retrospect her own assessment of Moore. She does so not only through her detailing of their differences and similarities, which carry with them assertions of value, but also through her account of her own expectations of Moore and how they were or were not fulfilled.[32]

For instance, describing her first meeting with Moore, Bishop remembers, "I had never seen a picture of Miss Moore; all I knew was that she had red hair and usually wore a wide-brimmed hat. I expected the hair to be bright red and for her to be tall and intimidating" (124). In fact, the only thing that *was* as she expected was Moore's hat: "[She was], I saw at once, not very tall and not in the least intimidating. . . . The large flat black hat was as I'd expected it to be" (124). This detailing of fashion and physical expectations—their fulfillment and frustration—forms one of the crucial undercurrents of Bishop's description of her relationship with Moore. What she can expect from Moore, how gradually her expectations develop as she gets to know her well—all this is part of Bishop's narrative, including descriptions of the moments when these expectations are not met. And along with expectations comes the idea of conventions, and whether they are upheld or not: literary, social, sexual, and gender conventions, as well as those of sartorial style. As Bishop remembers, "She wore a blue tweed suit that day and, as she usually did then, a man's 'polo shirt,' as they were called, with a black bow at the neck. The effect was quaint, vaguely Bryn Mawr 1909, but stylish at the same time" (124). Coyly, here, Bishop implies that Moore's outfit was out of fashion; in contrast to the "new spring suit" (124) that Bishop carefully chooses for their first meeting, Moore is wearing an outfit better suited for an era long passed, that of Moore's own college days at Bryn Mawr twenty-five years before. Such a detail seems simultaneously to express a moment of identification and of its refusal, because clothes stand in here for something else, as they will often continue to do for both Moore and Bishop. That is, Bishop's description of Moore's outfit signifies that to her, Moore's identity is also outdated as compared to Elizabeth's more "modern" attitudes and attire. But the detail about Moore's college years may also express an identification with her as well because Bishop herself attended a women's college, Vassar.[33] And after all, Bishop describes Moore as "stylish at the same time."[34]

Bishop is fascinated by Moore's outfit, just as she is by Moore's conversation, as she continues:

I sat down and she began to talk. It seems to me that Marianne talked to me steadily for the next thirty-five years, but of course that is nonsensical. . . . She must have been one of the world's greatest talkers: entertaining, enlightening, fascinating, and memorable; her talk, like her poetry, was quite different from anyone else's in the world. (124)

The narrative moves from a description of the uniqueness of Moore's outfit to the uniqueness of Moore's conversational style, and, by association, Moore's poetry. Like Moore's clothes, Moore's conversation is unique, slightly outdated, but also slightly queer.[35]

In other words, in this remembrance of Moore's dress the fact that Moore is cross-dressed stands out most vividly: she is wearing a "man's 'polo shirt,' as they were called" (124). Later in the memoir, Bishop writes:

Clothes were of course an endless source of interest to Marianne, increasingly especially so as she grew older. As she has written herself . . . her clothes were almost always hand-me-downs, sometimes very elegant ones from richer friends. These would be let out or, most frequently, let down (Marianne preferred clothes on the loose side, like the four-sizes-too-large "polo shirts"). The hats would be stripped of decorations, and ribbons changed so all was black or navy blue, and somehow perhaps *flattened*. There was the Holbein/Erasmus-type hat, and later the rather famous tricorne, but in the first years I knew her, only the large, flat, low-crowned hats of felt or summer straw. (132)

Once again we find images of "dressmaking," or in this case the "making over" of dresses and accessories, their transformation from one thing into another. The implications of this activity are multiple: Bishop's attention to this aspect of Moore's life unconsciously links her to Miss Gurley, as another model for negotiating a singular subjectivity. By extension, dress (read as both noun and verb) may continue to be a metaphor for (making) art, the art of poetry and the art of the self. And it is tempting to connect Moore's "making over" of clothes and hats to her famous "making over" of quotations by incorporating them into her poems.

This process of self-transformation is linked to gender: Bishop focuses again here on Moore's relation to self-display. To wear one's clothes "on the loose side" implies not only a need for comfort but also may signify a need to conceal or, less pejoratively, to modify one's body. Often, for example, women use loose-fitting clothes to "flatten" out or diminish signs of a "feminine" corporeality, including breasts and hips. Photos of Moore indicate that throughout her life, at least in public, she often wore slightly mannish suits, often with a "black bow tie at the neck."[36] To "strip [a hat] of decoration" and have the "ribbons changed so all was black or navy blue," is also a way of masculinizing or at least defeminizing one's accessories because excessive "decorations" are another way of signifying femininity.

Clothes were one of the main ways in which Moore sealed her reputation as what is usually referred to as an "eccentric": most renowned, of course, was her "George Washington crossing the Delaware" outfit, which included the "rather famous tricorne," the outfit that she wore to almost every public occasion of her later life. What does it mean for a prominent, female, modernist poet to assume as her public persona the "father of our Country"?[37] By impersonating George Washington, Moore cross-gender identifies with a national icon, and thereby implies that she herself is similarly important to the formation and sustenance of the nation. She performatively claims her own queerly productive poetic powers: she, through her poetry, "fathers" America. In so doing, she places herself outside the norms of bourgeois femininity and reproductive heterosexuality, allying herself instead with a vision of queer cultural reproduction. Here we find the spinster figure of the nineteenth century remade into an empowering and perhaps (auto)erotic public identity.[38]

That Moore herself viewed this as a *queer* position is clear from her own writing. "Marriage" (1923), as her famous poem of the same name remarks, "requir[es] all one's criminal ingenuity to avoid."[39] The word "criminal" echoes the medical and legal prohibitions of the turn of the century and the present, which classify any kind of existence outside of marriage as a crime: crimes against nature are sexual acts, the purpose of which is not heterosexual reproduction. Furthermore, "deviant" sexualities have been, for at least the last two centuries, consistently identified with criminality. Moore identifies herself as a "criminal," as someone who does not fit into the heterosexual social order.[40]

Elsewhere in "Efforts of Affection," Bishop details a conversation in which Moore expresses her views on marriage:

> [Moore] once remarked, after a visit to her brother and his family, that the state of being married and having children had one enormous advantage: "One never has to worry about whether one is doing the right thing or not. There isn't time. One is always having to go to market or drive the children somewhere. There isn't time to wonder, 'Is this *right* or isn't it?'" (154)

Moore comments slyly here on the ethical implications of marriage and conventional childrearing: one is so overwhelmed by daily obligations that one does not have time to contemplate one's actions, or at least one has this excuse. David Bergman, in his insightful reading of "Marriage," argues that Moore saw it as an ideological construct that caused even otherwise "thinking" people to enter into it blinded to its inherent problems and (gender) inequities.[41] By implication, then, those who are not married are able to resist this ideological interpellation—they do have this "time," and are therefore at least able to possess a modicum of self-consciousness. Once again Moore positions herself outside the heterosexual, reproductive family system—by reiterating this conversation in her memoir of their relationship, Bishop signals her identification with Moore in this positioning. What they have in common is their avoidance of both marriage and motherhood. Both imply that this positioning has some sort of constitutive effect on their writing and on their identities—if in no other way than to produce the kind of heightened self-awareness that Moore implies married parents lack.

Yet while Moore and Bishop may share this structural positioning, in many ways their relation to gender and sexuality is also quite different. Bishop identified as a "lesbian," a named sexual subjectivity with a history and subculture, of which she was clearly aware and in which she participated to a greater and lesser degree during her lifetime.[42] Throughout her life she concerned herself with developing alternative forms of female-female domesticity outside of both the space of the bourgeois family and the nation, as her longest relationship, with Lota de Macedo Soares, attests.[43] Finding such alternative spaces was for Bishop something of a necessity: born in 1911, left virtually an orphan by age five, she was raised first by relatives then by summer camps and boarding schools. Her subjectivity, as the letters that begin this chapter indicate, was thus constructed in large part in and through the semipublic/semiprivate spaces that by the time of her education were now American institutions, at least for the white, upper-middle class.[44]

To some degree throughout her life Bishop seems to have feared or at least avoided publicity as a lesbian.[45] As one of Bishop's old friends and flirtations, Mary Meigs, recalls,

Elizabeth, Marie-Claire, and I had dinner together from time to time in Cambridge and had animated conversations in which Elizabeth was conspicuously more discreet than Marie-Claire and I were. Elizabeth and I belonged to a generation of women who were terrified by the idea of being known as lesbians, and for Elizabeth as poet, the lesbian label would have been particularly dangerous. One of the side effects of lesbians' fear of being known to the world was our fear of being known to each other, so that a kind of caution was exercised (certainly it was by Elizabeth) that no longer seems necessary today.[46]

Thus, Bishop's own relation to "the private" and the domestic was shot through with the implications of the closet: for her, privacy included her relationships with women. In public Bishop upheld the proprieties of white, middle-class womanhood much more so than did Moore, perhaps to overcompensate for her sexuality and alcoholism, which, she rightly feared, if made wholly public would shatter such an image.[47] Perhaps this is one reason Bishop's biographers, as well as critics of her work, have remained reluctant fully to disclose the details of her personal life.[48] Only Gary Fountain and Peter Brazeau's edited collection, which presents personal accounts from many of Bishop's friends and acquaintances, begins to push at the boundaries of this genteel image: "As Katha Pollitt remembers Bishop's appearance, 'There was an aspect of the way Miss Bishop presented herself that permitted a dismissal of her as a sensual, passionate, and deeply feeling person.' In reality Bishop's private life was far different from this appearance."[49] To locate Bishop historically, her life seems increasingly structured, at least by the time she is an adult, by the imperative to "choose" one side or another of the hetero/homo divide, to "have" a sexual identity and in this case to "hide" it. Yet, at the same time, Bishop seems to have existed in a kind of implicit "I know that you know" agreement with her friends, a set of boundaries that Bishop crossed infrequently, usually at moments of crisis, especially when she had had too much to drink. At such times, as interviews from Fountain and Brazeau describe, she would discuss the details of her intimate life or even make passes at friends.[50] This account of Bishop's relation to her sexuality renders problematic any notion of Moore's thwarting of Bishop's need to "out" herself, and instead indicates that both women were engaged in a much more subtle form of acknowledgment/disavowal of one another's identities.

Moore, in contrast to Bishop, seems throughout her life to have resisted altogether the identificatory imperatives of the homo/hetero divide. Moore's letters from Bryn Mawr to her close friend Marcet Haldeman offer intimate details of Moore's female-female homoerotic encounters while in college, especially what she describes as a physically and emotionally intense relationship with Peggy James, daughter of William and niece of Henry.[51] Despite this relationship and the fact that while at Bryn Mawr and after Moore knew of and admired many lesbian-identified women (including the president of Bryn Mawr, M. Carey Thomas, and her partner, Mary Garrett, as well as H.D. and Bryher), there is no evidence that Moore ever openly identified herself as a lesbian, although it is clear that other women with whom she was intimately engaged did include her in this category, most notably H.D. and Bryher.[52] Instead, Moore's main (self-)identifications remained throughout her life those of (spinster) daughter and modernist poet. At first glance, one might be tempted to argue further that these identifications demarcated neatly Moore's occupation of "private" and "public" spaces: at home she performed the role of anachronistically dutiful daughter, while in the public realm of modernist literary foment she increasingly appeared as the queer poet and critic.

Certainly Moore's relationship with her mother resembles in its intensity those instances of maternal tutelage that I described in chapter 2, especially when one considers that, except for her undergraduate years at Bryn Mawr and one summer working away from home, Moore lived with her mother, first in Carlisle, Pennsylvania, then in New York in Greenwich Village and later in Brooklyn, until her mother's death in 1947.[53] And during the relatively brief time she was away at college, Marianne wrote to Mrs. Moore (and her brother, John Warner Moore) sometimes three or four times a week, and often these letters were long ones.[54]

The daughter of a Presbyterian minister, Mrs. Moore was in many ways similar to *Little Women*'s Mrs. March. She was known for her rigorous (and often rigid) religious ideals, as well as for her devotion to her children—she struggled after her father's death to support the family, working full time as a teacher rather than accept money (and therefore be obliged to have contact with) Moore's father's family. (She left Moore's father before Marianne was born due to his mental breakdown over the failure of a business investment, and it appears that none of the Moores ever had contact with him again.) As Moore's letters attest, her mother expected to participate fully in almost every decision made by her son Warner (his preferred name) and Marianne. She advises her children on everything from, in Marianne's case, which hat she should purchase to which word she should use in a poem. For Warner, who became a minister like his grandfather, as Linda Leavell notes, Mrs. Moore sent him ideas for sermons on a weekly basis, presuming that she should have a say in how he preached.[55]

That Mrs. Moore saw nothing unusual in her hold over her children is signified by the ease with which she assumes, in the letters exchanged while Warner and Marianne were in college and after, that they would all three continue to live together for the rest of their lives, in the rectory of whatever congregation hired Warner to be their minister. As the letters demonstrate, there was a crisis within the family when Warner first joined the navy, thereby ending Mrs. Moore's plan, and then proposed to a woman with whom Mrs. Moore did not get along.

Thus, while Warner was able to begin a family of his own, Marianne was left to the task of being her mother's lifelong companion.[56] Leavell records an excerpt from Moore's notebook of 1918, what she views as an unusual moment of self-revelation, in which Moore expresses her frustration at her situation:

> Well, there are reasons why it is better to live away from home—You want to go somewhere—come in at an unusual hour, or you don't want to eat, you want to be alone—my mother comes in 16 times a day bringing me apples & things to eat, and if you can't eat, she doesn't understand, the whole house is upset. Send for the doctor, insist on an exam. Oh my—Well—I can't have it.[57]

Leavell also points out the differences in Moore's account of her introduction to the modernist circles in which she would travel for much of the second and third decades of the twentieth century. While she writes pages and pages to Warner describing in minute detail her experiences, she writes her mother only a postcard, and uses generic and placating phrases to describe the artists with whom she was becoming acquainted:

> The K[reymborg]'s are the loveliest people I ever have met—gentle and full of fun and peaceful—very poor with some beautiful things, no Bohemian fierceness—Neither of them "smokes"—and they showed me photographs and read a few poems. . . . I've met [Stieglitz] and his is everything ideal, sane and modest. Imperturbable and kind."[58]

Leavell argues that Moore was trying to prepare her mother for what would become Moore's social milieu, to win her approval and assuage her mother's fears.[59] That Moore had to soft-pedal her modernist interests to her mother and that her mother saw her job as one of "protecting Marianne" are details that make it easy, then, to read Marianne as simply a frustrated, stifled daughter, occupying the position reserved in the nineteenth century for the spinster.[60]

Such a reading ignores the fact, however, that Mrs. Moore was a collaborator in Moore's writing: as much as Mrs. Moore presumed she would and should be involved in Marianne's creative process, Marianne also relied on her mother's guidance in composing and revising her poetry, so much so that her mother's death left her unsure of her own poetic abilities.[61] Moreover, the family was also a space for Moore to resist the norms of gender and sexuality that circulated in the larger culture, as Cristanne Miller has recently argued.[62] Not only do the letters exchanged between the three family members reveal playful inversions of the roles of children and adults, with, for instance, Mrs. Moore as "baby" or in the position of "niece" to Marianne's "Uncle," but as this example demonstrates, the letters also reveal the degree to which Marianne consistently cross-gender identified (and was referred to in "masculine" terms) within the family without any hint of sanction or disapproval.[63] In light of these biographical details, as well as the larger sociohistorical milieu of which Moore was a part, the era of the New Woman, Miller argues that familial support for what she terms Moore's "gender fluidity" may provide one reason that Moore was never eager to leave her mother, and that Moore found similar support in the communities of women she constructed through her extensive correspondence and personal interchanges, support that allowed her to feel that nothing was unusual in her choice not to marry.[64]

Although it is tempting to see Moore as occupying a position in what seems to be a version of Smith-Rosenberg's "female world," it ignores the fact that Moore also differed at least subtly from her mother in that, as I have demonstrated above, Moore seemed aware (and how could she not be) of the ways in which her choice to remain unmarried puts her outside the norms of gender and sexuality of her culture; that is, rendered her queer but not lesbian (self-)identified, as many of her intimate friends were. Although her mother may have relied on ideals of spiritual devotion and duty to underpin her own subjectivity and, in particular, to legitimate her own choice to leave her marriage and later to live within what, according to Bethany Hicok, seems to have been a romantic friendship of her own with Mary Norcross,[65] Moore's understanding of her own positioning seems to include her awareness of her perverse social marginality, a position she then performs and tries to reclaim, I would argue, by such strategies as impersonating George Washington. Did Moore's sense of her precarious position as woman in the male-dominated world of modernism lead her to renounce any form of interpersonal sexual intimacy?[66] Although at the time it was common for women to feel that they should decide between marriage and a career, many women of Moore's generation lived with other (unrelated) women instead. Why not Moore?[67] We will never know *for sure* Moore's reasons. What is certain is that in acquiescing to a lifelong companionship with her mother, all other intimacies were subordinated to this relationship.

Thus, just as it would be wrong to see Marianne as purely a passive victim or willing accomplice to her mother's disciplinary authority, so too would it be misguided to idealize her situation as somehow providing a utopian alternative to early-twentieth-century mores. As it seems to do for the Marches in Alcott's *Little Women* series, the tight-knit Moore family threesome, in particular the relationship between Mrs. Moore and Marianne, seems to uphold certain regulatory structures of gender and sexual identification while suspending them at the same time.

Given the fact that Mrs. Moore acted as a virtual collaborator on Moore's work by reading and revising drafts and contributing words and ideas, as well as adding her own corrections and additions to Moore's correspondence, it is not surprising that critics have made little or no effort to separate Marianne's sense of "manners and morals," in her life as well as her work, from those of her mother.[68] By contrast, one thing that distinguishes Bishop's descriptions of Moore from those of other critics is that she recognizes the differences between Marianne and her mother, an effort that is perhaps most eloquently expressed in Bishop's "Invitation to Miss Marianne Moore" (1948).[69] Requested to contribute a piece to a volume celebrating Moore, Bishop sent not only an essay but a poem. Modeled on Pablo Neruda's elegy for a drowned poet, Bishop's poem is quite literally a call to life after death, a loving incitement to Moore to put aside the death of her mother (who had died the year before) and to "please come flying" (82–83). But the fact that the piece is modeled on an elegy may also signal Bishop's call to Moore to come to life after herself being metaphorically dead, not just because Moore was to some degree stifled by her relationship with her mother, but also because Moore was feeling as if a part of herself had died *with* her mother.

Allusions to Mrs. Moore appear obliquely in the poem. As the penultimate stanza implores:

With dynasties of negative constructions
darkening and dying around you,
with grammar that suddenly turns and shines
like flocks of sandpipers flying,
    please come flying. (83)

In "Efforts of Affection," Bishop explicitly connects these negative constructions to Mrs. Moore's use of language: "Waiting for the conclusion of her longer statements, I grew rather nervous; nevertheless, I found her extreme precision enviable and thought I could detect echoes of Marianne's own style in it: the use of double or triple negatives, the lighter or wittier ironies—Mrs. Moore had provided a sort of ground base for them" (129). This description points to the central paradox of the Mrs. Moore/Marianne/Bishop relationship, the idea of the "double or triple negatives." A double negative can be characterized by its ambivalence—it proves, by intensifying the negative, the opposite, a positive. It is an example of a kind of linguistic inversion, a turning inside out. In using the term "negative," Bishop clearly alludes to what she refers to elsewhere as the "over-fastidious" moral prescriptions enforced by Moore and her mother, but she implies that, as in the lavish sentences of the later Henry James, these grammatical constructions, by their excessiveness and their performativity, often cancel out their regulatory force. Thus, although Bishop encourages Moore to shed the "negatives" of her own mother's influence, she also acknowledges the unstable and perhaps even productive effects of prohibition, both on Bishop and on Moore herself. Already we have a much more ambiguous representation of what has been taken at face value as Moore's unequivocal censoriousness of Bishop (and Mrs. Moore's hold over both of them). We also see in this passage a linking and yet a separateness maintained between Marianne and her mother.

In light of the picture of Moore I have drawn above, then, I would argue that we should read what are usually interpreted as moments of Moore's maternal prohibition as instead moments of culturally and temporally specific disagreement over what constitutes a female-female erotics or a "proper" poetic persona. By focusing on the famous "Roosters" incident as an example of such a disagreement, I will demonstrate how to understand this milestone not as an instance of simple censorship, but as a productive yet painful moment at which the differences between not just Moore and Bishop's perspectives but also between theirs and Mrs. Moore's are thrown into high relief. Such a moment also reveals Moore's own sense of the constraints of her ambiguous self-positioning as both poet and daughter.

"Lovingly, Rose Peebles"

Bishop experienced the multiplicitous effects of Moore's influence, as well as that of her mother, when in 1940 she sent Moore a copy of the poem "Roosters," which she was working on at the time.[70] Moore and her mother immediately revised the poem and were so exorcised by its apparent offensiveness that Moore telephoned Bishop, an unusual step, and then wrote her a letter detailing her own (and her mother's) criticisms and enclosing their revised version of the poem. Bishop replied by defending her poetic choices, and from then on Bishop claims she sent no one, Moore in particular, any drafts of her poetry. This moment is conventionally understood as the turning point at which Bishop makes her break from Moore and declares her poetic independence, and as the instance in which Moore's censoriousness and old-fashioned values overwhelmed Bishop.[71]

"Roosters" is divided into two parts. The first is most obviously a critique of the sex/gender system and its relation to other discourses of power: what one might term the public male violence that produces imperial conquest, militarism, war, and destruction, and the private male violence that characterizes compulsory heterosexuality. The second part describes most literally a statue that represents Peter's denial of Christ, and it explores themes of forgiveness and reconciliation in art. Although critics such as David Kalstone, for example, are reluctant to speculate on what Kalstone calls "the unexplained private suggestiveness of many of Bishop's dawn poems"[72] (a group of poems of which "Roosters" is a significant part), Erkkila is more forthright in her assessment of the motivations of the poem: "'Roosters' is a kind of veiled 'coming out' poem in which Bishop registers her personal protest against the 'senseless order' of marriage and heterosexuality that 'floats / all over town' and 'gloats' over the bed of lesbian love."[73]

Although clearly the poem represents, in some way, the relationship between what at first appears to be a private, enclosed lesbian sexuality and a public, phallic, patriarchal heterosexuality, Erkkila's use of the term "coming out" to describe the process of (self-)recognition in the poem is rhetorically and historically imprecise. The coming-out genre is usually characterized by a public revelation of self-knowledge: the kind of "I was blind but now I see" of lesbian life where the lesbian describes the moment or process of her self-recognition as a lesbian and her subsequent revelations to others. As George Chauncey has argued, "coming out" in 1940 would also have had very different connotations than it does post-Stonewall, signaling more a process of self-recognition and a coming into the larger gay community than a public declaration of one's sexuality.[74]

This is not what happens in "Roosters," at least at the level of a simple declaration of identity. Bishop is also not using the poem as a "coming-out" letter to Moore; as I have illustrated above, presumably Moore was fully aware of Bishop's sexual choices. Rather, "Roosters" describes the (very rude) awakening of the speaker into what for lack of a better phrase one might call the phallic order. The status of the speaker's relationship to it, as one member of a lesbian couple, the "we" whose sleep is disturbed, is what the poem debates: how are "we," the two women, lying in bed inside the house, affected by and/or implicated in the violence that begins outside? Or does it originate outside?[75]

As Susan Schweik notes, there are many instances in the poem where any sense of distance between the bed and the events outside is denied.[76] "Roosters" portrays a sudden yet somehow expected (as if routine) early-morning intrusion, unlike other Bishop poems that represent the safety and intimacy of the bed, as in the unpublished "It is marvellous to wake up together," which begins,

> It is marvellous to wake up together
> At the same minute; marvellous to hear
> The rain begin suddenly all over the roof,
> To feel the air clear
> As if electricity passed through it.[77]

The lines of "Roosters," written in rigid tercets, replicate a militaristic pulse even in their rhythms,[78] and contrast drastically with the more even, expansive tone of "It is marvellous." Lest we idealize the latter, however, even in Bishop's more tranquil and celebratory "dawn" or "predawn" poems, the lovers are still contained, or what I might term "mildly imprisoned," within the space of the bed, and still experience themselves as endangered:

> If lightning struck the house now, it would run
> From the four blue china balls on top
> Down the roof and down the rods all around us,

And we imagine dreamily
How the whole house caught in a bird-cage of lightning
Would be quite delightful rather than frightening.[79]

Although here the "bird-cage of lightning" is transformed from danger to delight, the lovers are still inside the cage, and the other side of this vision is the sudden flash of light, which illuminates that which was previously hidden: the revealing of a love usually concealed, the moment when the coed throws open the door and finds her roommate in bed with another woman. There is an irony here: the same lightning that ensnares also produces a feeling of intimacy, the desire between the two women. In other words, desire is generated by the threat of this (im)position, this revelation.[80]

"It is marvellous" continues:

And from the same simplified point of view
Of night and lying flat on one's back
All things might change equally easily,
Since always to warn us there must be these black
Electrical wires dangling. Without surprise
The world might change to something quite different,
As the air changes or the lightning comes without our blinking,
Change as our kisses are changing without our thinking.[81]

The stanza begins with an acknowledgment that this is a "simplified point of view," that the realities outside the bedroom belie the safety that the lovers create through transforming the lightning that imprisons them into a metaphor for, and the "electricity" of, their own sexual desire. Despite this, the poem cannot resist continuing with this fantasy, the "light falling of kisses" transformed in this stanza to a redemptive act that can disrupt and "change" the world.

This is not the first place where Bishop represents a changed world, transformed by the power of lesbian sexuality. In "Insomnia," she writes:

So wrap up care in a cobweb
and drop it down the well

into that world inverted
where left is always right,
where the shadows are really the body,

where we stay awake all night,
where the heavens are shallow as the sea
is now deep, and you love me.[82]

"Inverted" here connotes, among other things, homosexuality, and Bishop portrays a world transformed, made queer.[83] "It is marvellous" also expresses a desire for such a world, even as it is tempered by the speaker's recognition that escape is not possible.

"Roosters" does not participate in this utopian speculation. Already, in the second line, the "we" of the poem lies within the "gun-metal blue dark," not apart from it. The window itself is "gun-metal blue," the way one sees, one's vantage point, tinged itself with the color of violence. There is no space "outside," or in this case, "inside" patriarchal control. The poem insists on the "echoes" of the cock's crow, endless repetitions of the same, that spread all over town. The "we" are trapped within these echoes, which eventually establish a "senseless order" that "floats / all over town." This process of colonization, "active / displacement[s] in perspective" dislocates or relocates the "we" in a process that mimics soldiers rousting people from their beds and homes:

each screaming, "This is where I live!"

Each screaming
"Get up! Stop dreaming!"

.   .   .   .

what right have you to give
commands and tell us how to live,

cry "Here!" and "Here!"
and wake us here where are
unwanted love, conceit and war? (36)

At first, this appears to be a straightforward representation of the process of literal occupation, the conquest of the lesbian erotic space by imperial male violence. But the last line of the quote betrays an ambiguity that refuses the assignation of "unwanted love, conceit and war" to just the occupying force. "Wake us here where are" indicates that *here,* inside the house, in the bed, are also conflicts of desire and will. It refuses to romanticize the space of lesbian desire as one exempt from phallic law. In other words, unlike the preoedipal fantasy of Luce Irigaray's theories (not wholly without maternal/filial conflict) or the romantic mother/daughter space of Adrienne Rich's poetry, Bishop's poem refuses to idealize lesbianism as a place outside of power and domination, disappointment and perhaps even violence.[84] What, after all, are we to do with the term "unwanted love?"

In the second part of the poem, the poet examines the aestheticization of violence and denial through the creation of art. It begins with a discussion of sin—St. Peter's versus Mary Magdalen's. Although as a whore Magdalen sinned through "the flesh alone," Peter denied Christ and therefore committed a sin "of spirit." After describing Peter's fall, the poem then details several pieces of sculpture that represent this incident. In the first,

> Christ stands amazed,
> Peter, two fingers raised
> to surprised lips, both as if dazed.
>
> But in between
> a little cock is seen
> carved on a dim column in the travertine,
>
> explained by *gallus canit;*
> *flet Petrus* underneath it.
> There is inescapable hope, the pivot;
>
> yes, and there Peter's tears
> run down our chanticleer's
> sides and gem his spurs. (38)

Besides embodying, perhaps, the inevitability of phallic law, even in the homoerotics between two men,[85] this description concerns itself specifically with how representation functions. Phallic law, the "little cock," is always characterized by denial, the cause of Peter's tears; and denial, these tears, erotically adorn the cock, "our chanticleer." In other words, through denial and its pain, art is formed, and male violence is "spur[red] on." The cock's violence, his spurs, are aestheticized or made into art by Peter's tears and, more generally, by patriarchal religion's alliance with other forms of male dominance. The poem then describes the iconization of the rooster as a symbol of forgiveness: "his dreadful rooster came to mean forgiveness," which might be read as "came to"—that is, arrived at, "mean forgiveness," or forgiveness lacking in compassion or sincerity, a kind of cheap forgiveness. These symbols appear everywhere:

so the people and the Pope might see

that even the Prince
of the Apostles long since
had been forgiven, and to convince

all the assembly
that "Deny deny deny"
is not all the roosters cry. (38)

In a certain way, then, the rooster also embodies a continual process of denial, what Kalstone describes as "not something past but the moment of betrayal as eternal suspended action."[86] Representation becomes both a cover-up and an endless aestheticization of denial.[87]

The last part of the poem makes this clear. Invoking the old trope of the sunlight as redemptive and cleansing, the poem describes the recapturing of the "broccoli, leaf by leaf," by the rays, another form of aestheticization, "gilding the tiny / floating swallow's belly" (39). In the midst of this process of recreation, the poem asks, "How could the night have come to grief?" (39). The ambiguity of this question provides several dimensions to the scene. On the one hand, one might be tempted to read it as asking, "Since it is so beautiful now, how could any of that violence have happened last night?" And in one sense, the poem does ask this, leaving the question of to whom and by whom the violence occurred deliberately uncertain. This evasion hints at the trouble even within the women's bed, as well as gesturing more obviously toward the phallic battle that occurred outside. The cliché that accompanies this reading is that, of course, art has come along and cleaned all of it up. Like the tears that "gem" and the re-presentation, the echoes of the cock, the poem is restoring order to the world of the "we" and the entire town: "The cocks are now almost inaudible" (39).

Yet it is almost impossible not to see this as a process of denial in itself, a covering-up that leads right into the bedroom as "The sun climbs in, / following 'to see the end,' / faithful as enemy, or friend" (39). Here the power of art, as metaphorized by the sun, is ambiguous—"enemy, or friend"—and so is the status of each of the women. Are they enemies or friends? As Schweik points out, this line also alludes back to Peter, who was both "friend" and "enemy" to Christ, and thus the line brings issues of betrayal and crucifixion into the bedchamber.[88] As in her poem "One Art" (1976), Bishop undermines the power of aesthetic form—the sun— even as she valorizes it.[89]

In its critique of the state as being in the midst of intense national denial in the name of patriotism (it is no coincidence that the dominating colors in this poem are green and yellow, the colors of a World War II American army uniform, and the red and blue of the American flag), and in its linking of patriarchal and heterosexual violence with national security, the poem exposes the workings of pre–World War II ideology.[90] By refusing to exempt lesbianism from this critique, the poem demonstrates the effects of this violence on the women in the bed (there is no way to block it out) and refuses to rely on old stereotypes about women's "natural" niceness. In so doing, Bishop presents a vision of art that is not engaged in covering up or aestheticizing violence but in exposing and criticizing it.

Why did this vision of art so agitate Moore and her mother that they literally sat down and rewrote the poem? Aside from their well-documented objections to excrement, was their disapproval tinged by naïveté? Did Moore (and she may need to be separated from her mother here) miss the critique of heterosexuality and male dominance so entirely that she could have "innocently" recommended the change of title to "The Cock"? *Perhaps* she *was* unaware of the sexual connotations of the word. But Moore herself, in the 1935 edition of her *Collected Poems,* had written what is unmistakably a critique of militarism, "To Military Progress," which while it does not explicitly link the violence and waste of military conquest with patriarchal control, does indict the process.[91] And what about the references to "Peeter" which populate her letter to Bishop?:

> Dearest Elizabeth, the Pope-ian sagacity, as I was just now saying to you [on the telephone], and your justice to "Peeter," and such a crucially enviable consummation as
>> From strained throats
>> A senseless order floats,
> are like a din of churchbells in my ears, I am so excited (A little girl whom Mother had been teaching about the apostles said in one of her answers to a little written examination, "And don't forget Peeter.").[92]

Was Moore so ignorant as to have missed the phallic connotations of "Peter," especially when she exaggerates its more scatological function? Clearly she and her mother "cleaned up" Bishop's poem. They removed all references to the "water-closet" and its products, they tempered some of the language with which the roosters were portrayed, although they also left much of it intact—they cut the "cruel" of "cruel feet" and the "stupid" of "stupid eyes" and removed "the many wives" completely, yet they left such lines as "being courted and despised," one of the strongest indictments of heterosexual marriage in the poem. In other words, they softened the critique of the connections between national or state violence and individual male violence but left intact much of the commentary on compulsory heterosexuality and its relation to male dominance.[93]

In regard to the references to the internal scene, the relationship inside the house of the two women in bed, Marianne and Mrs. Moore changed "over our beds" to "across fastidious beds." Besides distancing the line from the speaker, what does it mean to have a "fastidious" bed? Is it a value? Perhaps this revision alludes to the ways in which household activities become ritualized, the fastidious making of beds every morning, the daughter supervised by the mother. Is there room for regret here? That is, having made one's fastidious bed, is one forced to lie in it and impose it on others? "Fastidious" also connotes a kind of obsessive cleanliness or neatness, which would contrast sharply with the mess being made outside the house—the carnage wreaked in the fighting and preening of the roosters. In this way the term proposes the order of private, bourgeois domesticity to the disorder of public male domination.[94]

Odder still is the substitution of "irrelevant" for "unwanted" in the line "unwanted love, conceit and war." By declaring the relationship between the two women "irrelevant," Moore and her mother do not, as many critics suggest, make it invisible or will it away.[95] Instead they remove it from any implication in the violence occurring around it—it is "irrelevant" to the scene outside.

It is fitting, then, that the Moores rewrite the lines about the signification of the rooster in Christian iconography to read:

There was always to be
a bronze cock on a porphyry
pillar so that people and Pope might see

that the Prince
of the apostles
was forgiven; to convince

them that "Deny deny deny"
is now now as it was, the rooster's cry. (268)

In this revision denial becomes the principal purpose of art. Moore and her mother make more explicit one of the strands of Bishop's argument, the idea that aesthetic activity must cover up or deny the violence that is its precondition.

After doing away with "how could the night have come to grief," Moore and her mother rewrite the last stanza to read:

> And climbing in to see the end,
> The faithful sin is here,
>   as enemy, or friend. (269)

The sun becomes "sin," which connects back to the sin of Magdalen, one of the flesh, as well as to Peter's sin of the spirit. Suddenly, the boundaries between the lesbian couple inside and the rest of the world break down, as sin enters the room. The ending reads almost like a tract: Is sin your enemy or your friend? Will the women inside the room allow the "sin" outside, the violence and destruction, to infect their own scene? This reading allows for the possibility that the "sin" does not come from within the room and that the poem is not making a comment on the morality of the relationship between the two women. Alternatively, if one reads this as a judgment, the implied question of the ending becomes "Have you made sin your enemy or your friend?" "Is sin something you already know well?"

Moore's mother, as Moore reminds Bishop in her letter cited above, taught Sunday school. One could imagine her dictating this revision to Moore, recycling a bit of her Sunday school diction. This would indicate that someone in the Moore household was savvy enough to understand the poem's sexual politics and to add a moralizing, homophobic retort. Or, alternatively, it indicates that Moore and her mother endeavored throughout the poem to keep the bedchamber sacrosanct and exempt from the critique.

Indeed, the rest of their revisions preserve the inside as sanctuary. In some ways, then, Moore and Mrs. Moore's critical position reflects nineteenth-century feminine ideals of (white, bourgeois) women's special role as peacemaker, nurturer, and one who is antiviolent,[96] as well as reflecting the nineteenth-century idealizations of female-female relationships. On the other hand, the hyperbole of "fastidious" and "sin," as well as the elimination altogether of the question of the ends of the night, make this reading too simple. Could we distinguish Moore from her mother here? Although Moore's mother certainly adheres to these nineteenth-century ideals, theories of lesbian desire also often replicate these stereotypes in their idealizations of lesbian relationships as being exempt from the gender inequities and sexual violence of heterosexuality. One might read this revision as a coming together of Mrs. Moore's morals with Moore's own ideals of desire between women. In a sense, then, Moore would be advocating a prototype of "lesbian modernism," and she is able to align herself with her mother because the historical roots of each identity, female exceptionalism and lesbian idealization, come from the same source: nineteenth-century white, bourgeois ideology.[97]

Earlier in the poem, Moore and/or her mother rewrite the stanza "over our churches / where the tin rooster perches, / over our little wooden northern houses," with the lines "crazily conjoined across white churches / on which the golden rooster perches." They gild, perhaps, the dull rooster to make his luster deeper, in much the same way Bishop criticizes later in her version, when Peter's tears gem the spurs of the cock.

In her poem about the role of the poet, "The Steeple-Jack" (1934),[98] Moore makes the title figure into a metaphor for the role of the poet in the community, or the nation. She describes a quintessential small American town, with houses very much like the "little white northern houses" of Bishop's "Roosters," a town that has its share of "presidents who have re-paid / sin-driven / / senators by not thinking about them" (7) and a church "made / modester by white-wash" (7), a church with a spire whose pitch is "not true" (6). It is the job of the steeple-jack to maintain this spire, to protect the citizens from its untruth:

It could not be dangerous to be living
    in a town like this, of simple people,
who have a steeple-jack placing danger-signs by the church
while he is gilding the solid-
    pointed star, which on a steeple
stands for hope. (7)

By "placing danger signs by the church," the steeple-jack warns the community that their values are suspect at the same time that he is "gilding the solid- / pointed star," using his (humble) ability to try to restore these same values, for they "[stand] for hope." The job of the poet in America is twofold: she must "warn" the community while struggling, through her aesthetic practice, to reformulate these values. John Slatin reads this job as one of participating in the "corruption" of the town.[99] Although the connotations of "gilding" imply an attempt to cover up, with a shiny surface, something that might otherwise be seen as it really is, Moore presents a more complicated situation. The steeple-jack is part of the community at the same time that, because of his unique job, he is able to have a view of the community from above—a survey of the country, so to speak. He is implicated in that which causes the "danger" (in fact, by climbing up the steeple he himself creates some of the danger) at the same time that it is his vocation to protect and restore the values of the community. We know that the spire of the church is "not true," but it is the job of the poet to maintain the illusion with the possibilities of writing. Thus, Moore's conception of the power of her vocation is extremely ambivalent—the view that it is necessary yet perhaps ultimately doomed to failure.

From the example of "The Steeple-Jack" one might conclude that Moore *did* endorse a poetics of repression, and that she was a moralistic force, (s)mothering Bishop until she submitted or rebelled. This reading does not do justice, however, to the complexities of Moore's self-positioning in this exchange. The famous "Roosters" letter, Bishop tells us, was notable as much for its self-presentation as for its contents: "I had had an English teacher at Vassar whom I liked very much, named Miss Rose Peebles, and for some reason this name fascinated Marianne. The revised poem had been typed out on very thin paper and folded into a small square, sealed with a gold star sticker and signed on the outside 'Lovingly, Rose Peebles'" (146). Interestingly, Kalstone complicates this narrative by adding Moore's impersonation of yet another woman. He relates that Moore wrote: "'I hope Dorothy Dix's enclosure will not, as I said to you on the telephone, mean that I am never to hear from you or see you again.'"[100]

Dorothy Dix is the pseudonym of a well-known woman journalist who wrote a syndicated advice column. Such writers are known for the bland, incorruptible responses they give to those who write for help. Their job is to enforce the most normative "solution" to whatever the advisee's problem might be. Traditionally, they have tried to save marriages, "cure" homosexuals, and repudiate any kind of perverse sexuality.[101] By aligning herself with such a figure, Moore makes a comment on her role as critic: like an advice columnist, her suggestions for revision reflect, perhaps, the most stereotypical of replies.

More specifically, at the time that Bishop sent her poem to the Moores, Dorothy Dix had just recently published a book titled *How to Win and Hold a Husband* (1939), which includes chapters such as "When Are You

Too Old to Marry?" and "Masculinity in Women." [102] The writer of the introduction, John Elfreth Watkins, offers glowing praise of Dix's persuasive powers:

> Often a tired and discouraged woman will write that something Miss Dix has written has made her see that raising a family is a great and glorious career for a woman, and that is has given her fresh courage to go on with the dull monotony of the daily grind in a poor household. Doctors often write her to tell her that they give her articles instead of pills and potions to their neurotic feminine patients. A girl will write to her that something she has written has kept her from setting her feet on the downward path. [103]

It is reasonable to assume, then, that Dorothy Dix carried a certain amount of cultural recognition. By referring to herself as Dix, Moore activates the power of the double or triple negative: she implies that her moralisms are simply the most bland, heterosexist stereotypes of the dominant culture, which are so ineffective as to endorse their opposite.

Further, by signing the letter "Lovingly, Rose Peebles," Moore makes over yet another identity for herself. Miss Rose Peebles, "'who was very proud of being an old-school Southern lady,'" [104] was one of Bishop's favorite English teachers at Vassar. She is yet another example of a woman who lived independently as a teacher of girls and a "role model." Like Miss Talbot, she influenced Bishop through her support and encouragement and her recognition of Bishop's talent, and in her singular existence she served as an example of the ways in which women could live outside of the family structure. Although Bishop was grateful for Peebles's support and tutelage, however, she often felt frustrated with her nineteenth-century ideas about poetry. [105]

By appropriating these women's identities, Moore distances her letter from "Marianne." I do not mean to imply that one *could* essentialize identity, only that in regard to the process of sending her own and her mother's criticisms to Bishop, Moore uses these two other characters as mouthpieces. In these performative, playful, yet painful, exchanges, Moore indicates her own distance from her criticisms: in the case of Miss Rose Peebles, she implies, first, that she views her relationship to Bishop in the light of such institutionalized models (teacher and student); and, second, that her ideas about sexuality in poetry are from the nineteenth century. In the case of Dorothy Dix, Moore indicates that her criticisms are intended to encourage Bishop to adopt a way of living that Moore herself has rejected. This makes it almost impossible to pin down her critical and/or political position. As Bishop muses in the passage from "Efforts of Affection" cited above, "Manners *as* morals? Or is it morals *as* manners?" Moore combines willed ignorance with a firm set of ideals regarding poetry and women's relationships, yet she deconstructs these values at the same time.

Bishop, confronting this, was forced to declare herself and define both her poetic style and her political sensibilities. She threw into harsh relief the historical differences between her own and Moore's positions. It would be impossible to deny, then, that this encounter was (re)productive for both of them, through the ways in which each multiply identified and disidentified, not only with each other but with a wide variety of cultural forms.

It is too easy to read the "Roosters" incident as simply a censorious encounter between Moore and Bishop. Instead, in her excessive use of "negatives" and in her impersonation of old maid prudery, Moore activates historically and culturally specific forms of gender and sexual identity (or, in the case of sexuality, its supposed absence). Furthermore, her critique of Bishop lies not in her reaction to Bishop's sexuality per se, but in a historically determined disagreement about how (and whether) female-female relationships should exist in language.

Viewed from the vantage point of post-Stonewall gay liberation, it is easy to narrate Moore's position as more "repressed" than Bishop's: after a brief hiatus at Bryn Mawr, Moore buries her desires for women and turns to writing instead. As my rereading of the "Roosters" exchange demonstrates, such an account cannot delineate the complexities of Moore's self-positioning, her crafting of a poetics *and* a persona famously built on reticence and silence, on the one side, and oblique overstatement on the other.[106] On the other hand, it would also be a mistake to romanticize Moore's location as somehow more liberating than Bishop's because it was somehow less defined by the imperatives of the regime of sexual identity. Moore, because she is "out-of-date," continually risks being dismissed as a poet and, as the "Roosters" incident demonstrates, as a mentor and intimate friend.

"Aunt Exemplary and Slim"

Bishop herself in turn acknowledges the complexities of Moore's subject position in what I would argue is perhaps her most extended meditation in poetry on Moore's influence—her uncollected poem of 1956, "Exchanging Hats."[107] The poem presents the reader with a series of detailed, almost photographic images that, because of the singsong nature of the meter, jerk along like frames in a home movie. Over the click of the projector comes the voice of the poet, a niece perhaps, who by the end of the poem directly addresses her "Unfunny uncles" and "Aunt exemplary and slim." It seems likely that for Bishop the term "aunt" as an appellation connotes a spinster relative—Bishop grew up surrounded by her aunts and uncles, including her neurasthenic Aunt Florence, on whom many argue "Aunt Consuelo" in "In the Waiting Room" is based.[108] But "aunt" may also carry wider, extrafamilial significance. As Mary McCarthy, in her memoir of her college acquaintance with Bishop, explains,

> There were several sort of droll characters in the smoking room at Cushing. There wasn't much input from Elizabeth, but she was certainly there. Louise [Crane] was part of the smoking room life in Cushing. She was known as "Auntie" because she had little old-maidish airs. At Vassar she was a comic butt. Elizabeth was devoted to her, and vice versa.[109]

Although McCarthy confines the connotations of "auntie" to "old-maidish airs," however, Bishop throughout her poem continually expands the possibilities of this subject position. The poem begins:

Unfunny uncles who insist
in trying on a lady's hat,
—oh, even if the joke falls flat,
we share your slight transvestite twist

in spite of our embarrassment.
Costume and custom are complex.
The headgear of the other sex
inspires us to experiment.

Anandrous aunts, who, at the beach
with paper plates upon your laps,
keep putting on the yachtsmen's caps
with exhibitionistic screech. (200)

In dialogue with these madcap actions, the poem's form, in particular its regular, nursery rhyme-like meter, stands in for precisely those conventions (social / sexual / political / religious) that uphold the sex/gender system, those mores the aunts and uncles flaunt.[110] Yet the form is also complicated by the exchanges and changes between words themselves. Certain syllabic constructions reappear and are transformed from word to word: "*un*funny *un*cles," "*in*sist / *in* trying"; "costume and custom;" "anandrous aunts." Just as Moore revels in such verbal and visual transformations, as in the shift in the same line from the name "Jubal" to the name "Jabal" in her poem of the late 1940s, "Efforts of Affection"[111] (from which Bishop took the title of her memoir), in "Exchanging Hats" Bishop exchanges and changes sounds and syllables from word to word in order to reflect the action described by the poem, the way wearing a hat can "inspire one to experiment" with cultural and historical norms of gender and sexuality. Language itself, the poem implies, can powerfully disrupt convention.[112]

At times the euphoria of these changes and exchanges even threatens to spin the poem out of control:

And if the opera hats collapse
and crowns grow draughty, then, perhaps,
he thinks what might a miter matter? (200)

The line "he thinks what might a miter matter," in its almost tongue-twisting alliteration and assonance (and one can't help but remember the description of the actions of the "unfunny uncles" cited above), mimics the implied chaos that might accompany drastic gender transvestism. The authority of the pope, as well as his bishops,[113] like that of the monarchy and of the opera goer, the upper- and upper-middle-class arbiters of society, might all be drastically undermined through this transvestism and, by implication, so might the grip that these omnipotents hold on the world: a miter (and perhaps also poetic meter, as metaphor for convention) might not matter at all. To make this explicit is to threaten political, religious, and class upheaval: these "unfunny uncles" and "anandrous aunts" may in fact destabilize the social order.

Of course, the irony of these descriptions is that each details a costume already rife with gender transvestism: the opera is the high cultural scene of gender crossing and its concomitant confusion of sexualities, as many recent writers on drag and on opera discuss.[114] This occurs not only on stage but in the audience, where queer opera queens sit side by side with bull dagger society dames in their excessive, feather-laden hats.

The other cultural sites described in the poem rival the opera in this confusion: the monarchy also connotes gay-male culture: Who is, in fact, the ultimate model for the drag queen but the queen mother herself? Or perhaps more accurately, isn't the queen herself the biggest drag artist in the land? And in the Roman Catholic hierarchy, often ridiculed by gay and homophobe alike, are the world's most powerful men in dresses.

The poem thus concedes that simply cross-dressing will not necessarily put one outside the status quo, but may in fact help consolidate a position as wielder of the law. As recent critics of drag and transvestism aptly point out, gender transvestism does not necessarily imply any other sort of challenge to the rigidities of gender.[115] It certainly does not indicate that one is or is not homosexual.

Bishop's poem, however, *does* include sexuality in its twists of convention:

> Or you who don the paper plate
> itself, and put some grapes upon it,
> or sport the Indian's feather bonnet,
> —perversities may aggravate
>
> the natural madness of the hatter. (200)

The word "unnatural" haunts the poem.[116] It is invoked, by inversion and antonym, in the last two lines of this quotation. What defines or demarcates the difference between "natural" and "unnatural" madness or "natural" and "unnatural" perversities? Like the crossing of racial boundaries that lingers behind the image of "sport[ing] the Indian's feather bonnet," these stanzas gesture toward other kinds of couplings that were, at the time of the writing of the poem, legally defined as "unnatural": racist prohibitions against miscegenation and the laws against "unnatural perversities" or crimes against nature. The connotations of madness itself are also significant here: until recently homosexuality was classified as a mental illness for which one could be institutionalized and "cured." Thus, these aunts and uncles, in their crossings of the lines of class and religion, politics and race, and gender and sexuality, threaten the underpinnings of bourgeois morality.

Bishop's poem celebrates the avuncular, what Sedgwick has termed the processes of "queer tutelage"; that is, the ways in which the relation within the family structure coded as "queer"—these "unfunny uncles" and "anandrous aunts"—offer their nieces and nephews models of alternative forms of subject formation.[117] Yet "Exchanging Hats" goes even further. In its descriptions of "anandrous" aunts, it also invokes the power of (self-)production: "Anandrous" means having the capability to asexually reproduce, which implies that one is able to reproduce one's self without heterosexual procreation. The aunts *and* uncles in the poem, through their changes and exchanges of hats and clothes and form and convention, achieve unexpected, transformative, even sublime effects:

> Unfunny uncle, you who wore a
> hat too big, or one too many,
> tell us, can't you, are there any
> stars inside your black fedora?
>
> Aunt exemplary and slim
> with avernal eyes, we wonder
> what slow changes they see under
> their vast, shady, turned-down brim. (200–1)

By employing one of Bishop's characteristic inversions, where in turning something inside out, or in some other way radically shifting the perspective (again, the homosexual connotations of inversion should not be ignored here),[118] the world suddenly opens up. Bishop inverts the image of the inside of the uncle's "black fedora," making it into a galaxy of sublime possibilities.

Moreover, these "exemplary and slim" aunts are transformed as the movement of metaphors spins off into another ever-widening vista. Their "avernal" eyes become hats, and the eyelids become "vast, shady, turned-down brim[s]." Bishop implies that vision, the way one sees the world, can be just as transgressive of gender, sexual, racial, and poetic norms as cross-dressing and same-sex relationships. At the same time, it is subject to fashion, to cultural and historical shapings: there is no "natural" way of seeing.[119]

This is not a wholly liberatory sequence of images, however: the origin of the word "avernal" is "Avernus," a lake in Italy that the Romans believed was the gateway to hell because of the water's poisonous gasses. The poem indicates here that these women's way of viewing the world places them in the position of the damned, at least in the eyes of those whose authority the poem seeks to undermine. "Avernal" also resonates with "averted," a looking away, and "perverse," an averting of one's sexuality from its supposedly "natural aim," heterosexual reproduction. And all of these words echo the central term, "verse."[120]

That Bishop details Moore's outfits (especially her hats) and the fashion dictates to which she slyly refuses to conform is no coincidence. Moore, whose performative examples of poetic costuming and twists and bends in (gender and sexual) convention that Bishop observes and tries out for herself, becomes one of her "old-maidish," anandrous aunts. Bishop does not just celebrate such models, however. She emphasizes the power of crossdressing to uphold, as well as to undermine, various norms; as I have argued above, Moore often does both simultaneously. And, although these aunts have transformative powers of vision (something that echoes comments about Moore's amazing "eye" for detail), this vision leads both to creation ("verse") *and* damnation. Thus, in "Exchanging Hats" Bishop recognizes the power *and* the danger involved in occupying such a position. The poem constitutes a working through or theorizing of the influence of such aunts and the costs of making an identification with them. Judith Butler describes "disidentification" as "an identification one fears to make only because one has already made it." [121] That Bishop has unconsciously made such an identification is revealed in the allusion to her own name the poem makes through the nod to "bishops." In other words, the poem indicates that Bishop herself reinforces as she undermines social norms. Yet her positioning of address as niece ultimately emphasizes her desire to *distance* herself from this ostentatiously performative model of gender and sexual subjectivity.

⋅⋅⋅

Diana Fuss defines subjectivity as "precisely [the] struggle to negotiate a constantly changing field of ambivalent identifications; indeed, subjectivity can be most concisely understood as *the history of one's identifications.*" [122] In this chapter I have concentrated mainly on the history of Bishop's identifications with Moore, as well as her disidentifications from her. I seek to elucidate the complex ways in which Bishop's subjectivity was formed both consciously and unconsciously through her encounter with Moore, the ways Bishop confronts the "*M* multiplying." But how does Moore's subjectivity shift, if at all, through her relationship with Bishop? My reading of "Roosters" emphasizes the self-consciousness with which Moore presents her own and her mother's critique of Bishop's poem, which indicates on Moore's part a high degree of self-knowing, as well as pain in her acknowledgment of her own limitations. Does Moore ever move beyond these limits? And should we expect her to, given the ways in which such limits may also function for both her and Bishop as productive forms of prohibition and refusal? In my next chapter, through an examination of what I consider to be key moments of self-definition in Moore's poems "An Octopus" (1924) and "The Paper Nautilus" (1940), I trace a history of Moore's identifications and the ways in which Moore herself is transformed through her encounter with Bishop.

Chapter 6

INFLUENCE AND INVITATION:

MARIANNE MOORE, ELIZABETH BISHOP, AND

THE PLEASURES OF INFLUENCE,

PART 2

᳁᷂᳀᷂᳁

My reading of Marianne Moore and Elizabeth Bishop's poetic and personal exchanges as exemplary of a queer model of literary influence is the focus of chapter 5. Although a queer framework helps loosen the hold of a narrowly circumscribed oedipal model owing to its foregrounding of identification, such a framework nevertheless raises its own problems of force and mastery. In this chapter I explore some of these problems by examining Moore's and Bishop's poetics in terms of the disagreements around the nature of influence itself, disagreements that, as I will demonstrate, reflect Moore's and Bishop's quite different understandings of poetic power. Moore bases her poetics on a singular, queer, autoerotics of incorporation, what for her is an aggressive and appropriative, yet simultaneously dispersed and decentered, form of identification, as her poem "An Octopus" illustrates. Bishop, on the other hand, increasingly in her poems seeks to find a way of representing a queer erotics of relation, or what I term "invitation," an erotics not based in subsuming the difference of the "other," but in preserving it. In other words, in moving from Moore to Bishop we shift from what I have argued are the problems of the erotics of identification—the fact that such identification is often inseparable from other forms of imperial recruitment—to an erotics that tries to resist this impulse to reform the "other" or the self. For Bishop, this erotics entails a move away from even a queer nationalism, just as she also rejects any version of queer or lesbian exceptionalism. Moore, on the other hand, as I will demonstrate, never abandons a self-legitimating vision of poetic and queer power based in her strategic appropriation of the national.

In revising the oedipal model and in emphasizing the mutability and temporality of identity, a queer reading of influence allows for identification and desire to go both ways, for what I have termed elsewhere in this book are the processes of "mimetic reversibility." After first identifying the ways in which Moore articulates a queer poetic subjectivity in her poem "An Octopus," as well as the ways in which Bishop's poem "Crusoe in England" may be read as a response to this version of queer poetic subjectivity, I go on to interpret one such moment of mimetic reversibility in Moore's own oeuvre, through reading her poem "The Paper Nautilus" as in part illustrative of her own view of her relationship with younger lesbian-identified women.

In chapter 5 I illustrate how bracketing the essentialized mother/daughter model may allow us to see the ways in which queer forms of influence produce queer subjects. Throughout this book, however, I have been emphasizing that it was the blurring between mothers and "others" that was so potent for the production of queer female identifications/desires. In this chapter I explore how Moore's "The Paper Nautilus" takes up this blurring as it evaluates both the rewards and limits of a queer (and a) maternal identity. The poem also represents an instance in which the queer "mother" is transformed through her relationship with her "children," and in the process calls into question the ethics of disciplinary intimacy. In other words, even as the poem acknowledges the coerciveness of lesbian pedagogy, it mourns the loss of this form of relation. This chapter might be best understood, then, as an analysis of how sentimental culture becomes incorporated into or is resisted by modern queer female identities and forms of interrelation.

"An Octopus"

In 1922, Moore and her mother traveled to Bremerton, Washington, to visit Moore's brother, Warner, on a trip that, as Charles Molesworth implies, was in part a means to reconcile with Warner after their disagreement over his marriage.[1] During this visit, Moore and her brother spent two nights in Mt. Rainier National Park.[2] In 1923, Moore began work on a long poem, which eventually became two of her most significant works, "Marriage" and "An Octopus."[3] Most critics have tended to interpret these poems as having very separate concerns. Although "Marriage," as I have noted above, is viewed as Moore's exploration and ultimate condemnation of the fundamental institution of compulsory heterosexuality,

"An Octopus" is at its most literal level, as Bishop puts it, "about a glacier."[4] The poem has been read by most critics as Moore's exploration of the unique power of American nature and, by extension, of the American sublime and of the inability of language to approximate or represent the real.[5]

"An Octopus" inarguably addresses issues of interpretation, in that the reader is placed in the position of the tourist who is attempting to explore (and by extension master) what Moore calls "Mount Tacoma" (the Native American name for Mt. Rainier), the poem's ostensible subject. The tourist's standpoint is continually disrupted and called into question as the poem repeatedly purports to offer him/her a conclusive view of the landscape and then rapidly switches perspective or closes down that view.[6] Moreover, as a final gesture of refusal, the poem ends with an "avalanche," "a curtain of powdered snow launched like a waterfall." This ending illustrates, for Bonnie Costello, the dialectic in Moore's poetry between her desire for "sincerity," what Costello defines as "an accurate rendering of objective reality, away from both discursive abstraction (rationality) and emotional abstraction (personality)," and "gusto," Moore's term, as Costello describes it, for "the feeling of pleasure accompanying bafflement, the energy released in the poem by the resistance of an object to each onslaught of form."[7] Although such a reading brilliantly illuminates the aesthetic dilemmas the poem addresses—that of the problem of representing the grandeur and multiplicity of a sublime nature—it misses the autobiographical layer that connects this image of sublimity to the poet herself.[8] Costello's reading assumes that Moore places herself within the poem as tourist; I would argue that, instead, the poem constitutes Moore's performative representation of her own poetic powers, which themselves cannot be fully known and thus contained.

Despite the shared origins of "Marriage" and "An Octopus" as a single poem, many critics find in "Marriage" an account of Moore's own personal dilemmas with the institution yet few critics allow for a similar autobiographical reading of "An Octopus." Costello, for instance, alludes to the possibility that the latter may be read as a self-reflexive commentary on Moore's poetics, but then rejects such a possibility as "too facile."[9] Such a New Critical refusal seems especially misplaced given the fact that for Moore, more than most other modernist writers, "public" and "private" meanings and references are almost always inextricably intertwined in her work, especially given both her mother's collaborative efforts during the process of composition and revision and Moore's voracious habit of quotation, in which the majority of her poems are made up of citations from other heterogeneous sources, including not just published works but also conversations and personal letters. For example, in "An Octopus" the *acknowledged* sources (putting aside the question of unacknowledged ones) include a brochure on the national parks put out by the Department of the Interior; several London newspapers; Ruskin; a tourist's guide to America; and a "comment overheard at the circus."[10] Moore also incorporates into the poem family nicknames: there are several references to one of Mrs. Moore's pet names, the ouzel, a bird similar to the blackbird, as well as to a rat, one of Moore's own appellations. And, as Patricia Willis notes, the marmot in the poem was originally a badger (a reference to Warner), which Moore then changed to reflect more accurately the indigenous animals of the region.[11]

Given the inseparability of public and private reference in Moore's work, I would contend, "An Octopus" can support a variety of readings, ranging from the autobiographical to the aesthetic and philosophical. Moore, in the period between 1910 and 1925 was struggling not only to accept her brother's decision to marry, but also to come to terms with the consequences of her own decision to stay with her mother, namely that it meant giving up the possibility of any other intimate relationships, as well as increased social mobility (as I argued in my last chapter) and even international travel. The writers H.D. and Bryher made several unsuccessful attempts during this period to persuade Moore to come and live with them in England, in what David Bergman has claimed would have been a ménage à trois.[12] After Moore repeatedly refused their offers, Bryher turned to a marriage of convenience with Robert McAlmon, another young aspiring writer, of whom Moore did not approve.[13] "Marriage" may be read as a pointed response to Bryher's choice and to H.D.'s and Moore's dismay in its aftermath.[14] Because "Marriage" and "An Octopus" began as one poem, I would contend that in the latter it is reasonable to assume that Moore may be considering these same dilemmas: although "Marriage" constitutes her critique of the institution, "An Octopus" is her representation of an alternative queer poetic subjectivity. In other words, "An Octopus" represents Moore's theorization not only of her poetic power but of her position vis-à-vis the gender and sexual norms she criticizes in "Marriage." More obliquely, the poem also illuminates Moore's aesthetic and political reasons for "staying at home" in America and refusing the life of the expatriate modernist that so many of her contemporaries were embracing.[15]

From the start, the poem mixes descriptions of nature with descriptions that allude to other discourses, creating layer upon layer of metaphoric association. "An octopus / of ice. Deceptively reserved and flat," read the title and first line (71). Ostensibly, Moore begins the poem with a reference to the glacier that covers much of Mt. Rainier, leading the reader to expect that what will come after is a description of this landscape. With the juxtaposition of "reserved," a word generally used to describe one's personality, and "flat," which indicates either topography or an affectless quality of speech, however, Moore anthropormorphizes this octopus and, by extension, this glacier. To be reserved is to hold things back, to not say too much. For "flat" to work in concert with this description it would have to refer to one's use of language.

Immediately, then, the "octopus of ice" becomes both a metaphor for the glacier and for a specific representational strategy, that of "deceptive," emotionless understatement. Later in the poem such descriptions recur, as in the lines that modify "'the main peak' of Mount Tacoma":

this fossil flower concise without a shiver,
intact when it is cut,
damned for its sacrosanct remoteness—
like Henry James "damned by the public for
    decorum";
not decorum, but restraint. (75–76)

Again, the poem connects a way of using language, "conscis[ion]," with a mode of personal behavior, "restraint," and here asserts that such a practice of what seems to be emotional "remoteness" (not analogous to, but related to "flat[ness]") "damn[s]" the "fossil flower." This flower is then connected to the writer Henry James.[16] It would be difficult to ignore in these lines references to the ways Moore herself was "damned" for her own "restraint"—for example, the "sacrosanct remoteness" that kept her from accepting Bryher and H.D.'s offer.[17] Almost as if anticipating Bishop's question in "Efforts of Affection" about Moore's poetry and personal philosophy—"Manners and morals; manners *as* morals? Or is it morals *as* manners?" (156)—Moore here provides one answer. The poem accuses the public of mistaking "a love of doing hard things," a productive holding back, for a simple conformity to social norms, "decorum." Silence, refusal, restraint, withdrawal—all words that have been associated with Moore's persona and her poetics—are recast here by the poem as generative and vital rather than merely signs of repression. Furthermore, the term "fossil flower" connotes a flower encased in rock. It literally refers to the mountain itself, a rock encased in ice that is inseparable from the glacier that covers it.[18]

Yet "fossil flower" also resonates with terms used to describe older, single women, ossified in their femininity, relics of another era. Bryher, first in her letters to Moore and then again in her roman à clef *West* (1924), which she was writing at the same time that Moore was beginning "An Octopus," repeatedly refers to Moore as a "(ptero)dactyl," an image both of Moore's anachronism—she is a "dinosaur" (in *West* Bryher also changes the Moores's last name to "Trollope," signaling that mother and daughter are more Victorian than modern)—and of her unique use of poetic meter. Moore describes this image and the context for its inception in a letter to Warner. In it Moore also describes her difference from Bryher and H.D. and, more openly than she does in a subsequent letter to Bryher, gives an account of her reasons for turning down their offer to accompany them on their travels:

> H.D.'s friend in California [Bryher], to my absolute stupefaction, has written me saying that she can't see the use of my being cooped up and kept to work [Moore was working part time in a library during this period] when I might be writing, or riding an elephant. She says she and H.D. are "fording about and *not* riding delicately about on a Tyrian-trapped elephant"—and that H.D. has reminded her that one cannot go on an adventure without gold, and that elephants cost about $5000.00 as she knows for her father has some in connection with a rice mill in Burma, and that the amount for an expedition shall be "extended on the point of a sword" if I will be a "good pterodactyl that will come out of its rock" and write a novel; H.D. wrote too, very much afraid I would take the offer amiss and feel that it was presumptuous, saying that Winifred [Bryher] has been rescued by her from a mansion in a fashionable part of London "refusing to meet any of her class." . . . This is surely very kind, isn't it? Of course I couldn't write a novel and wrote that I have none in the process of hatching and that I work and live here as much from choice as from necessity but put it better and more gratefully I hope.[19]

In *West,* Bryher also represents this exchange: she describes the Moore character's ("Anne Trollope") retreat into long narrative digressions of detailed description in the face of repeated offers to take Anne to Europe, until finally "Nancy," Bryher's pseudonym for herself, exclaims, "'You ought to be ashamed of yourself. Sitting here like a pterodactyl on a rock afraid to move. . . . Cut the masochism and come with us to England.'"[20] In its representation of Moore's isolation and deliberate withdrawal, this passage condemns Moore for her refusal to be drawn "off of her rock," away from her mother and America and into a relationship with Bryher and H.D. in Europe.

With the image of the "fossil flower," Moore rewrites criticisms of herself such as Bryher's into an image of natural, geologic, and poetic power, as first "an octopus of ice," another aged creature on a rock, and then, later in the poem, as the mountain itself (because the mountain *is* the glacier, just as the glacier *is part of* the mountain, the poem at times refers to Mt. Rainier as the "glass mountain," which indicates the inseparability of the ice and rock) and as a volcano (again, another aspect of the mountain, one usually kept hidden). Furthermore, Moore associates this mountain with feats of technological skill and development ("much needed invention[s]" [71]), and with mass production and with reproduction. By the end of the poem, it (and by extension the poet) has become a metaphor for the nation as a whole. In other words, the mountain and, by extension, Moore, like Whitman, "contains multitudes."[21]

Such shifts and layers of metaphor reflect what critics have described as Moore's habit of defining and redefining a central object in a poem through a series of sometimes contradictory associations. As is the case in such poems and in "An Octopus," these associative leaps require the reader to participate in making meaning from what are often seemingly disparate images, only to find, as in the case of the ending of this poem, that any final transcendent closure is withheld. Nevertheless, by linking together the disparate images in "An Octopus," a representation of the poet and of her unique poetic process begins to emerge.

For example, to return to the beginning of the poem, the first thirteen lines contain a set of metaphors that link the octopus to both the poet and to Moore's poetic process:

An octopus

of ice. Deceptively reserved and flat,
it lies "in grandeur and in mass"
beneath a sea of shifting snow-dunes;
dots of cyclamen-red and maroon on its clearly defined
                    pseudo-podia

made of glass that will bend—a much needed invention—
comprising twenty-eight ice-fields from fifty
    to five hundred
                feet thick,
of unimagined delicacy.
"Picking periwinkles from the cracks"
or killing prey with the concentric crushing
    rigor of the python,
it hovers forward "spider fashion
on its arms" misleadingly like lace;
its "ghostly pallor changing
to the green metallic tinge of an anemone-starred pool." (71)

Most immediately, these lines demonstrate the ways in which any sense of "reserve" in the octopus is matched by an equal sense of expansive, appropriative power. The lines move from the very general—"'in grandeur and in mass'"—to the particular—"dots of cyclamen-red and maroon on its clearly defined pseudo-podia"; from the snowy surface to icy depth—"twenty-eight ice fields from fifty to five hundred feet thick, of unimagined delicacy"; from the ability to "pick . . . periwinkles from the cracks," to "killing prey with the concentric crushing rigor of the python." This great power appears on the surface to be extremely fragile, "hover[ing] forward 'spider fashion / on its arms' misleadingly like lace," an image that recalls the deceptive frailty of the "fossil flower," yet this delicate "hover[ing]" signifies in actuality the powers of precision, the ability to deploy whatever force is necessary to pick the smallest shell from a crack or to kill. The abilities of this great power also extend to self-transformation, as evidenced in the ways in which it shifts from a "ghostly pallor" to "the green metallic tinge of an anemone-starred pool," depending, one would assume, on its surroundings.

At the most obvious level, all of these images denote the movements and abilities of a literal octopus, which is then made into a metaphor for the movement of a glacier. Yet all of these images point as well to poetic prowess. An octopus is a mollusk, but instead of dwelling within a shell, as do most of the other members of its phylum, the octopus shoots out ink from its body as a form of camouflage and protection. It recalls, then, many of Moore's other "armored" creatures, which critics usually interpret as stand-ins for the poet, creatures that reflect Moore's own supposed desire for self-protection and concealment, her need to hide herself in her poems and to avoid any form of self-disclosure.[22] Assuming that the octopus is thus another stand-in for Moore, it is too easy to see this image as simply reflecting a need for self-protection or concealment. Shooting ink also signifies an attack and a form of self-display, which connotes not just withdrawal but a combative, performative mode of (self-)representation. Ink also signifies writing, and it connects the octopus to the poet: here the actual body of the octopus/poet produces text, and this text is both a form of protection and revelation.

Another characteristic of the octopus, which distinguishes it from most other mollusks, is its abundance of feet. Already at the beginning of the poem, Moore begins to play with the connotations of this image, and here and throughout the poem references to feet recur again and again; for example, as "pseudo-podia," as a measurement of depth (the "twenty-eight ice fields from fifty to five hundred feet thick"), and later as the shape of "The Goat's Mirror," a compelling, foot-shaped pool of water that attracts the attention of the tourist/reader (71–72). In her poem "In the Days of Prismatic Color," Moore exploits the double meanings of the phrase a "multiplicity of feet," which signifies a line of verse, a collection of metric feet, and a creature with many appendages. Thus, as Costello explains, Moore "parodies meter as monster," because Moore's eccentric lines, which contain no regular metric patterns, often have such a "multiplicity of feet."[23] Although Moore's poems often appear to have some regular metric order, in fact they vary greatly in rhythm and in line length and usually contain only embedded or half-rhymes. For example, in "An Octopus," a glance at the words on the page reveals lines varying in length from six to seventeen syllables. In other words, Moore's poems are full of "false feet," or, as Moore terms it in the fourth line of "An Octopus," "pseudo-podia." Just as her poems resist or frustrate interpretation, formally they may, as "An Octopus" describes it, "[deceive you] into thinking you have progressed / under the polite needles of the larches," when in fact you are simply "completing a circle" (71).

But "pseudo-podia" can mean phagocytosis, a process of engulfment in which a cell devours all in its path; as *Webster's New Collegiate Dictionary* notes, it is also a word for the "slender leafless branch of the gametophyte" ("the individual or generation of a plant exhibiting alternation of generations that bear sex organs") "in various mosses that often bears gemmae" ("an asexual reproductive body that becomes detached from a parent plant"); or "a supposed or apparent psychic projection (as from a medium's body)." Read in relation to "feet" in the poetic sense, Moore makes an analogy between her writing and a devouring, incorporating process (compare this to the way an octopus devours its prey); a reproductive process that does not require sexual intercourse; and a psychic projection—as opposed to a process of incorporation—an extension of the self outside of the self, which recalls the way ink jets out of the body of the octopus.[24] Versification, the construction and extension of false feet, becomes a way of taking the world into one's body and regenerating, in solitude, one's self through writing. Here we also find a metaphor for Moore's notorious modernist project of "quotation," of incorporating all kinds of prosaic and poetic fragments into her poetry. Like a glacier, which swallows up everything in its path and encases it in ice, or an octopus, which shoots out ink as a form of attack and then devours its prey, the poet subsumes everything she encounters into herself and into her poetry (and in the process her art and her self become indistinguishable).[25]

Throughout this volume I have argued that the erotics of identification are rooted in the inseparability of being and having and that every identification also represents an act of power. Although the devouring action of the octopus/glacier/poet emphasizes the violence inherent in identification or what in this case is literal incorporation, Moore's vision of the octopus, as demonstrated in the "multiplicity of feet" of the poem, is also weirdly centerless and fragmented, monumental but also dispersed, what the poem terms "unegoistic action" (73).[26] This is introjection, but it is an introjection that seems to be trying to minimize its violence. This is Moore's vision of her modernist poetics: she is a deceptively reserved woman whose poetic powers queerly assimilate and then reproduce the "natural" world. In constructing this poetic persona, Moore replaces with an image of the poet as glacier, "an octopus / of ice. Deceptively reserved and flat," a stereotype of genteel, white (as signified through snow and ice), remote, isolated spinsterhood—the spinster as an older, polite woman whose life is without social utility because she does not reproduce children.[27]

As the poem continues, this image increasingly accrues more significance and power, as Moore adds layer upon layer of association. In the fourth and fifth lines she begins to mix the natural with the technological, with the image of "pseudo-podia / made of glass that will bend" (71). As her notes to the poem explain, "Sir William Bell, of the British Institute of Patentees, has made a list of inventions which he says the world needs," and this is one of them (273). The work of the poet expands beyond reproduction to production as well: the mountain is also in some way a machine that turns out "much needed invention[s]." In linking "pseudo-podia" to this marvel, Moore also makes her poetry analogous to a new technology, for these "false feet" "compris[e] ice fields from fifty to five hundred feet thick," lines of poetry, perhaps, whose varying lengths and cadences produce differing depths of meaning, a "much needed invention."[28] Poetry thus becomes analogous to other ambient processes of modernization such as industrialization, which are remaking America.

Elsewhere, the poem's language reinforces this connection between poetry and technological and scientific culture. Throughout the poem, allusions are made to various hidden "gems" yet uncut: the bear's den, which is "somewhere else, concealed in the confusion" (72), is "composed of calcium gems and alabaster pillars, / topaz, tourmaline crystals and amethyst quartz." In lines fifteen to twenty, the "vermilion and onyx and manganese-blue interior expensiveness" of the rock "seems frail compared with [the] dark energy of life" that springs from the fir trees (71). This rockbed, so to speak, of poetic creativity is filled with natural resources, "dumps of gold and silver ore" (71), just waiting to be converted by the poet into "much needed invention[s]."

Moreover, on the mountain there are "'thoughtful beavers / making drains which seem the work of careful men with shovels'" and "bears inspecting unexpectedly / ant-hills and berry-bushes" (72). With these allusions to a division of labor and to surprise inspections, the mountain becomes analogous to the factory, the quintessentially modern workplace. Thus, Moore indicates that her poetic processes are as valuable to the nation as any other productive activity.

Or more so, because Mt. Rainier is also a national park, one of the large tracts of land set aside as a "national treasure" in the early twentieth century. As Mark Seltzer points out in his critique of the production of masculinity at the turn of the century, with the closing of the frontier came the establishment of national parks, also called "nature museums."[29] On the mountain, existing side by side, we find "American royal families" (71), "ouzel[s]" (73), "white flowers of the rhododendron" (74), "mountain guide[s]" (73), and "beavers" (72), an "original American menagerie of styles" (74).[30] This reinforces the image of the mountain as a "museum," a "game preserve / where 'guns, nets, seines, traps and explosives, / hired vehicles, gambling and intoxicants are prohibited; / disobedient persons being summarily removed / and not allowed to return without permission in writing'" (75).[31] These parks were intended, like the Boy Scouts, to facilitate the process of "imperial subject production" in men by preserving a "wilderness space" in which men could engage in fantasies of imperial conquest, even after there was no more land on the American continent left to conquer. However, unlike the museums of natural history, which served to insure the primacy of man over all other beings, there is no cultural hierarchy on this mountain.[32] If anything, the poem satirizes man's (and I use "man" deliberately here) ability to influence his environment.

When men appear, they are usually included without any distinction in a larger list of the plants and animals:

> Big Snow Mountain is the home of a diversity of creatures:
> those who "have lived in hotels
> but who now live in camps—who prefer to";
> the mountain guide evolving from the trapper,
> "in two pairs of trousers, the outer one older,
> wearing slowly away from the feet to the knees";
> "the nine-striped chipmunk
> running with unmammal-like agility along a log";
> the water ouzel (73)

Amazingly, by wearing out their "trousers," the men appear to be undergoing a process of evolution, a "making of Americans" within the poem. This odd rewriting of evolution signals another larger movement in the poem, one that questions and criticizes the modern American ideal of progress: what does it mean to move from trapper to guide?[33]

By subsuming "man" within the account of the rest of the flora and fauna of the mountain, Moore does not preserve any hierarchy of value between men and animals, "businessmen" and trappers.[34] Animals perform work usually reserved for men, and men at best circulate but do not evolve. The poem implicitly critiques the ideal of white male domination, glorified as "progress," that is inscribed in many nature museums or parks. The earliest published version of the poem is even more forthright in its criticism of white masculinity, when it describes "this treacherous glass mountain" as "inimical to 'bristling, puny, swearing men / equipped with saws and axes,'"[35] and instead links the mountain to

> gentians, ladyslippers, harebells, mountain
> dryads,
> and "Calypso, the goat flower—
> that greenish orchid fond of snow"—

anomalously nourished upon shelving glacial
   ledges
where climbers have not gone or have gone
   timidly.[36]

In earlier versions of the poem, Moore juxtaposes a female intercon-
nectedness with (an albeit violent and cold) nature to a male rapacious-
ness. The mountain "anomalously nourishe[s]" and "admires" a feminine
nature while finding itself "inimical" to the men who seek to control it
through taking its resources for their own gain. That the peak itself is also
a (fossil) "flower," indicates the inherent connections between the Calypso
flower and the mountain, and perhaps emphasizes an erotic of sameness
over one of difference.[37] Here Moore signals once again her belief in female homoerotic exceptionalism; unlike the men who seek to conquer the
peak, the flower exists in a kind of symbiotic relationship with it. That
Moore cut this section from later published versions of the poem may not
necessarily indicate that she is trying to soften or tone down her feminist
vision, as Joanne Feit Diehl implies, but instead may signify her acknowledgment that femininity is not automatically exempt from power (Bishop's
argument in "Roosters"). Certainly the overarching argument of the poem
makes this point in its vision of the feminine mountain's enormous destructive and creative abilities.[38]

The power is expressed most obviously in the image of the mountain,
which is as much "white volcano" as glacier, "'a mountain with those
graceful lines which prove it a volcano,' / its top a complete cone like Fuji-
yama's / till an explosion blew it off" (73).[39] Like Dickinson's "vesuvius at
home," such images connote hidden explosive power, perhaps even in-
vaginated ones.[40] Like a volcano, an octopus also "explodes," and its ink
subsumes all in its path. One can also picture flows of lava running down
the sides of a mountain as the long appendages of the octopod. Such images connote the immense, autoerotic power of the poet, one that in its release can not only bring pleasure but immense destruction.

The last twenty-one lines of the poem bring together these disparate
images:

Relentless accuracy is the nature of this octopus
with its capacity for fact.
"Creeping slowly as with meditated stealth,
its arms seeming to approach from all directions,"

it receives one under winds that "tear the snow to bits
and hurl it like a sandblast,
shearing off twigs and loose bark from the trees."
Is "tree" a word for these things
"flat on the ground like vines"?
some "bent in half circle with branches on one side
suggesting dust-brushes, not trees;
some finding strength in union, forming little
    stunted groves
their flattened mats of branches shrunk in
    trying to escape"
from the hard mountain "planed by ice and polished by the
                        wind"—
the white volcano with no weather side;
the lightning flashing at its base,
rain falling in the valleys, and snow falling on the peak—
the glassy octopus symmetrically pointed,
its claw cut by the avalanche
"with a sound like a crack of a rifle,
in a curtain of powdered snow launched like a waterfall." (76)

The ending of this poem creates a sublime effect, a shutting down once
again of any possibility of ascending the mountain and, by metaphoric extension, of "knowing" it in its entirety.[41] This ending also recalls other moments in the poem of the poet's self-description, however, ones that emphasize endurance and strength. For example, the poem has already
provided the reader with evidence that the cutting of the glassy octopus's
claw will not destroy its power: the "fossil flower" remains "intact when
it is cut" (75). Through this image of sublime female self-sufficiency and
endurance,[42] Moore rewrites and reconceives the dominant cultural fears
surrounding single women that Stowe's novel articulates over fifty years
earlier, fears about both the effects of machine culture and of white,
middle-class women's entrance into the public sphere: would machines replace biological reproduction in the formation of social subjects? Were
bourgeois women somehow rendered "unfeminine" or "unfit" for motherhood through their participation in higher education, the work force,
and other realms of public life? In other words, would women become
"unnatural," sexually perverted, or queer? Were women, in effect, becoming machines? Moore replaces these fears with a fantasy of "natural" (al-

beit sometimes violent, self-mutilating) processes: on the mountain Americans are made and remade without biological labor. By comparing the role played by the queer woman poet to that played by a national monument or a factory, the poem implies that Moore's poetics ground and reproduce the nation. In so doing, Moore creates a space for herself within an ideology that did not recognize women, and certainly not spinsters such as Moore, as capable of influencing or reproducing culture.

This strategy recalls Moore's practice of impersonating George Washington: by making herself into the "father of our country" Moore implies that her place as poet fathers America. Here she extends that image even as she feminizes it: in uniting the natural and the technological, fire and ice, and man and animal, the "fossil flower" and, by extension, Moore as poet, makes and remakes the nation. In so doing, Moore creates a Whitmanian fantasy of queer citizenship: the queer poet becomes the model for the citizen, and the public embodiment of the nation, the nation in miniature. Inside this diorama, although Moore rejects hierarchizing Darwinian methods of organizing nature and, by implication, seeks radically to democratize the nation (with animals and men having the same status), she still allows for the spinster poet as national power, the one who brings the nation together and guarantees its union—not through symbolic or literalized representations of homosexual or heterosexual coupling, as in Whitman, but through an autoerotic, sometimes pleasurable, yet also painfully singular process.[43]

In other words, insofar as "An Octopus" expresses Moore's vision of her own queer body as nation, which is inseparable from her text as nation, she creates what is at once a quite radical and a profoundly reactionary ideology. In her simultaneous appropriation and subversion of white male imperial power, she still reproduces a fantasy of the "making of Americans," an engulfing, incorporating process in which the poet "contains multitudes." As Diana Fuss reminds us, "A certain element of colonization is structurally indispensable to every act of interiorization."[44] Moore's decentered vision of the creeping octopus tries to minimize this colonization, to preserve in its multiplicity the habitat of the mountain. Yet Moore still relies on the nation, and in particular the rhetoric of nation building, as a strategy of legitimation (and increasingly as she ages she will mobilize the rhetoric of patriotism as a self-authorizing strategy, especially because impersonating George Washington also implies that the impersonator is the ultimate patriot). That the nation is also the site of state-sanctioned violence and of a patriarchal heterosexuality, and that incorporation inevitably means a denial of the difference of the "other," are not issues "An Octopus" considers. Instead, the poem illustrates the limitations of what I have been arguing is a form of queer nationalism.

An Island

In contrast to Moore's work in "An Octopus," Bishop, in one of her last poems, "Crusoe in England" (1976), dramatizes through a retelling of the Robinson Crusoe story the problems with imperial gestures: Crusoe fails, as island castaway, at doing exactly what the poet succeeds at doing in "An Octopus": classifying, controlling, and reproducing (even if in a nonhierarchical way).[45] Instead, Bishop presents a vision of the queer as nationless.[46] In other words, if Moore represents the queer poet as sublime natural, national power, Bishop represents her as a tourist, whose travels lead her increasingly to question the stability of any identity—national, racial, sexual—as well as to seek ways of representing, in this case, cultural otherness, without trying to dominate or control the "other."[47]

To put it more specifically, in "Crusoe in England," Bishop refuses the space of the nation as one through which a queer identity can be articulated and, by extension, legitimated. She refuses to define the role of the poet as either the queer mother or father of a country,[48] the original reproducer of its citizenry. Instead, through her revision of Crusoe's experiences, she rewrites imperial domination and the romance of the market economy into an indictment of the imperial impulse, even when such an impulse includes queerly valenced attempts at reproduction.

Crusoe's problem, as he tells us over and over in the poem, is that he cannot get an image of himself reflected back from the flora and fauna of the island. Instead of striding manfully through the interior, naming and classifying everything he encounters (an activity Moore's poem both parodies and participates in), Crusoe finds that his sense of self is constantly shattered by the continually shifting landscape and the continually multiplying animals.[49]

In revising the romantic ideal that one finds one's self mirrored in nature, Bishop expresses the imperialist urge that lies behind such impulses. The attempt to (re)produce one's self becomes explicitly connected with violence when Bishop describes how Crusoe tries to make a baby goat his own child:

One day I dyed a baby goat bright red
with my red berries, just to see
something a little different.
And then his mother wouldn't recognize him.

Dreams were the worst. Of course I dreamed of food
and love, but they were pleasant rather
than otherwise. But then I'd dream of things
like slitting a baby's throat, mistaking it
for a baby goat. I'd have
nightmares of other islands
stretching away from mine, infinities
of islands, islands spawning islands,
like frogs' eggs turning into polliwogs
of islands, knowing that I had to live
on each and every one, eventually,
for ages, registering their flora,
their fauna, their geography. (165)

When Crusoe attempts to exert control over, through aesthetic reproduction, the baby goat, he makes the kid unrecognizable to his mother, and the image of slitting the throat of the goat makes explicit the baby's fate: it dies because its mother cannot identify it. Classification, another form of imperial reproduction, becomes a nightmare for Crusoe, an unbearable burden.[50] It is only when Friday arrives that he finds any solace or any possibility for stable subjectivity.[51]

Just when I thought I couldn't stand it
another minute longer, Friday came.
(Accounts of that have everything all wrong.)
Friday was nice.
Friday was nice, and we were friends.
If only he had been a woman!
I wanted to propagate my kind,
and so did he, I think, poor boy.
He'd pet the baby goats sometimes,
and race with them, or carry one around.
—Pretty to watch; he had a pretty body. (165–66)

Bishop attempts to replace or rewrite the traditional Crusoe story, which has usually been viewed as simply a narrative of Crusoe's imperialist power in miniature, with an account of the homoerotics between colonizer and colonized. Besides refusing the traditional colonial metaphors of the rape of the female land by the male conqueror,[52] which are replicated in much scholarship of orientalism, Bishop implies that through Crusoe's relationship with Friday, his anxieties about the island subside. Outside the realm of the national, homoerotic affiliation provides some kind of provisional sense of home.

Whatever the specificities of Crusoe and Friday's relationship, they cannot be spoken within the poem. Their interactions are described in flat, short, prosaic statements, which contrast markedly with the much more detailed descriptions of almost every other aspect of life on the island: "Friday was nice," "Friday was nice, and we were friends," "he had a pretty body."[53] It is as if language is not able to carry the weight of their relationship, because as soon as it is put into language it loses its meaning under the force of the imperial and heterosexual demands that would be placed on it. As Sara Suleri, in her evocative discussion of Forster's *A Passage to India,* puts it, "The logic of an imperial erotic [is one] in which intimacy is always too excessive or too scant."[54]

Although Crusoe makes an obligatory reference here to heterosexuality ("If he had only been a woman!"), the reader is not convinced.[55] Instead, the image of Friday carrying the goat implies that although they cannot biologically procreate, Crusoe and Friday's relationship is (re)productive: unlike Crusoe, who is not "native" to the landscape, Friday can "mother" the animals. But, through its refusal to represent their relationship, the poem does not allow Friday to become simply a colonial mirror through which the colonist finds himself restored. Bishop instead resorts to leaving Crusoe and Friday's relationship outside of representation. They exist in a liminal space, albeit a highly idealized one.

The tragedy, then, is that when Crusoe attempts to take Friday back to England, to return to the space defined as the national, Crusoe commits another act of violence: "And Friday, my dear Friday, died of measles / seventeen years ago come March" (166). Friday dies of the measles, a disease of imperialism, because he has no resistance to it—he is not "native" to England.[56] Crusoe is left in his own personal museum, which is meaningless without the homoerotic desire that underwrote it, as well as the specific, local island landscape that gave it meaning. He repudiates the utility of these objects outside of their own, specific island economy. He refuses, in Suleri's terms, "the ideology of the collector."[57] Within Britain's market economy these implements become useless, fetishized objects detached from their everyday use: museum pieces.

Bishop implies, then, that for queerness to succeed it cannot rely on the coherency of identity and identification offered by national identity. Furthermore, she implicates even the most benevolent attempts at reproducing one's self, however queerly, within an imperial context. Unlike Moore and the other late-nineteenth and early-twentieth-century women writers whose queer, protolesbian, and lesbian reproductive projects I have described in my earlier chapters, Bishop, at least in her later poems, rejects this imperial-pedagogical model. Instead, her portrayals of subjectivity in her poems increasingly foresee a different kind of subject formation, one based on movement and "travel" rather than on national, racial, or even sexual location.[58]

The Queer Maternal: Letting Go

Although Moore never relinquishes her attachment to the national, in "The Paper Nautilus" she rethinks her emphasis on incorporation. She also moves from a queer autoerotics of female singularity to an ambivalent representation of a queer maternal/filial relation.[59] That Moore is revisiting the issues of "An Octopus" is signaled most obviously in the literal connections between the two sea creatures: both are mollusks. The poem further links the two when it describes the process by which the paper nautilus guards her eggs:

> Buried eight-fold in her eight
>   arms, for she is in
>   a sense a devil-
> fish (121)

"Devil-fish" is another name for an octopus. Like the latter, the paper nautilus's form of protection and self-display connotes the processes of poetic creation: instead of shooting out ink, however, it makes a shell out of "paper," which then shelters the mother and her eggs. In fact, the distinctive reproductive process of the paper nautilus joins the processes of procreation and creation, for it produces from its body a paper shell, a

>   perishable
> souvenir of hope, a dull
>   white outside and smooth-

edged inner surface
glossy as the sea, (121)

only because it needs to protect its eggs. The need to mother compels the nautilus to create.

Once again, then, Moore connects the body itself to writing and chooses in this case what at first seems to be a much more traditional form of reproductivity as a metaphor for the poetic process. The poem draws on what appear to be the same tropes of sentimentalized maternality that I have argued above constitute dominant nineteenth-century idealizations of motherhood. For example, the concept of writing in "The Paper Nautilus" is represented as a form of (maternal) self-sacrifice:

> For authorities whose hopes
> are shaped by mercenaries?
> Writers entrapped by
> teatime fame and by
> commuters' comforts? Not for these
> the paper nautilus
> constructs her thin glass shell. (121)

Writing is not just a remunerative process of selling one's services to the highest bidder, nor is it an attempt to achieve "teatime fame" or "commuters' comforts," a need for fleeting, middlebrow recognition or quotidian security that then "entrap[s]" the writer.[60] Instead, this is a different form of self-imprisonment and reward because for the paper nautilus, maternity is a burden (and here is where the sentimental vision of motherhood starts to become more complicated): in constructing "her thin glass shell," the nautilus "entrap[s]" herself as well as her eggs. It is no wonder then, that "she scarcely / / eats until the eggs are hatched" (121). Only with their hatching is she able to move at all:

> the intensively
> watched eggs coming from
> the shell free it when they are freed (121)

The children literally free the mother, who has imprisoned herself and them within a paper shell until they hatch. We move from self-sacrifice to a form of confinement from which one needs to be liberated.

Critics connect this poem specifically to Moore's relationship with Bishop because of the circumstances of the poem's composition; erroneously, many readers have assumed that the poem was inspired by a gift from Bishop to Moore of a paper nautilus, an exotic shell, and that Moore wrote the poem (originally titled "A Glass-Ribbed Nest") as a gift in return. Although it is clear that for Bishop and Moore the rituals both of invitation and gift giving constituted a complicated negotiation of intimacy[61] (and perhaps even an erotic), in actuality the shell was a gift to Moore from Louise Crane, Bishop's lover at the time. Given the fact that the two young women were living together in Key West, however, Bishop surely had a hand in selecting the present. It also responds to as it rewrites one of Bishop's own poetic metaphors, the wasp's nest in "José's House" (later retitled "Jerónimo's House"), the draft of which Bishop had recently sent Moore (itself a kind of present to the older poet). Thus, Moore's poem *was* a reciprocal gift, but one presented to both young women (after all, the nautilus produces "eggs," hence more than one offspring).[62]

Given this biographical context, it would be hard to deny that the poem presents an unusual perspective on mothering. Moore, through writing this poem, implies that Bishop and Crane provide the inspiration for her creation: their influence seems to compel her to write. In other words, the impulse to mother finds its origin in female-female interactions (in this case nonfamilial in the biological sense). Thus, unlike representations of writing (and, by association, reproduction) in "An Octopus," in "The Paper Nautilus" such representations are not those of solitary (self-)regeneration, nor merely of a source of power.[63] Instead, writing comes from a desire to protect and nurture others as well as oneself. As metaphorized by the act of constructing a paper shell, then, creating a subjectivity through writing is simultaneously (self-)entrapping, protective, and nurturing but also potentially dangerous, for this maternal figure is a "devil- / fish," the enjambment of the line indicating that she is also a "devil"—a malevolent, perhaps even damned, figure.

Furthermore, the image of "her glass ram's horn-cradled freight" that "is hid but is not crushed," first describes the nautilus "cradl[ing]" her eggs, but it also tries to distinguish between a process of "hid[ing]" the eggs and "crush[ing]" them. Read biographically, this distinction recalls Moore's efforts to shelter and protect Bishop, efforts that, eventually, as evidenced by the "Roosters" exchange, felt to both of them like smothering. As Diehl puts it, "the danger, although here a danger evaded, is that [the mother] will crush what she strives to protect."[64] Other images in the poem, such as the nautilus's "intensive . . . watching," may also signal

Moore's desire to hide Bishop from the pressures of publication and professionalization, especially during the late 1930s, as well as her attempts to limit and control Bishop's poetic expressions, through a form of poetic surveillance. It may also connote specifically Moore's sense that her revisions of Bishop's more "vulgar" poems were in fact Moore's efforts to protect Bishop (and perhaps Crane as well) from the possibly negative public repercussions of Bishop's sexual self-disclosure.

Biographical context aside, Moore's representation of mothering may also be read as a critical interrogation of the workings of disciplinary intimacy: the poem repeatedly implies that there is a thin line between a maternal care that is simply a nurturing protectiveness and one that becomes a form of endangering control, as in the following lines:

> as Hercules, bitten
>
> by a crab loyal to the hydra,
> was hindered to succeed,
> the intensively
> watched eggs coming from
> the shell free it when they are freed (121)

The syntax of these lines is confusing: it is hard to tell whether "Hercules" refers to the paper nautilus or to the eggs. If we read the paper nautilus as analogous to Hercules, then like the crab the eggs at first "hinder" her progress but ultimately are the reason for her "succe[ss.]"[65] However, the reference to "hydra," a many-headed monster of Greek mythology, is also a reference to another sea animal, similar to the octopus in its multiplicity of appendages, and, by extension, to the nautilus itself. Perhaps we are to read the eggs as analogous to Hercules (and syntactically, this is probably more grammatically accurate). If so, the poem suggests that mothering "hinder[s]" the eggs' progress: not only must the eggs break out of the shell the mother has created to protect them but they must also fight her for their freedom.[66] In its deliberate syntactical confusion the poem supports both readings at once, which emphasizes that this relationship is one of discord and struggle but also that this conflict is ultimately productive.

In this way, I would argue, these lines connote more than the old oedipal battle, because instead of producing simple copies of the mother, this struggle produces what appears to be a new way of being for all involved. Its results are "free[dom]" for both the mother and her offspring. Yet this is an ambiguous representation of liberation, because the rest of the poem seems to mourn the loss of even such a fraught interrelationship, as evidenced especially in the description of the empty shell:

> its wasp-nest flaws
> of white on white, and close-
> laid Ionic chiton-folds
> like the lines in the mane of
> a Parthenon horse,
> round which the arms had
> wound themselves (122)

That the lines describing the way the arms held the shell (and by extension everything within them, the nautilus and the eggs) are written in the past tense indicates that this is a reference to the now-completed reproductive process, yet through the slippage from past to present implicit in these lines it also seems to express a kind of longing for this experience. This description also leads the reader to imagine the arms clutching a now-empty shell. As Sabine Sielke describes it, "Maternal love is depicted as an affection that cannot let go of its object." [67] It also reminds the reader that in protecting the eggs the mother was also in effect holding herself, and that with their departure her own (excuse for) self-protection is gone.

The poem then ends on what appears to be a sentimental note:

> as if they [the arms] knew love
> is the only fortress
> strong enough to trust to. (122)

At first reading, this end disappoints in its slip into what seem to be bland Victorian platitudes. But how are we to understand the nature of the "love" being celebrated here? Is the description of love as "the *only* fortress / strong enough to trust to" a contrast to the form of protectiveness and enclosure that the shell (and the maternal arms) offer the mother and her offspring? Or is it an extension or metaphor for it? In other words, the poem presents an interpretive problem: is ambivalent "maternal" love all one can trust, or is this *another* kind of love and another kind of protection that is ultimately a better choice? The word "fortress" also may have religious connotations—in it are echoes of the hymn "A Mighty Fortress is Our God," which would imply that love, rather than religious belief, is really what matters. What kind of love would necessitate such a contrast, especially since the love of parents for children, at least in Christian orthodoxy, is supposed to imitate that of God's love for humanity? If love forms a contrast to other kinds of fortresses, those inspired by religious example, including a self-abnegating/controlling ideal of maternal filiality, then maybe this word alludes to the kind of alternative love shared by Bishop and Crane, a love that for Moore might have meant choosing one form of intimacy—female-female homoerotic "love"—over spiritual certainty; that is, eros over agape.

These questions are impossible to resolve, given that, as in many of Moore's poems, the ending refuses the reader closure, even as its allusions to "love" seem also at first glance to mobilize a very traditional ending. Regardless of how one reads the last lines, there is a glaring contrast between what on the surface seems to be a Victorian piety and what is quickly an irresolvable sense of "love." A similar unraveling occurs when one tries to pin down the image of maternality and interrelationship presented by the poem as a whole. When read in the light of Moore's relationship with Bishop and Crane, however, it is clear that Moore here represents the inevitability that she will lose them because of her own efforts to influence their subjectivities and her own attempts at disciplinary intimacy, but that through losing them she will herself in some way be "freed."[68]

Moore also credits Bishop and Crane with providing the motivation for her art: unlike the singular spinster who regenerates the nation through incorporating all in her path, Moore indicates here a shift toward a subjectivity and poetics based in reciprocity, struggle, self-sacrifice, and redemption—attributes critics often associate with Moore's supposed Christian piety. But instead of coming from religion, "freedom" here comes from other people. Thus, Moore acknowledges the degree to which her own subjectivity can be transformed through her relationship to others, in particular her "love" for the two younger women. And although Moore clearly puts herself in the position of mother here, it would be hard not to see in this poem a retrospection, as well, of Moore's own ambivalent yet ultimately productive experience of being mothered herself.[69]

Read in the most positive light, the "eggs," in freeing themselves from the mother's ambivalent influence, also free her from the culturally inscribed limitations placed on imagining female-female relationships—which can only be construed in terms of a controlling maternality—into a more ambiguous "love." The images of loss that haunt the last stanza might then indicate the degree to which Moore cannot wholly embrace this freeing. And here, I would argue, is another reason for Moore's use of the maternal metaphor, not just to signal her easy identification of herself as "mother" but instead to signify its limitations, as well as its power as *the* overarching frame within which to locate female-female relations.

With this context in mind, one can perhaps also understand why contemporary critics often read Bishop's poetic "Invitation," written seven years after "The Paper Nautilus" and itself another explicit gift, as an attempt at "freeing" Moore; a call to Marianne to "come out" and to self-identify as lesbian now that she has been freed from her own mother's domineering influence.[70] As I have argued above such readings are historically inaccurate because "outing one's self" in the post-1969 sense is not equivalent to coming out in the 1920s and 1930s (or 1940s)—yet clearly this poem represents an eroticized appeal. As Bishop describes the anticipation of all of Manhattan for Moore's arrival, she includes in it, as Erkkila notes, allusions to her own "eager" first meeting with Marianne:[71]

> for whom the agreeable lions lie in wait
> on the steps of the Public Library,
> eager to rise and follow through the doors
> up into the reading rooms. (83)

Marianne has the power to charm, perhaps even seduce, all she comes into contact with.

The poem also makes reference to the disagreements that had changed irrevocably Moore and Bishop's relationship, most notably their falling out over Bishop's "Roosters":

> We can sit down and weep; we can go shopping,
> or play at a game of constantly being wrong
> with a priceless set of vocabularies,
> or we can bravely deplore, but please
>   please come flying. (83)

Deplore what? By making the dramatic setting for the poem the Brooklyn Bridge (the poem begins "From Brooklyn, over the Brooklyn Bridge, on this fine morning, / please come flying") Bishop offers to Moore the possibility of self-location within the lineage of American poetry that begins with Walt Whitman and includes Hart Crane. The irony of this moment of canon formation is that it is also a moment of *queer* canonization: as Bishop and Moore were well aware, many of the luminaries of American poetry had at best a marginal relationship to heterosexuality. Bishop, through this playful, teasing invocation, seeks to insert, perhaps even to seduce, Moore into both a poetic and a queer tradition. If we remember the metaphoric resonance of crossing in Whitman and Crane's texts, "Invitation" dramatizes the difficulties in "bridging" the generational, political, and identificatory distances between Elizabeth and Marianne. It is this difficulty (which, as I have argued, at various moments both poets acknowledge) that produces Bishop's ambivalent yet deeply affectionate portrayal of Moore—and is not simply, as some critics would have it, a dismissal of Moore's subjectivity or a full-scale rebellion against it.[72] Furthermore, here Bishop extends the possibility of a *queer* (not a lesbian) identification to Moore, a queer identification that in its careful representations of Moore's outfits (for example, Moore's "black capeful of butterfly wings and bon-mots" [82]) and diction (as in the lines that describe boats on the river as "countless little pellucid jellies / in cut-glass epergnes dragging with silver chains" [82]) does not seek to denigrate Moore or to delineate Bishop's "distance" from her,[73] but instead to acknowledge and preserve Moore's uniqueness.[74] Despite Moore's "mock ferocious" refusals, then, Bishop invites (rather than incorporates) Moore into a larger queer tradition.

In rereading Moore and Bishop's personal and poetic interactions, my project provides an alternative, queer model for theorizing poetic influence. Such a model provides us with a means of recognizing the ways in which queers reproduce other queers, not outside of but in complex relation to oedipal, heterosexual norms. Instead of narrowing influence to *the* mother and *the* daughter, a queer, identificatory theory of influence enables us to appreciate the historically specific nature of Moore and Bishop's subjectivities and their intimacy, while illuminating the differences between their poetic projects. As I illustrate in this chapter, these differences are not just formal divergences or disagreements over literary "fashion" but instead are complex debates over power, nurture, and identity.

CONCLUSION

❧❀❧

We recruit!
—Lesbian Avengers

Just when I thought I couldn't stand it
another minute longer, Friday came.
(Accounts of that have everything all wrong.)
Friday was nice.
Friday was nice, and we were friends.
—Elizabeth Bishop, "Crusoe in England"

Poems like "An Octopus," about a glacier, or "Peter," about a cat, or "Marriage," about marriage, struck me, as they still do, as miracles of language and construction.—Elizabeth Bishop, "Efforts of Affection"

One underlying implication of this book concerns the historic specificity of various forms of incitement to identification, which is perhaps a less pejorative term than subjection. Throughout this volume I have described the ways in which particular versions of intersubjective relations, namely those between mothers and daughters, become, through shifts in the organization of space, models for female-female intersubjective relations more generally. These models are then promulgated through the use of commodity forms such as the serial novel, the handbook, and the accessories of identity that a movement such as the Girl Scouts creates and distributes. Literally then, commodity capitalism helps to promulgate particular models of subject formation through marketing particular commodities.

But I am also arguing something more theoretical about the relation of identification/desire and capitalism. Judith Butler has been criticized for the ways in which her model of the subject as performative echoes the ideals of consumerism. In the most severe critique of her work, performativity becomes another version of the supposed "freedom" of the marketplace, in which subjects can, through purchasing and displaying commodities, supposedly achieve agency and liberation.[1] Such a view, as I have argued in this book, relies on very narrow conceptions of what counts as actual work or labor, conceptions that have at their heart a heterosexist and essentialist vision of what counts as true (re)productivity. Butler has in her later works elaborated a complex theory of the subject, one that is careful to emphasize the limits of subjection. Her account, in my opinion, refutes any accusation of her model of the performativity of the subject as just another version of free agency.[2]

Yet all of these critics, including Butler, overlook what I assert is a key historical/theoretical connection that emerges at the turn of the twentieth century between the serial production of commodities and the serial production of individuals. There is some historical connection, in other words, between queer subjects and capitalism. Insofar as subjectivity becomes something that can be mass produced, it also becomes something distanced from heterosexual reproductivity, the oedipal family, and the "natural" body. Commodity culture allows for forms of "unnatural" subject production that challenge the supremacy of heterosexual reproduction.

Materially, emergent industrial capitalism opens up new semipublic/semiprivate spaces within which women are able to encounter other women and form homoerotic attachments through the dynamics of an "identificatory erotics." This erotics was originally intended to serve the needs of a new capitalist economy in which women would play a larger role outside the home. Ideologically, modernization provides new models of subject formation based on mass production, machines rather than bodies. Protolesbian figures such as the spinster, this book argues, were represented in the nineteenth century as harbingers and/or embodiments of this vision of modernization. In the early twentieth century, lesbian-identified modernists such as Gertrude Stein look to such figures to create a reverse discourse of lesbian identity.

More speculatively, this book raises but does not attempt fully to answer the question of the inherent queerness of *any* form of modern subject formation that relies on the blurring of the desire to be/have to produce in the subject an internalization of particular norms, whether or not it leads to a lesbian or gay public self-identification. Michael Warner, as I have noted above, addresses this question as it applies to (white) male modern subjects; I have described the specific conditions in which white (and to some degree African American) female subjects might have been able to utilize the queer desires produced through disciplinary intimacy toward more, or at times less, normalizing ends.

That African American women's experience of identificatory erotics has had different, racially specific limits indicates that although all forms of modern subject formation may include the possibility of the blurring of being/having, not all such subjects can easily embrace this erotics or find in lesbian identity a mode of resistance, rather than just an extension, of subjection. Furthermore, as I have noted above, although at times the protolesbian figure of the spinster, a specifically white identity, is linked, because of her "unnatural" relation to production and reproduction, to other minority subjects, her identity is still racially marked. Therefore, we should not expect to find in modernist African American lesbian-identified culture the same emphasis on the spinster as a reverse discourse that we do in the work of a white, lesbian-identified modernist such as Stein.[3] In this book I point out the degree to which fantasies of queer female autonomy (including self-making) are always already racialized because of the disparities between the ability of white women to take on the rhetoric of "independence" or "self-reliance" and the cultural, economic, and political reasons that African Americans have often been either unable or unwilling to find in this rhetoric avenues for imagining agency. Thus, although all forms of modern subject formation may produce (homo)erotic effects, we cannot claim that these effects are experienced identically by all subjects.

In chapter 6 I discuss what I term Bishop's idea of "invitation," of a model of affiliation that does not require assimilation. Such a model resembles other poststructuralist attempts to ameliorate or overcome the effects of power. Her version of Crusoe's description of Friday reflects a similar strategy. His language becomes distinctively flat and clichéd: "Friday was nice. / Friday was nice, and we were friends." Helen Vendler, describing this moment in the poem, writes, "Speechless with joy, Crusoe can speak only in the most vacant and consequently the most comprehensive of words. . . . Love escapes language."[4] Vendler, although she recognizes the great "love" between Crusoe and Friday, misses the larger point. In refusing to describe their relationship in language, Crusoe attempts to shield it from the gaze of the reader/colonizer, who can only reinscribe it into his/her own signifying system and thus deny its singular meaning. In other words, Crusoe tries to preserve the specificity and the reciprocity of a (homoerotic) relation that, within language and the signifying systems of

"English" versus "native," can only view Friday, and their relationship, as part of an imperial economy and worldview.

Oddly similar are Bishop's one-word glosses of Moore's poems. Although she declares Moore's poems "miracles of language and construction," she refuses to detail (and therefore presumably to circumscribe or co-opt) their actual content. She again retreats into a flatness of description designed, I believe, to preserve the specificity, complexity, and multiplicity of Moore's work.

Such strategies anticipate the valorization of silence and/or extreme understatement with which many postmodern artists and writers have engaged when struggling with the limits of language and the social. In terms of my argument in this book, one way out of the double bind of identification—the paradox that identificatory erotics, although they may produce queer desires, identifications, and sometimes identities, also seek to regulate and limit the subject—is to try to refuse to engage in any form of subjection. As Bishop's poem illustrates, however, to do so is often to refuse representation. Bishop's poem tries to maintain or preserve a sense of outside, an "island" space that resists, in its multiplicity, any attempts to conquer and control it. Given that this island space is also one that enables Crusoe and Friday's love to exist, we might think of this representational ethics as a version of a queer and/or postcolonial postmodernism. Similarly, Stein's idealization of erotic and economic reciprocity and (re)productivity in *Tender Buttons* might also constitute another aspect of such a postmodernism, especially in its multiple possibilities for interpretation. In its emphasis on excess signification and on constant change, we might argue, Stein's prose poem refuses any singular interpretation and therefore resists being (mis)appropriated and thus controlled.

It would be tempting to end this book on this idealist note, but such representational strategies are few and far between when we examine what might be termed lived experience in the social. Within a disciplinary structure of subject formation, as theorists such as Butler have asserted, resistance lies in how one performs or, to use José Muñoz's terms, disidentifies with dominant social norms. Identification becomes a way of negotiating the demands of power, a tactic, even as it also may reinscribe some aspects of the dominant structure. Because we cannot know in advance the ways in which subjects will identify queerly, we cannot know in advance the effects of the disciplinary. As I have discussed, intense subject-forming attempts at self-regulation such as the Girl Scouts', which also are attempting to produce a specifically white and middle-class version of the female subject, may end up instead producing a subject eager to identify with other social movements organized around less-normative aims. Desire to have produced out of, and inseparable from, desire to be, may lead to other kinds of identifications. In other words, queerness is one possible effect of normalization.

But of equal concern to my project has been the possibility that normalization is one effect of queerness, or at least of a lesbian identity that carries with it a set of norms into which one may be recruited. In constructing a genealogy of modern lesbian identity out of nineteenth-century sentimental culture, I in part have worked to emphasize the close historical connections between forms of subject formation that we have come to regard as imperial and those that we often regard as liberatory. At its most historically specific, this book details my argument that modern lesbian identity has its roots in an identificatory erotics that was explicitly designed to control and regulate the female subject, and that it constitutes in many ways an extension, rather than a departure, from this tradition. Nevertheless, the workings of power within modern lesbian or queer social movements also may have a multiplicity of effects. For example, a statement such as the Lesbian Avengers's intentionally ambiguous declaration, "We Recruit!" works both on and against the imperial and liberatory currents that I have described above. The statement signals a possible denial of difference implicit in the action of recruitment and, more positively perhaps, simultaneously provokes the fears and indicates the pleasures inherent in the idea that one can be seduced into an identity and a movement.[5]

NOTES

❧

Introduction

1 Louisa May Alcott, *Little Women* (New York: Modern Library, 1983), 537.

2 Lisa Duggan, "The Trials of Alice Mitchell: Sensationalism, Sexology, and the Lesbian Subject in Turn-of-the-Century America," *Signs* 18 (1993): 791.

3 For other examples of historical work that criticize an exclusive focus on the role of medical and sexological discourse in the formation of homosexual identity, see George Chauncey's discussion of a vernacular street culture that precedes medicalization in his *Gay New York: Gender, Urban Culture, and the Making of the Gay Male World, 1890–1940* (New York: Basic Books, 1994), or Lisa Duggan's understanding of the cross-textual influence of people's stories, sensationalist journalism, and sexology in *Sapphic Slashers: Sex, Violence, and American Modernity* (Durham: Duke University Press, 2000).

4 Richard Brodhead, *Cultures of Letters: Scenes of Reading and Writing in Nineteenth-Century America* (Chicago: University of Chicago Press, 1994).

5 Lisa L. Moore, *Dangerous Intimacies: Toward a Sapphic History of the British Novel* (Durham: Duke University Press, 1997), 11. Indeed, as David Halperin has recently argued, Foucault himself may have overestimated the extent to which the rise of the homosexual (and the heterosexual) was the first instance of sexual identity (Halperin, "Forgetting Foucault: Acts, Identities, and the History of Sexuality," *Representations* 63 [summer 1998]: 93–120).

6 For a related critique of this problem, see Martha Vicinus, "'They Wonder to Which Sex I Belong': The Historical Roots of the Modern Lesbian Identity," *Feminist Studies* 18 (1992): 467–97.

7 Marylynne Diggs, "Romantic Friends or a 'Different Race of Creatures?' The Representation of Lesbian Pathology in Nineteenth-Century America," *Fem-*

inist Studies 21.2 (summer 1995): 2; Terry Castle, *The Apparitional Lesbian: Female Homosexuality and Modern Culture* (New York: Columbia University Press, 1993).

8   Aside from the fact that this dangerously reproduces stereotypes about lesbian and, I would argue, queer invisibility (once again, lesbians are always invisible, not quite there, or hiding wraithlike), it also obscures the historical specificities of gender and sexual identity, a point Moore makes most forcefully in *Dangerous Intimacies* (7). On reading Castle's book, perhaps the most notable example of this trend, one discovers that the author's promises in the introduction never really pan out: most notably she states that she will prove that lesbians with clearly articulated identities, in some way analogous to those of lesbians of the 1920s and today, existed prior to the turn of the century. Although Castle tells quite well the story of Anne Lister, the cross-dressing English rake whose diaries reveal an intense set of desires for and relationships with women, she never explains how Lister possessed a sense of a lesbian identity; nor does Castle explain, as Amanda Berry has argued, how Lister's clear cross-gender identification (Lister fantasized that she was a man and took great pleasure in being mistaken for one) might have in fact been the location of whatever erotic identity she understood herself to have (Berry, "The Lesbian Focus," *Lesbian and Gay Studies Newsletter* [July 1994]: 25 – 26). For another critique of Castle, see Julie L. Abraham, "A Case of Mistaken Identity?" *Women's Review of Books* 11.10–11 (July 1994): 36–37.

More productively, Valerie Rohy argues for a focus on the workings of what she terms "lesbian desire" as a recurring trope or figure in American literature, and she sees this desire as linked to "the instability of figural language," what she terms "lesbian impossibility" (Rohy, *Impossible Women: Lesbian Figures and American Literature* [Ithaca: Cornell University Press, 2000], 147). Constituted through absence, abjection, or "as a set of sexual and discursive effects that patriarchal culture displaces onto figures of perverse female desire," lesbian desire for Rohy is the site of resistance to hegemonic, or what she calls "patriarchal," attempts to define reality (9). But it is also necessary for "sustain[ing] the symbolic order" as its other (15). Rohy's nuanced readings locate more specifically than Castle the rewards and problems of locating lesbian existence within absence.

9   Any list of such contributors would include Eve Kosofsky Sedgwick, *Between Men: English Literature and Male Homosocial Desire* (New York: Columbia University Press, 1985); Michael Moon, *Disseminating Whitman: Revision and Corporeality in "Leaves of Grass"* (Cambridge: Harvard University Press, 1991); and James Creech, *Closet Writing/Gay Reading: The Case of Melville's "Pierre"* (Chicago: University of Chicago Press, 1994).

10 Carroll Smith-Rosenberg, "The Female World of Love and Ritual," in *Disorderly Conduct: Visions of Gender in Victorian America* (New York: Ox-

ford University Press, 1985), 53–76; Lillian Faderman, *Surpassing the Love of Men: Romantic Friendship and Love between Women from the Renaissance to the Present* (New York: William Morrow, 1981).

11 Adrienne Rich, "Compulsory Heterosexuality and Lesbian Existence," in *Blood, Bread, and Poetry: Selected Prose, 1979–1985* (New York: Norton, 1986), 23–75.

12 For related critiques of Smith-Rosenberg, ones that inform my own, see Leila J. Rupp, "'Imagine My Surprise': Women's Relationships in Historical Perspective," *Frontiers* 5.3 (1981): 61–70, and Lisa Moore, "'Something More Tender Still Than Friendship': Romantic Friendship in Early-Nineteenth-Century England," *Feminist Studies* 18.3 (fall 1992): 499–520, and *Dangerous Intimacies,* esp. chapter 1.

13 Molly McGarry, "Female Worlds," *Journal of Women's History* 12.3 (2000): 9–12.

14 See Eve Kosofsky Sedgwick, *Epistemology of the Closet* (Berkeley: University of California Press, 1990), 2. See also Jonathan Ned Katz, *The Invention of Heterosexuality* (New York: Dutton, 1995).

15 For a related point, see Moore, *Dangerous Intimacies,* 11.

16 This is challenged by recent work in queer female homoerotic intimacies prior to the twentieth century: see especially Diggs, "Romantic Friends," and Karen Hansen, "'No *Kisses* Is Like Youres': An Erotic Friendship between Two African-American Women during the Mid-Nineteenth-Century," in *Lesbian Studies: A Feminist Studies Reader,* ed. Martha Vicinus (Bloomington: Indiana University Press, 1996), 178–207.

17 Moore, *Dangerous Intimacies,* 9–10.

18 Moore makes a similar point in "'Something More Tender Still Than Friendship,'" 503.

19 Recent reassessments of romantic friendship have found a wider range of societal responses to female-female intimacy than the blanket acceptance assumed by Smith-Rosenberg and Faderman, including responses that display anxiety about the degree to which such relationships might displace heterosexual marriage. There is also evidence that the women within these friendships at times seemed to recognize that there was a limit or a boundary to what they might safely express publicly without fear of sanction, which implies that there was a general social awareness of the possible transgressiveness of female-female relationships, at least if they crossed certain racial, class, and gender boundaries. As Duggan demonstrates in her analysis of the Alice Mitchell case, in late-nineteenth-century American culture when romantic friendships were formed across class or racial lines and/or when they transgressed the norms of gender they were considered to be outside the bounds of bourgeois respectability (see Duggan, "The Trials of Alice Mitchell" and *Sapphic Slashers*).

20 Brodhead, *Cultures of Letters*, esp. 43. Michel Foucault, *Discipline and Punish: The Birth of the Prison*, trans. Alan Sheridan (New York: Vintage Books, 1979).

21 Elaine Showalter even goes so far as to assert that maternality *was* sexuality for nineteenth-century (white, middle-class) women (Showalter, *Sister's Choice: Tradition and Change in American Women's Writing* [Oxford: Clarendon Press, 1991], 14).

22 Judith Butler, *The Psychic Life of Power: Theories in Subjection* (Stanford: Stanford University Press, 1997).

23 Ibid., 83–105.

24 Diana Fuss, *Identification Papers* (New York: Routledge, 1995), 4. For accounts of these theories of sympathy as they emerge in the eighteenth century and apply to both late-eighteenth- and early to mid-nineteenth-century American fiction, including "sentimental fiction," see Elizabeth Barnes, *States of Sympathy: Seduction and Democracy in the American Novel* (New York: Columbia University Press, 1997), and Lori Merish, *Sentimental Materialism: Gender, Commodity Culture, and Nineteenth-Century American Literature* (Durham: Duke University Press, 2000). Although in both cases these critics argue that previous theorists of sentimentality, including Brodhead, have failed adequately to explain the (psycho)dynamics of sentimental identification, neither connects the Scottish accounts of sympathy they outline to a psychoanalytic account of identification per se, although Merish does use the term "subjection" to describe one effect of sentimental identification. Furthermore, her account of what she terms "sentimental materialism" resembles to some degree a notion of female commodity fetishism based in lack, not of castration but of social power. Barnes's account of sentimental subject formation, on the other hand, seems to accept Brodhead's account of disciplinary intimacy, which Barnes juxtaposes against the daughter's heterosexual relation to a (father) figure. In other words, her description of the scene of female subject formation in sentimental fiction matches exactly the Freudian account of oedipalization: a daughter exchanges an essentially regressive and reactionary relation with a mother for one with a father substitute, rendering impossible any hope of resistance or agency. The girl merely becomes a copy of her mother, living with a father substitute in a family that mirrors the nation.

25 Sigmund Freud, *Group Psychology and the Analysis of the Ego* (New York: Norton, 1989), 46.

26 See especially Freud, "Three Essays on the Theory of Sexuality," in *On Sexuality: Three Essays on the Theory of Sexuality and Other Works*, ed. James Strachey and Angela Richards (Harmondsworth, Eng.: Penguin, 1986), 33–169; "The Ego and the Id," in *The Essentials of Psychoanalysis*, selected by Anna Freud (Harmondsworth, Eng.: Penguin, 1986), 439–83; "On Narcis-

sism," in *On Metapsychology: The Theory of Psychoanalysis,* ed. James Strachey and Angela Richards (Harmondsworth, Eng.: Penguin, 1984), 59–97; "Some Psychical Consequences of the Anatomical Distinction between the Sexes," in *On Sexuality,* 323–43; "Female Sexuality," in *On Sexuality,* 367–92; "Fragment of an Analysis of a Case of Hysteria: Dora," in *Case Histories I,* ed. James Strachey and Angela Richards (Harmondsworth, Eng.: Penguin, 1985), 31–164; "The Psychogenesis of a Case of Homosexuality in a Woman," *Case Histories II,* ed. James Strachey and Angela Richards (Harmondsworth, Eng.: Penguin, 1984), 367–400.

27 Freud, *Group Psychology,* 51.

28 As Freud insists: "It is easy to state in a formula the distinction between an identification with the father and the choice of the father as an object. In the first case one's father is what one would like to *be,* and in the second he is what one would like to *have*" (Freud, *Group Psychology,* 47).

29 In addition to Fuss and Butler, my work has been most influenced by Elin Diamond, *Unmaking Mimesis: Essays on Feminism and Theater* (New York: Routledge, 1997); José Esteban Muñoz, *Disidentifications: Queers of Color and the Performance of Politics* (Minneapolis: University of Minnesota Press, 1999); Ann Pellegrini, *Performance Anxieties: Staging Psychoanalysis, Staging Race* (New York: Routledge, 1997); Eve Kosofsky Sedgwick, "Tales of the Avunculate: *The Importance of Being Earnest,*" in *Tendencies* (Durham: Duke University Press, 1993), 52–72; and Michael Warner, "Homo-Narcissism; or, Heterosexuality," in *Engendering Men: The Question of Male Feminist Criticism,* ed. Joseph A. Boone and Michael Cadden (New York: Routledge, 1990), 190–206.

30 And this is often (but not always) defined in his work as gendered and (hetero)sexualized in advance of any encounter with the social.

31 See Julia Kristeva, "Woman's Time," in *The Kristeva Reader,* ed. Toril Moi (New York: Columbia University Press, 1986), 187–213, and "Stabat Mater," in *The Kristeva Reader,* 160–86, for quintessential examples of this trend.

32 See Leo Bersani, *Homos* (Cambridge: Harvard University Press, 1995), and Teresa de Lauretis, *The Practice of Love: Lesbian Sexuality and Perverse Desire* (Bloomington: Indiana University Press, 1994).

33 This is a point Muñoz makes quite forcefully in regard to de Lauretis in his recent transformative book, *Disidentifications* (13–15). Here my work most clearly signals its difference from that of de Lauretis, not only in my emphasis on media other than the visual but also in my insistence on identification as a model for subject formation. De Lauretis refuses identification and instead builds a theory of lesbian "perverse desire." Her rewriting of Freud's work on sexuality as without a normalizing hierarchy of psychosexual development (de Lauretis views "neurosis," "perversion," and "normal oedi-

palization" as existing on a continuum, not in a hierarchy as in Freud's work) seems ultimately untenable, especially in its inability to historicize the rise of psychoanalysis in relation to other social and cultural developments. More-over, de Lauretis's rejection of identification leads her finally to be unable to account for her own theory of subject formation: after numerous, often intriguing, critiques of classical psychoanalysis, feminist theory, and lesbian cultural texts, her chapter on her own alternative theory of perverse les-bian desire seems incomplete and without the persuasive force of the rest of critique.

34 See especially Fuss, *Identification Papers* and Muñoz, *Disidentifications.*

35 Here I am referring to Freud's formulation of (male) society as predicated on the repression of homosexuality, most notably in his *Group Psychology.*

36 Fuss, *Identification Papers,* 10.

37 And in this regard, my work draws on those queer theorists who have begun to analyze other sites of subject production. See, for example, Sedgwick, "Tales of the Avunculate," in which she revises the role of aunts and uncles, elucidating how through what she terms "queer tutelage" they offer children (queer) identificatory alternatives to the parental dyad.

38 Judith Butler, "Imitation and Gender Subordination," in *Inside/Out: Lesbian Theories, Gay Theories,* ed. Diana Fuss (New York: Routledge, 1991), 26.

39 Mikkel Borch-Jacobsen, *The Freudian Subject,* trans. Catherine Porter (Stan-ford: Stanford University Press, 1988). He writes, "If desire is satisfied in and through identification . . . it is not in the sense in which a desire somehow precedes its 'gratification,' since no desiring subject (no 'I,' no ego) precedes the mimetic identification: identification brings the desiring subject into be-ing, and not the other way around" (172). For detailed genealogies of these revisions of Freudian identification, ones to which I am greatly indebted, see Fuss, *Identification Papers;* Ruth Leys, "The Real Miss Beauchamp: The His-tory and Sexual Politics of the Multiple Personality Concept," in *Feminists Theorize the Political,* ed. Judith Butler and Joan W. Scott (New York: Rout-ledge, 1992), 167–214; and Diamond, *Unmaking Mimesis.*

40 Her work forms the basis of my thinking here: although its impressive tra-jectory resists summary, it could be viewed as an attempt to bring together the philosophical tradition, most notably Foucault (and increasingly Al-thusser), with a revised psychoanalysis that undoes the primacy of normative ideals of heterosexuality and of gender. See Butler, *Gender Trouble: Femi-nism and the Subversion of Identity* (New York: Routledge, 1989), *Bodies That Matter: On the Discursive Limits of "Sex"* (New York: Routledge, 1993), and especially *The Psychic Life of Power.*

41 This is a criticism Diana Fuss in *Identification Papers* (71) makes of Borch-Jacobsen, which could also be extended both to Butler and to some degree to

Fuss as well, who often herself implicitly draws on this revised account of the subject.

42 Most notably, Freud draws this mistaken conclusion in his analysis in "Fragment of an Analysis of a Case of Hysteria: Dora."

43 And it seems worth noting here that perhaps the inauguration of this disagreement comes from the famous "Douglas-Tompkins debate" over the effects of sentimental fiction (see Ann Douglas, *The Feminization of American Culture* [New York: Knopf, 1977], and Jane Tompkins, *Sensational Designs: The Cultural Work of American Fiction, 1790–1860* [New York: Oxford University Press, 1985]).

44 Moon's *Disseminating Whitman* is just one distinguished example.

45 For notable examples of this trend, see Barnes, *States of Sympathy*; Dana D. Nelson, "'No Cold or Empty Heart': Polygenesis, Scientific Professionalization, and the Unfinished Business of Male Sentimentalism," *differences: A Journal of Feminist Cultural Studies* 11.3 (1999): 29–56; and Glenn Hendler, "Tom Sawyer's Masculinity," *Arizona Quarterly* 49.4 (winter 1993): 33–59.

46 For a related critique of theories of sentimentality and domesticity, one that has deeply influenced my own, see Lora Romero, *Home Fronts: Domesticity and Its Critics in the Antebellum United States* (Durham: Duke University Press, 1997).

47 Tompkins, afterword to *The Wide, Wide World*, by Susan Warner (1850; New York: Feminist Press, 1987). Brodhead, *Cultures of Letters*, esp. 13–47.

48 For discussions of the novel, see especially Tompkins, *Sensational Designs*, 147–85, and Brodhead, *Cultures of Letters*. G. M. Goshgarian briefly notes the possibility of female-female desire, but his real focus is the quasi-incestuous relationship between father and daughter figures, and he views all relationships in the novel as always already about reproducing the oedipal father-daughter connection (Goshgarian, *To Kiss the Chastening Rod: Domestic Fiction and Sexual Ideology in the American Renaissance* [Ithaca: Cornell University Press, 1992], 80–81). Similarly, Barnes sees mother-daughter relationships in the sentimental novel as preoedipal forms of seduction, which lead only to the daughter's further entrapment within the patriarchal family through the mother's seductive influence, which motivates the daughter to follow her example (Barnes, *States of Sympathy*, esp. 107).

49 Michael Moon, "'The Gentle Boy from the Dangerous Classes': Pederasty, Domesticity, and Capitalism in Horatio Alger," in *The New American Studies,* ed. Philip Fisher (Berkeley: University of California Press, 1991), 261.

50 Warner, *The Wide, Wide World,* 152.

51 Sedgwick mentions the possible links between tears and masturbation in her essay "Jane Austen and the Masturbating Girl," in *Tendencies,* 109–29.

Tompkins is the only critic to even discuss (although it is only in passing) the possible effects of sentimentality and identification on sexuality: in her afterword to *The Wide, Wide World* she notes, "The tears that flow when Ellen is embraced by her mother and Alice Humphreys, and the physical intimacy that subsists between her and them, hint at an alternative to the brutal sexuality embodied by her male masters" (600).

52 Warner, *The Wide, Wide World,* 152.

53 This is a point that Barnes argues most forcefully, but in a way that reiterates a "blame the victim" ideology (*States of Sympathy,* 107). Daughters in her analysis of the sentimental novel have no way out, as motherly influence merely leads to further entrapment within a patriarchal family. See Chapter 2 of this volume, notes 8 and 10 for further discussion of this problem.

54 See especially Sedgwick, "Tales of the Avunculate," and Muñoz, *Disidentifications.*

55 Sedgwick, *Epistemology of the Closet.*

56 This is as opposed to Rich's idea of the continuum described in "Compulsory Heterosexuality and Lesbian Existence," in which all relationships between women are viewed as lesbian.

57 Nancy Fraser, "Rethinking the Public Sphere: A Contribution to the Critique of Actually Existing Democracy," in *Habermas and the Public Sphere,* ed. Craig Calhoun (Cambridge: MIT Press, 1993), 123.

58 As Fraser puts it, "Public spheres are not only arenas for the formation of discursive opinion; they are arenas for the formation and enactment of social identities" ("Rethinking the Public Sphere," 125).

59 This is true even as Miriam Hansen admits that it may be difficult to tell "partial publics," those that are simply part of industrial capitalist culture, from "counterpublics." Mary P. Ryan in her history of "women in public" in nineteenth-century U.S. culture also echoes this move (Hansen, foreword to *Public Sphere and Experience: Toward an Analysis of the Bourgeois and Proletarian Public Sphere,* by Oskar Negt and Alexander Kluge [Minneapolis: University of Minnesota Press, 1993], esp. xxxviii; Mary Ryan, *Women in Public: Between Banners and Ballots, 1825–1880* [Baltimore: Johns Hopkins University Press, 1990]).

60 For two feminist revisions of the private sphere, see Ryan, *Women in Public,* and Linda Kerber, "Separate Spheres, Female Worlds, Woman's Place: The Rhetoric of Women's History," *Journal of American History* 75 (June 1989): 9–39. As Gillian Brown notes as well, to valorize the private sphere is also to risk reiterating a dangerous fantasy of the supposed division of social spaces, one that perpetuates the "othering" of the private as outside the purview of the political (Brown, *Domestic Individualism: Imagining Self in Nineteenth-Century America* [Berkeley: University of California Press, 1990]).

At least since the time of Jacksonian democracy, as Ryan has illustrated, women were active in the public sphere, albeit in ways that were not always recognized by the masculinist arbiters of publicity (and by women themselves, albeit for different reasons) as *public*. For women, claiming public power was often a dangerous and self-defeating option. Instead, they created spheres of public influence through mobilizing the ideology of the domestic sphere for political aims. Furthermore, as Kerber, among others, notes, maintaining a "domestic sphere" allowed these white, middle-class women to articulate their supposed differences from working-class white and African American women, who did not have the privilege of occupying such a space but had to work and display themselves "in public" (Kerber, "Separate Spheres").

Chapter 1. *"Single White Female": The Sexual Politics of Spinsterhood in Harriet Beecher Stowe's* Oldtown Folks

1 Brodhead, *Cultures of Letters,* esp. 18–27, 74.

2 Stowe, *Oldtown Folks* (1869; New Brunswick: Rutgers University Press, 1987). Subsequent citations appear as parenthetical page references in the text.

3 Hortense Spillers, "Interstices: A Small Drama of Words," in *Power and Danger: Exploring Female Sexuality,* ed. Carole S. Vance (London: Pandora Press, 1984), 73–100, and "Mama's Baby, Papa's Maybe: An American Grammar Book," *Diacritics* 17.2 (summer 1987): 65–81. Interestingly, one might see this struggle as having similarities to the present-day fight for gay and lesbian marriages, where the same kinds of arguments about citizenship are advanced.

4 And this difference in regard to marriage is rewritten in the mid-twentieth century, when white, middle-class women once again start agitating for the "right to a career" and "freedom from the household," whereas for black women the right to stay home and care for their own children, as opposed to those of their white employers, is a much more pressing concern. For one discussion of this difference and its implications for black women's relationship to white, middle-class feminism, see bell hooks, "Homeplace: A Site of Resistance," in *Yearning: Race, Gender, and Cultural Politics* (Boston: South End Press, 1990), 41–49.

5 A point that Hazel Carby was perhaps the first to argue in her influential study *Reconstructing Womanhood: The Emergence of the Afro-American Woman Novelist* (New York: Oxford University Press, 1987), esp. 79–80. See also Ann duCille, *The Coupling Convention: Sex, Text, and Tradition in Black Women's Fiction* (New York: Oxford University Press, 1993), 45–47.

6　I have found only one spinster character in a nineteenth-century novel written by an African American woman that replicates the same stereotypes. In
Mrs. A. E. Johnson's *Clarence and Corinne; or, God's Way* (1890; New York:
Oxford University Press, 1988), Miss Rachel Penrose's inability to mother
the orphan girl Corinne and, in particular, her abuse of Corinne's labor mirrors Miss Asphyxia's failures with Tina. Corinne is eventually rescued by a
kind set of spinster sisters, Mary and Helen Grey. Although Helen Grey is a
teacher, an approved occupation, Mary is an invalid, an identity the status of
which one could argue is centrally connected to issues of labor and leisure.
The sister-couple act as a foil to Miss Penrose. But in this novel, as in many
of the others written by African American women during this period, all of
the characters are not racially marked, which makes it difficult to claim Miss
Penrose as an example of an African American spinster who follows the same
tropes as those established for white characters. Within African American
women's novels written with explicitly black characters during the postbellum period, no such spinster characters exist.

7　Berlant develops Bhabha's understanding of the ideological function of the
stereotype, what she specifically terms "stereotypic embodiment" (Berlant,
The Queen of America Goes to Washington City, [Durham: Duke University
Press, 1997], 83–144). Homi Bhabha writes that "the stereotype . . . is a
form of knowledge and identification that vacillates between what is always
'in place,' already known, and something that must be anxiously repeated"
(Bhabha, *The Location of Culture* [New York: Routledge, 1994], 66).

8　See Berlant, *The Queen of America*, esp. 83–144.

9　Bhabha, *The Location of Culture*, 67.

10　This is Berlant's term for the ways in which subjects identify with what seem
to be harmful and often devastating signifiers (*The Queen of America*, 103).

11　And, as Cathy N. Davidson notes, even in the late eighteenth century the
"pervasive cultural ridicule" surrounding spinsterhood "drove more than
one sentimental heroine into the arms of the seducer" (Davidson, *Revolution
and the Word: The Rise of the Novel in America* [New York: Oxford University Press, 1986], 121). For a groundbreaking anthology of American
short fiction about unmarried women, see Susan Koppelman, ed., *Old
Maids: Short Stories by Nineteenth Century U.S. Women Writers* (London:
Pandora Press, 1984), in which Sedgwick's "Old Maids" is reprinted.

12　My definition of "spinster" includes unmarried women but does not include
widows or adolescent girls, as some critics do. I would also distinguish the
spinster from the "bachelor-girl" type identified by Lynn Wardley, a postbellum American young woman who self-identifies as outside the marriage
market and as "before marriage" in a way that may or may not open up alternative gender and sexual possibilities for her. According to Wardley,
the bachelor-girl also identifies herself against the old maid or spinster type

(Wardley, "Bachelors in Paradise: The State of a Theme," in *The Return of Thematic Criticism*, ed. Werner Sollors [Cambridge: Harvard University Press, 1993], 217–41).

13 Dale Bauer, after analyzing representations of spinsters in nineteenth-century writing, concludes that "remaining outside the marriage market promises a way to subvert a rigidified nineteenth-century culture" (Bauer, "The Politics of Collaboration in *The Whole Family*," in *Old Maids to Radical Spinsters: Unmarried Women in the Twentieth-Century Novel,* ed. Laura L. Doan [Urbana: University of Illinois Press, 1991], 108).

14 Coverture laws, which subsumed married women's identities under those of their husbands and thereby denied such women the right to own, inherit, or bequeath property, did not apply to single women, but spinsters did not have the rights of citizenship afforded to male property owners. And rarely did they inherit property in the first place. For more on the *feme covert* and the *feme sole*, see Linda Kerber, *Women of the Republic: Intellect and Ideology in Revolutionary America* (New York: Norton, 1980), esp. 120–21, and Nancy F. Cott, *The Bonds of Womanhood: 'Woman's Sphere' in New England, 1780–1835* (New Haven: Yale University Press, 1977).

15 Alice Kessler-Harris, *Out to Work: A History of Wage-Earning Women in America* (New York: Oxford University Press, 1982), 98.

16 Ibid., 98. Indeed, the "problem of single women" had been a visible part of public debate in both England and the United States since at least the 1830s.

17 For more on this, see Martha Banta, *Imaging American Women: Idea and Ideals in Cultural History* (New York: Columbia University Press, 1987); Smith-Rosenberg, *Disorderly Conduct*, esp. 245–96; and Faderman, *Surpassing the Love of Men*, esp. 231–94.

18 Joan D. Hedrick, *Harriet Beecher Stowe: A Life* (New York: Oxford University Press, 1994), 342. It also combines a number of genres: while ostensibly it is a historical romance, in its attention to the local it is often read as an early example of regionalism. I am arguing here that it also extends as it modifies the conventions of antebellum sentimental fiction.

19 Catharine E. Beecher and Harriet Beecher Stowe, *The American Woman's Home, or, Principles of Domestic Science; Being A Guide to the Formation and Maintenance of Economical, Healthful[,] Beautiful and Christian Homes* (1869; Hartford: Stowe-Day Foundation, 1991).

20 Joseph S. Van Why, in his introduction to the recent reprint of *The American Woman's Home*, argues that Harriet Beecher Stowe herself had little to do with writing the book but that because of her popularity following the publication of *Uncle Tom's Cabin* in 1852, Catharine Beecher wanted to capitalize on her sister's fame by using her name to help sales. This is not to say that Stowe was not aware of and involved in the ideas and ideals outlined in the guide; on the contrary, her own writings in the *Atlantic Monthly* of the same

period and earlier reflect the values expressed in *The American Woman's Home:* thrift, frugality, love, and guidance, but always in moderation (Van Why, introduction to *American Woman's Home,* n.p.). For examples of this writing, see Stowe [Christopher Crowfield, pseud.], *House and Home Papers* (Boston: Fields and Osgood, 1864).

21 Beecher and Stowe, *American Woman's Home,* 20.

22 Stowe and Beecher were certainly not alone in their professionalization of motherhood: as many critics have noted, professionalizing motherhood was a dominant concern of many nineteenth-century women writers and social activists (for one example, see Elizabeth K. Helsinger, Robin Lauterbach Sheets, and William Veeder, eds., *The Woman Question. Vol. 2: Social Issues, 1837–1883* (New York: Garland Publishing, 1983), esp. 140–43).

23 Dorothy Yost Deegan even goes so far as to create a category of spinster characters based solely on these "quaint" names, as outlined in her *The Stereotype of the Single Woman in American Novels: A Social Study with Implications for the Education of Women* (New York: King's Crown Press, 1951), 82–83. We might gather from her ideas that naming itself, the process of quaint/queer naming of spinsters, is part of the signifying process of establishing stereotypes.

24 These descriptions of Miss Asphyxia's nature match what Bauer, writing in reference to Mary Wilkins Freeman, has argued is the significance of the unmarried woman in postbellum writing. She states: "The spinster . . . was invented in the nineteenth century, coincident with the change from household production to production at 'the Works'" (Bauer, "The Politics of Collaboration," 115). The descriptions also make Miss Asphyxia an embodiment of the original definition of a "spinster." As Julie A. Matthei notes, the term finds its beginnings in extradomestic labor: "Due to the prevalence of husbandless women in spinning, the word spinster, originally appended to a woman's name to denote her occupation, came to mean an unmarried woman" (Matthei, *An Economic History of Women in America: Women's Work, the Sexual Division of Labor, and the Development of Capitalism* [New York: Schocken Books, 1982], 64).

25 Brodhead, *Cultures of Letters,* 31.

26 Ibid.

27 For accounts of the transformation of this sphere, see, among others, Matthei, *An Economic History of Women,* 101–40.

28 I am not alone in identifying Miss Asphyxia's form of childrearing as tied to specific ideas of both economics and discipline. For a somewhat different analysis of these issues, one that attributes her views to Calvinism and patriarchy, see Berkson, introduction to *Oldtown Folks,* xxxiii.

29 Gillian Brown, *Domestic Individualism,* 18. Stowe is certainly not the only writer for whom this distinction held true; for example, as Karen Sanchez-

Eppler has recently argued, Lydia Maria Child viewed women and slaves as linked through the economic effects of marriage/bondage, another kind of mixing of what was supposedly sacred; that is, marriage, through patriarchy, gets intermingled with the corruption of the market (Sanchez-Eppler, *Touching Liberty: Abolition, Feminism, and the Politics of the Body* [Berkeley: University of California Press, 1993], esp. 14–49). That this often led to the empowerment of white women at the expense of black women is central to Hazel Carby's and, most recently, Robyn Wiegman's critique of sentimentality.

As Wiegman uncomfortably yet accurately points out, even contemporary feminist work that tries to articulate the complex interrelationships between race and gender ideology may end up sacrificing one at the expense of the other. Her book charts the ways in which black women are elided by both black male and white feminist discourse at the same time that each endeavor invokes black femininity for its own purposes. Although Wiegman indicts this critical practice, she also notes that the narrative and political strategy of illuminating or "making visible" one identity through another is an inevitable consequence of modern and postmodern white feminist critical practice, one that repeats even as it critiques nineteenth-century white women for doing the same things. I cannot help but be struck by the proximity of Wiegman's criticism, as well as the methods of her project, to my own: in finding sexuality through its relation to ideologies of race and gender and labor in nineteenth-century texts, I, too, run the risk of rendering one less visible at the same time that I foreground what in this case are the urgencies of an antihomophobic project. At the same time, my hope for this analysis is that although it may repeat this inevitable chain of substitution it may also signal the points at which racializing, sexualizing, and gender-producing discourses overlap, and the points at which a coalitional politics of resistance might find its inspiration. For Wiegman's argument, see especially *American Anatomies: Theorizing Race and Gender* (Durham: Duke University Press, 1995), 179–202. See also Carby, *Reconstructing Womanhood*.

30 Lora Romero, "Bio-Political Resistance in Domestic Ideology and *Uncle Tom's Cabin*," *American Literary History* 1.4 (winter 1989): 715–34. See also Romero's *Home Fronts*, 70–88, for a revised and slightly different version of this argument.

31 Hedrick, *Harriet Beecher Stowe*, 343.

32 In other words, already in 1869 we have an example of what Mark Seltzer has termed, in *Bodies and Machines* (New York: Routledge, 1992), "the machine-body complex."

33 Native Americans are more complicated in the novel because while they, too, seem to be overly reproductive they are also continuously described as dying out or as extinct already.

34 For a discussion of the tradition of these kinds of representations, see Spillers, "Mama's Baby, Papa's Maybe"; Wiegman, *American Anatomies;* and
Sanchez-Eppler, *Touching Liberty.*

35 Brown, *Domestic Individualism,* 30.

36 Ibid., 41–42.

37 Significantly, this is the only representation approaching slavery that the
book allows, even though it is set in the post-Revolutionary period. That
Stowe would make this an example of black-on-black enslavement thus
seems particularly troubling. At the same time, it was not entirely uncommon
for free black women in the antebellum South to purchase black male slaves
as husbands; for descriptions of such relationships, see Suzanne Lebsock,
The Free Women of Petersburg: Status and Culture in a Southern Town,
1784–1860 (New York: Norton, 1985).

38 Smith-Rosenberg, *Disorderly Conduct,* 235.

39 Michel Foucault, *The History of Sexuality. Vol. 1: An Introduction,* trans.
Robert Hurley (London: Penguin, 1978).

40 Interestingly, "brooding" also connotes mental activity, thinking, and self-
reflection—the kinds of activities Stowe's middle-class mothers are supposed
to practice. I am grateful to Michael Moon for pointing this out.

41 That old maids were centrally defined by their supposed lack of interest in
male/female sexual interactions seems to have been a cultural trope throughout the nineteenth century. In his discussion of how country bumpkins were
thought to embody a more active heterosexuality in nineteenth-century
American writing, Alfred Habegger cites a passage that makes old maids the
opposite of female heterosexual availability: "'I don't mean to say that Judy
had any thing agin sparking in a re'lar way, on Sunday nights in the east
room, when the paper curtains was all down and the old folks had gone to
bed. It cum kinder nateral to set up til two or three o'clock, and Judy warnt
by no means old-maidish.'" (Ann Stephens, *High Life in New York. By Jona-*
than Slick, Esq., of Weathersfield, Connecticut [New York: Edward Stephens, 1843], 12), cited in Habegger, *Gender, Fantasy, and Realism in Ameri-*
can Literature (New York: Columbia University Press, 1982), 307 n. 4.

42 Romero, "Bio-Political Resistance," 720.

43 G. J. Barker-Benfield, *The Horrors of the Half-Known Life: Male Attitudes*
toward Women and Sexuality in Nineteenth-Century America (New York:
Harper and Row, 1976), esp. 118.

44 Eve Kosofsky Sedgwick, "Jane Austen and the Masturbating Girl" and "Epidemics of the Will," both in *Tendencies.*

45 Brown, *Domestic Individualism,* 47.

46 Moreover, the similarities between this scene and the scene in *Uncle Tom's*
Cabin where Simon Legree burns the lock of Little Eva's hair that Tom had
preserved connect Miss Asphyxia directly to Legree, emphasizing her impli-

cation in a market in people—an implication that in Legree's case paradoxically also racializes him (I am grateful to Benjamin Weaver for pointing this out to me). In other words, Legree, and by analogy Miss Asphyxia, are connected to African Americans because both are viewed by Stowe as complicit and caught in market relations, just as are slaves.

47 In this way, Miss Mehitable bears a strong resemblance to the New Woman, whose desire to enter the public sphere was also thought to masculinize her.

48 Romero, *Home Fronts*, 22.

Chapter 2. *"Trying All Kinds": Louisa May Alcott's Pedagogic Erotics*

1 Martha Vicinus's work in Britain remains the most comprehensive in this area, see her *Independent Women: Work and Community for Single Women, 1850–1920* (Chicago: University of Chicago Press, 1985). For historical accounts of this shift in the U.S. context, with which my work is in dialogue, see among others, Smith-Rosenberg, *Disorderly Conduct*, 245–96; Estelle Freedman, "Separatism as Strategy: Female Institution Building and American Feminism, 1870–1930," *Feminist Studies* 5 (fall 1979): 512–29; Kathryn Kish Sklar, "Hull House in the 1890s: A Community of Women Reformers," *Signs* 10 (summer 1985): 658–77; Joanne J. Meyerowitz, *Women Adrift: Independent Wage Earners in Chicago, 1880–1930* (Chicago: University of Chicago Press, 1988); Kessler-Harris, *Out to Work*; Helen Lefkowitz Horowitz, *Alma Mater: Design and Experience in the Women's Colleges from Their Nineteenth-Century Beginnings to the 1930s* (New York: Knopf, 1984) and *The Power and Passion of M. Carey Thomas* (New York: Knopf, 1994); Brodhead, *Cultures of Letters*; Barbara Sicherman, "Sense and Sensibility: A Case Study of Women's Reading in Late-Victorian America," in *Reading in America: Literature and Social History*, ed. Cathy N. Davidson (Baltimore: Johns Hopkins University Press, 1989), 201–25, "Reading *Little Women*: The Many Lives of a Text," in *U.S. History as Women's History: New Feminist Essays*, ed. Linda K. Kerber, Alice Kessler-Harris, and Kathryn Kish Sklar (Chapel Hill: University of North Carolina Press, 1995), 245–66, and "Reading and Ambition: M. Carey Thomas and Female Heroism," in *American Quarterly* 45.1 (March 1993): 73–103; Nancy Sahli, "Smashing: Women's Relationships before the Fall," *Chrysalis* 8 (1977): 18–27; Blanche Wiesen Cook, "Female Support Networks and Political Activism: Lillian Wald, Crystal Eastman, Emma Goldman," *Chrysalis* 3 (1977): 43–61; Mari Jo Buhle, *Women and American Socialism, 1870–1920* (Urbana: University of Illinois Press, 1981); and Molly Ladd-Taylor, *Mother-Work: Women, Child Welfare, and the State, 1890–1930* (Urbana: University of Illinois Press, 1994).

For an illuminating and thorough account of the importance of the Civil War itself as providing a literal and symbolic form of access to the public sphere for women and for Alcott in particular, and one whose analysis of Alcott's relation herself to gender and sexuality at times is significantly parallel to my own readings of its workings within Alcott's texts, see Elizabeth Young, *Disarming the Nation: Women's Writing and the American Civil War* (Chicago: University of Chicago Press, 1999). Young convincingly argues that these forms of access "inverted" (to use her terms), however temporarily, conventional gender, sexual, class, and even racial boundaries.

2 Alcott, *Little Men: Life at Plumfield with Jo's Boys* (1871; New York: Signet, 1986), *Jo's Boys, and How They Turned Out* (1886; New York: Signet, 1987), and *An Old-Fashioned Girl* (1870; New York: Grosset and Dunlap, 1980). Subsequent citations of these works appear as parenthetical page references in the text.

3 Alcott, *Diana and Persis* (1879; New York: Arno Press, 1978), and *Work: A Story of Experience,* ed. Sarah Elbert (1873; New York: Schocken Books, 1977). Subsequent citations appear as parenthetical page references in the text.

4 See Glenn Hendler, "The Limits of Sympathy: Louisa May Alcott and the Sentimental Novel," *American Literary History* 3 (winter 1991): 685–706, for a related reading of the ending of this novel.

5 Besides Brodhead (who in *Cultures of Letters* argues that Marmee and the March family represent a relaxing of disciplinarity—a post–Civil War liberalization, so to speak), see Carolyn Heilbrun, *Reinventing Womanhood* (New York: Norton, 1979), esp. 212, and Linda K. Kerber, who in "Can a Woman Be an Individual? The Limits of Puritan Tradition in the Early Republic," *Texas Studies in Literature and Language* 25.1 (spring 1983): 165–78, sees in Alcott the remnants of the Puritan insistence on "restraint, resignation, and endurance" (166).

6 Elizabeth Barnes, "The Whipping Boy of Love: Atonement and Aggression in Alcott's Fiction," *Journal X: A Journal in Culture and Criticism* (1997): 12. In so doing, Barnes extends her critique of antebellum sentimental fiction, which she views as always reinforcing the patriarchal family and, by extension, a model of national politics based on this family, in which "sympathy" / identification can only mean repression/oppression (see Barnes, *States of Sympathy,* esp. xi). I am arguing instead that at least in the postbellum period, the family begins to be replaced and interpenetrated by other semipublic/semiprivate spheres, which challenge its centrality and its normative power even as they at times repeat it.

7 Young, *Disarming the Nation,* 107–8, 83. Young's interpretation remains perhaps the most nuanced and comprehensive discussion of Alcott's construction of gender, especially in regard to race and class; however, she can-

not fully account for the ways in which sexuality operates as a reverse discourse in Alcott's texts (as opposed to in Alcott's own life), which then, I would argue, in turn challenges to some degree domesticity's attempts to stabilize gender and social relations. Nevertheless, as will become more clear below, Young's critique of the limits of Jo's family-nation underlines the degree to which queer forms of gender and sexual identification can be complicit in, rather than challenging of, other kinds of normalization.

8 Barnes's unironic, repeated use of the term "self-abuse" as a synonym for the identificatory subject-forming structure of Alcott's fiction, without any acknowledgment of its nineteenth-century connotations as a pejorative term for masturbation, epitomizes this inability to consider pleasure, even the pleasures of power. What distinguishes the (self-)abuse of disciplinary identification from (self-)pleasure? In her emphasis only on the violence of the disciplinary structure, Barnes reiterates an account of the (female) subject as inherently a victim and as always contributing to her own victimization. In other words, such a view of power can only be negative: it cannot imagine a positive view of its workings, and in so doing it risks perpetuating this negative structure. Nevertheless, I agree with Barnes that in submitting to the dictates of disciplinary power, the self must reform itself in ways that often require a denial of various kinds of difference.

9 Butler, *Gender Trouble.* As her work argues, there is no "outside" to power, thus, I am not looking for a model of the subject that posits such an outside to the market, disciplinary culture, etc.

10 My understanding of this dichotomy is based on the work, most centrally, of G. Brown, *Domestic Individualism;* Seltzer, *Bodies and Machines;* and in relation to Alcott specifically, Hendler, "The Limits of Sympathy." Brown traces the term "possessive individualism" to the work of C. B. McPherson. As she describes it, "According to this concept of self evolving from the seventeenth century, every man has property in himself and thus the right to manage himself, his labor, and his property as he wishes" (2). Brown notes that this was most obviously a masculine form of subjectivity—women legally were the possessions of their husbands, rendering self-possession an impossibility—but she convincingly argues that that did not mean that the domestic sphere was free from what she terms "possessive" relations. Describing subjectivity at the turn of the century, Seltzer details what he terms "tension . . . between laissez-faire or *possessive individualism and market culture,* on the one side, and what might be called *disciplinary individualism and machine culture,* on the other, that is perpetually reenacted in the paradoxical economy of consumption" (58). Most notably, in his insightful essay on *Work,* Hendler discusses what he terms the "novel's attempt to reconcile normative femininity with individuality" (700), and reiterates the gendered oppositions between a feminine self-loss and the ideals of liberal individual-

ism (which he never explicitly identifies as "masculine" but associates with the nonfeminine). However, while Hendler sees these two forms of subjectivity as ultimately irreconcilable in Alcott except at two moments of what he terms "feminine—even feminist—collectivity" (699), I read Alcott's texts as deconstructing what is shown to be a false opposition between self-loss and self-possession. When I argue that these seemingly distinct models of subjectivity carry gendered valences, that is not to say that they do not also reach across the lines of gender. For example, much of domestic ideology (and its criticism) idealizes self-loss in men (as antipatriarchal and antimarket) (Tompkins, *Sentimental Designs*); such forms of self-loss are also often read by critics of sentimentality as dangerous forms of (ef)feminization (as indicative of an absorption in commodified, cheapened emotion) (Douglas *Feminization of American Culture*).

11 This is a paradox that both Brown and Howard Horwitz's work makes abundantly evident: to make yourself is to erase yourself and to erase yourself is to make yourself. Increasingly, in the late nineteenth century, I would argue, this becomes also the paradox of what Seltzer terms "market" versus "machine" culture: to make yourself is always already to submit to another's image, what for Seltzer becomes paradigmatically the manufactured "type" (G. Brown, *Domestic Individualism;* Horwitz, *By the Law of Nature: Form and Value in Nineteenth-Century America* [New York: Oxford University Press, 1991]; Seltzer, *Bodies and Machines*).

12 Harriet Beecher Stowe, *Uncle Tom's Cabin* (1851; New York: Norton, 1994); Kelley, *Megda* (1891; New York: Oxford University Press, 1988). Subsequent citations appear as parenthetical page references in the text.

13 Claudia Tate, *Psychoanalysis and Black Novels: Desire and the Protocols of Race* (New York: Oxford University Press, 1998), 23.

14 I am not the only critic to notice the similarities between Alcott's project and earlier examples of sentimental fiction. In addition to Brodhead, *Cultures of Letters,* Susan K. Harris views *Work* as a "late didactic novel" in her *Nineteenth-Century American Women's Novels: Interpretive Strategies* (Cambridge: Cambridge University Press, 1990), 163; Donna M. Campbell argues that *Little Women* subverts as it recycles the conventions of the sentimental genre, and in particular those established by *The Wide, Wide World,* see her "Sentimental Conventions and Self-Protection: *Little Women* and *The Wide, Wide World*," *Legacy* 11.2 (1994): 118–29. See also Barnes, "The Whipping Boy of Love," and Young, *Disarming the Nation.*

15 Ann B. Murphy, "The Borders of Ethical, Erotic, and Artistic Possibilities in *Little Women,*" *Signs: Journal of Women in Culture and Society* 15.3 (1990): 564.

16 Smith-Rosenberg, *Disorderly Conduct,* 53–76.

17 Judith Fetterley, "*Little Women*: Alcott's Civil War," *Feminist Studies* 5.2 (summer 1979): 379.

18 Showalter simply calls relationships between women in Alcott "passionate friendships" and leaves it at that, demonstrating how Smith-Rosenberg's refusal to investigate what counts as sexuality and sex in nineteenth-century white women's relationships lets critics merely pay lip service to such homoerotic intensities (Showalter, ed., introduction to *Alternative Alcott*, by Louisa May Alcott [New Brunswick: Rutgers University Press, 1988], ix–xliii).

19 Showalter (*Sister's Choice*, 14) attributes to sentimental fiction the status of the "preoedipal" mother/daughter bliss; however, I would not go so far as to make it a prototype for psychoanalysis, in part because of my need to think historically about identification, and in part because although Marmee's relationship to her "girls" is often extremely tender/erotic, it is also fraught with the urgencies and disappointments of power, impoverishment, and anger—attributes that feminist psychoanalytic accounts sometimes, but not always, leave out.

20 Horowitz, *Alma Mater*, 17.

21 Vicinus, *Independent Women*, 163–210.

22 Stephen Mailloux links Alcott to the counterpublic space of the girls' reform schools in order to demonstrate the ways in which reading and disciplinarity were explicitly linked, both for Alcott and for postbellum nineteenth-century U.S. culture (see Mailloux, "The Rhetorical Use and Abuse of Fiction: Eating Books in Late-Nineteenth-Century America," *boundary* 2 17.1 (1990): 133–57).

23 Borch-Jacobsen, *The Freudian Subject*, 45.

24 For two notable examples, see Linda Zwinger, *Daughters, Fathers, and the Novel: The Sentimental Romance of Heterosexuality* (Madison: University of Wisconsin Press, 1991), 52–75, and Barnes, "The Whipping Boy of Love," 9.

25 Karen Haltunnen, "The Domestic Drama of Louisa May Alcott," *Feminist Studies* 10.2 (summer 1984): 250.

26 Barnes, "The Whipping Boy of Love," 6.

27 A. Murphy, "Borders," 576.

28 Campbell, "Sentimental Conventions." I find this analysis useful in elucidating Alcott's use of genre conventions to "queer" ends.

29 Brodhead also makes this point, although he does not notice the complexities of identification and desire that this process of becoming enables (Brodhead, *Cultures of Letters*, 71). Jennifer Doyle mobilizes Judith Butler's psychoanalytically informed idea of melancholic identification to argue that, in fact, Jo becomes Beth after Beth's death. Although this is a persuasive reading of Jo's transformation into a more domesticated "little woman," a read-

ing whose understanding of the erotics of identification informs my own, it also challenged me to consider more fully Jo's narrative trajectory from girl to mother/teacher as a whole, and to try to place the processes of identification within the specific historical context of postbellum U.S. culture (Doyle, "Jo March's Love Poems," paper delivered at the Duke University Women's Studies Program Graduate Conference, Durham, October 11, 1994).

30 Unlike the model of the spinster (an unmarried woman) I employed in my first chapter, Aunt March is a widow. That her relationship to married heterosexuality has fully ended is symbolized by the fact that she can no longer fit into her wedding ring: it is "too small now for her fat finger" (*Little Women*, 238), although the memory of her marriage is obviously a treasured one.

31 To which Amy is shown to respond with much more success, in part because she is motivated by the idea of material rewards. This competition between the girls culminates in the moment when Aunt March chooses Amy over Jo to go Europe, enabling Amy to pursue her artistic longings.

32 Sharon O'Brien contextualizes Louisa May Alcott and, by proxy, Jo's persona through a discourse of the "tomboyism" that predominated in late-nineteenth-century bourgeois culture. As I discussed above, white, middle-class society was concerned with what it perceived to be the dying out of the "white race," in part because of the "constitutional" weaknesses of many white, middle-class women. Encouraging girls to be "tomboys," to run and play like boys, was thought to make them healthier, more stable mothers. Certainly Jo reflects this trend; however, O'Brien does not examine the ways in which gender and sexual identifications might intersect or diverge in the "tomboy" as Alcott portrays her (O'Brien, "Tomboyism and Adolescent Conflict: Three Nineteenth-Century Case Studies," in *Woman's Being, Woman's Place: Female Identity and Vocation in American History*, ed. Mary Kelley [Boston: G. K. Hall, 1979], 351–72).

Alternatively, Lisa Duggan in *Sapphic Slashers* discusses the ways in which romantic friendships between white, middle-class girls were tolerated as long as they did not cross over the boundaries of race and class, which included the association of cross-dressing or male identification with African American and (white and black) working-class culture, and the idea of marriage between the "male" female partner and the more "feminine" one. Thus, Jo walks the line, I would argue, between genteel tomboyism and its dangerous working-class connotations. It may also be interesting to view her in light of recent discussions of "female masculinity" in U.S. culture. See especially Judith Halberstam, *Female Masculinity* (Durham: Duke University Press, 1998).

33 Bedell, introduction to *Little Women*, xiii.

34 Sarah Elbert, in *A Hunger for Home: Louisa May Alcott and "Little Women"* (Philadelphia: Temple University Press, 1984), 144, remarks on this fluidity of gender but does not connect it to sexual identity, except so as to assume compulsory heterosexuality.

35 Elbert refers to him as a "fifth sister" (Elbert, *A Hunger for Home*, 144).

36 A point Doyle, "Jo March's Love Poems," among other critics, illustrates quite well.

37 In contrast to Barnes, I would argue that the family thus becomes not just a repressive microcosm of forced national unity but a space for gender and sexual fluidity, at least in its postbellum incarnation (Barnes, "The Whipping Boy of Love," 12, xn. 14–15).

38 See Hendler, "The Limits of Sympathy," 687.

39 Or, as Hendler puts it, an example of " 'the affective intensification of the family space,' Foucault argues 'characterizes bourgeois society's regime of sexuality' " ("The Limits of Sympathy," 689), in which (heterosexual) incest acts as a limit to how far relations of "sympathetic equivalence" can be extended.

40 It is tempting here to remember that Louisa May Alcott herself suffered through at least one attempt to set up such a school/family when her father and several other men established what they termed a "consociate family," which Haltunnen argues "would replace the exclusive nuclear household with universal domestic love" (Haltunnen, "The Domestic Drama," 237).

41 Hendler makes a similar point when he asserts that "sentimental novels' use of familial rhetoric risks incestuous implications in part because sympathy implies that family ties can be voluntary, based on affective not biological or conventional bonds. At this point such ties cease to be bonds of kinship, and the family as a normative category becomes incoherent" ("The Limits of Sympathy," 690). Yet he goes on to read such moments in Alcott as fleeting, perhaps because he is more interested in "collective" and feminist, rather than homoerotic, forms of affiliation, and because he argues that relations of sympathy have a limit: heterosexual incest. In contrast, I see them as precisely without limit, and therefore as much more radically destabilizing of the family than even Hendler does.

42 And here my argument differs most strongly from Young's: although Young recognizes Jo's masculine, cross-gender identifications and, interestingly, links them to Alcott's own sense of gender and sexual identity, she is only able to read Jo's relation to the maternal, while adopting a role and not as biologically determined, as simply a recapitulation, finally, to the norms of domesticity. This inability to read maternality itself as a cross-gendered practice comes, I would argue, from Young's methodological emphasis on privileging a feminist antipatriarchal critique of domesticity, an emphasis that

ultimately can only then read Jo as a victim of such a structure (Young, *Disarming the Nation*, esp. 107).

43 And Jo is certainly not the only heroine in Alcott's oeuvre to do so; so also, one might argue, does Rose (in *Eight Cousins* [1875] and in *Rose in Bloom* [1876]) and, most obviously, Polly, in *An Old-Fashioned Girl*, who marries her "younger brother," Tom, whom she has disciplined for most of the novel.

44 For example, Ann Murphy asserts that Jo cannot completely give up her love for her mother, something Murphy sees as not the euphoric, homoerotic utopia hypothesized by many lesbian-feminist critics but instead as an effect of Marmee's almost stifling attempts at subject formation. Because Jo cannot completely rid herself of her homoerotic longings, she must marry her father, in the guise of Professor Bhaer, as opposed to a "real" man, Laurie (but isn't he "that adorable girl"?). Jo develops, in Murphy's words, a "terror of heterosexuality" ("Borders," 576). According to this account, women become lesbians because of their overbearing mothers—they cannot let go of their preoedipal attachments enough to firmly enter the symbolic and take up their position as "heterosexual woman"; they are frigid and unable to "mature" enough to enjoy heterosexual pleasure. Such a reading imposes Freudian, heterosexist limits on gender and sexual identification, and it denies the queerly laden, historically specific vicissitudes of desire.

45 Young, *Disarming the Nation*, 104. Concentrating solely on gender identification, Young reads Nan as Alcott's attempt to reconcile male/female characteristics into a new, mostly unrepresented (and unrepresentable) model for female/feminist subjectivity within the text (104–5).

46 Robert Stein, "Girls' Cooperative Boarding Homes," *The Arena* (1898): 398.

47 Ibid., 410.

48 Kessler-Harris, *Out to Work*, 102; Meyerowitz, *Women Adrift*, xvii–xviii. Although Meyerowitz focuses on a period that begins after most of Alcott's novels were written, her analysis of "women adrift" seems extremely helpful in contextualizing Alcott's fantasies about the possibilities of such spaces.

49 As Jean Fagan Yellin has pointed out, although Christie's struggles in *Work* are in some ways reflective of the problems encountered by working-class women of the period, Alcott largely ignores the plight of the industrial proletariat and actively dissociates herself from it through her anti-Irish sentiments (Yellin, "From Success to Experience: Louisa May Alcott's *Work*," *Massachusetts Review* [fall 1980]: 537).

50 See Christine Stansell's *City of Women: Sex and Class in New York, 1789–1860* (Urbana: University of Illinois Press, 1987), 85–86, and Kathy Peiss's *Cheap Amusements: Working Women and Leisure in Turn-of-the-Century New York* (Philadelphia: Temple University Press, 1986), for discussions of

the ways in which these new semi- or counterpublic spaces offered opportunities for heterosexual encounters.

51 Moon, "'The Gentle Boy from the Dangerous Classes,'" 261–62.

52 For discussions of these counterpublic spaces, see Buhle, *Women and American Socialism;* Cook, "Female Support Networks"; Freedman, "Separatism as Strategy"; and Sklar, "Hull House."

For a reading of the importance of both these new homosocial spaces and identification/desire in *Work* that at times substantially parallels my own, see Gregory Eiselein, "Sentimental Discourse and the Bisexual Erotics of *Work,*" *Texas Studies in Literature and Language* 41.3 (fall 1999): 203–35. Although Eiselein recognizes both the erotics of the workplace and that between Rachel and Christie, he falls back into limiting Freudian terms when describing their identifications with one another: identifications must be "active" (male) or "passive" (female). Having and being are always then associated with gendered (and ultimately, biologically based) positions.

53 Eiselein ("Sentimental Discourse," 224–25) reads these shifts as indicative of a bisexual triangle, but I am less convinced of the importance of the male-female romance and see it more as a narrative means to a protolesbian end.

54 Yellin, "From Success to Experience," 528.

55 As Janet S. Zehr explains in "The Response of Nineteenth-Century Audiences to Louisa May Alcott's Fiction," *American Transcendental Quarterly* 1.4 (December 1987): 323–42, nineteenth-century (mostly male) reviewers found this ending somewhat implausible.

56 Lee Chambers-Schiller, "The Single Woman: Family and Vocation among Nineteenth-Century Reformers," in *Woman's Being, Woman's Place: Female Identity and Vocation in American History,* ed. Mary Kelley (Boston: G. K. Hall, 1979), 337.

57 See Hendler ("The Limits of Sympathy," 699) for a related interpretation of this ending, to which I am indebted.

58 As Natania Rosenfeld puts it, "Onto this scene of *jouissance,* the august father intrudes, clearly threatened by the spectacle of his wife 'hard at it' with another woman. Diana and Percy have been, in effect, creating a baby together: a female Cupid who revels in prelapsarian immodesty." Although I might take issue with Rosenfeld's reliance on a psychoanalytic model that relegates relationships with women to the preoedipal, she is right to notice the reclaiming of reproductivity itself as a female-female pursuit, another form of artistry (Rosenfeld, "Artists and Daughters in Louisa May Alcott's *Diana and Persis,*" *New England Quarterly* 64.1 [March 1991]: 15).

59 Luce Irigaray, *Speculum of the Other Woman,* trans. Gillian C. Gill (Ithaca: Cornell University Press, 1984).

60 Warner, "Homo-Narcissism," 206.

61 Irigaray, *Speculum of the Other Woman*.

62 Hendler, "The Limits of Sympathy," 699.

63 Seltzer, *Bodies and Machines*, 58.

64 And indeed, in the first situation Christie encounters when she works as a domestic servant, the first thing the mistress does is change her name to "Jane."

65 Susan Harris sees it as just another "experience" among experiences; this interpretation, it seems to me, denies the economic equivalencies between marriage and other forms of "work" that Alcott implicitly wants to draw (Harris, *Nineteenth-Century Novels*, 181).

66 Alcott, *Behind a Mask: The Unknown Thrillers*, ed. Madeleine B. Stern (London: Hogarth Press, 1985).

67 Jean Muir is not the only one who obviously "performs" femininity in Alcott's oeuvre; so, too, do Jo and Amy March. Amy begs Jo to behave as they pay calls on the neighboring society; Jo replies, " 'Let me see; "calm, cool and quiet"! yes, I think I can promise that. I've played the part of a prim young lady on the stage, and I'll try it off' " (358).

68 As Judith Fetterley aptly describes it, "*Behind a Mask* asserts that there is no honest way for a woman to make a living; survival depends on one stratagem or another—sell your hair, sell your body, sell your soul; all are equivalent moves in the same game" (Fetterley, "Impersonating 'Little Women': The Radicalism of Alcott's *Behind a Mask*," *Women's Studies* 10 [1983]: 2). Haltunnen argues that the trope of the mask represents "a mask that disguises a rebellion against the cult of true womanhood" ("Domestic Drama," 242). She sees theatricality functioning in *Little Women* as a form of social control: "Family life itself was presented as a form of theater, a continuing drama in which the evil forces of passion were ritualistically subdued by the forces of perfectionist domesticity" (245). I am not as convinced by the idea of rebellion, of a drama of liberal individualism against domesticity, especially because both Fetterley and Haltunnen imply that there is a true self, distinct from the cult of true womanhood and/or theatricality, to be found somewhere, usually in liberal self-realization. Instead, I am interested in the overlaps between the ideologies of sentimentalism and capitalism and what prospects for identity and sexuality these overlaps present.

69 For a related discussion of Alcott's unsuccessful attempts to separate female identity from "theatricality," see Hendler, "The Limits of Sympathy," 694–97.

70 G. K. Chesterton, "Louisa Alcott," in *Critical Essays on Louisa May Alcott*, ed. Madeleine B. Stern (Boston: G. K. Hall, 1984), 214.

71 Elizabeth Janeway, "Meg, Jo, Beth, Amy, and Louisa," in *Critical Essays on Louisa May Alcott*, ed. Stern, 97–98.

72 See Barnes, "The Whipping Boy of Love."

73 Philip Fisher, *Hard Facts: Setting and Form in the American Novel* (New York: Oxford University Press, 1985).

74 See Saidiya V. Hartman, *Scenes of Subjection: Terror, Slavery, and Self-Making in Nineteenth-Century America* (Oxford: Oxford University Press, 1997) for the most notable example of this argument.

75 Marianne Noble, "An Ecstasy of Apprehension: The Gothic Pleasures of Sentimental Fiction," in *American Gothic: New Interventions in a National Narrative,* ed. Robert K. Martin and Eric Savoy (Iowa City: University of Iowa Press, 1998), 163–82.

76 For a recent discussion of Jo March's effects on one particular lesbian reader, see Catharine Stimpson, "Reading for Love: Canons, Paracanons, and Whistling Jo March," *New Literary History* 21 (1990): 957–76, in which Stimpson hints at Jo's "lesbian pedagogical" influence.

77 Sicherman, "Sense and Sensibility." My arguments here are deeply indebted to Sicherman's meticulous research and searching analysis.

78 Sicherman, "Reading *Little Women*," 245–66.

79 Ibid., 73–103. For a related discussion of M. Carey Thomas's reading and its relationship to identity formation, see Horowitz, *The Power and Passion,* esp. 16–73.

80 Sicherman, "Reading and Ambition," 93.

81 And, importantly, whether they acknowledge it or not, many of these theories contain an implicit theory of reading that assumes that it has an effect on subject formation.

82 Sicherman, "Reading and Ambition," 77.

83 Significantly, Sicherman emphasizes that this form of reading experience was unique to white, middle-class girls. She reminds us of the working-class reading audiences described in Dorothy Richardson's *The Long Day;* readers who, Sicherman notes, found *Little Women* too "realistic," too much about the minute details of middle-class life. Sicherman speculates that the novel did not offer working-class women the fantasy of escape from class and toil that other books (penny-dreadfuls) often did (Sicherman, "Reading *Little Women*," 257–59).

Taking this idea a step further, Vicinus links this inspirational power to the origins of modern feminism. She sums up her discussion of the effects of women's biographies on late-Victorian girl readers with a question: "Is it too far fetched to speculate that formulaic biographies for girls may have engendered powerful fantasies that empowered the first feminist movement?" (Vicinus, "What Makes a Heroine? Nineteenth-Century Girls' Biographies," *Genre* 20 [summer 1987]: 185). Similarly, Jane H. Hunter examines the role of writing, specifically diary keeping, in the construction of female identity. As she describes it, "As both discipline and technique, diary-keeping contributed to the process by which late-Victorian girls amassed fragments of experience into identity" (Hunter, "Inscribing the Self in the Heart of the Family: Diaries and Girlhood in Late-Victorian America," *American Quarterly* 44.1 [March 1992]: 51). Using Alcott's own journal as an example, Hunter illustrates well the paradox of disciplinary intimacy I have discussed in greater detail above: Alcott's journal was a space for (self-)regulation, filled not only with her goals for self-improvement but also her mother's words themselves, as Alcott willingly shares her diary with her mother and asks for her response (another form of confession). At the same time, the journal was also a forum to explore the options offered by the ideologies of individualism and vocation. As Sicherman notes in "Reading and Ambition" (83), M. Carey Thomas as a youth began keeping a diary in the voice of Jo March herself, adopting her "tomboy" identity as a persona for her own journal.

84 Alcott, *The Journals of Louisa May Alcott,* eds. Joel Myerson and Daniel Sheahy (Boston: Little Brown, 1989), 196.

85 Brodhead reads this scene and its fictional counterpart in *Jo's Boys* as Alcott's representation of a standard scene in postbellum fiction, in which the feminine private sphere of the domestic author is invaded literally and metaphorically by the adoring public, and in which the female author submits herself to public scrutiny and adoration for the greater good of profit. Although this reading accurately describes the workings of publicity, it cannot account for the erotics of female-female fandom: the closest Brodhead gets to this topic is when he asserts, "The public [Jo] courts wants not just to read her works but to see and symbolically possess the author of her works" (*Cultures and Letters,* 70).

86 Alcott, *Journals,* 188.

87 See Harris for another, quite different, interpretation of this incident (Harris, *Nineteenth-Century American Women's Novels,* 178).

88 Despite her denials to the contrary, Sicherman often *implies* that reading *created,* as well as nurtured, ambitions.

89 In her revised preface to *Reading the Romance: Women, Patriarchy, and Popular Literature,* rev. ed. (Chapel Hill: University of North Carolina Press, 1993), 14–16, Janice Radway reinforces the idea that the form of the genre itself may at least question, even as it reinstates, the inevitability of heterosexuality.

90 As Donna Campbell's provocative reading in "Sentimental Conventions and Self-Protection" of Alcott's use of sentimental convention exposes.

91 Alcott, *Journals,* 167.

92 Laura Mulvey, "Visual Pleasure and Narrative Cinema," *Screen* 16.3 (autumn 1975): 6–18.

93 Cora Kaplan, "*The Thorn Birds:* Fiction, Fantasy, Femininity," in *Sea Changes: Essays on Culture and Feminism* (London: Verso, 1986), 120.

94 Alison Light, "'Returning to Manderley'—Romance Fiction, Female Sexuality, and Class," *Feminist Review* 16 (April 1984): 8, 13.

95 And I would include Sicherman, despite her historical rigor, in this as well.

96 See especially A. Murphy, "Borders."

97 Judith Butler, "The Force of Fantasy: Feminism, Mapplethorpe, and Discursive Excess," *differences: A Journal of Feminist Cultural Studies* 2.2 (1990): 105–25.

98 Ibid., 114.

99 Ibid., 119.

100 A point I am certainly not the first to make (see Butler, *Gender Trouble*). In Butler's *Bodies That Matter,* she attempts to address the critique of her work as modeling relations in late capitalism: "Gender performativity cannot be theorized apart from the forcible and reiterative practice of regulatory sexual regimes. . . . The account of agency conditioned by those very regimes of discourse/power cannot be conflated with voluntarism or individualism, much less with consumerism, and in no way presupposes a choosing subject" (15). Although this may be true, I will demonstrate below how Butler's project could not exist without the ideology of machine production.

101 A project with which Fuss's "Fashion and the Homospectatorial Look," *Critical Inquiry* 18 (summer 1992): 713–37, seems tacitly to ally itself even as it evades it.

102 As Kaplan and Butler note. J. Laplanche and J.-B. Pontalis, *The Language of Psychoanalysis,* trans. Donald Nicholson-Smith (New York: Norton, 1973), 314–18; Pierre Bourdieu, *Distinction: A Social Critique of the Judgment of Taste* (Cambridge: Harvard University Press, 1984).

103 John D'Emilio, "Capitalism and Gay Identity," in *Powers of Desire: The Politics of Sexuality,* ed. Ann Snitow, Christine Stansell, and Sharon Thompson (New York: Monthly Review Press, 1983, 100–13).

104 Brodhead, *Cultures of Letters,* 96–98.

105 Nina Auerbach, *Communities of Women: An Idea in Fiction* (Cambridge: Harvard University Press, 1978), 60.

106 Tate (*Psychoanalysis and Black Novels,* 35–36) views such eroticization of luxuries as a "semiotic" undercurrent of the text, which relegates them to a regressive, preoedipal and presocial space. See below for an extended critique of this strategy.

107 For a related reading of eroticized domesticity in Pauline Hopkins's *Contending Forces: A Romance Illustrative of Negro Life North and South* (1900; New York: Oxford University Press, 1988), see Siobhan Somerville,

Queering the Color Line: Race and the Invention of Homosexuality in American Culture (Durham: Duke University Press, 2000), 89–93. As Somerville notes, however, for African American women, because of the political necessity of marriage, such spaces were even more fleeting.

108 Although this form of female homoerotics seems particularly enabled by the "female space" of white, bourgeois culture in the United States, it is by no means confined to it, as I will discuss in greater detail below.

109 Radway, *Reading the Romance,* 14–16.

110 For a searing analysis of the imperial underpinnings of domesticity, see Laura Wexler, *Tender Violence: Domestic Visions in an Age of U.S. Imperialism* (Chapel Hill: University of North Carolina Press, 2000).

111 Sicherman, "Reading *Little Women.*"

112 As Stimpson puts it, "*Little Women* seeks to be radical about race and class, but it is the radicalism of philanthropy. Its benevolence demands the needy, lesser other to justify its existence" ("Reading for Love," 966–67).

113 Young, *Disarming the Nation,* 104–5.

114 David R. Roediger, *The Wages of Whiteness: Race and the Making of the American Working Class* (London: Verso, 1992).

115 For several notable examples, see G. Brown, *Domestic Individualism,* 55–58.

116 See ibid., as well as Spillers, "Changing the Letter: The Yokes, the Jokes of Discourse, or, Mrs. Stowe, Mr. Reed," in *Slavery and the Literary Imagination,* ed. Deborah McDowell and Arnold Rampersad (Baltimore: Johns Hopkins University Press, 1989), 25–61.

117 And here, in addition to *Iola Leroy or Shadows Uplifted* (1892; Boston: Beacon Press, 1987), I am referring to Emma Dunham Kelley (Hawkins), *Megda* and *Four Girls at Cottage City* (1898; New York: Oxford University Press, 1988); Mrs. A. E. Johnson's *Clarence and Corinne; or God's Way* and *The Hazeley Family* (1894; New York: Oxford University Press, 1988), and Pauline Hopkins's *Contending Forces.* I use the term same in quotations to signal the fact that in the Kelley and Johnson's texts the racial identities of the characters described are not clearly defined. See below for further discussion of this issue.

118 Tate, in *Domestic Allegories of Political Desire: The Black Heroine's Text at the Turn of the Century* (New York: Oxford University Press, 1992) and in *Psychoanalysis and Black Novels,* and duCille (*The Coupling Convention*) differ, however, in the degree to which they also see these novels as advocating a more equitable vision of relations between the sexes than those promulgated in sentimental texts authored by white women and as presenting a more or less matriarchal, black feminist domesticity.

119 duCille, *The Coupling Convention,* 13–14.

120 Somerville, *Queering the Color Line*, 82–83. See also duCille, *The Coupling Convention*, 14.

121 Tate, *Psychoanalysis and Black Novels*, 197 n.5.

122 Ibid., 23, 29–30. I put the term black in parentheses because the characters in *Medga* lack racial specificity, an issue I discuss in detail below.

123 Tate, *Psychoanalysis and Black Novels*, 30.

124 Tate (*Psychoanalysis and Black Novels*, esp. 33) does an excellent job of historicizing the latter, and her readings of Megda's encounters with Mr. Stanley bring out the specific cultural codes for representing heterosexual attraction that the novel deploys, in ways that challenge any notion of this novel as "passionless." But she cannot do the same for Megda's relationship with Ethel, even as she recognizes their intimacies as at heart about desires to have and to be.

125 Tate notes the similarity to the March family (*Psychoanalysis and Black Novels*, 29).

126 Ibid., esp. 33.

127 As Tate (*Psychoanalysis and Black Novels*, esp. 29) and duCille (*The Coupling Convention*, esp. 61), albeit in different ways, also note.

128 Hite, introduction to *Megda*, xxxv.

129 Hite (introduction to *Megda*, xxvii) also notices the nostalgia the narrator expresses.

130 Certainly Toni Morrison's *Beloved* (New York: New American Library, 1987) implies that this is one reason Sethe refuses to discipline her daughters.

131 Although there are some significant moments in the novel where both Meg's brother, Hal, and her sister do model for her versions of self-regulation that she takes seriously.

132 Tate, *Psychoanalysis and Black Novels*, 34.

133 Ibid., 33.

134 Ibid., 34.

135 Indeed, Meg's relationship with Laurie constitutes another example of the same kind of disciplinary intimacy. Meg first harshly dismisses Laurie, but after her conversion her relationship with her changes: "She loved [Laurie] with her whole heart; loved her for her own invaluable little self, and for the many lessons that she had been unconsciously teaching her. And Laurie returned her love in full—when had she ever done anything else but love her?—and dreaded to leave her as much as Meg dreaded to have her go" (354). In fact, Laurie loves Megda so much that she refuses to accept Hal's proposal until Meg "withdraw[s] all opposition" (354).

136 McDowell also notes the importance of this image in her introduction to *Four Girls at Cottage City*, xxxv, as does duCille (*The Coupling Convention*, 59).

137 Tate, *Psychoanalysis and Black Novels*, 30–31.

138 See also duCille (*The Coupling Convention*, 59) for a discussion of the connections between marriage and death in the novel.

139 For discussions of the significance of the use of Cottage City, see especially Hite, introduction to *Megda*, xxx–xxxi.

140 duCille, *The Coupling Convention*, 54.

141 Ibid., 55; Tate, *Psychoanalysis and Black Novels*, 24.

142 Tate, *Psychoanalysis and Black Novels*, 30.

143 See McDowell, introduction to *Quicksand; and, Passing* by Nella Larsen (New Brunswick: Rutgers University Press, 1986), xxiii–xxxi, and Butler, *Bodies That Matter*, 167–85, for two queer readings of this novel that have influenced my perspective.

144 Audre Lorde, "The Uses of the Erotic: The Erotic as Power," in *The Lesbian and Gay Studies Reader*, ed. Henry Abelove, Michèle Aina Barale, and David M. Halperin (New York: Routledge, 1993), 339–43.

145 Muñoz, *Disidentifications*, 95.

146 Ibid., 11–12.

147 Tate, *Psychoanalysis and Black Novels*, 44–46. That the text also kills off the blackest (and seemingly, inherently connected to that, most evil) character, a point Tate overlooks, must necessarily I believe temper any impulse to see the novel as some unproblematic celebration of color.

148 A death that Tate's reading of the ending overlooks entirely, and one that I think most seriously calls into question her claims.

149 Muñoz, *Disidentifications*, 108.

150 What McDowell (introduction to *Four Girls at Cottage City*, xxxi), following Smith-Rosenberg, refers to as "the female world." (By this point, Kelley had married and changed her name to Hawkins.) See also duCille's reading of the four girls' interactions (*The Coupling Convention*, 56–59). Even Somerville's reading of Sappho and Dora's relationship overemphasizes, I would argue, the degree to which this intimacy is "closeted" or not openly erotic (*Queering the Color Line*, 89–93). Although their intimacies take place in the bedroom, this is not simply a family home but a boardinghouse, and Sappho is not a sister but a boarder to Dora. Thus, I would argue that Hopkins's novel, like Alcott's, is exploring the erotic effects of the permeability of the boundary between public and private, family and sisterhood and unrelated female-female intimacies.

151 duCille, *The Coupling Convention*, 55.

152 DuCille points, however, to one important exception: Flora Hazeley, the main character of Johnson's *The Hazeley Family*, remains unmarried, and in so doing represents a "social function for women independent of marriage, but a function still decidedly domestic" (*The Coupling Convention*, 63).

Chapter 3. "Scouting for Girls": Reading and Recruitment
in the Early Twentieth Century

1 The first edition of the handbook, titled *How Girls Can Help Their Country: Handbook for Girl Scouts* (New York: Girl Scouts of America, 1913), was written by W. J. Hoxie, a friend of Juliette Gordon Low. It imported much of its bases from the British Girl Guide movement, and as Elizabeth Israels Perry notes, reflected less of Low's ideological emphases. By comparison, the second edition, *Scouting for Girls: Official Handbook of the Girl Scouts* (New York: Girl Scouts of America, 1920), was the first to demonstrate a distinctly "American" version of Scouting (as evidenced by the proto-American and American role models discussed above). For more on the differences between the early handbooks, see Elizabeth Israels Perry, "From Achievement to Happiness: Girl Scouting in Middle Tennessee, 1910s-1960s," *Journal of Women's History* 5.2 (fall 1993): 75–94, an essay to which this chapter is indebted.

2 *Scouting for Girls*, 20–27.

3 Ibid., 24.

4 Djuna Barnes, *Ladies Almanack* (1928; Elmwood Park: Dalkey Archive Press, 1992). Subsequent citations appear as parenthetical page references in the text.

5 Not all historians agree that queer subjects found sexology pathologizing, however. Jay Prosser and Laura Doan have argued that in fact queers such as Radclyffe Hall had a much more ambivalent relation to this uneven discourse, finding in it ways to explain and narrate identity rather than just images to organize against (Prosser, *Second Skins: The Body Narratives of Transsexuality* [New York: Columbia University Press, 1998], and Doan, *Fashioning Sapphism: The Origins of a Modern English Lesbian Culture* [New York: Columbia University Press, 2001]).

6 Martha Banta, *Imaging American Women*, 16–17. Banta's work represents just one example of a much larger critical project, which often includes investigating the ways that race and ethnicity themselves were becoming codified into "identities" or "types" in this period. For several notable and controversial examples, see Werner Sollors, ed., *The Invention of Ethnicity* (New York: Oxford University Press, 1989); Kwame Anthony Appiah, *In My Father's House: Africa in the Philosophy of Culture* (New York: Oxford University Press, 1992), esp. chapter 2, "Illusions of Race," 28–46; Weigman, *American Anatomies;* and Walter Benn Michaels, *Our America: Nativism, Modernism, and Pluralism* (Durham: Duke University Press, 1995).

7 For more detailed discussions of the rise of cultural hierarchy in the United States, see, for example, Lawrence Levine, *Highbrow/Lowbrow: The Emergence of Cultural Hierarchy in America* (Cambridge: Harvard University

Press, 1988); Christopher Wilson, *The Labor of Words: Literary Profession-alism in the Progressive Era* (Athens: University of Georgia Press, 1985); and Janice Radway, *A Feeling for Books: The Book-of-the-Month Club, Literary Taste, and Middle-Class Desire* (Chapel Hill: University of North Carolina Press, 1997).

8 Banta, *Imaging American Women*, 46–47.

9 For a biography of Low intended for a Girl Scout readership, see Anne Hyde Choate and Helen Ferris, *Juliette Low and the Girl Scouts: The Story of an American Woman, 1860–1927* (New York: Doubleday, Doran, 1928).

10 Seltzer, *Bodies and Machines*, 150.

11 Ibid., 140.

12 Michael Rosenthal, *The Character Factory: Baden-Powell and the Origins of the Boy Scout Movement* (New York: Pantheon Books, 1984).

13 See, for example, *Scouting for Girls*, 24.

14 Although other historians note Low's emphasis on domesticity and moth-erhood, none question or even remark on her reinforcement of hetero-sexuality.

15 My understanding of these events has been shaped in part by Mary Aickin Rothschild, "To Scout or to Guide? The Girl Scout–Boy Scout Controversy, 1912–1941," *Frontiers* 6.3 (1982): 115–21, and Charles E. Strickland, "Juliette Low, the Girl Scouts, and the Role of American Women," in *Wom-an's Being, Woman's Place: Female Identity and Vocation in American His-tory*, ed. Mary Kelley (Boston: G. K. Hall, 1979), 252–64. See also Lau-reen Tedesco, "Making a Girl into a Scout: Americanizing Scouting for Girls," in *Delinquents and Debutantes: Twentieth-Century American Girls' Cultures*, ed. Sherrie A. Inness (New York: New York University Press, 1998), 19–39.

16 Sir Robert Baden-Powell, "Girl Scouts or Girl Guides," *Jamboree* (Octo-ber 1921): as quoted in Rothschild, "To Scout or to Guide?" 119.

17 Quoted in Strickland, "Juliette Low," 259.

18 Smith-Rosenberg, *Disorderly Conduct*, esp. 245–96; Chauncey, "From Sex-ual Inversion to Homosexuality: Medicine and the Changing Conception of Female Deviance," *Salmagundi* 58/59 (fall 1982 / winter 1983): 114–45.

19 Havelock Ellis, *Sexual Inversion* (1897; New York: Arno Press, 1975), 99–100, as quoted in Sahli, "Smashing," 25.

20 Recently, Doan has argued in regard to England that it was only with Rad-clyffe Hall's obscenity trial in 1928 that female masculinity was connected to sexual inversion by the general public. Prior to that, at least in the 1920s, she asserts that masculinity was a fashion trend in Britain and signified the larger category "modern" (Doan, *Fashioning Sapphism*, xiv–xv). Elsewhere in this chapter I argue that "modern" itself connoted "queer" when used to describe women. Furthermore, in the context of the United States, in her analysis of

the Alice Mitchell trial, Lisa Duggan in *Sapphic Slashers* asserts that the publicity surrounding this event linked female masculinity and lesbianism. Given that any connection between female masculinity and lesbianism is an uneven development because, as Doan notes, access and familiarity with sexology itself as well as to various other descriptions of sapphism differed greatly among classes and among nations, it still seems from Duggan's account that by the second decade of the twentieth century in the United States female masculinity might have connoted deviant sexuality. Certainly Gulick's language indicates moral corruption.

21 Hoxie, *How Girls Can Help Their Country*, 12.

22 Ibid., viii.

23 Bhabha, *The Location of Culture*, 85–92. Bhabha writes: "It is from this area between mimicry and mockery, where the reforming, civilizing mission is threatened by the displacing gaze of its disciplinary double, that my instances of colonial imitation come. What they all share is a discursive process by which the excess of slippage produced by the *ambivalence* of mimicry (almost the same, *but not quite*) does not merely 'rupture' the discourse, but becomes transformed into an uncertainty which fixes the colonial subject as a 'partial' presence. By 'partial' I mean both 'incomplete' and 'virtual.' It is as if the very emergence of the 'colonial' is dependent for its representation upon some strategic limitation or prohibition *within* the authoritative discourse itself. The success of colonial appropriation depends on a proliferation of inappropriate objects that ensure its strategic failure, so that mimicry is at once resemblance and menace" (86).

24 *Scouting for Girls*, 4. In Hoxie, *How Girls Can Help Their Country*, the promise reads "your" instead of "my" (3).

25 *Scouting for Girls*, 4.

26 The added clause exists only in the first edition (Hoxie, *How Girls Can Help Their Country*, 5).

27 *Scouting for Girls*, 4–12. The first edition reads, "A Girl Scout Keeps herself Pure," and this law comes sixth in the list, rather than last (*How Girls Can Help Their Country*, 5).

28 *Scouting for Girls*, 60–61.

29 Ibid., 63.

30 Ibid., 60–65.

31 Ibid., 497–533.

32 Ibid., 510.

33 A point Perry makes most forcefully in her examination of the history of one particular Girl Scout council. See also Tedesco ("Making a Girl into a Scout," 19–39) who argues that the Girl Scouts' emphasis on militarism is what in particular attracted young women to the movement, and that the early handbooks mixed more "male" pursuits with domestic ones in order to

implicitly argue for the girls' equality with boys, while at the same time reinforcing the norms of domesticity.

34 Tim Jeal, *The Boy-Man: The Life of Lord Baden-Powell* (New York: William Morrow, 1990), 390–91.

35 Here I am adapting Benedict Anderson's famous description of nations as "imagined communities" from his *Imagined Communities: Reflections on the Origin and Spread of Nationalism* (London: Verso, 1983).

36 Historians of the Boy Scouts debate the degree to which the organization is more or less democratic or imperialist. For the former view, see especially Jeal, *The Boy-Man;* for the latter, see especially Rosenthal, *The Character Factory.*

37 Historians of the Boy Scouts also debate the degree to which Baden-Powell was a liberal and antimilitarist (at least in relation to the Boy Scouts) and genuinely interested in the progress of each individual boy, and the degree to which his movement constituted an effort at social control and an extension of militarist ideology. Jeal's view in *The Boy-Man* (esp. 409–23) tends to place Baden-Powell on the liberal side, which is not surprising given that Jeal sees Baden-Powell himself as an individual and does not tend to locate him inside or as representative of larger social forces. I find Rosenthal's argument in *The Character Factory* (esp. 191–229) much more persuasive, as it focuses more on Baden-Powell's implication in ideologies of race, class, empire, and character, despite Baden-Powell's occasional protests to the contrary.

38 *Scouting for Girls,* 6–7.

39 Hoxie, *How Girls Can Help Their Country,* 5.

40 Ibid., viii.

41 Lavell, *The Girl Scouts' Good Turn* (New York: A. L. Burt Company, 1922).

42 Lavell, *The Girl Scouts' Canoe Trip* (New York: A. L. Burt Company, 1922).

43 Lavell, *The Girl Scouts' Rivals* (New York: A. L. Burt Company, 1922).

44 Lilian Garis, *The Girl Scout Pioneers, or Winning the First B.C.* (New York: Cupples and Leon Company, 1920).

45 Ibid., 53.

46 Ibid., 57.

47 For a related discussion of this process within the novel, see Sherrie A. Inness, "Girl Scouts, Camp Fire Girls, and Wood Craft Girls," in *Nancy Drew and Company: Culture, Gender, and Girls' Series,* ed. Sherrie A. Inness (Bowling Green, Ohio: Bowling Green State University Popular Press, 1997), 89–100.

48 Perry, "From Achievement to Happiness," 77.

49 *Scouting for Girls,* 12.

50 Ibid., 5.

51 And the emphasis on it being something one carries in one's hand seems important here (Rosenthal, *The Character Factory,* 185–90). Jeal discusses the fact that Baden-Powell throughout his lifetime apparently carried on exten-

sive private correspondence with individual Boy Scouts in which he coun-
seled them on how to avoid masturbation (Jeal, *The Boy-Man,* 100).

52 Hoxie, *How Girls Can Help Their Country,* 107.

53 Lavell, *The Girl Scouts at Camp* (New York: A. L. Burt, 1922), 54. For a related discussion of this passage, one that carries the analysis of Scouting into
the later part of the twentieth century, see Kathryn R. Kent, "No Trespassing: Girl Scouting and the Limits of the Counterpublic Sphere," *Women and
Performance: A Journal of Feminist Theory* 8.2 (1996): 185–203.

54 Sherrie A. Inness, *Intimate Communities: Representation and Social Transformation in Women's College Fiction, 1895–1910* (Bowling Green, Ohio:
Bowling Green State University Popular Press, 1995), 47.

55 Ibid., 53.

56 Ibid., 47.

57 Although in this novel Marjorie's actual title is "assistant director," she is the
de facto director of a large Girl Scout organization (Lavell, *The Girl Scout
Director* [New York: A. L. Burt, 1925]).

58 Lavell, *The Girl Scouts on the Ranch* (New York: A. L. Burt, 1923), and *The
Girl Scouts' Motor Trip* (New York: A. L. Burt, 1924). For examples by other
writers, see also Lillian Elizabeth Roy, *Girl Scouts in the Rockies* (New York:
Grosset and Dunlap, 1921). In other books in her series, Girl Scouts also go
to Arizona, New Mexico, and California (Roy, *Girl Scouts in Arizona and
New Mexico* [New York: Grosset and Dunlap, 1920], and *Girl Scouts in the
Redwoods* [New York: Grosset and Dunlap, 1920]).

59 Sedgwick, *Between Men* and *Epistemology of the Closet.*

60 Elsewhere I have hypothesized that later in the twentieth century the identity
"Girl Scout" *did* serve as a substitute for either a homosexual or heterosexual identification, while at the same time allowing for a much wider range
of homoerotic expression between women than what has been recognized
as "normal" within the larger culture. I have also noted the similarities between the Girl Scout movement and emerging second-wave lesbian-femi-
nism. There exists to my knowledge no historical documentation that the
early Girl Scouts "made" girls into lesbians, however. See Kent, "No Trespassing," 185–203, for a discussion of how this process occurs in the late
twentieth century.

61 Karla Jay, "The Outsider among the Expatriates: Djuna Barnes's Satire on
the Ladies of the *Almanack,*" in *Silence and Power: A Reevaluation of Djuna
Barnes,* ed. Mary Lynn Broe (Carbondale: Southern Illinois University Press,
1991), 184–93.

62 For examples of this strategy, see Susan Sniader Lanser, "Speaking in
Tongues: *Ladies Almanack* and the Discourse of Desire" (156–68), and
Frann Michel, "All Women Are Not Women All: *Ladies Almanack* and Fem-
inine Writing" (170–83), both in *Silence and Power,* ed. Broe.

63 One notable exception to this gap is Julie L. Abraham, *Are Girls Necessary? Lesbian Writing and Modern Histories* (New York: Routledge, 1996), 121–38.

64 Anderson, *Imagined Communities*, esp. 3–5.

65 Michael Warner, *The Letters of the Republic: Publication and the Public Sphere in Eighteenth-Century America* (Cambridge: Harvard University Press, 1990).

66 Davidson, *Revolution and the Word.*

67 For more on this, see David Harvey, *The Condition of Postmodernity: An Enquiry into the Origins of Social Change* (Cambridge: Blackwell, 1989), 228–29.

68 Catharine Stimpson, afterword to *Silence and Power,* ed. Broe, 371.

69 In the same vein it is interesting to note the cultural resonances of Radclyffe Hall's name itself, which connotes the privileges of the established aristocracy at the same time that it echoes the names of early women's educational seminaries and, later, colleges ("Lady Margaret Hall" at Oxford is one such example).

70 See Vicinus, *Independent Women,* for a discussion of such sisterhoods in Britain. In the United States, the closest equivalent to such organizations, although more secularized, were the settlement houses (which sought to "convert" poor and immigrant women and children into "good Americans") and, during the early twentieth century, the maternity home movement. See Regina G. Kunzel, *Fallen Women, Problem Girls: Unmarried Mothers and the Professionalization of Social Work, 1890–1945* (New Haven: Yale University Press, 1993).

71 It is interesting to note that Gertrude Stein, Alice B. Toklas, and Radclyffe Hall all worked on or near the front lines during World War I; Stein and Toklas transported medical supplies and Hall served as an ambulance driver. See Diane Souhami, *Gertrude and Alice* (London: Pandora Press, 130–39), and Michael Baker, *Our Three Selves: The Life of Radclyffe Hall* (New York: Morrow, 1985).

72 With its emphasis on a collective mission and "work," this image parodies most obviously the women's maternity home movement, which is itself an offspring of women's late-nineteenth-century evangelical efforts. As Kunzel describes such women, "Whether ministering to prostitutes, widows, homeless women, and single mothers, evangelical women understood their work to be a collective and emphatically missionary effort and one that they were uniquely suited to do as women" (Kunzel, *Fallen Women,* 11).

73 Seltzer, *Bodies and Machines,* 32.

74 And this is true even as it appropriates and idealizes an image of wage laborers that has little to do with the conditions of women in factories.

75 Smith-Rosenberg, *Disorderly Conduct* (263); and it is also a point Kunzel echoes in her description of women's social work in *Fallen Women* (10–11).

76 We should be suspicious of how this works, however, because Barnes is also interrogating what it means to be "born" a lesbian, or to be "born again" as one: the woman who springs out of the egg is both "born" and "made" at the same time, leading one to ask if "born" and "made" are really that different.

77 And the language of this discussion is also reminiscent of Teresa de Lauretis's argument regarding lesbians and sexual difference; that is, that it is precisely because sexual difference is only conceived of in terms of phallic possession or lack that lesbian-lesbian sexuality and representation cannot be represented or, even more important, is not thought to carry any cultural, rhetorical, political, or historical significance (de Lauretis, "Sexual Indifference and Lesbian Representation," in *The Lesbian and Gay Studies Reader,* ed. Henry Abelove, Michèle Aina Barale, and David M. Halperin (New York: Routeledge, 1993), 141–58, and *The Practice of Love*). Although I think de Lauretis's point is very important, I am more convinced by Butler and others' reclamation of the phallus for lesbian sexuality and representation. In particular, Butler, in *Bodies That Matter,* challenges us to "consider that 'having' the phallus can be symbolized by an arm, a tongue, a hand (or two), a knee, a thigh, a pelvic bone, an array of purposefully instrumentalized bodylike things" (88). She goes on to say, "If a lesbian 'has' [the phallus], it is also clear that she does not 'have' it in the traditional sense; her activity furthers a crisis in the sense of what it means to 'have' one at all. The phantasmatic status of 'having' is redelineated, rendered transferable, substitutable, plastic; and the eroticism produced within such an exchange depends on the displacement from traditional masculinist contexts as well as the critical redeployment of its central figures of power" (88–89). This emphasis on the transferability of the phallus resembles very much Barnes's strategy, and again begs the question of what the rise of commodity capitalism has to do with possibilities for "transferability."

78 A point of much contention in scholarship on Barnes. See, for example, Jay, "The Outsider among the Expatriates," and Abraham, *Are Girls Necessary?* For a more general discussion of the construction of such a figure in the early-twentieth-century United States and in Britain, see Esther Newton, "The Mythic Mannish Lesbian: Radclyffe Hall and the New Woman," in *Hidden from History: Reclaiming the Gay and Lesbian Past,* ed. Martin Duberman, Martha Vicinus, and George Chauncey Jr. (New York: Meridian, 1989), 281–93.

79 D. H. Lawrence, *The Rainbow* (1915; New York: Penguin Books, 1981), 336.

80 Jill Johnston, *Lesbian Nation: The Feminist Solution* (New York: Simon and Schuster, 1973).

81 Muñoz, *Disidentifications*, 95.

82 And this may indicate that she stands in for the author of *Ladies Almanack* herself, because Djuna Barnes used this same appellation in place of an author's name when publishing the novella.

83 Muñoz, *Disidentifications*, 78.

Chapter 4. *"Excreate a No Since"*: The Erotic Currency of Gertrude Stein's Tender Buttons

1 Gertrude Stein, *Tender Buttons: Objects Food Rooms* (1914; Los Angeles: Sun and Moon Press, 1994); 37–38. Subsequent citations appear as parenthetical page references in the text.

2 *Scouting for Girls,* 509.

3 Lydia Maria Child, *The American Frugal Housewife* (New York: Wood, 1844). For a fascinating discussion of the tradition of the domestic manual, see Kathleen Anne McHugh, *American Domesticity: From How-to Manual to Hollywood Melodrama* (New York: Oxford University Press, 1999).

4 Alice B. Toklas, *The Alice B. Toklas Cookbook* (1954; Garden City: Anchor Books, 1960). For accounts of this relationship, to which this chapter is particularly indebted, see Linda Wagner-Martin, *"Favored Strangers": Gertrude Stein and Her Family* (New Brunswick: Rutgers University Press, 1995), and Diane Souhami, *Gertrude and Alice.*

5 Stein, as quoted in Jayne L. Walker, *The Making of a Modernist: Gertrude Stein from "Three Lives" to "Tender Buttons"* (Amherst: University of Massachusetts Press, 1976), 128.

6 For more information on this reading, see Harriet Scott Chessman, *The Public Is Invited to Dance: Representation, the Body, and Dialogue in Gertrude Stein* (Stanford: Stanford University Press, 1989), 88–89; Elizabeth Fifer, *Rescued Readings: A Reconstruction of Gertrude Stein's Difficult Texts* (Detroit: Wayne State University Press, 1992), 46–58; and Shari Benstock, *Women of the Left Bank: Paris, 1900–1940* (Austin: University of Texas Press, 1986), 162–63.

7 For accounts, to which this chapter is indebted, of Toklas's arrival and the departure of Leo Stein from 27 rue de Fleurus, see, among others, John Malcolm Brinnin, *The Third Rose: Gertrude Stein and Her World* (New York: Grove Press, 1959); James R. Mellow, *Charmed Circle: Gertrude Stein and Company* (New York: Praeger Publishers, 1974); and Souhami, *Gertrude and Alice.*

8 Ellen Berry, *Curved Thought and Textual Wandering: Gertrude Stein's Postmodernism* (Ann Arbor: University of Michigan Press, 1992), 11–35.

9   In reading Stein's writing as simply uninterpretable, some critics have lauded this supposed opacity as an example of how her work resists reification by signifying, in its unintelligibility, the labor of interpretation itself, what we might think of as a kind of zero-degree materialism of reading. For some, like Fredric Jameson, this forms the basis of these critics' disdain for mass culture: high modernist texts are those that somehow resist the effects of commodity capitalism, whereas mass cultural texts are simply products of this system and attempt to placate their readers into accepting it through their manipulation of utopian fantasy. See, for example, Marjorie Perloff, *The Poetics of Indeterminacy: Rimbaud to Cage* (Princeton: Princeton University Press, 1981), and Jameson, classroom lecture, Duke University, fall 1990.

10   Richard Bridgman, as quoted in E. Berry, *Curved Thought*, 3.

11   Sedgwick, *Epistemology of the Closet*, 3–10.

12   For one example of this reading of Stein's work, in particular of *Tender Buttons*, see Margaret Dickie, "Recovering Repression in Stein's Erotic Poetry," *Gendered Modernisms: American Women Poets and Their Readers*, ed. Margaret Dickie and Thomas Travisano (Philadelphia: University of Pennsylvania Press, 1996), 3–25. Despite her insistence on reading the poem as "encoding" Stein's lesbianism and her desire for Toklas, much of Dickie's reading of *Tender Buttons* identifies the poem as centrally focused on the Stein/Toklas relationship. For a somewhat more pejorative critique of what she calls Stein's "lesbian lie," see Catharine R. Stimpson, "Gertrude Stein and the Lesbian Lie," *American Women's Autobiography: Fea(s)ts of Memory*, ed. Margo Culley (Madison: University of Wisconsin Press, 1992), 152–66. For a critique of this "decoding" trend in regard to readings of "Lifting Belly," see Susan Holbrook, "Lifting Bellies, Filling Petunias, and Making Meanings through the Trans-Poetic," *American Literature* 71.4 (December 1999): 751–71.

13   Seltzer, *Bodies and Machines*, 3. For discussions of Stein's work and reception in relation to her possible connection to or comment on a feminized mass culture, see E. Berry, *Curved Thought*, 133–52, and Nicola Pitchford, "Unlikely Modernism, Unlikely Postmodernism," *American Literary History* 11.4 (winter 1999): 642–67.

14   Houston A. Baker, *Modernism and the Harlem Renaissance* (Chicago: University of Chicago Press, 1987).

15   In many ways this was not a rupture in the domestic ideal but a continuity from the ideology, prevalent in the nineteenth century, of the domestic sphere as haven from a heartless world. See Smith-Rosenberg, *Disorderly Conduct*, and Christopher Lasch, *Haven in a Heartless World: The Family Betrayed* (New York: Basic Books, 1977).

16   Seltzer, *Bodies and Machines*, 13.

17   Ibid., 40.

18 It is important to note here, however, that even Seltzer's use of the term sexual seems to mean *heterosexual,* in particular heterosexual reproduction. Although he continually invokes the terms production and reproduction, natural and unnatural, Seltzer is silent on the subject of queer sexualities. When he reads sexuality at all it remains firmly linked to gender and often becomes a substitute for it. For example, he reads images of machines as mothers as dangerous and antifemale, as opposed to moments that open up possibilities for an unhinging of the link between heterosexuality and (re)production. Although it is true that certain fantasies of reproduction without women represent misogynist desires to replace or take over the maternal function as an assertion of power, Seltzer's book opens up many other possibilities, ones he himself does not pursue.

19 The classic example of this is D'Emilio, "Capitalism and Gay Identity." Vicinus makes the most salient critique of this form of economic determinism in her essay "'They Wonder to Which Sex I Belong,'" 467–97.

20 Toklas, *The Alice B. Toklas Cookbook,* 42–43; emphasis mine.

21 And this occurs throughout the cookbook and her memoir.

22 See Alice B. Toklas, *What Is Remembered* (San Francisco: North Point Press, 1985), 24, 34.

23 Stein, as quoted in Walker, *The Making of a Modernist,* 128.

24 And certainly it must be pointed out that whatever her labor it is not that of a French peasant woman but of a middle-class expatriate in Paris.

25 Richard Wightman Fox and T. J. Jackson Lears, eds., *The Culture of Consumption: Critical Essays in American History 1880–1980* (New York: Pantheon Books, 1983).

26 And it may indicate the degree to which life in Paris was "less" modernized than that in America.

27 Alan Trachtenberg, *The Incorporation of America* (New York: Hill and Wang, 1982), 129.

28 Richard Ohmann, "Where Did Mass Culture Come From? The Case of Magazines," in *Politics of Letters* (Middletown, Conn.: Wesleyan University Press, 1987), 148.

29 See especially Leigh Gilmore, *Autobiographics: A Feminist Theory of Women's Self-Representation* (Ithaca: Cornell University Press, 1994). For other readings of their relationship, see Fifer, *Rescued Readings,* esp. 46–58. Lisa Ruddick cites from Stein's journals fascinating passages describing the Stein/Toklas relationship, but she cannot account for their complexity. She ends up concluding that Stein simply "dominat[ed]" Toklas as a substitute for Stein's lost mother (Ruddick, *Reading Gertrude Stein* [Ithaca: Cornell University Press, 1990], 185). Kay Turner's introduction to her edited volume of Stein and Toklas's correspondence provides the most nuanced discussion of their "marriage," seeing their use of the appellations of traditional

reproductive heterosexuality as a playful reinscription and representation of domestic intimacy, as well as an exchange of various forms of power that are not at all interested in dominance (Turner, *Baby Precious Always Shines: Selected Love Notes between Gertrude Stein and Alice B. Toklas* [New York: St. Martin's Press, 1999], esp. 11).

30 For a discussion of the relationship between *Tender Buttons* and the magazine and cookbook culture in particular (which also focuses on its "public exploration of a gendered world"), see Mary O'Connor, "The Objects of Modernism: Everyday Life in Women's Magazines, Gertrude Stein, and Margaret Watkins," in *American Modernism across the Arts*, ed. Jay Bochner and Justin D. Edwards (New York: Peter Lang, 1999), 97–123. See also Marguerite S. Murphy, "'Familiar Strangers': The Household Words of Gertrude Stein's *Tender Buttons*," *Contemporary Literature* 32.3 (1991): 383–402.

31 Neil Harris, *Cultural Excursions: Marketing Appetites and Cultural Tastes in Modern America* (Chicago: University of Chicago Press, 1990), 56–81, 174–97.

32 Trachtenberg, *Incorporation of America*, 132.

33 For an early definition of this term, see Rich, "Compulsory Heterosexuality," 23–75.

34 Souhami, *Gertrude and Alice*, 206–7.

35 Ibid., 12.

36 Ibid., 11.

37 For the reading that formed the departure point for my own work, and the one that makes the most of this idea, see Chessman, *The Public Is Invited*, 88–111.

38 For one analysis of these connections, see Sue Ellen Case, "Tracking the Vampire," *differences: A Journal of Feminist Cultural Studies* 3 (1991): 3–4.

39 For an argument about the lesbian machine-body in late-twentieth-century culture, see Cathy Griggers, "Lesbian Bodies in the Age of (Post)mechanical Reproduction," in *Fear of a Queer Planet: Queer Politics and Social Theory*, ed. Michael Warner (Minneapolis: University of Minnesota Press, 1993), 178–92.

40 Again, Chessman's work in *The Public Is Invited* (88–111) represents one of the strongest analyses that takes this reading as its basis.

41 For perhaps the best discussion of reading relations to Stein's work, see E. Berry, *Curved Thought*, 11–35.

42 Douglas's *The Feminization of American Culture* is perhaps the most predominant of the literary critical examples of this view. For a continuation of these ideas into the twentieth century, see, for instance, Stuart Ewen and Elizabeth Ewen, *Channels of Desire: Mass Images and the Shaping of American Consciousness* (Minneapolis: University of Minnesota Press, 1992).

43 Although many critics have commented on the similarity of buttons to coins, none notices the connection between this fact and the connotations of "tender," which recall the phrase, "legal tender." For one particularly interesting example of this, see Neil Schmitz, *Of Huck and Alice: Humorous Writing in American Literature* (Minneapolis: University of Minnesota Press, 1983).

44 For accounts of this revisionary view of modernism, see, among many others, Marcus Klein, *Foreigners: The Making of American Literature, 1900–1940* (Chicago: University of Chicago Press, 1981); Sandra Gilbert and Susan Gubar, *No Man's Land: The Place of the Woman Writer in the Twentieth Century. Vol. 1: The War of the Words* (New Haven: Yale University Press, 1988); Andreas Huyssen, "Mass Culture as Woman: Modernism's Other," in *Studies in Entertainment: Critical Approaches to Mass Culture,* ed. Tania Modleski (Bloomington: Indiana University Press, 1986), 188–207; and Aldon Lynn Nielsen, *Reading Race: White American Poets and the Racial Discourse in the Twentieth Century* (Athens: University of Georgia Press, 1988).

45 Maria Damon is perhaps the only critic to analyze Stein's use of language in relation to Stein's Jewishness. Against the work of those such as Richard Bridgman, who, as Damon notes, dismisses Stein's possible relation to Jewish identity and culture because Stein was not "observant," Damon argues for the cultural effects of Jewishness or any other ethnicity on those seemingly "assimilated" (Damon, *The Dark End of the Street: Margins in American Poetry* [Minneapolis: University of Minnesota Press, 1993], 235). Damon convincingly argues that Stein, through her use of doggerel, "deterritorializes English" (229) and at times parodies or deconstructs the boundaries of the nation in order to create a space for the Jewish lesbian body, a strategy that produces what Damon terms "a different kind of homeland in language" (235).

46 Marc Shell, *The Economy of Literature* (Baltimore: Johns Hopkins University Press, 1978), 91.

47 Ibid., 85.

48 *Jean Baudrillard: Selected Writings,* ed. Mark Poster (Stanford: Stanford University Press, 1988), 72.

49 Martyn J. Lee, *Consumer Culture Reborn: The Cultural Politics of Consumption* (New York: Routledge, 1994), 21.

50 Walter Benjamin, "The Work of Art in the Age of Mechanical Reproduction," in *Illuminations: Essays and Reflections,* ed. Hannah Arendt (New York: Schocken Books, 1968), 217–51; Fredric Jameson, *Postmodernism, or, The Cultural Logic of Late Capitalism* (Durham: Duke University Press, 1991).

51 Karl Marx, "The German Ideology," in *The Marx-Engels Reader,* ed. Robert C. Tucker (New York: Norton, 1978), 156. One might also want to re-

mark on the curiousness of this passage itself because it appears to endorse its own fantasy of male-male reproduction in its strange locution, where "men . . . make other men" and women seem a kind of afterthought.

52 Georges Bataille, "The Notion of Expenditure," in *Visions of Excess: Selected Writings, 1927–1939,* ed. Allan Stoekl (Minneapolis: University of Minnesota Press, 1985), 117.

53 Karl Marx, *Capital,* volume 1 (New York: International Publishers, 1967), 41.

54 Andrew Parker, "Unthinking Sex: Marx, Engels, and the Scene of Writing," in *Fear of a Queer Planet: Queer Politics and Social Theory,* ed. Warner, 35. Miranda Joseph, in "The Performance of Production and Consumption," *Social Text* 54, 16.1 (spring 1998): 25–61, makes the most serious critique of Parker. She asserts that Parker posits queer sex as "unproductive," as outside of relations of production. This is in part because she disagrees with Parker's reading of Marx: she argues that Marx is not "productivist" and that his vision of production (and of use value) is socially constructivist and therefore, one would assume, not based in visions of the "natural." I think Joseph misses what Parker is pointing out, however, which is not that queer sex or theatricality are not productive, but only that they have not been viewed that way because of the narrow limits that Marx (and marxism) puts on what counts as productive, which is basically what she is also arguing. I find her defense of Marx unconvincing given the connections I (and Parker) have articulated above—Joseph herself acknowledges Marx's "[indisputable] homophobia" (49). Joseph also takes issue with what she sees as Baudrillard's efforts along the same line, to posit an exterior to production (she notes that Baudrillard's idea of "final consumption" is used by "contemporary capitalism . . . to make room for more production" [51]). Given my emphasis on a Foucauldian notion of discursivity, which emphasizes that there is no "outside" to power, in arguing for queer forms of (re)production, I am not arguing for an exterior to production but a redefinition of it. In so doing, however, I fall prey (or I am showing how Stein falls prey) to what Joseph, following Spivak, indicts as analogies "between representation and production, and . . . between political and symbolic representation" (51). Joseph seems to find these analogies problematic because they then favor to a greater or lesser degree, depending on who wields them, the "free play of the signifier" and "non-realist" (51) forms of representation over realist ones, as well as symbolic action over political action. They also seem to long for, at least in Joseph's critique of Peggy Phelan, an unrealizable Real. In other words, it seems less the analogies themselves that are the problem than in how they are used to posit an outside to production. In fact, Joseph's notion of performance makes the same kinds of analogies (and in its claims for the productivity of performance sees it as simultaneously symbolic and political),

but because she sees it as a form of production rather than a challenge to production, she argues that her vision of performance is distinctive.

55 Aristotle's *Politics,* as quoted in Shell, *Economy of Literature,* 94.

56 These same issues—usury, sodomy, gift exchange—are discussed with reference to Renaissance sodomy in Jody Greene's "'You Must Eat Men': The Sodomite Economy of Renaissance Patronage," *GLQ: A Journal of Lesbian and Gay Studies* 1.2 (1994): 163–97. In particular Greene's conception of "(un)natural breeding" resonates in some ways with my own conception of queer reproduction. It is clear that Stein was an avid, even obsessive, reader of Shakespeare, among others. The overwhelming majority of these representations of "unnatural breeding" in Greene and in other readings of Renaissance writings, however, are male-male. If Stein is revaluing this tradition, she is also reclaiming sodomy for women.

57 See also Schmitz, *Of Huck and Alice.*

58 Gertrude Stein, *The Geographical History of the United States, or, The Relation of Human Nature to the Human Mind* (New York: Random House, 1936), 165.

59 Marc Shell, *Money, Language, and Thought: Literary and Philosophical Economies from the Medieval to the Modern Era* (Berkeley: University of California Press, 1982), 22.

60 This "use" of identity becomes much more obvious in "Lifting Belly" and "Patriarchal Poetry."

61 Gilbert and Gubar, *No Man's Land,* 188; Catharine Stimpson, "Gertrude Stein and the Transposition of Gender," in *The Poetics of Gender,* ed. Nancy K. Miller (New York: Columbia University Press, 1986), 1–18.

62 Butler, *Gender Trouble,* 121.

63 For an early reading of the significance of "difference," see Pamela Hadas, "Spreading the Difference: One Way to Read Gertrude Stein's *Tender Buttons,*" *Twentieth-Century Literature* 24 (1978): 57–78.

64 For another, somewhat related, analysis of the way "masculine" and "feminine" objects work in *Tender Buttons,* see Ruddick, *Reading Gertrude Stein,* esp. 190–213. See also Holbrook, "Lifting Bellies," for an interpretation of "Lifting Belly" that reads Stein's experiments with the indeterminacy of language as ways to avoid the problems of representing lesbian visibility when such representations immediately then become an occasion for surveillance and control of lesbian sexuality. Holbrook also draws on Butler's notion of the iterability of sexual difference and of repetition as a way to intervene in normative systems of sexual and gender regulation, and, interestingly, she connects Butler's wariness about taxonomy to Stein's project in ways that resonate with my own analysis above.

65 For challenges to this ideology, see Lewis Hyde, *The Gift: Imagination and the Erotic Life of Property* (New York: Vintage Books, 1979), and Georges

Bataille, *The Accursed Share*, trans. Robert Hurley (New York: Zone Books, 1988).

66 I am grateful to Eve Sedgwick for calling this to my attention.

67 For a related, yet somewhat universalizing, discussion of the slippage between use and usury and its relation to coinage and metaphor, see Jacques Derrida, "White Mythology: Metaphor in the Text of Philosophy," in *Margins of Philosophy,* trans. Alan Bass (Chicago: University of Chicago Press, 1982), esp. 217–18. Derrida makes no attempt to discuss the historical connection of usury with anti-Semitism or with sodomy. He does, however, employ it as a way to describe how metaphor uses language.

68 Studies of "primitive" societies have often enforced this romanticization of gift giving. However, Bataille, writing on potlatch in *The Accursed Share,* dissolves the difference between gift giving and usury. Noting that such rituals of giving create an expectation of a greater return on the part of the giver, he observes that "wealth is multiplied in *potlatch* civilizations in a way that recalls the inflation of credit in banking civilizations" (122).

69 In a complex reading of Ezra Pound's poetry, Andrew Parker calls upon the usury/sodomy/money/language connection in Aristotle and the usury/metaphor connection in Derrida to demonstrate Pound's anti-Semitic critique of the transferability of the sign. He argues that Pound tried to create a "natural" form of writing based on a "natural" form of correspondence between money and things, in order to combat the "unnatural" slippage between signifier and signified. Stein was certainly aware of Pound's writing, and the fact that she also employs these same Aristotelian moments to opposite effect signals that some forms of modernism may at base be a struggle over "unnatural" forms of signification and subjectivity (Parker, "Ezra Pound and the 'Economy' of Anti-Semitism," in *Postmodernism and Politics,* ed. Jonathan Arac [Minneapolis: University of Minnesota Press, 1986], 70–90). Mena Mitrano, although she identifies Stein's project as one of "shifting [writing] toward dirt or profitless meaning," can only read this shift in terms of expressing alienation, and not in terms of a queer poetics that challenges the modernist trope of alienation in the first place (Mitrano, "Linguistic Exoticism and Literary Alienation: Gertrude Stein's *Tender Buttons,*" *Modern Language Studies* 28.2 [1998]: esp. 99).

70 Bataille, "The Notion of Expenditure," 116–17.

71 (Most statutes prohibiting sodomy in the United States include these definitional acts.) In the last few years there has been a critical outpouring of work on sodomy, in particular on its unstable definition. For several notable examples, see Janet Halley's two essays, "*Bowers v. Hardwick* in the Renaissance," in *Queering the Renaissance,* ed. Jonathan Goldberg (Durham: Duke University Press, 1993), and "The Construction of Heterosexuality," in *Fear of a Queer Planet,* ed. Warner, 82–102. See also Jonathan Goldberg, *Sodom-*

otries (Stanford: Stanford University Press, 1992), and his edited volume, *Reclaiming Sodom* (New York: Routledge, 1994).

72 As John Boswell explains in his history of the Christian Church's position on homosexuality: "By the fourteenth century usury incurred more severe penalties in church law than 'sodomy' did and was derogated in exactly the same terms" (Boswell, *Christianity, Social Tolerance, and Homosexuality: Gay People in Western Europe from the Beginning of the Christian Era to the Fourteenth Century* [Chicago: University of Chicago Press, 1980], 331). For a more historically detailed account of representations of usury and their connection to sodomy in early modern England in particular, see Greene, "'You Must Eat Men,'" esp. 170–78.

73 Schmitz, *Of Huck and Alice*, 180.

74 The connection between oral sex and writing is one of the themes of Stein's later work, "Lifting Belly."

75 Stein's relationship to her own Jewishness has long been a subject of debate, and in making this argument about her linking of sodomy and usury in *Tender Buttons* I am not attempting to resolve the issue in advance in regard to Stein's later work and actions, but rather only to argue it as it emerges in this poem. In addition to Damon's *Dark End of the Street*, see also her "Gertrude Stein's Jewishness, Jewish Social Scientists, and the 'Jewish Question,'" *Modern Fiction Studies* 42.3 (1996), in which she ponders the question of Stein's possible anti-Semitism, especially given Stein's deep interest in Weininger. Damon writes, "Stein . . . in her very challenge to the concept or desirability of identity, in her very claim that identity is relational rather than innate and autonomous, enacted and affirmed a kind of Jewishness that eschewed fixed categories and unilinear ways of thinking, thus instantiating Weininger's charges of Jews' faulty reasoning-cum-being-in-the-world while championing that psychic style as valid, liberating, and intellectually and aesthetically rewarding" (495). See also Wanda Van Dusen's recent discussion of Stein's collaboration with the Vichy regime and its relationship to shifts in her literary and philosophical positions. Although Van Dusen illuminates Stein's support of Pétain, she also points out the ways in which Stein may have undertaken this collaboration for her and Toklas's own personal safety. Nevertheless, Van Dusen's work makes clear the degree to which Stein separated herself publically, at least during World War II, from her Jewish identity (Van Dusen, "Portrait of a National Fetish: Gertrude Stein's 'Introduction to the Speeches of Maréchal Pétain,'" *Modernism/Modernity* 3.3 [1996]: 69–92). Phoebe Stein Davis, in an essay discussing the complexity of Stein's representations of World War II, hints at the degree to which Stein may have been (self-)critical of her own collaboration, and also points to moments where Stein demonstrates a clear understanding of the danger she, Toklas, and other Jews living in France were in (Davis, "'Even Cake Gets to Have An-

other Meaning': History, Narrative, and 'Daily Living' in Gertrude Stein's World War II Writings," *Modern Fiction Studies* 44.3 [1998]: 568–607). In so doing, Davis argues that, for Stein, history, the political, and the aesthetic were never separable. My essay does the same for Stein's theory of language as she presents it in *Tender Buttons*.

76 As Schmitz (*Of Huck and Alice,* 181), for one, has noted.

77 Ibid., 181–82. See also Pitchford, "Unlikely Modernism" (645–49), for another, at times substantially parallel, reading of this section.

78 Schmitz, *Of Huck and Alice,* 181.

79 I am grateful to Michael Moon for pointing out this detail.

80 Schmitz, *Of Huck and Alice,* 166–67.

81 I am not the only critic to notice how the poem repeatedly puns on Alice's name. For one notable example, see Hadas, "Spreading the Difference," 69.

82 Of course, Alice is also the "third" in the unholy trinity of Gertrude, Leo, and Alice, which soon leads to Leo's departure.

83 As noted above, the collaborative relationship between Stein and Toklas has formed the basis of many critical analyses, although none read it as (re)productive in quite the same way, and most, like Stimpson, fault Stein for her "male-identification" and the supposedly unequal gender roles she and Toklas occupied. See, for example, Stimpson, "Gertrude Stein and the Transposition of Gender," as well as her "Gertrice/Altrude: Stein, Toklas, and the Paradox of the Happy Marriage," in *Mothering the Mind: Twelve Studies of Writers and their Silent Partners,* ed. Ruth Perry and Martine Watson Brownley (New York: Holmes and Meier, 1984), 123–39.

84 Ruddick, in *Reading Gertrude Stein* (esp. 145–47), reads this metaphor as evidence of Stein's preoedipal fantasies. Using feminist psychoanalytic theory, she traces in Stein's writing a revaluation of the presymbolic and of the mother-daughter relationship, and ultimately she declares Stein a "gnostic writer." Although aspects of this approach may be useful, my work attempts to reclaim Stein's erotics from the totalizing effects of such readings, which, in their need to reduce all textual complexities to the bourgeois heterosexual reproductive family, cannot account for the sexual and historical specificities of her project. Turner, in *Baby Precious* (26–36), also sees Stein's and to a lesser degree, Toklas's, focus on "cows" as metaphors for Alice's bowel movements in their private correspondence and as in part a recuperation of Stein's relationship with her mother, but she also recognizes the crucial link in these letters between the "natural" processes of elimination, writing, and Stein and Toklas's "caretaking" relationship (28), as well as their female-female erotics. Although she mentions somewhat enigmatically that "Lifting Belly" may be read as a poem about "an enema" (35), and connects Stein's interest in "the bottom nature" of individuals in *The Making of American* with a naturalism grounded in the metaphor of shitting as writing and vice

versa, she does not extend this discussion to deal in any real depth with the erotic/excrement connection in Stein's literary works, nor does she notice the connections to prohibitions against sodomy, etc.

85 For several examples, see Angela McRobbie, "Dance as Social Fantasy," in *Gender and Generation,* ed. Angela McRobbie and Mica Nava (London: Macmillan, 1984), 131–61, and Paul Gilroy, *There Ain't No Black in the Union Jack* (Chicago: University of Chicago Press, 1991).

86 Michel de Certeau, *The Practice of Everyday Life,* trans. Stephen Rendall (Berkeley: University of California Press, 1984), esp. 165–76. See also Butler, "Merely Cultural," *Social Text* 52/53, 15.3–4 (fall/winter 1997): 265–77.

87 In aligning consumption and production I am not arguing that they are equivalent. As Joseph notes, "'Consumptive' labor is productive, but it is organized very differently than 'productive' labor: it is not organized, procured, or exploited as wage labor." Consequently, she argues, "In expanding production to include women's work, private activity, and signification or performance, the definition of the technology of oppression, what Marx called exploitation, also must be expanded" (Joseph, "Performance of Production," 35).

88 McRobbie's work is just one of numerous examples.

89 For one notable example of this, see W. F. Haug, *Critique of Commodity Aesthetics: Appearance, Sexuality, and Advertising in Capitalist Society* (Minneapolis: University of Minnesota Press, 1986).

90 Smith-Rosenberg, *Disorderly Conduct,* 221–25.

Chapter 5. The M Multiplying: Marianne Moore, Elizabeth Bishop,
and the Pleasures of Influence, Part 1

1 Elizabeth Bishop, *One Art: Letters,* selected and edited by Robert Giroux (New York: Farrar, Straus and Giroux, 1994), 3 (and footnote). I reproduce this letter as the editor has written it; all italics and parenthetical citations are his. In addition to Bishop's letters, in this chapter I draw on biographical studies of Bishop by Lorrie Goldensohn, *Elizabeth Bishop: The Biography of a Poetry* (New York: Columbia University Press, 1992); David Kalstone, *Becoming a Poet: Elizabeth Bishop with Marianne Moore and Robert Lowell,* ed. Robert Hemenway (New York: Farrar, Straus and Giroux, The Noonday Press, 1989); Brett Millier, *Elizabeth Bishop: Life and the Memory of It* (Berkeley: University of California Press, 1993); and Gary Fountain and Peter Brazeau, eds., *Remembering Elizabeth Bishop: An Oral Biography* (Amherst: University of Massachusetts Press, 1994). It also draws on Charles Molesworth's biography of Moore, *Marianne Moore: A Literary Life* (New

York: Atheneum, 1990), and on Moore's *Selected Letters,* ed. Bonnie Costello, with Celeste Goodridge and Cristanne Miller (New York: Knopf, 1997).

2 This is due, in part, to the suppression or destruction of many of the most intimate letters. After Bishop's longtime lover, Lota de Macedo Soares, committed suicide, all of Bishop's letters to her were destroyed.

3 Frani Blough Muser, interviewed in Fountain and Brazeau (*Remembering
Elizabeth Bishop,* 25) misidentifies the teacher as a Miss Prentiss, who Muser
describes as too sentimental in many ways for Bishop's taste, yet who she
says Bishop admitted influenced her as a poet. Thus, we might see Bishop's
tone as somewhat ironic. Regardless, however, Bishop here experiments with
the (sentimental) erotics of silence that Miss Talbot sets in motion. Bethany
Hicok argues that Miss Prentiss (Miss Talbot?) actually pursued Bishop ro-
mantically, and that Bishop was "working through [her] perceived advances"
(Hicok, "'Some Realm of Reciprocity': Moore, Bishop, and the Women's
College," Ph.D. diss., University of Rochester, 1996, 158).

4 This urge is reminiscent of Whitman's fantasies about his readers' relationships to "Leaves of Grass," in which he imagines that his readers, by pos-
sessing his book, also possess him—what Michael Moon in *Disseminating
Whitman* (69) refers to as the practice of "specular incorporation."

5 Giroux, in Bishop, *One Art,* 3.

6 Two of the most nuanced examples of this trend, which I discuss in this chapter and the next, are Joanne Fiet Diehl, *Elizabeth Bishop and Marianne
Moore: The Psychodynamics of Creativity* (Princeton: Princeton University
Press, 1993), and Betsy Erkkila, *The Wicked Sisters: Women Poets, Literary
History, and Discord* (New York: Oxford University Press, 1992). In both
cases, I would argue, these critics' inability to see Moore as anything but a
repressive censor, as opposed to exploring her own queer positioning, limit
severely the ways in which they can appreciate the intensity and complexity
of Moore and Bishop's interactions. A less-dominant strain in studies of
Moore and Bishop's relationship, and one that Diehl and Erkkila position
themselves against, is that of reading their intimacies as simply examples of
an essentially female sense of "nurture." For the most notable example of this
trend, see Bonnie Costello, "Marianne Moore and Elizabeth Bishop: Friendship and Influence," *Twentieth-Century Literature* 30 (summer/fall 1984):
130–49. To a large degree, in chapters five and six I take it for granted that
such an idealized vision of female-female interactions overlooks the degree to
which power operates within women's relationships, as Erkkila pointedly
notes in *The Wicked Sisters* (108). Other critics, such as Langdon Hammer,
have argued that we should read the Moore/Bishop relationship as just one
example of the uniquely twentieth-century "mentor/protégé" type. Although
Hammer acknowledges the specificity of the female-female context Moore

thus provided for Bishop, he is not able to address the issues of gender and sexuality that were, I would assert, so central to both their commonalities and their differences, except when he argues that Moore's femininity provided Bishop with an alternative to the intensely competitive "heterosexual" literary world (Hammer, "Useless Concentration: Life and Work in Elizabeth Bishop's Letters and Poems," *American Literary History* 9.1 [1997]: 166). Jeredith Merrin also argues for the "mentor/protégé" paradigm: her study of the intertextualities and formal overlaps and differences in their work in light of literary history remains exemplary (Merrin, *An Enabling Humility: Marianne Moore, Elizabeth Bishop, and the Uses of Tradition* [Rutgers University Press, 1990]).

7 In order to avoid confusion, throughout this chapter I will refer to Marianne Moore as "Marianne" (Bishop's choice of appellation in "Efforts of Affection") or "Moore," and to Marianne's mother as "Mrs. Moore."

8 In describing Moore (and Bishop's) relationship to white, middle-class, bourgeois standards of gender and sexuality, I rely on Butler's idea of the *performativity* of identity. As she cogently describes it in *Gender Trouble*, "Consider gender, for instance, as *a corporeal style,* an 'act,' as it were, which is both intentional and performative, where *'performative'* suggests a dramatic and contingent construction of meaning" (139).

9 Kirstin Hotelling argues that Moore refuses the conventions of the traditional lyric "I," and that she practices a form of "situated" or "partial" knowledge/vision, which reveals the partialness of any perspective while still striving for limited objectivity. More relevant to this project, Hotelling also links Moore's theory of gender in her poetry to Butler's project of understanding the ways in which gender and sex are both discursively constructed and nonessential. Such an understanding of Moore's "poetic persona" removes Moore from the endless "is she 'feminine' or is she 'masculine'?" debate of much feminist criticism of the poet, yet Hotelling often confuses sex and sexuality in her discussion, arguing that Moore is not "asexual" when I think she means not "gender neutral" or "androgynous" (Hotelling, " 'The I of each is to the I of each, a kind of fretful speech which sets a limit on Itself': Marianne Moore's Strategic Selfhood," *Modernism/Modernity* 5.1 [1998]: 75–96). Cristanne Miller, whose brilliant book *Marianne Moore: Questions of Authority* (Cambridge: Harvard University Press, 1995), informs this study throughout, also sees Moore's poetry (and her own persona) as embodying "fluid gender identification" (127), although at times this seems to become for Miller a "gender neutrality," or an avoidance of gender, inspired by the early-twentieth-century discourse of female professionalism, as opposed to an investigation of the workings of gender and sexuality in language and form. Still, Miller traces the ways in which critics' "depiction's of [Moore's] anxiety and her femininity have been exaggerated," and argues in-

stead that "Moore's confidence in her abilities to perform the kind of gender transformational work she pursues in her poetry was both remarkably and anomalously strong" (104). Miller focuses primarily, however, on Moore's "transformation" of gender, and she shies away from discussion of Moore's sexuality. For three other feminist interpretations of Moore to which this study is indebted, see Sabine Sielke, *Fashioning the Female Subject: The Intertextual Networking of Dickinson, Moore, and Rich* (Ann Arbor: University of Michigan Press, 1997); Jeanne Heuving, *Omissions Are Not Accidents: Gender in the Art of Marianne Moore* (Detroit: Wayne State University Press, 1992); and Hicok, *Some Realm of Reciprocity.*

10 Elizabeth Bishop, "Efforts of Affection," in *The Collected Prose,* ed. Robert Giroux (New York: Farrar, Straus and Giroux, The Noonday Press, 1984), 156. Subsequent citations appear as parenthetical page references in the text.

11 Diehl, *Elizabeth Bishop and Marianne Moore,* 41.

12 Gilbert and Gubar, *The Madwoman in the Attic: The Woman Writer and the Nineteenth-Century Literary Imagination* (New Haven: Yale University Press, 1979), 49.

13 Teresa de Lauretis, *The Practice of Love,* 171. De Lauretis, whose critique of traditional psychoanalytic interpretations of the mother/daughter relationship matches most closely my own, still cannot avoid replicating these same problems even as she tries to avoid them. Her attempts at including racial (and even less so, class) specificities into her overarching model of the psychic construction of lesbian subjectivity end up getting subsumed into the totalizing power of the psychoanalytic machine, and she cannot at all address the questions of either the historical formation of modern lesbian identity or its relation to other national, imperial, and racial forms of identification. See Margaret Homans, *Women Writers and Poetic Identity: Dorothy Wordsworth, Emily Brontë, and Emily Dickinson* (Princeton: Princeton University Press, 1980), and Gilbert and Gubar, *The Madwoman in the Attic,* for perhaps the inaugurating examples of this dominant critical current.

14 Even from the very first essays on Bishop's poetry, Moore's influence was thought to be central to understanding the young poet. Randall Jarrell, for example, when reviewing Bishop's first book, *North and South,* writes: "When you read Miss Bishop's 'Florida' . . . you don't need to be told that the poetry of Marianne Moore was, in the beginning, an appropriately selected foundation for Miss Bishop's work" (Jarrell, "On *North and South,*" in *Elizabeth Bishop and Her Art,* ed. Lloyd Schwartz and Sybil P. Estes [Ann Arbor: University of Michigan Press, 1979], 180). Influence does not automatically entail mothering, however.

15 For example, even David Kalstone, arguably one of their most sensitive critics, interprets Bishop's riff on Moore cited above as clear "evidence" of Moore as mother: "Moore is taken up in an alliterative blur of childhood

associating with the remote Nova Scotia village where Bishop grew up: the coiling initial letters that fascinated Bishop in her beloved grandfather's Bible; his old-fashioned village lessons in behavior revisited in one of a planned series of poems on "manners"; and beneath it all the unspoken fact of Bishop's childhood: an absent mother" (Kalstone, *Becoming a Poet,* 5).

16 See Bonnie Costello, afterword to *Remembering Elizabeth Bishop: An Oral Biography,* ed. Gary Fountain and Peter Brazeau (Amherst: University of Massachusetts Press, 1994), 354, for just one example of this argument.

17 Erkkila, *The Wicked Sisters,* 110.

18 How many of us have not had such an encounter? As a young, lesbian-identified college student, full of political excitement and ire, I encountered older women whose relationships to their sexualities were not mediated or invigorated by politics, and for whom an erotics of silence, of upholding various proprieties, especially in relation to younger girls, was both a source of great pleasure, and at moments, great pain. It would be a mistake to romanticize this position as some kind of pre-Stonewall utopia, just as it would also be wrong to imagine that because things are now spoken, made public, the position of gays and lesbians and queers in the United States is necessarily "better," as the controversy over gays in the military illustrates.

19 And her reasons for disliking Crane ostensibly circled around her highly publicized conflicts with him over her criticism of his poetry, as Moore's biographer, Charles Molesworth, acknowledges (*Marianne Moore,* 219–20). His assessment of Moore's relation to homosexuality, in particular to Auden, Kallman, Wheeler, and Westcott, as well as to knowing and "unknowing," most resembles my own:

> [Auden and Kallman] were highly aesthetic writers, very involved with the gossip and goings-on of the literary scene. The homosexual style and aesthetic sensibility of these men did not discernibly make Moore uncomfortable. In fact, there were among her good friends and acquaintances several homosexuals or bachelors, many of whom were also bibliophiles, and they treated Moore with great deference while at the same time being playful and artistically very knowing. This combination of knowingness, which at times approached pedantry, and a playful teasing was, of course, evident in Moore's poetry. . . . Because Moore chose to remain single all her life, she was perhaps disposed to be more than tolerant of those who had not started a family of their own. This would include many of her female friends, such as Elizabeth Bishop and Louise Crane, as well. But in many if not all of such instances, Moore was able to give her friends, as they gave her, a very intense and complex emotional support. (363–64)

20 For example, as Moore's recently published letters attest, she maintained long-lasting, intense epistolary and interpersonal exchanges with a large

group of women, including the openly lesbian writers H.D. and Bryher, Louise Crane (Bishop's lover of the 1930s), as well as many other women who lived in intimate relationships with other women.

21 I am grateful to Barry Sarchett for pointing this out.

22 Lee Edelman, "The Geography of Gender: Elizabeth Bishop's 'In the Waiting Room,'" in *Elizabeth Bishop: The Geography of Gender*, ed. Marilyn May Lombardi (Charlottesville: University Press of Virginia, 1993), 91–107.

23 Bishop, "In the Waiting Room," in *The Complete Poems: 1927–1979* (New York: Farrar, Straus and Giroux, 1983), 160.

24 Bishop, "In the Village," in *The Collected Prose*, 251–74. Subsequent citations appear as parenthetical page references in the text.

25 Of these, Kalstone's is perhaps the most compelling example (*Becoming a Poet*, 156–66).

26 For notable exceptions to this trend, see Susan McCabe, *Elizabeth Bishop: Her Poetics of Loss* (University Park: Pennsylvania State University Press, 1994), 12–13, and Diehl, *Elizabeth Bishop and Marianne Moore*, 98–100.

27 Although the connotations of this term are also, of course, dependent on the context in which it is employed: within communities of African American women, for example the term "girl" is also one of affection and alliance.

28 Diehl goes so far as to read the kitten image as one of "infanticide," and she is only able to read Miss Gurley as an example of the preoedipal, dangerous maternal. By confining Miss Gurley to this presymbolic realm, Diehl denies her power to influence Bishop's subject formation, except as another emblem of "malevolent" femininity to which the male blacksmith offers an oedipalizing alternative (Diehl, *Elizabeth Bishop and Marianne Moore*, 100).

29 McCabe also notices the connection of dressmaker to artist, although she sees the gift of the coin as a metonym for "'original' loss," the loss of the mother, which for McCabe is always the underlying signified of Bishop's work (*Elizabeth Bishop*, 12–13). In so doing, McCabe overlooks the significance of Miss Gurley's social-sexual position: the coin becomes simply a regressive reminder of maternal absence and a signifier of Bishop's endless struggle to master maternal loss through language.

30 As McCabe perhaps most compellingly argues, it also presents the blacksmith as a "male" model for poetic production, but *not* in a way that supplants or replaces the maternal or, I might add, Miss Gurley's influence (*Elizabeth Bishop*, 7–8, 11–12).

31 Apparently Moore had chosen such locations carefully to allow her an easy exit, but as Bishop surmises, Moore must have been interested in Bishop enough not to propose an assignation at the information booth of Grand Central Station, something she had done when meeting with less-promising young women, which would have made any real conversation almost impossible. For various retellings of this meeting, accounts that have influ-

enced my own, see, among others, Millier, *Elizabeth Bishop;* Erkkila, *The Wicked Sisters;* Kalstone, *Becoming a Poet;* and Diehl, *Elizabeth Bishop and Marianne Moore.* At the time, Moore was living in Brooklyn with her mother.

32 Miller reads this memoir as not-so-subtly condescending and belittling of Moore, especially in the ways in which it reveals "private" details of Moore's life, such as discussions of her underwear, which Miller argues would never characterize a memoir of a male modernist (*Marianne Moore,* 240 n.49). Thus, Miller argues that Bishop succumbs to the predominant view of Moore as somehow strange, "nonhuman . . . , fantastic . . . , and fragile . . . [;] not a person but a phenomenon" (23). I would argue instead that by emphasizing Moore's "old maidish" qualities as well as her uniqueness, Bishop reveals the complexity of Moore's positioning as both genteel spinster daughter and powerfully queer modernist poet. Miller tries to play down both of these aspects of Moore's subjectivity, instead focusing on Moore as what ultimately seems to be a liberal feminist (what Miller sees as Moore's belief in the power of the individual [25]).

33 For an illuminating and, at times, somewhat parallel reading of Moore and Bishop's relationship, one that pays particular attention to the importance of the women's college to the development of their individual gendered subjectivities and poetics, but still sees them as ultimately in a mother/daughter relation, see Hicok, *Some Realm of Reciprocity.*

34 And I would argue that, in general, this ambivalence of tone is reflected throughout the memoir, not as a way of belittling Moore or making her seem ridiculous (as Miller argues, see note 32 above), but, as Diehl remarks in *Elizabeth Bishop and Marianne Moore* (esp. 29), as a complex negotiation of Bishop's feelings of identification and refusal of that identification. Even at Bishop's most distanced point in the memoir, reflected in the satirizing of Moore, there is an undercurrent of affection that I would argue undercuts any reading of it as belittling or dismissive, or even, as Diehl asserts, aggressively distancing.

35 Again, as I do in earlier chapters, I use this term generally to connote any sexual practice or identity that falls outside the boundaries of bourgeois reproductive heterosexuality, but I also deliberately intend at this moment in my discussion of Moore and Bishop for it to remain somewhat undefined.

36 See, for example, "Moore" by Cecil Beaton or "Moore" by Cartier-Bresson, both reproduced in Molesworth, *Marianne Moore.*

37 Molesworth anxiously assures us that this habit was not one connected with a kind of political or poetic radicalism, and he asserts that Moore was already wearing this outfit before she left college. By reiterating this bit of personal history, it appears he believes that since Moore had cross-dressed be-

fore she was recognized as a poet, her penchant for impersonating George Washington had absolutely nothing to do with her sense of her importance to American letters (Molesworth, *Marianne Moore,* 30). Miller sees this outfit as contributing to Moore's increasing dismissal by the literary establishment as simply an eccentric, slightly ridiculous old woman. Such a reading misses completely the strategic ways in which Moore deploys gender and sexuality in her deliberate donning of such outfits. Such a question has led other feminist critics, when examining the habits of self-(re)presentation employed by prominent women modernists such as Moore and Gertrude Stein, to assume that these women just "wanted to be men," to garner male authority and renounce their femininity. Any evidence of cross-gender identification is taken as a straightforward assumption and by extension acceptance, of "male," and therefore negative, values.

Queer theory has challenged such a dismissal of "male identification" by arguing that it overlooks the complexities of the relationship (or non-relationship) between gender identification, biological sex, and sexuality (see Sedgwick, *Epistemology of the Closet,* and Butler, *Gender Trouble*). Throughout the twentieth century, female masculinity has represented a self-identification with the discourse of inversion (as in the case of Radclyffe Hall), as well as a deeply felt sense of essential masculinity (as in a man trapped in a woman's body, or what is now often labeled gender dysphoria or gender identity disorder). At other times, female masculinity has also provided a way for "biological women" subversively to reinscribe and simultaneously co-opt male (sexual) power—to make masculinity a matter of performance, not of nature. Or it may also simply connote a desire to wear men's clothes. For discussions of these issues, see especially Newton, "The Mythic Mannish Lesbian"; Halberstam, *Female Masculinity;* and Prosser, *Second Skins.*

It seems unlikely that Moore identified as anything resembling what we would now call a "butch" lesbian, or even, to be more historically precise, an "invert." Her practices of male impersonation are hyperbolically performative (i.e., they do not strive for "realness"), inconsistent, and perhaps *because* of their obvious performativity, were and still are viewed simply as "odd" and "anachronistic," (not coincidentally, I would argue) a throwback to the old maid of the nineteenth century.

38 For a related discussion of this outfit, see Sandra Gilbert, "Marianne Moore as Female Female Impersonator," *Marianne Moore: The Art of a Modernist,* ed. Joseph Parisi (Ann Arbor: UMI Research Press, 1990), 27–46.

39 Moore, *The Complete Poems of Marianne Moore* (New York: Viking, 1967), 62. Subsequent references to the poems appear as parenthetical references in the text.

40 David Bergman is the only other critic to notice this connection; see his groundbreaking essay "Marianne Moore and the Problem of 'Marriage,'" *American Literature* 60.2 (May 1988): 250.

41 Ibid., 250–51.

42 As Fountain and Brazeau's *Remembering Elizabeth Bishop* reveals.

43 For the most extensive account of this relationship, see Millier, *Elizabeth Bishop,* 236–398.

44 For historical discussions of this generation of lesbian women, see Newton, "The Mythic Mannish Lesbian," 298–93, and Faderman, *Odd Girls and Twilight Lovers,* esp. 37–61. For an account that focuses specifically on working-class lesbian culture, see Elizabeth Lapovsky Kennedy and Madeline D. Davis, *Boots of Leather, Slippers of Gold: The History of a Lesbian Community* (New York: Penguin, 1993).

45 She also tried for years to control and hide her alcoholism from all but her closest friends (a task at which she invariably failed, partly due her habit of calling them, as well as acquaintances, late at night when she had had too much to drink) (Millier, *Elizabeth Bishop,* 150).

46 Fountain and Brazeau, *Remembering Elizabeth Bishop,* 86, 336.

47 Thus, I would argue that critics consistently exaggerate Bishop's "need" to confess to Moore her own sexual identity, overlooking the complexity with which Bishop herself existed in relation to the closet. For example, Diehl continually assumes that Bishop wanted to "out" herself explicitly to Moore. Ironically, this assumption of the need for greater personal openness is matched by an overemphasis of the workings of the closet in regard to Bishop's poetry, which Diehl reads as indebted to Moore's own techniques of self-distancing. Such an interpretation cannot then adequately account for the ways in which Bishop's poems consistently represent relationships between women (Diehl, *Elizabeth Bishop and Marianne Moore,* esp. 12, 24, 33–34).

48 It is in many ways no surprise, then, that most of her biographers, including David Kalstone and Brett Millier, have been reluctant to reveal the details of Bishop's relationships with women.

49 Fountain and Brazeau, *Remembering Elizabeth Bishop,* 327–28.

50 Ibid., 118.

51 As one such letter confides:

> Peggy [James]—to return, is *comme usual.* I get nervous as a horse though when [I] get to touching certain parts of her. I don't believe she has "understanding" or the shadow of it. Alas some deficiencies do not however keep one from being a Circe, if the instinct to please, and a gentle, feeling aspect, and a mind over which passions show color as they run, are present. I hate to make Peggy an *objet d'art* and it is her fault that I

do—but if she *can*not acknowledge me a man without giving me a black, she *can*not. (Moore, *Selected Letters*, 38)

In light of such writings, against those critics who either insist on Moore's asexuality, or, more recently, retreat when describing even these intimacies behind the line of "romantic friendship," I would argue that Moore herself, at least within the intense atmosphere of Bryn Mawr, did have what even at the time would have been labeled by some as "lesbian" relationships. In its description of what seems to be a repeated "touching," the letter grounds this instance of the seemingly ubiquitous college "crush" in the physical (at least for Moore). Furthermore, Moore encountered other examples of openly lesbian couples at Bryn Mawr and after, which would make it hard to assert that she was ignorant or "innocent," as some critics maintain, as to the implications of her own intimacies. But why should one have to go to such great lengths to "prove" Moore's familiarity with female-female intimacy in the first place? For a brilliant reading of Moore's early fiction in light of her relationship with Peggy James, see Hicok, "'To Work Lovingly': Marianne Moore at Bryn Mawr, 1905–1909," *The Journal of Modern Literature* 23.4 (spring/summer 2000): 483–501.

52 Cyrena Pondrom, "Marianne Moore and H.D.: Female Community and Poetic Achievement," in *Marianne Moore: Woman and Poet*, ed. Patricia C. Willis (Orono: University of Maine, National Poetry Foundation, 1990), 379.

53 My understanding of the inner workings of the Moore family is most indebted to Leavell's groundbreaking archival research, which she uses primarily not to discuss the intricacies of sexuality and gender but to chart Moore's relationship to emerging aesthetic theories and movements; see Leavell, *Marianne Moore and the Visual Arts: Prismatic Color* (Baton Rouge: Louisiana State University Press, 1995). See also Molesworth, *Marianne Moore*, and Miller, *Marianne Moore*, esp. 94–97.

54 For examples of these letters, see Moore, *Selected Letters*, esp. 3–72.

55 Leavell, *Marianne Moore*, 12.

56 Although it should be noted that he continued to help support his mother and sister financially and (through his numerous letters) emotionally throughout their lives.

57 As quoted in Leavell, *Marianne Moore*, 41 (MM, summer 1918, Notebook 1250/23 [Rosenbach VII:10:06], 67).

58 As quoted in Leavell, *Marianne Moore*, 26 (MM to MWM, December 2, 1915 [Rosenbach VI:21:13]).

59 That Moore's mother disapproved of the bohemian circles within which Moore traveled is clear but, as Leavell notes, this disapproval seemed to stem more from how one conducted one's self than from what one did (Leavell, *Marianne Moore*, 44 n.69).

60 This is Erkkila's position (*The Wicked Sisters*). For a related critique of such views of Moore's mother, see Hicok, "To Work 'Lovingly,'" 485–88.

61 Leavell, *Marianne Moore*, 12–13.

62 Although Miller is still uncomfortable with what she terms the "undoubted masculism in the family choice to empower Marianne by making her male rather than by reconstructing the feminine so as to empower her as female" (*Marianne Moore*, 97). Miller, it seems to me, misses some of the playfulness and complexity of these nicknames—why should we expect the family to revalue the feminine? Could their masculine terms of endearment for Moore instead recognize her own ambiguous sense of gender identity?

63 A point the editors of the letters make in their introduction, as does Miller (*Marianne Moore*, 97).

64 Interestingly, Miller even goes so far to assert that Moore's whole poetic was a representation of this community ethic. She asserts that Moore would have felt comfortable choosing a professional life as a poet over marriage because of the fact that a high percentage of her female peers were also doing so. Although it is true that many middle-class, white women of Moore's generation chose, or were forced, not to marry (Miller's statistics indicate that 55 percent of Bryn Mawr graduates in 1909 did not marry), this does not mean that such women found widespread social acceptance for this decision (Miller, *Marianne Moore*, 99). In fact, increasingly during this period (and already in the late nineteenth century, as I have argued above), single women were viewed with suspicion, as "unnatural." Furthermore, deciding not to marry and deciding not to engage in object-directed sexual activity are two different things, and as illustrated by Moore's conflicts with H.D. and Bryher, discussed in detail below, even her closest women friends questioned her decision to prioritize her relationship with her mother over all others. I do agree with Miller, however, that within Moore's own family much of what I would term her "queer" performative identifications were accepted, and that therefore her family served as a counter to public expressions of disapprobation at what were perceived as transgressions of gender and sexual norms.

65 Leavell, *Marianne Moore*, 14–15. That Mrs. Moore had experienced such a relationship might indicate that she even provided Marianne a context for appreciating her "smashes" at Bryn Mawr and for supporting Marianne's later friendships with a wide range of other women. Hicok terms Mrs. Moore's relationship with Norcross a "Boston marriage," and she reproduces a letter from Mrs. Moore to Norcross that appears extremely erotic (Hicok, *Some Realm of Reciprocity*, 101–2). Such a letter begs the same question I ask above: What counts as sex for such women? Is their eroticism something other than sex, and therefore legitimate? Regardless of the answer, by the time Moore was in college the beginning of the emergence of the

identity category lesbian, along with its deviant connotations, would have made it increasingly difficult to maintain any such distinction.

66 Interestingly, Bergman traces Moore's thinking on marriage and contextualizes her view of it (and its concomitant reproductive heterosexuality) as incompatible with a career (see "Marianne Moore," esp. 241–43). Other forms of erotic expression may not be opposed to a career, however. As John Vincent convincingly argues, the formal construction of Moore's poetry itself may constitute a form of erotic expression for her (Vincent, *Queer Lyrics: Difficulty and Closure in American Poetry* [New York: Palgrave, forthcoming]).

67 Were her intense epistolary relationships a "substitute" for or, less pejoratively, an expression of an erotic interrelationship? Pondrom hints at this possibility, pointing provocatively to the last lines of a relatively late letter from Moore to H.D.: "'Shall I see you?' Moore inquired in 1956, 'It's too soon to know. . . . A blessing is it not, that the mind has wings—that the page is the person. Could I live if it were not so?'" (Moore to H.D. August 27, 1956, as quoted in Pondrom, "Marianne Moore and H.D.," 393). While Miller uses this discussion as a basis for her assertions about Moore's communal poetics, in the process the specifically erotic component of these exchanges, in my opinion, is minimized.

68 Usually this means that Marianne ends up being subsumed within her mother's religiosity, and by extension critics assume that Marianne shared her mother's social and political conservatism, a trend Miller also refutes.

69 Bishop, *The Complete Poems*, 82–83. Subsequent citations appear as parenthetical references in the text.

70 Bishop, *The Complete Poems*, 35–39. Subsequent citations appear as parenthetical page references in the text.

71 My understanding of this "incident" is indebted to the accounts in Millier, *Elizabeth Bishop*, 158–60; Diehl, *Elizabeth Bishop and Marianne Moore*, 24; Kalstone, *Becoming a Poet*, 76–101; Erkkila, "Elizabeth Bishop," 99–151; and Goldensohn, *Elizabeth Bishop*, 133–61, which each have a slightly different interpretation of this event.

72 Kalstone, *Becoming a Poet*, 82.

73 Erkkila, *The Wicked Sisters*, 126.

74 See Biddy Martin, "Lesbian Identity and Autobiographical Difference[s]," in *Life/Lines: Theorizing Women's Autobiography,* ed. Bella Brodzki and Celeste Schenck (Ithaca: Cornell University Press, 1988), 77–103, for the best description to date of the "coming out" genre. See also Chauncey, *Gay New York*, 6–7.

75 Most critics who acknowledge the lesbian content of "Roosters," if they do at all, read the lovers as totally separated from and not implicated in the

violence that ostensibly occurs outside the window. They isolate lesbianism as somehow outside the structures of power and violence that characterize what are usually its monolithic opposition: "patriarchy" and "heterosexuality." Butler, in discussing theories of lesbian identity, labels this way of thinking "lesbian modernism" and asserts instead that "there are structures of psychic homosexuality within heterosexual relations, and structures of psychic heterosexuality within gay and lesbian sexuality and relationships" (Butler, *Gender Trouble,* 121). Lesbianism is not somehow free from power but instead reinscribes it.

76 Susan Schweik, *A Gulf So Deeply Cut: American Women Poets and the Second World War* (Madison: University of Wisconsin Press, 1991), 231–32. Schweik elegantly elucidates, in ways that often match my own analysis, the forms in which love and war in the poem are made analogous, not held separate.

77 This "lost" Bishop poem is published, along with her narrative of its recovery, in Goldensohn, *Elizabeth Bishop,* 27–28.

78 A point that many critics have noticed. See for example, Costello, *Elizabeth Bishop: Questions of Mastery* (Cambridge: Harvard University Press, 1991), 65.

79 Bishop, as quoted in Goldensohn, *Elizabeth Bishop,* 28.

80 Interestingly, Hicok ties this to the spatial significance of the closet; see her "Elizabeth Bishop's 'Queer Birds': Vassar, *Con Spirito,* and the Romance of Female Community," *Contemporary Literature* 40.2 (1999): 306. She reads what she calls moments of "enclosure" in Bishop's work as ways of establishing and often celebrating lesbian subcultural community. I am more interested in the ways in which such a moment in Bishop's work explores both the erotic restrictions and the possibilities produced by prohibition and/or surveillance. In other words, I am concerned with the ways in which for Bishop's poetry, desire is often connected to danger and the threat of exposure.

81 Bishop; as quoted in Goldensohn, *Elizabeth Bishop,* 28.

82 Bishop, *The Complete Poems,* 70.

83 My reading here is indebted to Goldensohn (*Elizabeth Bishop,* 27–28), whose careful interpretation of "It is marvellous" remains one of the most nuanced lesbian-focused readings of Bishop's poetry.

84 Luce Irigaray, *This Sex Which Is Not One,* trans. Catherine Porter (Ithaca: Cornell University Press, 1985), esp. chapter 11. I am thinking specifically here, for example, of Rich's "Transcendental Etude," in *The Dream of a Common Language* (New York: Norton, 1978), 72–77. See Margaret Dickie, *Stein, Bishop, and Rich: Lyrics of Love, War, and Place* (Chapel Hill: University of North Carolina Press, 1997), for an extended discussion of Bishop's war poems and their relation to "love." Dickie spends little time on

"Roosters," but in general she also argues for refusing any idealization of lesbian intimacy because of what she views as the duplicitous, damaging (yet also productive) effects of the closet.

85 I would rather not read this as a flaunting of homosexuality, a kind of privileged relation to the phallus, à la Irigaray (*Speculum of the Other Woman; This Sex Which Is Not One*).

86 Kalstone, *Becoming a Poet*, 83.

87 And here my interpretation differs significantly from critics such as Alicia Suskin Ostriker, who prefer to read this aestheticization as *simply* a withdrawal from the scene of violence; see her *Stealing the Language: The Emergence of Women's Poetry in America* (Boston: Beacon, 1986), 54.

88 Schweik, *A Gulf So Deeply Cut*, 231–32.

89 In "One Art" (*The Collected Poems*, 178), Bishop equates form itself with a kind of staying power: against an incessant series of losses, culminating in the loss of a lover (which many critics read to be Bishop's allusion to the suicide of the woman with whom she had the most significant relationship of her life, Lota de Macedo Soares), writing itself, in this case the poetic form of a villanelle, is the frame that holds things together even as they are continually being carried away by various kinds of losses. The irony of "One Art" is that the injunction that invokes writing as a way to stave off utter (self-)loss interrupts or disrupts the form, which is itself supposed to guarantee stability:

> —Even losing you (the joking voice, a gesture
> I love) I shan't have lied. It's evident
> the art of losing's not too hard to master
> though it may look like (*Write* it!) like disaster. (178)

This interruption dramatizes the way in which the poem can barely contain the loss of the "you," which in the list of things lost, as it telescopes out from keys, to watches, to houses, to continents, comes as the crowning loss, the most significant. "*Write* it!" interrupts the easy flow of the rhyme, and indicates that even as it provides the solution to mastering loss, it also always threatens to destabilize this mastery. Writing always endangers form: in this poem, the conventions of grief.

90 See Schweik, *A Gulf So Deeply Cut*, for the most extended discussion of this context.

91 And she continued to write antimilitarism poems into the mid-to-late 1940s (Schweik, *A Gulf So Deeply Cut*, 232).

92 Kalstone, *Becoming a Poet*, 79.

93 Moore and her mother's rewriting of "Roosters" appears in the appendix of Kalstone's biography (*Becoming a Poet*, 265–69); as well as in Moore's *Selected Letters*, 403–4.

94 Interestingly, Bishop notes in "Efforts of Affection" that she prefers the term "over-fastidious" to "prudish," the term others have chosen, to describe Mrs. Moore and Marianne, and she then argues that Marianne was less so than Mrs. Moore, especially as she aged. The example Bishop uses to illustrate Marianne's increasing lack of "fastidiousness" is her ability to "call a spade a spade," and then Bishop raises the issue of homosexuality (130). When we remember the minute attention that both poets paid to word choice, and the ways in which they exchanged words like gifts, the significance of Bishop's choice, harkening back as it does to this famous interchange, becomes even more intriguing.

95 Kalstone, *Becoming a Poet,* 81.

96 See Erkkila (*The Wicked Sisters,* 101) for another, related analysis of their relationship to nineteenth-century, white, bourgeois femininity.

97 This is a point that in chapter 3 I explore in much greater detail.

98 Moore, *The Complete Poems,* 5–7. Subsequent citations appear as parenthetical page references in the text.

99 Slatin, *The Savage's Romance: The Poetry of Marianne Moore* (University Park: Pennsylvania State University Press, 1986), 12.

100 Kalstone, *Becoming a Poet,* 81. (The style of the note itself is another comical example of Moore's exaggerated hyperbole.)

101 Although, to be fair, in the last ten years or so columnists such as Ann Landers have begun to challenge pathologizing stereotypes of homosexuals.

102 Dix (Elizabeth Meriwether Gilmer), *How to Win and Hold a Husband* (1939; New York: Arno Press, 1974).

103 Watkins, introduction to *How to Win and Hold a Husband,* xv.

104 Bishop; as quoted in Millier, *Elizabeth Bishop,* 332.

105 Millier, *Elizabeth Bishop,* 43–44.

106 Costello, *Marianne Moore: Imaginary Possessions* (Cambridge: Harvard University Press, 1981).

107 Bishop, *The Complete Poems,* 200–1. Subsequent citations appear as parenthetical page references in the text. Diehl mentions this poem briefly in her essay, "Bishop's Sexual Poetics," in *The Geography of Gender,* ed. Marilyn May Lombardi (Charlottesville: University of Virginia Press, 1993) 31–32.

108 Fountain and Brazeau, *Remembering Elizabeth Bishop,* 15.

109 McCarthy; quoted in ibid., 43.

110 I take the term sex/gender system from Gayle Rubin's influential essay "The Traffic in Women: Notes on the 'Political Economy' of Sex" (in *Toward an Anthropology of Women,* ed. Rayna R. Reiter [New York: Monthly Review Press, 1975]), where she uses it to replace an ahistoric "patriarchy," which signals the historic and cultural differences in the ways in which sexuality and gender are experienced, as well as the differing ways in which power is

distributed within these systems (157–210). Sedgwick utilizes and extends the possibilities of this term in her books *Between Men; Epistemology of the Closet;* and *Tendencies.*

111 Moore, *The Complete Poems,* 147.

112 In other words, the poem demonstrates that, as Butler has famously argued, "There is no gender identity behind the expressions of gender; that identity is performatively constituted by the very 'expressions' that are said to be its results" (Butler, *Gender Trouble,* 23).

113 And here we see Bishop writing herself into the poem as another cross-dresser. Her sense of self is metaphorized as one of the quintessential representatives of social and moral order. Yet, as I demonstrate here, she simultaneously elucidates how at the core, this identity is always already in question. I am grateful to Michael Moon for calling this to my attention.

114 For several excellent discussions of the relationship between drag, queer sexualities, and/or opera, see Marjorie Garber, *Vested Interests: Cross-Dressing and Cultural Anxiety* (New York: Routledge, 1992); Sedgwick and Moon, "Divinity," in *Tendencies,* (Durham: Duke University Press, 1993), 215–51; and Wayne Koestenbaum, *The Queen's Throat: Opera, Homosexuality, and the Mystery of Desire* (New York: Vintage Books, 1994).

115 Sedgwick and Moon, "Divinity," 219.

116 And it also uncannily resonates with the "unfunny uncles."

117 Sedgwick, "Tales of the Avunculate," 52–72.

118 As both Adrienne Rich and Goldensohn note in their readings of other Bishop poems. See Rich, "The Eye of the Outsider: Elizabeth Bishop's *Complete Poems, 1927–1979,*" in *Blood, Bread, and Poetry: Selected Prose, 1979–1985* (New York: Norton, 1986), 129, and Goldensohn, *Elizabeth Bishop,* esp. 32.

119 I am grateful to Mark Simpson for helping me to clarify this point.

120 I am thankful to Eve Sedgwick for helping me to understand these connections.

121 Butler, *Bodies That Matter,* 112, as cited in Fuss, *Identification Papers,* 7.

122 Fuss, *Identification Papers,* 34.

Chapter 6. Influence and Invitation: Marianne Moore, Elizabeth Bishop, and the Pleasures of Influence, Part 2

1 Molesworth, *Marianne Moore,* 182–85; Patricia Willis, as interviewed in Rebecca Newth, "'Marriage' by Marianne Moore: An Interview with Patricia Willis," *Arkansas Review: A Journal of Criticism* 3.2 (fall 1994): 193–207.

2 I am also indebted to Willis's invaluable article "The Road to Paradise: First Notes on Marianne Moore's 'An Octopus,'" *Twentieth-Century Studies* 30.2–3 (summer/fall 1984): 242–72, for the details of both this trip and of Moore's earliest work on the poem.

3 Moore, *The Complete Poems*, 71–79 ("An Octopus"); 62–70 ("Marriage"). Subsequent citations appear as parenthetical page references in the text.

4 Bishop, *The Collected Prose*, 123.

5 Diehl is the only critic who explores the connection between the two poems and sees both of them as Moore's attempts to understand "questions of sexual identity, culturally encoded gender roles, and the female self's relation to all beyond it" (Diehl, *Women Poets and the American Sublime* [Bloomington: Indiana University Press, 1990], 61).

6 Costello, *Marianne Moore*, 87.

7 Ibid., 2, 3.

8 Costello, for instance, admits that "we find that most poems have a private as well as a public layer—that they contain allusions and references that only her [Moore's] family and friends would recognize—references that are unessential to an appreciation of most poems, but which endow them with a personal dimension missed by the uninitiated reader" (*Marianne Moore*, 6). I would argue that in maintaining such a New Critical line, Costello misses or willfully overlooks the clear connections Moore presents between her own subjectivity as poet and the "octopus."

9 Costello, *Marianne Moore*, 91. Heuving, in her brief analysis of the poem, notes, following Willis, that "the poem consists of twenty-eight sentences, corresponding in number to the mountains' twenty-eight ice fields" and that "the qualities she praises as the 'nature of this octopus' are the same qualities she strives to attain in her collage poetry" (Heuving, *Omissions Are Not Accidents*, 133). Yet she does not then connect the image of the octopus to the poet herself.

10 Moore, *The Complete Poems*, 273.

11 Willis, "The Road to Paradise," 244–45.

12 Bergman, "Marianne Moore," 256.

13 For a complete account of these events, see Barbara Guest, *Herself Defined: The Poet H.D. and Her World* (Garden City, N.Y.: Doubleday, 1984), 131–43.

14 As Laurence Stapleton was the first to argue, in her *Marianne Moore: The Poet's Advance* (Princeton: Princeton University Press, 1978, esp. 40–42).

15 Only Diehl, in her elegant book *Women Poets*, explores the biographical context of the poem. As she notes, "Despite the easily amassed differences between 'Marriage' and 'An Octopus,' on another level both poems engage similar questions relating not simply to the authority of the imagination over

experience, but also, more specifically, to a woman poet's understanding of her possible authority in the world" (74). Her reading of "An Octopus" focuses, however, on what she terms "a sublime confrontation" with a "female centered Family Romance" (74), and she reads the mountain and glacier as "good mother" versus "bad mother" images of Mrs. Moore (78). Moore herself, Diehl argues, is represented in a passage later cut from the poem, as "'Calypso, the goat flower— / that greenish orchid fond of snow.'"

Such a reading is limited first by its assumption that mother/daughter relationships must always lie at the heart of female creativity, and, second, by its concomitant heterosexualizing of the Calypso image (75–79). Although, as I have noted above, Moore's intimate relationship with her mother makes it difficult, at times, to distinguish one from the other, the ways in which the poem theorizes poetic power and authority indicate that Moore makes an extended metaphor of *herself* as mountain, divided, rather than as a flower frozen by her mother's greater power over her. Diehl's reading repeats exactly the same problem she attributes to Moore, namely that of understanding Moore's difference from her mother. In doing this it fails to recognize the incredibly subversive and hubristic way in which Moore appropriates the sublime for her own poetic project, allying her powers as poet with the sublime effects of the natural world. The focus on the mother/daughter relationship obscures the degree to which the poem articulates Moore's own incorporative, destructive, and creative fantasies of queer poetic (re)production. Despite my serious differences with Diehl's interpretation, however, my reading of "An Octopus" is indebted to Diehl's discussion of the ways in which the poem alludes to Moore's biography, as well as to issues of poetic authority.

16 Interestingly, Diehl argues, using Willis's notes to the poem, that this quote is in essence a reference, cross-gender encoded, again to Moore's mother in part because Moore's notes for the poem indicate both that her mother read her this description of James, and because in the same notebook, as Willis explains, Moore quotes her mother as saying, "'The deepest feeling ought to show itself in restraint'" (Willis, as quoted in Diehl, *Women Poets,* 82). That Moore would inscribe her mother's influence into the poem is hardly surprising, especially because in part it was from her mother that she learned the power of restraint. Nevertheless, Moore converts this moralistic restraint into something much more empowering and strange in her poetics. That Moore would include quotes from male as well as female figures of influence does not indicate that she is trying to hide or degender her poetics (by making James a spokesperson for her mother) but instead indicates the degree to which Moore identified across the lines of gender and sexuality. It may also signal her desire to include herself by association with one of the most significant members of the American literary canon.

17 And here we begin to find places where Bishop, in "Exchanging Hats," may be echoing Moore's own self-description, as in the resonances between this quote and the allusions to "avernus" in Bishop's poem.

18 And, originally, it seems this image of "concis[ion]" was directly connected to the octopus, for, as Willis describes in "The Road to Paradise," Moore's notes for the poem reveal that the quote from Moore's notebook that became "the fossil flower" actually reads "the cuttle fish concise . . . without a shiver" (248). The cuttle fish is another cephalopod mollusk, with ten arms. In *Women Poets* Diehl also notices this connection, and links the fossil flower and the octopus to the image of the Calypso orchid later in the poem, which she reads as "an image of the woman poet confronting an adversarial readership and the abandonment of her beloved" (76). Yet Diehl goes on to revise this reading, arguing instead that the orchid is Moore's representation of her own frozen, denied, and lost desire in the face of her *mother* as octopus (77–78). I argue instead below that the flower represents a moment of female-female desire.

19 Moore, letter to John Warner Moore, January 23, 1921, *Selected Letters,* 141. Interestingly, the letter also contains one of Moore's hyperbolic, performative statements of feigned ignorance, as she describes herself as "absolutely stupef[ied]" to receive such an offer.

20 Bryher [Winifred Ellerman], *West* (London: Jonathan Cape, 1924), 150. I am grateful to John Vincent, whose work first brought this quote to my attention.

21 In *Women Poets,* Diehl argues that "Moore's investment in propriety, her shock at Whitman's overt, erotic art, conveys, I would suggest, a will to power as great as his own" (60), but she sees this power as "resisting" "poetry as body" (46). In other words, because Diehl repeats stereotypes of Moore as asexual and as avoiding the erotic, she must see Whitman and Moore as opposed, at least in terms of the degree to which the body and sexuality enter into their work.

22 See chapter 5, n.9.

23 Costello, *Marianne Moore,* 180.

24 Once again, there are echoes of this image in Bishop's "Exchanging Hats"— her use of the term "anandrous" alludes to a similar asexual reproductive process.

25 For a discussion of Moore's technique as a form of collage, or what Lynn Keller calls "mosaic," see Keller's essay, " 'For Inferior Who Is Free?' Liberating the Woman Writer in Marianne Moore's 'Marriage,' " in *Influence and Intertextuality in Literary History,* ed. Jay Clayton and Eric Rothstein (Madison: University of Wisconsin Press, 1991), 219–44 and Heuving, *Omissions Are Not Accidents,* 112–13. Most notably, Cristanne Miller, in *Marianne Moore,* sees Moore's unique poetics as one based centrally in com-

munality: through her use of quotation, Moore, Miller asserts, creates a poetics that acknowledges a whole community (especially of women) and denies traditional hierarchical distinctions between different kinds of voices and is thus, by implication, nonhierarchical and antiauthoritarian. She compares Moore's style to gossip, which she claims is a particularly feminine form of communication, and she contends that Moore saw her aesthetic as more one of "borrowing" and "selecting" than creating (189–90). Although I also see Moore incorporating multiplicity into her text, I think her ambitions are more about asserting her unique poetic (and national) power and less about recognizing and honoring what Miller describes as a kind of subjective interdependence among women, although Moore's descriptions of life on the mountain certainly include this aspect of existence. Miller's somewhat idealized vision of female community and her desire to locate Moore's poetics within it misses, I think, such moments where Moore claims for herself immense poetic power. Leavell, in *Marianne Moore*, with whom Miller is especially in dialogue, argues that Moore's use of collage was "American—for the impulse of collage is anti-hierarchical and democratic" (117), yet I would argue within that democratic impulse is also a claim for the role of the poet as organizing authority of the nation.

26 I am grateful to Christopher Pye for helping me think this through.

27 This description becomes even more poignant when we realize that Moore was only in her early thirties when she wrote the poem.

28 Lisa Steinman identifies this link between poetry and technology as a defining characteristic of modern American poetry; see her *Made in America: Science, Technology, and American Modernist Poets* (New Haven: Yale University Press, 1987), 5.

29 Seltzer, *Bodies and Machines*, 149–50.

30 Willis, "The Road to Paradise," 250.

31 For another interpretation of this warning sign, as an allusion to the Fall, see Diehl, *Women Poets*, 72.

32 Donna Haraway, *Primate Visions: Gender, Race, and Nature in the World of Modern Science* (New York: Routledge, 1990), 26–58.

33 For fascinating discussions of the impact of Darwin on Moore's form and her poetics, see David Kadlec, "Marianne Moore, Immigration, and Eugenics," *Modernism/Modernity* 1.2 (1994): 21–49, and Robin G. Schulze, "Textual Darwinism: Marianne Moore, the Text of Evolution, and the Evolving Text," *Text* 11 (1998): 270–305.

34 Indeed, the only hierarchy on the mountain seems to be that of natural habitat: as Willis points out, often the order in which animals appear in the poem reflects a move upward through habitats from sea level past the timber line ("The Road to Paradise," 249–51).

35 Moore, *Observations* (New York: Dial, 1924), 87.

36 Ibid. As Heuving remarks suggestively about the poem as a whole, "it allowed Moore to affirm and celebrate a community which is not based on the marriage contract" (*Omissions Are Not Accidents*, 136).

37 And here my interpretation disagrees most decisively with Diehl's ultimate decision that Calypso and the glacier/mountain are metaphors for Moore and her mother, respectively.

38 Diehl, *Women Poets*, 81–82.

39 This is an image that also links Moore to Dickinson. For illuminating discussions of the connections between their poetics, see Diehl, *Woman Poets*, 44–57, as well as Sielke, *Fashioning the Female Subject*, 19–90.

40 See, for one notable example of this argument, Adrienne Rich, "Vesuvius at Home: The Power of Emily Dickinson," in *On Lies, Secrets, and Silence: Selected Prose, 1966–1978* (New York: Norton, 1979), 157–83.

41 Costello, *Marianne Moore*, 92; Diehl, *Women Poets*, 81.

42 And also, perhaps, through the ability of Moore's poetry to endure the increasingly drastic forms of "cutting" that constituted for her a process as key to creation as the actual composition of the lines in the first place. Writing poetry, in other words, once again is linked to the body, and both are connected with pain.

43 Here I disagree most sharply with the claims of Diehl (and others) that there is no sexuality in Moore's work (see Diehl's, *Women Poets*, 46). In "An Octopus," also, we can see that Moore is moving toward a kind of queer nationalism, a vision of the power of her writing that in some way matches Barnes's fantasy in *Ladies Almanack*. What is troubling, as I have discussed above in relation to the Girl Scouts and to Barnes, is the way these images appropriate the machinery of national subject production for their own queer ends. For a contemporary discussion of queer nationality, see Lauren Berlant and Elizabeth Freeman, "Queer Nationality," in *Fear of a Queer Planet*, ed. Warner, 193–229.

44 Fuss, *Identification Papers*, 9.

45 Bishop, *The Complete Poems*, 162–66. Subsequent citations appear as paranthetical page references in the text. Recently critics have begun to summarize Moore's and Bishop's differences in terms of a modern versus a postmodern poetics, but usually this signifies a recognition, on Bishop's part, of the inherent subjectivity of vision and the impossibility of objective representation (a distinction that does not do justice to the complexity of Moore's understanding of this problem); or an awareness on Bishop's part of the lack of spiritual or moral absolutes (which once again sees Moore's own moral-spiritual vision as much simpler and certain than it is, with Moore as unconflicted Christian or Platonic idealist); or of the inherent division of the subject (something I would argue Moore also recognizes, as her representa-

tion of the poet as mountain, which includes glacier and volcano, explores). Instead, I would argue that Bishop's postmodernism stems from her refusal to privilege the nation as a legitimating prosthesis for the queer poet. I take this term "prosthesis" from Berlant, who uses it in discussing how black women's bodies become trademarks for white women's ascendancy. In the process, they also become national symbols ("prostheses") for the intersections and overlappings of racial, gender, and class inequities that characterize African American women's status (or lack of it) in the United States (Berlant, "National Brands/National Body: *Imitation of Life,*" in *Comparative American Identities: Race, Sex, and Nationality in the Modern Text,* ed. Hortense J. Spillers [New York: Routledge, 1990], 110–40).

46 Furthermore, Bishop's strategy differs dramatically from both Stein's and Barnes's. Stein uses her expatriate status as a way paradoxically to get closer to American culture and to intensify her relationship to it (she argues in *Paris, France* that in order to write in American English she has to live in a country where it is not the spoken and written national language and that in so doing she is able to clarify and concentrate her Americanness). Stein, especially in her later writings, continually reasserts the central power of the nation in assuring her queer writerly power. Barnes, on the other hand, is not as tied specifically to the nation: her fantasies of recruitment (and simultaneous critique of it) are global.

47 As Erkkila argues in regard to Bishop's "Brazil" poems, "Bishop's dialectical approach to cultural encounter—her willingness to reverse, question, destabilize, and ironize the gaze of the colonizer, including her own, and thus to pose resistant points of view—keeps her Brazil poems from becoming mere exercises in political and aesthetic tourism" (Erkkila, "Elizabeth Bishop, Modernism, and the Left," *American Literary History* 8.2 [1996]: 297). I would argue that Bishop similarly explores the dynamics of "cultural encounter" in this poem.

48 And, by extension, in the case of the United States, of an empire—the Dame Evangeline Musset role.

49 This is what Diehl, in *Elizabeth Bishop and Marianne Moore* (41), terms their "oppressive replication."

50 Goldensohn (*Elizabeth Bishop,* 249) cites Fiona Shaw's unpublished dissertation, where Shaw names Darwin, among others, as a precursor to the poem.

51 See Goldensohn (*Elizabeth Bishop,* 247–49) for a slightly different interpretation of this arrival, a reading to which mine is indebted.

52 For her critique of this impulse, see Sara Suleri, *The Rhetoric of English India* (Chicago: University of Chicago Press, 1992), 133.

53 Goldensohn, *Elizabeth Bishop,* 68.

54 Suleri, *Rhetoric of English India*, 242.

55 McCabe reads this utterance as instead "subversively refer[ing] to homosexual passion" (*Elizabeth Bishop*, 199), because she takes the whole poem as a
comment on the "position of the lesbian writer, castaway from the main-
stream tradition, thrown upon her own resources. By revealing lesbians as si-
lenced and made unnameable by tradition, Bishop refutes the new Adam and
inscribes the absence that books have not gotten right" (198). By making
Crusoe simply a metaphor for lesbian existence, McCabe risks overlooking
the imperial context of the poem. Certainly Bishop is describing the dilemmas of representing the unrepresentable, including queer desire, yet she is
also attempting to delineate and critique unequal relations of power between
colonizer and colonized.

56 Goldensohn reads these events slightly differently. She writes, "By implication, the death of Friday renders even Crusoe's triumphant return to England
sterile" (*Elizabeth Bishop*, 249). What she misses in this description is the
way Crusoe refuses any kind of reproduction (and this oversight is related to
her silence on the imperial context of the poem).

57 Suleri, *Rhetoric of English India*, 143.

58 But this is not to say they are all free from the problems of colonial vision
and incorporation.

59 Moore, *The Collected Poems*, 121–22. Subsequent citations appear as parenthetical page references in the text.

60 Sielke, *Fashioning the Female*, 121.

61 See Diehl, *Elizabeth Bishop and Marianne Moore*, esp. 106–9; Pondrom,
"Marianne Moore and H.D.," 381–82; C. Miller, *Marianne Moore*, 193–
94; and Sielke, *Fashioning the Female*, 121–23.

62 Furthermore, Crane herself was at the time beginning an intimate friendship
with Moore, a friendship that would eventually include Crane's patronage
of her. The gift of the shell, in fact, marks the early stages of what would be
a lifelong habit of giving materially on Crane's part and of return gifts of
poems on Moore's (one reason that *The Complete Poems* is dedicated to
Crane). (For a related discussion of Crane's significance to the poem, see
Sielke, *Fashioning the Female*, 122–23.)

63 Although the poem concerns itself with the relationship between literary and
other forms of reproduction, its take on this process is much more ambivalent than most critics acknowledge: certainly it is no celebration of motherhood. Costello's reading in "Marianne Moore and Elizabeth Bishop," (131)
is one influential example.

64 Diehl, *Women Poets*, 86. Erkkila also remarks on the ambivalence of these
lines (*The Wicked Sisters*, 123–24).

65 And this appears to be Diehl's reading of these lines (*Women Poets*, 86).

66 Sielke argues that this passage equates the eggs with "heroes" through the analogy to Hercules, and mothering thus becomes only a way to give birth to heroism, rather than a form of heroism in itself. She also sees the mother as a possible hydra, writing that it "both symbolizes the fear-inflicting part of female reproductive powers and embodies female lack. [The hydra] gets displaced, however, by the nautilus, whose eight arms 'knew love' before loss and lack" (Sielke, *Fashioning the Female*, 129). In other words, the maternal's limits are that it can only (re)produce others who will assert agency.

67 Sielke, *Fashioning the Female*, 126.

68 For a related discussion of these last stanzas, see ibid., 124–26.

69 As Diehl notes in *Women Poets* (86).

70 Erkkila, *The Wicked Sisters*, 135.

71 Ibid.

72 Diehl, *Marianne Moore and Elizabeth Bishop*, 18.

73 Erkkila, *The Wicked Sisters*, 131–32.

74 As McCabe hints in *Elizabeth Bishop* (135).

Conclusion

1 For one notable example, see Kath Weston, "Do Clothes Make the Woman? Gender, Performance Theory, and Lesbian Eroticism," *Genders* 17 (fall 1993): 1–21.

2 See especially Butler, *Bodies That Matter*, 15.

3 On the other hand, Stein's celebration of unnatural forms of signification and economy might line up with similar African American modernist interventions, for example, Zora Neale Hurston's examination of female sexual subjectivity and its relation to various forms of economic existence in *Their Eyes Were Watching God* (1937; New York: Harper and Row, 1990). Critics have struggled to read Hurston's text as "lesbian," despite the famous line of the frame narrative that mixes images of female-female erotic intimacy with speech, indicating that the character Janie finds inspiration for her story in her desire for her friend or that her erotic relationship with her friend (and her reader, because we are positioned in her place as audience for her tale) is what allows her to speak or create at all. Perhaps one reason for this confusion as to how to locate Hurston's text is because of the way it does not follow the expectations that white, lesbian modernist texts set up, but instead traces what I would argue is the first African American female narrative of eroticized self-making. In so doing, the text cannot simply co-opt the rhetoric of self-reliance, but must instead trace the pain and violence Janie experiences as she is able little by little to understand and claim any form of female self-sufficiency.

4 Helen Vendler, "Elizabeth Bishop: Domestication, Domesticity, and the Otherworldly," in *Part of Nature, Part of Us* (Cambridge: Harvard University Press, 1980), 106.

5 For a discussion of the politics of the Lesbian Avengers, see Ann Cvetkovitch, "Fierce Pussies and Lesbian Avengers: Dyke Activism Meets Celebrity Culture," in *Feminist Consequences: Theory for the New Century,* ed. Elisabeth Bronfen and Misha Kavka (New York: Columbia University Press, 2001), 283–318.

BIBLIOGRAPHY

Abel, Elizabeth, Marianne Hirsch, and Elizabeth Landland, eds. *The Voyage In: Fictions of Female Development*. Hanover, N.H.: University Press of New England, 1983.

Abraham, Julie L. *Are Girls Necessary? Lesbian Writing and Modern Histories*. New York: Routledge, 1996.

———. "A Case of Mistaken Identity?" *The Women's Review of Books* 11 (July 1994): 36–37.

Alcott, Louisa May. *Alternative Alcott*. Edited by Elaine Showalter. New Brunswick: Rutgers University Press, 1988.

———. *Behind a Mask: The Unknown Thrillers*. Edited by Madeleine B. Stern. London: Hogarth Press, 1985.

———. *Diana and Persis*. 1870. New York: Arno Press, 1978.

———. *A Double Life: Newly Discovered Thrillers of Louisa May Alcott*. Edited by Madeleine B. Stern. Boston: Little, Brown, 1989.

———. *Eight Cousins; or, The Aunt-Hill*. 1875. Boston: Little, Brown, 1910.

———. *Jack and Jill: A Village Story*. Boston: Roberts Brothers, 1880.

———. *Jo's Boys, and How They Turned Out*. 1886. New York: Signet, 1987.

———. *The Journals of Louisa May Alcott*. Edited by Joel Myerson and Daniel Shealy. Boston: Little Brown, 1989.

———. *Little Men: Life at Plumfield with Jo's Boys*. 1871. New York: Signet, 1986.

———. *Little Women*. 1868–69. New York: Modern Library, 1983.

———. *A Modern Mephistopheles and Taming a Tartar*. Edited by Madeleine B. Stern. New York: Praeger, 1987.

———. *An Old-Fashioned Girl*. 1870. New York: Grosset and Dunlap, 1980.

———. *Plots and Counterplots: More Unknown Thrillers of Louisa May Alcott*. Edited by Madeleine B. Stern. New York: William Morrow, 1976.

———. *Rose in Bloom*. Boston: Roberts Brothers, 1876.

———. *Under the Lilacs*. Boston: Roberts Brothers, 1878.

———. *Work: A Story of Experience*. 1873. Edited by Sarah Elbert. New York: Schocken Books, 1977.

Ammons, Elizabeth. *Conflicting Stories: American Women Writers at the Turn into the Twentieth Century*. New York: Oxford University Press, 1991.

———. ed. *Critical Essays on Harriet Beecher Stowe*. Boston: G. K. Hall, 1980.

Anderson, Benedict. *Imagined Communities: Reflections on the Origin and Spread of Nationalism*. London: Verso, 1983.

Appiah, Kwame Anthony. *In My Father's House: Africa in the Philosophy of Culture*. New York: Oxford University Press, 1992.

Armstrong, Frances. "'Here Little, and Hereafter Bliss': *Little Women* and the Deferral of Greatness." *American Literature* 64 (1992): 453–74.

Armstrong, Nancy. *Desire and Domestic Fiction: A Political History of the Novel*. New York: Oxford University Press, 1987.

Auerbach, Nina. *Communities of Women: An Idea in Fiction*. Cambridge: Harvard University Press, 1978.

———. *Woman and the Demon*. Cambridge: Harvard University Press, 1982.

Baden-Powell, Robert. "Girl Scouts or Girl Guides." *Jamboree* (October 1921): n.p.

Baker, Houston A. *Modernism and the Harlem Renaissance*. Chicago: University of Chicago Press, 1987.

Baker, Michael. *Our Three Selves: The Life of Radclyffe Hall*. New York: Morrow, 1985.

Banta, Martha. *Imaging American Women: Idea and Ideals in Cultural History*. New York: Columbia University Press, 1987.

———. *Taylored Lives: Narrative Production in the Age of Taylor, Veblen, and Ford*. Chicago: University of Chicago Press, 1993.

Barker-Benfield, G. J. *The Horrors of the Half-Known Life: Male Attitudes toward Women and Sexuality in Nineteenth-Century America*. New York: Harper and Row, 1976.

Barnes, Djuna. *Ladies Almanack*. 1928. Elmwood Park, Illinois: Dalkey Archive Press, 1992.

Barnes, Elizabeth. *States of Sympathy: Seduction and Democracy in the American Novel*. New York: Columbia University Press, 1997.

———. "The Whipping Boy of Love: Atonement and Aggression in Alcott's Fiction." *Journal X: A Journal in Culture and Criticism* (1997): 1–17.

Bataille, Georges. *The Accursed Share*. Translated by Robert Hurley. New York: Zone Books, 1988.

———. "The Notion of Expenditure." In *Visions of Excess: Selected Writings, 1927–1939*, edited by Allan Stoekl. Minneapolis: University of Minnesota Press, 1985. 116–29.

Baudrillard, Jean. *Jean Baudrillard: Selected Writings*. Edited by Mark Poster. Stanford: Stanford University Press, 1988.

Bauer, Dale. "The Politics of Collaboration in *The Whole Family*." In *Old Maids to Radical Spinsters: Unmarried Women in the Twentieth-Century Novel*, edited by Laura L. Doan. Urbana: University of Illinois Press, 1991. 107–22.

Baym, Nina. *Novels, Readers, and Reviewers: Responses to Fiction in Antebellum America*. Ithaca: Cornell University Press, 1984.

Bedell, Madelon. *The Alcotts: Biography of a Family*. New York: Clarkson N. Potter, 1980.

Beecher, Catharine E. and Harriet Beecher Stowe. *The American Woman's Home, or, Principles of Domestic Science; Being A Guide to the Formation and Maintenance of Economical, Healthful[,] Beautiful and Christian Homes*. 1869. Hartford: The Stowe-Day Foundation, 1991.

Benjamin, Walter. "The Author as Producer." In *Reflections: Essays, Aphorisms, Autobiographical Writings*. New York: Schocken Books, 1978. 220–38.

———. "The Work of Art in the Age of Mechanical Reproduction." In *Illuminations: Essays and Reflections*. Edited by Hannah Arendt. New York: Schocken Books, 1968. 217–51.

Bennett, Paula. "Lesbian Poetry in the United States, 1890–1990: An Overview." In *Professions of Desire: Gay and Lesbian Studies in Literature*, edited by George E. Haggerty and Bonnie Zimmerman. New York: Modern Language Association of America, 1995. 98–110.

Benstock, Shari. *Women of the Left Bank: Paris, 1900–1940*. Austin: University of Texas Press, 1986.

Bergman, David. "Marianne Moore and the Problem of 'Marriage.'" *American Literature* 60.2 (May 1988): 241–54.

Berkson, Dorothy. Introduction to *Oldtown Folks,* by Harriet Beecher Stowe. 1869. New Brunswick: Rutgers University Press, 1987. ix–xxxviii.

Berlant, Lauren. *The Anatomy of National Fantasy: Hawthorne, Utopia, and Everyday Life*. Chicago: University of Chicago Press, 1991.

———. "The Female Complaint." *Social Text* 19/20 (1988): 237–59.

———. "National Brands/National Body: *Imitation of Life*." In *Comparative American Identities: Race, Sex, and Nationality in the Modern Text*, edited by Hortense J. Spillers. New York: Routledge, 1990. 110–40.

———. "Poor Eliza." *American Literature* 70.3 (September 1998): 635–68.

———. *The Queen of America Goes to Washington City: Essays on Sex and Citizenship*. Durham: Duke University Press, 1997.

———. "'68, or Something." *Critical Inquiry* 21 (1994): 124–55.

Berlant, Lauren, and Elizabeth Freeman. "Queer Nationality." In *Fear of a Queer Planet: Queer Politics and Social Theory*, edited by Michael Warner. Minneapolis: University of Minnesota Press, 1993. 193–229.

Berry, Amanda. "The Lesbian Focus." *Lesbian and Gay Studies Newsletter* (July 1994): 25–26.

Berry, Ellen. *Curved Thought and Textual Wandering: Gertrude Stein's Postmodernism.* Ann Arbor: University of Michigan Press, 1992.

Bersani, Leo. *Homos.* Cambridge: Harvard University Press, 1995.

Bhabha, Homi. *The Location of Culture.* New York: Routledge, 1994.

Bishop, Elizabeth. "As We Like It." *Quarterly Review of Literature* 4 (1948): 129–35.

———. *The Collected Prose.* Edited by Robert Giroux. New York: Farrar, Straus and Giroux, The Noonday Press, 1984.

———. *The Complete Poems: 1927–1979.* New York: Farrar, Straus and Giroux, 1983.

———. *One Art: Letters.* Selected and edited by Robert Giroux. New York: Farrar, Straus and Giroux, 1994.

———. "A Sentimental Tribute." *Bryn Mawr Alumnae Bulletin* 3 (spring 1962): 3.

Bloom, Harold, ed. *Marianne Moore.* New York: Chelsea House, 1987.

Borch-Jacobsen, Mikkel. *The Freudian Subject.* Translated by Catherine Porter. Stanford: Stanford University Press, 1988.

Boswell, John. *Christianity, Social Tolerance, and Homosexuality: Gay People in Western Europe from the Beginning of the Christian Era to the Fourteenth Century.* Chicago: University of Chicago Press, 1980.

Bourdieu, Pierre. *Distinction: A Social Critique of the Judgement of Taste.* Translated by Richard Nice. Cambridge: Harvard University Press, 1984.

Bowers, Jane Palatini. *Gertrude Stein.* New York: St. Martin's Press, 1993.

Brackett, Anna C. *The Education of American Girls.* New York: G. P. Putnam's Sons, 1879.

Bridgman, Richard. *Gertrude Stein in Pieces.* New York: Oxford University Press, 1970.

Brinnin, John Malcolm. *The Third Rose: Gertrude Stein and Her World.* New York: Grove Press, 1959.

Brodhead, Richard. *Cultures of Letters: Scenes of Reading and Writing in Nineteenth-Century America.* Chicago: University of Chicago Press, 1994.

Broe, Mary Lynn, ed. *Silence and Power: A Reevaluation of Djuna Barnes.* Carbondale: Southern Illinois University Press, 1991.

Bromwich, David. "Elizabeth Bishop's Dream-Houses." *Raritan* 1 (1984): 5–16.

Brown, Gillian. *Domestic Individualism: Imagining Self in Nineteenth-Century America.* Berkeley: University of California Press, 1990.

Brown, Herbert Ross, *The Sentimental Novel in America.* Durham: Duke University Press, 1940.

Bryher [Winifred Ellerman]. *West.* London: Jonathan Cape, 1924.

Buhle, Mari Jo. *Women and American Socialism, 1870–1920.* Urbana: University of Illinois Press, 1981.

Burke, Carolyn. "Getting Spliced: Modernism and Sexual Difference." *American Quarterly* 39.1 (spring 1987): 98–121.

Burns, Edward, ed. *Staying On Alone: Letters of Alice B. Toklas.* New York: Liveright, 1973.

Butler, Judith. *Bodies That Matter: On the Discursive Limits of "Sex."* New York: Routledge, 1993.

———. "The Force of Fantasy: Feminism, Mapplethorpe, and Discursive Excess." *differences: A Journal of Feminist Cultural Studies* 2.2 (1990): 105–25.

———. *Gender Trouble: Feminism and the Subversion of Identity.* New York: Routledge, 1989.

———. "Imitation and Gender Insubordination." In *Inside/Out: Lesbian Theories, Gay Theories,* edited by Diana Fuss. New York: Routledge, 1991. 13–21.

———. "Merely Cultural." *Social Text* 52/53, 15.3–4 (fall/winter 1997): 265–77.

———. *The Psychic Life of Power: Theories in Subjection.* Stanford: Stanford University Press, 1997.

Calhoun, Craig, ed. *Habermas and the Public Sphere.* Cambridge: MIT Press, 1992.

Campbell, Donna M. "Sentimental Conventions and Self-Protection: *Little Women* and *The Wide, Wide World.*" *Legacy* 11.2 (1994): 118–29.

Campbell, Helen. "Is American Domesticity Decreasing, and If So, Why?" *The Arena* (1897): 86–96.

Cappetti, Carla. "Deviant Girls and Dissatisfied Women: A Sociologist's Tale." In *The Invention of Ethnicity,* edited by Werner Sollors. New York: Oxford University Press, 1989. 124–57.

Carby, Hazel V. *Reconstructing Womanhood: The Emergence of the Afro-American Woman Novelist.* New York: Oxford University Press, 1987.

Carlson, Erin G. *Thinking Fascism: Sapphic Modernism and Fascist Modernity.* Stanford: Stanford University Press, 1998.

Case, Sue Ellen. "Tracking the Vampire." *differences: A Journal of Feminist Cultural Studies* 3 (1991): 1–20.

Castle, Terry. *The Apparitional Lesbian: Female Homosexuality and Modern Culture.* New York: Columbia University Press, 1993.

Chambers-Schiller, Lee. *Liberty, A Better Husband, Single Women in America: The Generations of 1780–1940.* New Haven: Yale University Press, 1984.

———. "The Single Woman: Family and Vocation among Nineteenth-Century Reformers." In *Woman's Being, Woman's Place: Female Identity and Voca-*

tion in American History, edited by Mary Kelley. Boston: G. K. Hall, 1979. 334–50.

Chapman, Mary, and Glenn Hendler, eds. *Sentimental Men: Masculinity and the Politics of Affect in American Culture.* Berkeley: University of California Press, 1999.

Chartier, Roger. "Texts, Printing, Readings." In *The New Cultural History,* edited by Lynn Hunt. Berkeley: University of California Press, 1989. 154–75.

Chauncey, George Jr. "From Sexual Inversion to Homosexuality: Medicine and the Changing Conception of Female Deviance." *Salmagundi* 58/59 (fall 1982/winter 1983): 114–45.

———. *Gay New York: Gender, Urban Culture, and the Making of the Gay Male World, 1890–1940.* New York: Basic Books, 1994.

Cheney, Ednah D., ed. *Louisa May Alcott: Her Life, Letters, and Journals.* Cambridge: University Press, 1889.

Chessman, Harriet Scott. *The Public Is Invited to Dance: Representation, the Body, and Dialogue in Gertrude Stein.* Stanford: Stanford University Press, 1989.

Chester, Eliza. *The Unmarried Woman.* New York: Dodd Mead, 1892.

Chesterton, G. K. "Louisa Alcott." In *Critical Essays on Louisa May Alcott,* edited by Madeleine B. Stern. Boston: G. K. Hall, 1984. 214.

Child, Lydia Maria. *The American Frugal Housewife.* New York: Wood, 1844.

Choate, Anne Hyde, and Helen Ferris. *Juliette Low and the Girl Scouts: The Story of an American Woman, 1860–1927.* New York: Doubleday, Doran, 1928.

Clarke, Edward Hammond. *Sex in Education; or, A Fair Chance for the Girls.* New York: Arno Press, 1972.

Cook, Blanche Wiesen. "Female Support Networks and Political Activism: Lillian Wald, Crystal Eastman, Emma Goldman." *Chrysalis* 3 (1977): 43–61.

———. "Women Alone Stir My Imagination: Lesbianism in the Cultural Tradition." *Signs* 4 (1979): 718–39.

Costello, Bonnie. Afterword to *Remembering Elizabeth Bishop: An Oral Biography,* edited by Gary Fountain and Peter Brazeau. Amherst: University of Massachusetts Press, 1994. 353–56.

———. *Elizabeth Bishop: Questions of Mastery.* Cambridge: Harvard University Press, 1991.

———. "The Feminine Language of Marianne Moore." In *Marianne Moore,* edited by Harold Bloom. New York: Chelsea House Publishers, 1987. 98–99.

———. "Marianne Moore and Elizabeth Bishop: Friendship and Influence." *Twentieth-Century Literature: A Scholarly and Critical Journal* 30 (summer/ fall 1984): 130–49.

———. *Marianne Moore: Imaginary Possessions.* Cambridge: Harvard University Press, 1981.

Cott, Nancy F. *The Bonds of Womanhood: "Woman's Sphere" in New England, 1780–1835.* New Haven: Yale University Press, 1977.

Coultrap-McQuin, Susan. *Doing Literary Business: American Women Writers in the Nineteenth Century.* Chapel Hill: University of North Carolina Press, 1990.

Creech, James. *Closet Writing / Gay Reading: The Case of Melville's "Pierre."* Chicago: University of Chicago Press, 1994.

Crow, Duncan. *The Victorian Woman.* New York: Stein and Day, 1972.

Crozier, Alice C. *The Novels of Harriet Beecher Stowe.* New York: Oxford University Press, 1969.

Cutter, Martha J. "Beyond Stereotypes: Freeman's Radical Critique of Nineteenth-Century Cults of Femininity." *Women's Studies* 21 (1992): 383–95.

Cvetkovitch, Ann. "Fierce Pussies and Lesbian Avengers: Dyke Activism Meets Celebrity Culture." In *Feminist Consequences: Theory for the New Century,* edited by Elisabeth Bronfen and Misha Kavka. New York: Columbia University Press, 2001. 283–318.

Dalke, Anne. "'The House-Band': The Education of Men in *Little Women.*" *College English* 47 (October 1985): 571–78.

Damon, Maria. *The Dark End of the Street: Margins in American Poetry.* Minneapolis: University of Minnesota Press, 1993.

———. "Gertrude Stein's Jewishness, Jewish Social Scientists, and the 'Jewish Question.'" *Modern Fiction Studies* 42.3 (1996): 489–506.

Davidson, Cathy N. "No More Separate Spheres!" *American Literature* 70.3 (September 1998): 444–63.

———. *Revolution and the Word: The Rise of the Novel in America.* New York: Oxford University Press, 1986.

———, ed. *Reading in America: Literature and Social History.* Baltimore: Johns Hopkins University Press, 1989.

Davis, Phoebe Stein. "'Even Cake Gets to Have Another Meaning': History, Narrative, and 'Daily Living' in Gertrude Stein's World War II Writings." *Modern Fiction Studies* 44.3 (1998): 568–607.

de Certeau, Michel. *The Practice of Everyday Life.* Translated by Stephen Rendall. Berkeley: University of California Press, 1984.

Deegan, Dorothy Yost. *The Stereotype of the Single Woman in American Novels: A Social Study with Implications for the Education of Women.* New York: King's Crown Press, 1951.

de Lauretis, Teresa. *The Practice of Love: Lesbian Sexuality and Perverse Desire.* Bloomington: Indiana University Press, 1994.

———. "Sexual Indifference and Lesbian Representation." In *The Lesbian and Gay Studies Reader,* edited by Henry Abelove, Michèle Aina Barale, and David M. Halperin. New York: Routledge, 1993. 141–58.

D'Emilio, John. "Capitalism and Gay Identity." In *Powers of Desire: The Politics of Sexuality,* edited by Ann Snitow, Christine Stansell, and Sharon Thompson. New York: Monthly Review Press, 1983. 100–13.

D'Emilio, John, and Estelle Freedman. *Intimate Matters: A History of Sexuality in America.* New York: Harper and Row, 1988.

Denning, Michael. *Mechanic Accents: Dime Novels and Working Class Culture in America.* London: Verso, 1987.

Derrida, Jacques. "White Mythology: Metaphor in the Text of Philosophy." In *Margins of Philosophy.* Translated by Alan Bass. Chicago: University of Chicago Press, 1982.

Diamond, Elin. *Unmaking Mimesis: Essays on Feminism and Theater.* New York: Routledge, 1997.

Dickie, Margaret. "Recovering Repression in Stein's Erotic Poetry." In *Gendered Modernisms: American Women Poets and Their Readers,* edited by Margaret Dickie and Thomas Travisano. Philadelphia: University of Pennsylvania Press, 1996. 3–25.

———. *Stein, Bishop, and Rich: Lyrics of Love, War, and Place.* Chapel Hill: University of North Carolina Press, 1997.

Diehl, Joanne Fiet. "Bishop's Sexual Poetics." In *Elizabeth Bishop: The Geography of Gender,* edited by Marilyn May Lombardi. Charlottesville: University of Virginia Press, 1993. 17–45.

———. *Elizabeth Bishop and Marianne Moore: The Psychodynamics of Creativity.* Princeton: Princeton University Press, 1993.

———. *Women Poets and the American Sublime.* Bloomington: Indiana University Press, 1990.

Diggs, Marylynne. "Romantic Friends or a 'Different Race of Creatures?' The Representation of Lesbian Pathology in Nineteenth-Century America." *Feminist Studies* 21.2 (summer 1995): 317–40.

———. "Surveying the Intersection: Pathology, Secrecy, and the Discourses of Racial and Sexual Identity." *Journal of Homosexuality* 26.2–3 (1993): 1–19.

Dix, Dorothy (Elizabeth Meriwether Gilmer). *How to Win and Hold a Husband.* 1939. New York: Arno Press, 1974.

Doan, Laura L. *Fashioning Sapphism: The Origins of a Modern English Lesbian Culture.* New York: Columbia University Press, 2001.

———, ed. *Old Maids to Radical Spinsters: Unmarried Women in the Twentieth-Century Novel.* Urbana: University of Illinois Press, 1991.

Donovan, Josephine. *New England Local Color Literature: A Women's Tradition.* New York: Frederick Ungar Publishing, 1983.

Douglas, Ann. *The Feminization of American Culture.* New York: Knopf, 1977.

Doyle, Jennifer. "Jo March's Love Poems." Paper delivered at the Duke University Women's Studies Program Graduate Conference, Durham, October 11, 1994.

Dubnick, Randa. *The Structure of Obscurity: Gertrude Stein, Language, and Criticism.* Urbana: University of Illinois Press, 1984.

duCille, Ann. *The Coupling Convention: Sex, Text, and Tradition in Black Women's Fiction.* New York: Oxford University Press, 1993.

Duggan, Lisa. *Sapphic Slashers: Sex, Violence, and American Modernity.* Durham: Duke University Press, 2000.

———. "The Trials of Alice Mitchell: Sensationalism, Sexology, and the Lesbian Subject in Turn-of-the-Century America." *Signs* 18 (1993): 791–814.

Dydo, Ulla E., ed. *A Stein Reader.* Evanston: Northwestern University Press, 1993.

Edelman, Lee. "The Geography of Gender: Elizabeth Bishop's 'In the Waiting Room.'" In *Elizabeth Bishop: The Geography of Gender,* edited by Marilyn May Lombardi. Charlottesville: University of Virginia Press, 1993. 91–107.

Eiselein, Gregory. "Sentimental Discourse and the Bisexual Erotics of *Work.*" *Texas Studies in Literature and Language* 41.3 (fall 1999): 203–35.

Elbert, Sarah. *A Hunger for Home: Louisa May Alcott and "Little Women."* Philadelphia: Temple University Press, 1984.

Ellis, Havelock. *Sexual Inversion.* 1897. New York: Arno Press, 1975.

Erkkila, Betsy. "Elizabeth Bishop, Modernism, and the Left." *American Literary History* 8.2 (1996): 284–310.

———. *The Wicked Sisters: Women Poets, Literary History, and Discord.* New York: Oxford University Press, 1992.

Ewen, Stuart, and Elizabeth Ewen. *Channels of Desire: Mass Images and the Shaping of American Consciousness.* Minneapolis: University of Minnesota Press, 1992.

Faderman, Lillian. *Odd Girls and Twilight Lovers: A History of Lesbian Life in Twentieth-Century America.* New York: Penguin Books, 1991.

———. *Surpassing the Love of Men: Romantic Friendship and Love between Women from the Renaissance to the Present.* New York: William Morrow, 1981.

Fetterley, Judith. "Impersonating 'Little Women': The Radicalism of Alcott's *Behind a Mask.*" *Women's Studies* 10 (1983): 1–14.

———. "*Little Women:* Alcott's Civil War." *Feminist Studies* 5.2 (summer 1979): 369–83.

Fiedler, Leslie. *Love and Death in the American Novel.* Cleveland: Criterion Books, 1960.

Field, Andrew. *Djuna: The Formidable Miss Barnes.* Austin: University of Texas Press, 1985.

Fields, Annie. *Life and Letters of Harriet Beecher Stowe.* Boston: Houghton Mifflin, 1897.

Fifer, Elizabeth. *Rescued Readings: A Reconstruction of Gertrude Stein's Difficult Texts.* Detroit: Wayne State University Press, 1992.

Fisher, Philip. *Hard Facts: Setting and Form in the American Novel.* New York: Oxford University Press, 1985.

———. *The New American Studies: Essays from "Representations."* Berkeley: University of California Press, 1991.

Fluck, Winifred. "The Power and Failure of Representation in Harriet Beecher Stowe's *Uncle Tom's Cabin." New Literary History* 23 (1992): 319–38.

Flynn, Elizabeth A., and Patrocinio P. Schweikart, eds. *Gender and Reading: Essays on Readers, Texts, and Contexts.* Baltimore: Johns Hopkins University Press, 1986.

Foreman, P. Gabrielle. "'This Promiscuous Housekeeping': Death, Transgression, and Homoeroticism in *Uncle Tom's Cabin." Representations* 43 (summer 1993): 51–72.

Foucault, Michel. *Discipline and Punish: The Birth of the Prison.* Translated by Alan Sheridan. New York: Vintage Books, 1979.

———. *The History of Sexuality. Vol. 1: An Introduction.* Translated by Robert Hurley. London: Penguin, 1978.

Fountain, Gary, and Peter Brazeau, eds. *Remembering Elizabeth Bishop: An Oral Biography.* Amherst: University of Massachusetts Press, 1994.

Fox, Richard Wightman, and T. J. Jackson Lears, eds. *The Culture of Consumption: Critical Essays in American History 1880–1980.* New York: Pantheon Books, 1983.

Frankel, Noralee, and Nancy S. Dye, eds. *Gender, Class, Race, and Reform in the Progressive Era.* Lexington: University Press of Kentucky, 1992.

Fraser, Nancy. "Rethinking the Public Sphere: A Contribution to the Critique of Actually Existing Democracy." In *Habermas and the Public Sphere,* edited by Craig Calhoun. Cambridge: MIT Press, 1993. 109–42.

Freedman, Estelle. "Separatism as Strategy: Female Institution Building and American Feminism, 1870–1930." *Feminist Studies* 5 (fall 1979): 512–29.

Freud, Sigmund. "The Ego and the Id." In *The Essentials of Psychoanalysis.* Selected by Anna Freud. Harmondsworth, Eng.: Penguin, 1986. 439–83.

———. "Female Sexuality." In *On Sexuality: Three Essays on the Theory of Sexuality and Other Works.* Edited by James Strachey and Angela Richards. Harmondsworth, Eng.: Penguin, 1986. 367–92.

———. "Fragment of an Analysis of a Case of Hysteria: Dora." In *Case Histories I.* Edited by James Strachey and Angela Richards. Harmondsworth, Eng.: Penguin, 1985. 31–164.

———. *Group Psychology and the Analysis of the Ego.* New York: Norton, 1989.

———. "On Narcissism." In *On Metapsychology: The Theory of Psychoanalysis.* Edited by James Strachey and Angela Richards. Harmondsworth, Eng.: Penguin, 1984. 59–97.

———. "The Psychogenesis of a Case of Homosexuality in a Woman." In *Case Histories II.* Edited by James Strachey and Angela Richards. Harmondsworth, Eng.: Penguin, 1984. 367–400.

———. "Some Psychical Consequences of the Anatomical Distinction Between the Sexes." In *On Sexuality,* edited by James Strachey and Angela Richards. Harmondsworth, Eng.: Penguin, 1986. 323–43.

———. "Three Essays on the Theory of Sexuality." In *On Sexuality,* edited by James Strachey and Angela Richards. Harmondsworth, Eng.: Penguin, 1986. 33–169.

Frith, Gill. " 'The Time of Your Life': The Meaning of the School Story." In *Language, Gender and Childhood,* edited by Carolyn Steedman, Cathy Urwin, and Valerie Walkerdine. London: Routledge and Kegan Paul, 1985. 113–36.

Fuller, Margaret. *The Essential Margaret Fuller.* Edited by Jeffrey Steele. New Brunswick: Rutgers University Press, 1992.

Fuss, Diana. "Fashion and the Homospectatorial Look." *Critical Inquiry* 18 (summer 1992): 713–37.

———. *Identification Papers.* New York: Routledge, 1995.

Gallup, Donald, ed. *The Flowers of Friendship: Letters Written to Gertrude Stein.* New York: Knopf, 1953.

Garber, Marjorie. *Vested Interests: Cross-Dressing and Cultural Anxiety.* New York: Routledge, 1992.

Garis, Lilian. *The Girl Scout Pioneers, or Winning the First B.C.* New York: Cupples and Leon Company, 1920.

Gever, Martha. "What Becomes a Legend Most?" *GLQ* 1 (1993): 209–19.

Gilbert, Sandra. "Marianne Moore as Female Female Impersonator." In *Marianne Moore: The Art of a Modernist,* edited by Joseph Parisi. Ann Arbor: UMI Research Press, 1990. 27–46.

Gilbert, Sandra, and Susan Gubar. *The Madwoman in the Attic: The Woman Writer and the Nineteenth-Century Literary Imagination.* New Haven: Yale University Press, 1979.

———. *No Man's Land: The Place of the Woman Writer in the Twentieth Century.* Vol. 1: *The War of the Words.* New Haven: Yale University Press, 1988.

Gilmore, Leigh. *Autobiographics: A Feminist Theory of Women's Self-Representation.* Ithaca: Cornell University Press, 1994.

Gilroy, Paul. *There Ain't No Black in the Union Jack.* Chicago: University of Chicago Press, 1991.

Goldberg, Jonathan. *Sodomotries.* Stanford: Stanford University Press, 1992.

———, ed. *Queering the Renaissance.* Durham: Duke University Press, 1993.

———, ed. *Reclaiming Sodom.* New York: Routledge, 1994.

Goldensohn, Lorrie. *Elizabeth Bishop: The Biography of a Poetry.* New York: Columbia University Press, 1992.

Goodloe, Abbe Carter. "A Short Study in Evolution." *Scribner's* 17 (1895): 588–94.

Gordon, Lynn D. *Gender and Higher Education in the Progressive Era.* New Haven: Yale University Press, 1990.

Goshgarian, G. M. *To Kiss the Chastening Rod: Domestic Fiction and Sexual Ideology in the American Renaissance.* Ithaca: Cornell University Press, 1992.

Greenblatt, Stephen. "Towards a Poetics of Culture." In *The New Historicism,* edited by H. Aram Veeser. New York: Routledge, 1989. 1–14.

Greene, Jody. "'You Must Eat Men': The Sodomite Economy of Renaissance Patronage." *GLQ: A Journal of Lesbian and Gay Studies* 1.2 (1994): 163–97.

Griggers, Cathy. "Lesbian Bodies in the Age of (Post)mechanical Reproduction." In *Fear of a Queer Planet: Queer Politics and Social Theory,* edited by Michael Warner. Minneapolis: University of Minnesota Press, 1993. 178–92.

Guest, Barbara. *Herself Defined: The Poet H.D. and Her World.* Garden City, N.Y.: Doubleday, 1984.

Habegger, Alfred. *Gender, Fantasy, and Realism in American Literature.* New York: Columbia University Press, 1982.

Habermas, Jürgen. *The Structural Transformation of the Public Sphere: An Inquiry into a Category of Bourgeois Society.* Translated by Thomas Burger. Cambridge: MIT Press, 1989.

Hadas, Pamela. "Spreading the Difference: One Way to Read Gertrude Stein's *Tender Buttons.*" *Twentieth-Century Literature* 24 (1978): 57–78.

Halberstam, Judith. *Female Masculinity.* Durham: Duke University Press, 1998.

Halley, Janet. "*Bowers v. Hardwick* in the Renaissance." In *Queering the Renaissance,* edited by Jonathan Goldberg. Durham: Duke University Press, 1993. 33–57.

———. "The Construction of Heterosexuality." In *Fear of a Queer Planet: Queer Politics and Social Theory,* edited by Michael Warner. Minneapolis: University of Minnesota Press, 1993. 82–102.

Halperin, David. "Forgetting Foucault: Acts, Identities, and the History of Sexuality." *Representations* 63 (summer 1998): 93–120.

Haltunnen, Karen. "The Domestic Drama of Louisa May Alcott." *Feminist Studies* 10.2 (summer 1984): 233–54.

Hammer, Langdon. "Useless Concentration: Life and Work in Elizabeth Bishop's Letters and Poems." *American Literary History* 9.1 (1997): 162–80.

Hansen, Karen. "'No *Kisses* Is Like Youres': An Erotic Friendship between Two African-American Women during the Mid-Nineteenth-Century." In *Lesbian Studies: A Feminist Studies Reader,* edited by Martha Vicinus. Bloomington: Indiana University Press, 1996. 178–207.

Hansen, Miriam. *Babel and Babylon: Spectatorship in American Silent Film.* Cambridge: Harvard University Press, 1991.

———. Foreword to *Public Sphere and Experience: Toward an Analysis of the Bourgeois and Proletarian Public Sphere,* by Oskar Negt and Alexander Kluge. Minneapolis: University of Minnesota Press, 1993. ix–xli.

Haraway, Donna. *Primate Visions: Gender, Race, and Nature in the World of Modern Science.* New York: Routledge, 1990.

———. "Teddy Bear Patriarchy: Taxidermy in the Garden of Eden, New York City, 1908–1936." In *Cultures of United States Imperialism,* edited by Amy Kaplan and Donald E. Pease. Durham: Duke University Press, 1993. 237–91.

Harper, Frances E. W., *Iola Leroy or Shadows Uplifted.* 1892; Boston: Beacon Press, 1987.

Harper, Philip Brian. *Framing the Margins: The Social Logic of Postmodern Culture.* New York: Oxford University Press, 1994.

Harris, Bertha. "The More Profound Nationality of Their Lesbianism: Lesbian Society in Paris in the 1920s." In *Amazon Expedition,* edited by Phyllis Birkby, Bertha Harris, Jill Johnston, Esther Newton, and Jane O'Wyatt. Albion, Calif.: Times Change Press, 1973. 77–88.

Harris, Neil. *Cultural Excursions: Marketing Appetites and Cultural Tastes in Modern America.* Chicago: University of Chicago Press, 1990.

Harris, Susan K. "The Female Imaginary in Harriet Beecher Stowe's *The Minister's Wooing*." *New England Quarterly* 66 (June 1993): 179–98.

———. *Nineteenth-Century American Women's Novels: Interpretive Strategies.* Cambridge: Cambridge University Press, 1990.

Harrison, Victoria. *Elizabeth Bishop's Poetics of Intimacy.* Cambridge: Cambridge University Press, 1993.

Hartman, Saidiya V. *Scenes of Subjection: Terror, Slavery, and Self-Making in Nineteenth-Century America.* Oxford: Oxford University Press, 1997.

Harvey, David. *The Condition of Postmodernity: An Enquiry into the Origins of Social Change.* Cambridge: Blackwell, 1989.

Haug, W. F. *Critique of Commodity Aesthetics: Appearance, Sexuality, and Advertising in Capitalist Society.* Minneapolis: University of Minnesota Press, 1986.

Hedrick, Joan D. *Harriet Beecher Stowe: A Life.* New York: Oxford University Press, 1994.

———. "Parlor Literature: Harriet Beecher Stowe and the Question of 'Great Women Artists.'" *Signs* 17 (1992): 275–303.

Heilbrun, Carolyn. *Reinventing Womanhood.* New York: Norton, 1979.

Helly, Dorothy O., and Susan M. Reverby. *Gendered Domains: Rethinking Public and Private in Women's History.* Ithaca: Cornell University Press, 1992.

Helsinger, Elizabeth K., Robin Lauterbach Sheets, and William Veeder, eds. *The Woman Question. Vol. 2: Social Issues, 1837–1883*. New York: Garland Publishing, 1983.

———. *The Woman Question. Vol. 3: Literary Issues, 1837–1883*. New York: Garland Publishing, 1983.

Hendler, Glenn. "The Limits of Sympathy: Louisa May Alcott and the Sentimental Novel." *American Literary History* 3 (winter 1991): 685–706.

———. "Pandering in the Public Sphere: Masculinity and the Market in Horatio Alger." *American Quarterly* 48.3 (1996): 415–38.

———. "Tom Sawyer's Masculinity." *Arizona Quarterly* 49.4 (winter 1993): 33–59.

Heuving, Jeanne. *Omissions Are Not Accidents: Gender in the Art of Marianne Moore*. Detroit: Wayne State University Press, 1992.

Hewitt, Nancy A., and Suzanne Lebsock, eds. *Visible Women: New Essays on American Activism*. Urbana: University of Illinois Press, 1993.

Hicok, Bethany. "Elizabeth Bishop's 'Queer Birds': Vassar, *Con Spirito*, and the Romance of Female Community." *Contemporary Literature* 40.2 (1999): 286–310.

———. "'Some Realm of Reciprocity': Moore, Bishop, and the Women's College." Ph.D. diss., University of Rochester, 1996.

———. "'To Work Lovingly': Marianne Moore at Bryn Mawr, 1905–1909." *The Journal of Modern Literature* 23.4 (spring/summer 2000): 483–501.

Hite, Molly. Introduction to *Megda*, by Emma Dunham Kelley. 1891. New York: Oxford University Press, 1988. xxvii–xxxvii.

Holbrook, Susan. "Lifting Bellies, Filling Petunias, and Making Meanings through the Trans-Poetic." *American Literature* 71.4 (December 1999): 751–71.

Homans, Margaret. *Women Writers and Poetic Identity: Dorothy Wordsworth, Emily Brontë, and Emily Dickinson*. Princeton: Princeton University Press, 1980.

hooks, bell. "Homeplace: A Site of Resistance." In *Yearning: Race, Gender, and Cultural Politics*. Boston: South End Press, 1990. 41–49.

Hopkins, Pauline E. *Contending Forces: A Romance Illustrative of Negro Life North and South*. 1900. New York: Oxford University Press, 1988.

———. *The Magazine Novels of Pauline Hopkins*. New York: Oxford University Press, 1988.

Horowitz, Helen Lefkowitz. *Alma Mater: Design and Experience in the Women's Colleges from Their Nineteenth-Century Beginnings to the 1930s*. New York: Knopf, 1984.

———. *The Power and Passion of M. Carey Thomas*. New York: Knopf, 1994.

Horwitz, Howard. *By the Law of Nature: Form and Value in Nineteenth-Century America*. New York: Oxford University Press, 1991.

Hotelling, Kirstin. "'The I of Each Is to the I of Each, a Kind of Fretful Speech Which Sets a Limit on Itself': Marianne Moore's Strategic Selfhood." *Modernism/Modernity* 5.1 (1998): 75–96.

Hounshell, David A. *From the American System to Mass Production, 1800–1932: The Development of Manufacturing Technology in the United States.* Baltimore: Johns Hopkins University Press, 1984.

Howard, June. "What Is Sentimentality?" *American Literary History* 11.1 (spring 1999): 63–81.

Howard, Richard. "Marianne Moore and the Monkey Business of Modernism." In *Marianne Moore: The Art of a Modernist,* edited by Joseph Parisi. Ann Arbor: UMI Research Press, 1990. 1–12.

Howe, Julia Ward, ed. *Sex and Education: A Reply to Dr. Clarke's "Sex in Education".* Cambridge, Mass.: Roberts Brothers, 1874.

Hoxie, W. J. *How Girls Can Help Their Country: Handbook for Girl Scouts.* New York: Girl Scouts of America, 1913.

Humphries, Mary Gay. "Women Bachelors in New York." *Scribner's* 18 (1895): 626–36.

———. "Women Bachelors in London." *Scribner's* 19 (1896): 600–11.

Hunter, Jane H. "Inscribing the Self in the Heart of the Family: Diaries and Girlhood in Late-Victorian America." *American Quarterly* 44.1 (March 1992): 51–81.

Hurston, Zora Neale. *Their Eyes Were Watching God.* 1937. New York: Harper and Row, 1990.

Huyssen, Andreas. "Mass Culture as Woman: Modernism's Other." In *Studies in Entertainment: Critical Approaches to Mass Culture,* edited by Tania Modleski. Bloomington: Indiana University Press, 1986. 188–207.

Hyde, Lewis. *The Gift: Imagination and the Erotic Life of Property.* New York: Vintage Books, 1979.

Inness, Sherrie A. "Girl Scouts, Camp Fire Girls, and Wood Craft Girls: The Ideology of The Girl's Scouting Novels, 1910–1935." In *Nancy Drew and Company: Culture, Gender, and Girls' Series,* edited by Sherrie A. Inness. Bowling Green, Ohio: Bowling Green State University Popular Press, 1997. 89–100.

———. *Intimate Communities: Representation and Social Transformation in Women's College Fiction, 1895–1910.* Bowling Green, Ohio: Bowling Green State University Popular Press, 1995.

Irigaray, Luce. *Speculum of the Other Woman.* Translated by Gillian C. Gill. Ithaca: Cornell University Press, 1984.

———. *This Sex Which Is Not One.* Translated by Catherine Porter. Ithaca: Cornell University Press, 1985.

Jacobs, Harriet. *Incidents in the Life of a Slave Girl.* 1861. New York: Harcourt Brace, 1983.

Jameson, Fredric. Classroom lecture, Duke University, fall 1990.

———. "Pleasure: A Political Issue." In *The Ideologies of Theory: Essays 1971–1986. Vol. 2: Syntax of History*. Minneapolis: University of Minnesota Press, 1988. 61–74.

———. *Postmodernism, or, The Cultural Logic of Late Capitalism*. Durham: Duke University Press, 1991.

———. "Reification and Utopia in Mass Culture." *Social Text* 1 (1979): 23–58.

Janeway, Elizabeth. "Meg, Jo, Beth, Amy, and Louisa." *Critical Essays on Louisa May Alcott*, edited by Madeleine B. Stern. Boston: G. K. Hall, 1984. 97–98.

Jarrell, Randall. "On *North and South*." In *Elizabeth Bishop and Her Art*, edited by Lloyd Schwartz and Sybil P. Estes. Ann Arbor: University of Michigan Press, 1979. 180.

Jay, Karla. "The Outsider among the Expatriates: Djuna Barnes's Satire on the Ladies of the *Almanack*." In *Silence and Power: A Reevaluation of Djuna Barnes*, edited by Mary Lynn Broe. 184–93.

Jeal, Tim. *The Boy-Man: The Life of Lord Baden-Powell*. New York: William Morrow, 1990.

Jeffrys, Sheila. *The Spinster and Her Enemies: Feminism and Sexuality, 1880–1930*. London: Pandora Press, 1985.

Johns, Barbara A. "'Love-Cracked': Spinsters as Subversives in 'Anna Malaan,' 'Christmas Jenny,' and 'An Object of Love.'" *Colby Library Quarterly* 23 (March 1987): 4–15.

———. "Some Reflections on the Spinster in New England Literature." In *Regionalism and the Female Imagination: A Collection of Essays*, edited by Emily Toth. New York: Human Sciences Press, 1985. 29–64.

Johnson, Mrs. A. E. *Clarence and Corinne; or, God's Way*. 1890. New York: Oxford University Press, 1988.

———. *The Hazeley Family*. 1894. New York: Oxford University Press, 1988.

Johnson, Deirdre. *Edward Stratemeyer and the Stratemeyer Syndicate*. New York: Twayne, 1993.

———, ed. *Stratemeyer Pseudonyms and Series Books: An Annotated Checklist of Stratemeyer and Stratemeyer Syndicate Publications*. Westport, Conn.: Greenwood Press, 1982.

Johnston, Jill. *Lesbian Nation: The Feminist Solution*. New York: Simon and Schuster, 1973.

Joseph, Miranda. "The Performance of Production and Consumption." *Social Text* 54, 16.1 (spring 1998): 25–61.

Kadlec, David. "Marianne Moore, Immigration, and Eugenics." *Modernism/ Modernity* 1.2 (1994): 21–49.

Kalstone, David. *Becoming a Poet: Elizabeth Bishop with Marianne Moore and Robert Lowell*. Edited by Robert Hemenway. New York: Farrar, Straus and Giroux, Noonday Press, 1989.

Kaplan, Amy. "'Left Alone with America': The Absence of Empire in the Study of American Culture." In *Cultures of United States Imperialism*, edited by Amy Kaplan and Donald E. Pease. Durham: Duke University Press, 1993. 3–21.

Kaplan, Amy, and Donald E. Pease, eds. *Cultures of United States Imperialism*. Durham: Duke University Press, 1993.

Kaplan, Cora. "*The Thorn Birds*: Fiction, Fantasy, Femininity." In *Sea Changes: Essays on Culture and Feminism*. London: Verso Press, 1986. 117–46.

Katz, Jonathan Ned. *Gay/Lesbian Almanac: A New Documentary History*. New York: HarperCollins, 1983.

———. *The Invention of Heterosexuality*. New York: Dutton, 1995.

Keller, Lynn. "'For Inferior Who Is Free?' Liberating the Woman Writer in Marianne Moore's 'Marriage.'" In *Influence and Intertextuality in Literary History*, edited by Jay Clayton and Eric Rothstein. Madison: University of Wisconsin Press, 1991. 219–44.

Kelley, Emma Dunham. *Megda*. 1891. New York: Oxford University Press, 1988.

Kelley (Hawkins), Emma D. *Four Girls at Cottage City*. 1898. New York: Oxford University Press, 1988.

Kelley, Mary. *Private Woman, Public Stage: Domesticity in Nineteenth-Century America*. New York: Oxford University Press, 1984.

———, ed. *Woman's Being, Woman's Place: Female Identity and Vocation in American History*. Boston: G. K. Hall, 1979.

Kellner, Bruce, ed. *A Gertrude Stein Companion: Content with the Example*. New York: Greenwood Press, 1988.

Kellner, Douglas, ed. *Baudrillard: A Critical Reader*. Oxford: Blackwell, 1994.

Kennedy, Elizabeth Lapovsky, and Madeline D. Davis. *Boots of Leather, Slippers of Gold: The History of a Lesbian Community*. New York: Penguin, 1993.

Kensinger, Faye Riter. *Children of the Series and How They Grew; or, A Century of Heroines and Heroes, Romantic, Comic, Moral*. Bowling Green, Ohio: Bowling Green State University Popular Press, 1987.

Kent, Kathryn R. "No Trespassing: Girl Scouting and the Limits of the Counterpublic Sphere." *Women and Performance: A Journal of Feminist Theory* 8.2 (1996): 185–203.

Kerber, Linda K. "Can a Woman Be an Individual? The Limits of Puritan Tradition in the Early Republic." *Texas Studies in Literature and Language* 25 (spring 1983): 165–78.

———. "Separate Spheres, Female Worlds, Woman's Place: The Rhetoric of Women's History." *Journal of American History* 75 (June 1989): 9–39.

———. *Women of the Republic: Intellect and Ideology in Revolutionary America*. New York: Norton, 1980.

Kerber, Linda, Alice Kessler-Harris, and Kathryn Kish Sklar, eds. *U.S. History as*

Women's History: New Feminist Essays. Chapel Hill: University of North Carolina Press, 1995.

Kessler-Harris, Alice. *Out to Work: A History of Wage-Earning Women in America*. New York: Oxford University Press, 1982.

Keyser, Elizabeth Lennox. *Whispers in the Dark: The Fiction of Louisa May Alcott*. Knoxville: University of Tennessee Press, 1993.

Klein, Marcus. *Foreigners: The Making of American Literature, 1900–1940*. Chicago: University of Chicago Press, 1981.

Koestenbaum, Wayne. *The Queen's Throat: Opera, Homosexuality, and the Mystery of Desire*. New York: Vintage Books, 1994.

Koppelman, Susan, ed. *Old Maids: Short Stories by Nineteenth Century U.S. Women Writers*. London: Pandora Press, 1984.

——, ed. *Two Friends and Other Nineteenth-Century Lesbian Stories by American Women Writers*. New York: Meridian Press, 1994.

Kristeva, Julia. "Stabat Mater." In *The Kristeva Reader*. Edited by Toril Moi. Oxford: Basil Blackwell, 1986. 160–86.

——. "Women's Time." In *The Kristeva Reader*. Edited by Toril Moi. Oxford: Basil Blackwell, 1986. 187–213.

Kunzel, Regina G. *Fallen Women, Problem Girls: Unmarried Mothers and the Professionalization of Social Work, 1890–1945*. New Haven: Yale University Press, 1993.

Ladd-Taylor, Molly. *Mother-Work: Women, Child Welfare, and the State, 1890–1930*. Urbana: University of Illinois Press, 1994.

Landes, Joan. *Woman and the Public Sphere in the Age of the French Revolution*. Ithaca: Cornell University Press, 1988.

Langland, Elizabeth. "Female Stories of Experience: Alcott's *Little Women* in Light of *Work*." In *The Voyage In: Fictions of Female Development*, edited by Elizabeth Abel, Marianne Hirsch, and Elizabeth Langland. Hanover, N.H.: University Press of New England, 1983. 112–27.

Lanser, Susan Sniader. "Speaking in Tongues: *Ladies Almanack* and the Discourse of Desire." In *Silence and Power: A Reevaluation of Djuna Barnes*, edited by Mary Lynn Broe. Carbondale: Southern Illinois University Press, 1991. 156–68.

Laplanche, J., and J.-B. Pontalis. *The Language of Psychoanalysis*. Translated by Donald Nicholson-Smith. New York: Norton, 1973.

Larsen, Nella. *Quicksand; and, Passing*. Edited by Deborah E. McDowell. New Brunswick: Rutgers University Press, 1986.

Lasch, Christopher. *Haven in a Heartless World: The Family Betrayed*. New York: Basic Books, 1977.

Lavell, Edith. *The Girl Scout Director*. New York: A. L. Burt, 1925.

——. *The Girl Scouts at Camp*. New York: A. L. Burt, 1922.

——. *The Girl Scouts' Canoe Trip*. New York: A. L. Burt, 1922.

———. *The Girl Scouts' Good Turn.* New York: A. L. Burt, 1922.

———. *The Girl Scouts' Motor Trip.* New York: A. L. Burt, 1924.

———. *The Girl Scouts on the Ranch.* New York: A. L. Burt, 1923.

———. *The Girl Scouts' Rivals.* New York: A. L. Burt, 1922.

Lawrence, D. H. *The Rainbow.* 1915. New York: Penguin Books, 1981.

Leavell, Linda. *Marianne Moore and the Visual Arts: Prismatic Color.* Baton Rouge: Louisiana State University Press, 1995.

Lebsock, Suzanne. *The Free Women of Petersburg: Status and Culture in a Southern Town, 1784–1860.* New York: Norton, 1985.

Lee, Martyn J. *Consumer Culture Reborn: The Cultural Politics of Consumption.* New York: Routledge, 1994.

Levine, Lawrence. *Highbrow/Lowbrow: The Emergence of Cultural Hierarchy in America.* Cambridge: Harvard University Press, 1988.

Leys, Ruth. "The Real Miss Beauchamp: The History and Sexual Politics of the Multiple Personality Concept." In *Feminists Theorize the Political,* edited by Judith Butler and Joan W. Scott. New York: Routledge, 1992. 167–214.

Light, Alison. " 'Returning to Manderley'—Romance Fiction, Female Sexuality, and Class." *Feminist Review* 16 (April 1984): 1–10.

Lister, Anne. *I Know My Own Heart: The Diaries of Anne Lister, 1791–1840.* Edited by Helena Whitbread. New York: New York University Press, 1992.

Liu, Alan. "Local Transcendence: Cultural Criticism, Postmodernism, and the Romanticism of Detail." *Representations* 32 (fall 1990): 75–113.

———. "The Power of Formalism: The New Historicism." *ELH* 56 (winter 1989): 721–71.

Lombardi, Marilyn May, ed. *Elizabeth Bishop: The Geography of Gender.* Charlottesville: University Press of Virginia, 1993.

Lorde, Audre. "The Uses of the Erotic: The Erotic as Power." In *The Lesbian and Gay Studies Reader,* edited by Henry Abelove, Michèle Aina Barzle, and David M. Halperin. New York: Routledge, 1993. 339–43.

MacKay, Anne, ed. *Wolf Girls at Vassar: Gay and Lesbian Experiences, 1930–1990.* New York: Ten Percent Publishing, 1992.

Madison, Charles Allan. *Book Publishing in America.* New York: McGraw Hill, 1966.

Mailloux, Stephen. *Interpretive Conventions: The Reader in the Study of American Fictions.* Ithaca: Cornell University Press, 1982.

———. "The Rhetorical Use and Abuse of Fiction: Eating Books in Late Nineteenth-Century America." *boundary* 2 17.1 (1990): 133–57.

Martin, Biddy. "Lesbian Identity and Autobiographical Difference[s]." In *Life/Lines: Theorizing Women's Autobiography,* edited by Bella Brodzki and Celeste Schenck. Ithaca: Cornell University Press, 1988. 77–103.

Martin, Taffy. *Marianne Moore: Subversive Modernist.* Austin: University of Texas Press, 1986.

Marx, Karl. *Capital*. Volume 1. New York: International Publishers, 1967.

———. *The German Ideology*. In *The Marx-Engels Reader*, edited by Robert C. Tucker. New York: Norton, 1978.

Matthei, Julie A. *An Economic History of Women in America: Women's Work, the Sexual Division of Labor, and the Development of Capitalism*. New York: Schocken Books, 1982.

Matthews, Glenna. *The Rise of Public Woman: Woman's Power and Woman's Place in the United States, 1630–1970*. New York: Oxford University Press, 1992.

McCabe, Susan. *Elizabeth Bishop: Her Poetics of Loss*. University Park: Pennsylvania State University Press, 1994.

McDowell, Deborah. Introduction to *Four Girls at Cottage City*, by Emma D. Kelley (Hawkins). 1898. New York: Oxford University Press, 1988. xxvii–xxxvii.

———. Introduction to *Quicksand; and, Passing*, by Nella Larsen. New Brunswick: Rutgers University Press, 1986. xxiii-xxxi.

McGarry, Molly. "Female Worlds." *Journal of Women's History* 12.3 (2000): 9–12.

McHugh, Kathleen Anne. *American Domesticity: From How-to Manual to Hollywood Melodrama*. New York: Oxford University Press, 1999.

McKinstry, Susan Jaret. "A Ghost of An/Other Chance: The Spinster-Mother in Toni Morrison's *Beloved*." In *Old Maids to Radical Spinsters: Unmarried Women in the Twentieth-Century Novel*, edited by Laura L. Doan. Urbana: University of Illinois Press, 1991. 259–74.

McRobbie, Angela. "Dance as Social Fantasy." In *Gender and Generation*, edited by Angela McRobbie and Mica Nava. London: Macmillan, 1984. 131–61.

Mellow, James R. *Charmed Circle: Gertrude Stein and Company*. New York: Praeger, 1974.

Merish, Lori. *Sentimental Materialism: Gender, Commodity Culture, and Nineteenth-Century American Literature*. Durham: Duke University Press, 2000.

Merrin, Jeredith. *An Enabling Humility: Marianne Moore, Elizabeth Bishop, and the Uses of Tradition*. New Brunswick: Rutgers University Press, 1990.

Meyerowitz, Joanne J. *Women Adrift: Independent Wage Earners in Chicago, 1880–1930*. Chicago: University of Chicago Press, 1988.

Michaels, Walter Benn. *The Gold Standard and the Logic of Naturalism: American Literature at the Turn of the Century*. Baltimore: Johns Hopkins University Press, 1987.

———. *Our America: Nativism, Modernism, and Pluralism*. Durham: Duke University Press, 1995.

Michel, Frann. "All Women Are Not Women All: *Ladies Almanack* and Feminine Writing." In *Silence and Power: A Reevaluation of Djuna Barnes*, edited by Mary Lynn Broe. Carbondale: Southern Illinois University Press, 1991. 170–83.

Miller, Cristanne. *Marianne Moore: Questions of Authority.* Cambridge: Harvard University Press, 1995.

Miller, D. A. *The Novel and the Police.* Berkeley: University of California Press, 1988.

Millier, Brett C. *Elizabeth Bishop: Life and the Memory of It.* Berkeley: University of California Press, 1993.

Mitchell, Sally. *The New Girl: Girls' Culture in England, 1880–1915.* New York: Columbia University Press, 1995.

Mitrano, Mena. "Linguistic Exoticism and Literary Alienation: Gertrude Stein's *Tender Buttons.*" *Modern Language Studies* 28.2 (1998): 87–102.

Moers, Ellen. *Literary Women.* Garden City, N.Y.: Doubleday, 1976.

Molesworth, Charles. *Marianne Moore: A Literary Life.* New York: Atheneum, 1990.

Montague, Susan P. "How Nancy Gets Her Man: An Investigation of Success Models in American Adolescent Pulp Literature." In *The American Dimenson: Cultural Myths and Social Realities,* edited by Susan P. Montague and W. Arens. Sherman Oaks, Calif.: Alfred Publishing, 1981. 77–90.

Montrose, Louis A. "Professing the Renaissance: The Poetics and Politics of Culture." In *The New Historicism,* edited by H. Aram Veeser. New York: Routledge, 1989. 15–36.

Moody, Helen Watterson. "The Unquiet Sex: First Paper—the Woman Collegian." *Scribner's* 22 (1897): 150–56.

Moon, Michael. *Disseminating Whitman: Revision and Corporeality in "Leaves of Grass."* Cambridge: Harvard University Press, 1991.

———. "'The Gentle Boy from the Dangerous Classes': Pederasty, Domesticity, and Capitalism in Horatio Alger." In *The New American Studies: Essays from "Representations,"* edited by Philip Fisher. Berkeley: University of California Press, 1991. 260–83.

Moore, Lisa L. *Dangerous Intimacies: Toward a Sapphic History of the British Novel.* Durham: Duke University Press, 1997.

———. "'Something More Tender Still Than Friendship': Romantic Friendship in Early-Nineteenth-Century England." *Feminist Studies* 18 (fall 1992): 499–520.

Moore, Marianne. *The Complete Poems of Marianne Moore.* New York: Viking, 1967.

———. *Observations.* New York: Dial, 1924.

———. *Selected Letters.* Edited by Bonnie Costello, with Celeste Goodridge and Cristanne Miller. New York: Knopf, 1997.

———. *Selected Poems.* London: Faber and Faber, 1935.

Morrison, Toni. *Beloved.* New York: New American Library, 1987.

Mott, Frank Luther. *Golden Multitudes: The Story of Best Sellers in the United States.* New York: Bowker, 1947.

Mulvey, Laura. "Visual Pleasure and Narrative Cinema." *Screen* 16.3 (autumn 1975): 6–18.

Muñoz, José Esteban. *Disidentifications: Queers of Color and the Performance of Politics.* Minneapolis: University of Minnesota Press, 1999.

Murphy, Ann B. "The Borders of Ethical, Erotic, and Artistic Possibilities in *Little Women*." *Signs: Journal of Women in Culture and Society* 15.3 (1990): 562–85.

Murphy, Marguerite S. "'Familiar Strangers': The Household Words of Gertrude Stein's *Tender Buttons*." *Contemporary Literature* 32.3 (1991): 383–402.

Myerson, Joel, and Daniel Sheahy, eds. *The Journals of Louisa May Alcott.* New York: Little, Brown, 1989.

Nackenoff, Carol. *The Fictional Republic: Horatio Alger and American Political Discourse.* New York: Oxford University Press, 1994.

Nelson, Dana D. "'No Cold or Empty Heart': Polygenesis, Scientific Professionalization, and the Unfinished Business of Male Sentimentalism." *differences: A Journal of Feminist Cultural Studies* 11.3 (1999): 29–56.

Neuman, Shirley. *Gertrude Stein: Autobiography and the Problem of Narration.* Victoria, Canada: E.L.S. Monograph Series, 1979.

Neuman, Shirley, and Ira B. Nadel, eds. *Gertrude Stein and the Making of Literature.* Boston: Northeastern University Press, 1988.

Newcomer, Mabel. *A Century of Higher Education for American Women.* New York: Harper and Row, 1959.

Newth, Rebecca. "'Marriage' by Marianne Moore: An Interview with Patricia Willis." *Arkansas Review: A Journal of Criticism* 3.2 (fall 1994): 193–207.

Newton, Esther. "The Mythic Mannish Lesbian: Radclyffe Hall and the New Woman." In *Hidden from History: Reclaiming the Gay and Lesbian Past,* edited by Martin Duberman, Martha Vicinus, and George Chauncey Jr. New York: Meridian, 1989. 281–93.

Nielsen, Aldon Lynn. *Reading Race: White American Poets and the Racial Discourse in the Twentieth Century.* Athens: University of Georgia Press, 1988.

Noble, Marianne. "An Ecstasy of Apprehension: The Gothic Pleasures of Sentimental Fiction." In *American Gothic: New Interventions in a National Narrative,* edited by Robert K. Martin and Eric Savoy. Iowa City: University of Iowa Press, 1998. 163–82.

Norris, Mary Harriott. *The Golden Age of Vassar.* Poughkeepsie, N.Y.: Vassar College, 1915.

Norton, Mary Beth, and Carol Groneman, eds. *"To Toil the Livelong Day": America's Women at Work, 1780–1980.* Ithaca: Cornell University Press, 1987.

O'Brien, Sharon. "Tomboyism and Adolescent Conflict: Three Nineteenth-Century Case Studies." In *Woman's Being, Woman's Place: Female Identity and Vocation in American History*, edited by Mary Kelley. Boston: G. K. Hall, 1979. 351–72.

O'Connor, Mary. "The Objects of Modernism: Everyday Life in Women's Magazines, Gertrude Stein, and Margaret Watkins." In *American Modernism Across the Arts*, edited by Jay Bochner and Justin D. Edwards. New York: Peter Lang, 1999. 97–123.

Ohmann, Richard. "Where Did Mass Culture Come From? The Case of Magazines." In *Politics of Letters*. Middletown, Conn.: Wesleyan University Press, 1987. 135–51.

Ostriker, Alicia Suskin. *Stealing the Language: The Emergence of Women's Poetry in America*. Boston: Beacon, 1986.

Papashvily, Helen Waite. *All the Happy Endings*. New York: Harper, 1956.

Parker, Andrew. "Ezra Pound and the 'Economy' of Anti-Semitism." In *Postmodernism and Politics*, edited by Jonathan Arac. Minneapolis: University of Minnesota Press, 1986. 70–90.

———. "Unthinking Sex: Marx, Engels, and the Scene of Writing." In *Fear of a Queer Planet: Queer Politics and Social Theory*, edited by Michael Warner. Minneapolis: University of Minnesota Press, 1993. 19–41.

Peiss, Kathy. *Cheap Amusements: Working Women and Leisure in Turn-of-the-Century New York*. Philadelphia: Temple University Press, 1986.

———. "Going Public: Women in Nineteenth-Century Cultural History." *American Literary History* 3 (1991): 817–28.

Pellegrini, Ann. *Performance Anxieties: Staging Psychoanalysis, Staging Race*. New York: Routledge, 1997.

Perloff, Marjorie. *The Poetics of Indeterminacy: Rimbaud to Cage*. Princeton: Princeton University Press, 1981.

Perry, Elizabeth Israels. "From Achievement to Happiness: Girl Scouting in Middle Tennessee, 1910s–1960s." *Journal of Women's History* 5.2 (fall 1993): 75–94.

Pitchford, Nicola. "Unlikely Modernism, Unlikely Postmodernism." *American Literary History* 11.4 (winter 1999): 642–67.

Pondrom, Cyrena. "Marianne Moore and H.D.: Female Community and Poetic Achievement." In *Marianne Moore: Woman and Poet*, edited by Patricia C. Willis. Orono: University of Maine, The National Poetry Foundation, 1990. 371–402.

Pratt, Annis, with Barbara White and Mary Wyer. *Archetypal Patterns in Women's Fiction*. Bloomington: Indiana University Press, 1981.

Prosser, Jay. *Second Skins: The Body Narratives of Transsexuality*. New York: Columbia University Press, 1998.

Radway, Janice. *A Feeling for Books: The Book-of-the-Month Club, Literary Taste, and Middle-Class Desire*. Chapel Hill: University of North Carolina Press, 1997.

———. *Reading the Romance: Women, Patriarchy, and Popular Literature*. Rev. ed. Chapel Hill: University of North Carolina Press, 1993.

Reid, B. L. *Art by Subtraction: A Dissenting Opinion of Gertrude Stein*. Norman: University of Oklahoma Press, 1958.

Rich, Adrienne. "Compulsory Heterosexuality and Lesbian Existence." In *Blood, Bread, and Poetry: Selected Prose, 1979–1985*. New York: Norton, 1986. 23–75.

———. *The Dream of a Common Language*. New York: Norton, 1978.

———. "The Eye of the Outsider: Elizabeth Bishop's *Complete Poems, 1927–1979*." In *Blood, Bread, and Poetry: Selected Prose, 1979–1985*. New York: Norton, 1986. 124–35.

———. "Vesuvius at Home: The Power of Emily Dickinson." In *On Lies, Secrets, and Silence: Selected Prose, 1966–1978*. New York: Norton, 1979. 157–83.

Rigsby, Mary. "'So Like Women!': Louisa May Alcott's *Work* and the Ideology of Relations." In *Redefining the Political Novel: American Women Writers, 1797–1901*, edited by Sharon M. Harris. Knoxville: University of Tennessee Press, 1995. 109–27.

Robbins, Bruce, ed. *The Phantom Public Sphere*. Minneapolis: University of Minnesota Press, 1993.

Roediger, David R. *The Wages of Whiteness: Race and the Making of the American Working Class*. London: Verso, 1992.

Rogers, W. G. *Gertrude Stein Is Gertrude Stein Is Gertrude Stein: Her Life and Work*. New York: Thomas Y. Crowell, 1973.

Rohy, Valerie. *Impossible Women: Lesbian Figures and American Literature*. Ithaca: Cornell University Press, 2000.

Romero, Lora. "Bio-Political Resistance in Domestic Ideology and *Uncle Tom's Cabin*." *American Literary History* 1.4 (winter 1989): 715–34.

———. *Home Fronts: Domesticity and Its Critics in the Antebellum United States*. Durham: Duke University Press, 1997.

———. "Vanishing Americans: Gender, Empire, and New Historicism." In *The Culture of Sentiment: Race, Gender, and Sentimentality in Nineteenth-Century America*, edited by Shirley Samuels. New York: Oxford University Press, 1993. 115–27.

Rosenberg, Rosalind. *Beyond Separate Spheres: Intellectual Roots of Modern Feminism*. New Haven: Yale University Press, 1982.

Rosenfeld, Natania. "Artists and Daughters in Louisa May Alcott's *Diana and Persis*." *New England Quarterly* 64.1 (March 1991): 3–21.

Rosenthal, Michael. *The Character Factory: Baden-Powell and the Origins of the Boy Scout Movement.* New York: Pantheon Books, 1984.

Rothblum, Esther, and Kathleen Brehony, eds. *Boston Marriages: Romantic but Asexual Relationships among Contemporary Lesbians.* Amherst: University of Massachusetts Press, 1993.

Rothschild, Mary Aickin. "To Scout or to Guide? The Girl Scout–Boy Scout Controversy, 1912–1941." *Frontiers* 6.3 (1982): 115–21.

Roy, Lillian Elizabeth. *Girl Scouts in Arizona and New Mexico.* New York: Grosset and Dunlap, 1920.

———. *Girl Scouts in the Redwoods.* New York: Grosset and Dunlap, 1920.

———. *Girl Scouts in the Rockies.* New York: Grosset and Dunlap, 1921.

Rubin, Gayle. "The Traffic in Women: Notes on the 'Political Economy' of Sex." In *Toward an Anthropology of Women,* edited by Rayna R. Reiter. New York: Monthly Review Press, 1975. 157–210.

Ruddick, Lisa. *Reading Gertrude Stein.* Ithaca: Cornell University Press, 1990.

Rupp, Leila J. "'Imagine My Surprise': Women's Relationships in Historical Perspective." *Frontiers* 5 (1981): 61–70.

Russett, Cynthia Eagle. *Sexual Science: The Victorian Construction of Womanhood.* Cambridge: Harvard University Press, 1989.

Ryan, Mary. *Women in Public: Between Banners and Ballots, 1825–1880.* Baltimore: Johns Hopkins University Press, 1990.

Sahli, Nancy. "Smashing: Women's Relationships before the Fall." *Chrysalis* 8 (1979): 18–27.

Samuels, Shirley, ed. *The Culture of Sentiment: Race, Gender, and Sentimentality in Nineteenth-Century America.* New York: Oxford University Press, 1992.

Sanchez-Eppler, Karen. *Touching Liberty: Abolition, Feminism, and the Politics of the Body.* Berkeley: University of California Press, 1993.

Saxton, Martha. *Louisa May.* Boston: Houghton Mifflin, 1977.

Schmitz, Neil. *Of Huck and Alice: Humorous Writing in American Literature.* Minneapolis: University of Minnesota Press, 1983.

Schulte-Sasse, Jochen. "Can the Disempowered Read Mass-Produced Narratives in Their Own Voice?" *Cultural Critique* 10 (fall 1988): 171–99.

Schultz, Jane E. "Embattled Care: Narrative Authority in Louisa May Alcott's *Hospital Sketches.*" *Legacy* 9 (1992): 104–17.

Schultz, Nancy Lusignan. "The Artist's Craftiness: Miss Prissy in *The Minister's Wooing.*" *Studies in American Fiction* 20 (spring 1992): 33–44.

Schulze, Robin G. "Textual Darwinism: Marianne Moore, the Text of Evolution, and the Evolving Text." *Text* 11 (1998): 270–305.

Schwartz, Lloyd. "Annals of Poetry (Elizabeth Bishop and Brazil)." *New Yorker* 67.32 (September 30, 1991): 5–97.

Schwartz, Lloyd, and Sybil P. Estes. *Elizabeth Bishop and Her Art*. Ann Arbor: University of Michigan Press, 1979.

Schweik, Susan. *A Gulf So Deeply Cut: American Women Poets and the Second World War*. Madison: University of Wisconsin Press, 1991.

Scouting for Girls: Official Handbook of the Girl Scouts. New York: Girl Scouts of America, 1920.

Sedgwick, Catharine Maria. "Old Maids." In *Old Maids: Short Stories by Nineteenth-Century U.S. Women Writers,* edited by Susan Koppelman. London: Pandora Press, 1984. 11–26.

Sedgwick, Eve Kosofsky. *Between Men: English Literature and Male Homosocial Desire*. New York: Columbia University Press, 1985.

———. "Epidemics of the Will." In *Tendencies*. Durham: Duke University Press, 1993. 130–42.

———. *Epistemology of the Closet*. Berkeley: University of California Press, 1990.

———. "Jane Austen and the Masturbating Girl." In *Tendencies*. Durham: Duke University Press, 1993. 109–29.

———. "Privilege of Unknowing: Diderot's *The Nun*." In *Tendencies*. Durham: Duke University Press, 1993. 23–51.

———. "Tales of the Avunculate: *The Importance of Being Earnest*." In *Tendencies*. Durham: Duke University Press, 1993. 52–72.

Sedgwick, Eve Kosofsky, and Michael Moon. "Divinity." In *Tendencies*. Durham: Duke University Press, 1993. 215–51.

Segal, Elizabeth. "'As the Twig is Bent . . .': Gender and Childhood Reading." In *Gender and Reading: Essays on Readers, Texts, and Contexts,* edited by Elizabeth A. Flynn and Patrocinio P. Schweikart. Baltimore: Johns Hopkins University Press, 1986. 165–86.

Seltzer, Mark. *Bodies and Machines*. New York: Routledge, 1992.

———. *Serial Killers: Death and Life in America's Wound Culture*. New York: Routledge, 1998.

Sheahy, Daniel, Madeleine B. Stern, and Joel Myerson, eds. *Louisa May Alcott: Selected Fiction*. Boston: Little, Brown, 1990.

Shell, Marc. *The Economy of Literature*. Baltimore: Johns Hopkins University Press, 1978.

———. *Money, Language, and Thought: Literary and Philosophical Economics from the Medieval to the Modern Era*. Berkeley: University of California Press, 1982.

Showalter, Elaine, ed. Introduction to *Alternative Alcott*, by Louisa May Alcott. New Brunswick: Rutgers University Press, 1988. ix-xiii.

———. *Sister's Choice: Tradition and Change in American Women's Writing*. Oxford: Clarendon Press, 1991.

Sicherman, Barbara. "Sense and Sensibility: A Case Study of Women's Reading in Late-Victorian America." In *Reading in America: Literature and Social History,* edited by Cathy N. Davidson. Baltimore: Johns Hopkins University Press, 1989. 201–25.

———. "Reading and Ambition: M. Carey Thomas and Female Heroism." *American Quarterly* 45.1 (March 1993): 73–103.

———. "Reading *Little Women:* The Many Lives of a Text." In *U.S. History as Women's History: New Feminist Essays,* edited by Linda K. Kerber, Alice Kessler-Harris, and Kathryn Kish Sklar. Chapel Hill: University of North Carolina Press, 1995. 245–66.

Sielke, Sabine. *Fashioning the Female Subject: The Intertextual Networking of Dickinson, Moore, and Rich.* Ann Arbor: University of Michigan Press, 1997.

Sklar, Kathryn Kish. "Hull House in the 1890s: A Community of Women Reformers." *Signs* 10 (summer 1985): 658–77.

Slatin, John M. *The Savage's Romance: The Poetry of Marianne Moore.* University Park: Pennsylvania State University Press, 1986.

Smith-Rosenberg, Carroll. *Disorderly Conduct: Visions of Gender in Victorian America.* New York: Oxford University Press, 1985.

Sollors, Werner, ed. *The Invention of Ethnicity.* New York: Oxford University Press, 1989.

Solomon, Barbara Miller. *In the Company of Educated Women.* New Haven: Yale University Press, 1985.

Somerville, Siobhan. *Queering the Color Line: Race and the Invention of Homosexuality in American Culture.* Durham: Duke University Press, 2000.

Souhami, Diane. *Gertrude and Alice.* London: Pandora Press, 1991.

Spillers, Hortense. "Changing the Letter: The Yokes, the Jokes of Discourse, or, Mrs. Stowe, Mr. Reed." In *Slavery and the Literary Imagination,* edited by Deborah McDowell and Arnold Rampersad. Baltimore: Johns Hopkins University Press, 1989. 25–61.

———. "Interstices: A Small Drama of Words." In *Pleasure and Danger: Exploring Female Sexuality,* edited by Carole S. Vance. London: Pandora Press, 1984. 73–100.

———. "Mama's Baby, Papa's Maybe: An American Grammar Book." *Diacritics* 17 (summer 1987): 65–81.

Sprigge, Elizabeth. *Gertrude Stein: Her Life and Work.* New York: Harper and Brothers, 1957.

Stallybrass, Peter. "Marx and Heterogeneity: Thinking the Lumpenproletariat." *Representations* 31 (summer 1990): 69–95.

Stansell, Christine. *City of Women: Sex and Class in New York, 1789–1860.* Urbana: University of Illinois Press, 1987.

Stapleton, Laurence. *Marianne Moore: The Poet's Advance.* Princeton: Princeton University Press, 1978.

Steedman, Carolyn. *Landscape for a Good Woman.* New Brunswick: Rutgers University Press, 1987.

Steedman, Carolyn, Cathy Urwin, and Valerie Walkerdine, eds. *Language, Gender, and Childhood.* London: Routledge and Kegan Paul, 1985.

Stein, Gertrude. *Fernhurst, Q.E.D., and Other Early Writings.* New York: Liveright, 1971.

———. *The Geographical History of the United States, or, The Relation of Human Nature to the Human Mind.* New York: Random House, 1936.

———. *Lectures in America.* Boston: Beacon, 1985.

———. *Tender Buttons: Objects Food Rooms.* 1914. Los Angeles: Sun and Moon Press, 1994.

Stein, Robert. "Girls' Cooperative Boarding Homes." *Arena* (1898): 397–417.

Steinman, Lisa. *Made in America: Science, Technology, and American Modernist Poets.* New Haven: Yale University Press, 1987.

Stephens, Ann. *High Life in New York. By Jonathan Slick, Esq., of Weathersfield, Connecticut.* New York: Edward Stephens, 1843.

Stern, Madeleine B., ed. *Critical Essays on Louisa May Alcott.* Boston: G. K. Hall, 1984.

———. *Louisa May Alcott.* Norman: University of Oklahoma Press, 1950.

Stevenson, Louise L. *The Victorian Homefront: American Thought and Culture, 1860–1880.* New York: Twayne, 1991.

Stewart, Susan. *Nonsense: Aspects of Intertextuality in Folklore and Literature.* Baltimore: Johns Hopkins University Press, 1978.

Stimpson, Catharine. Afterword to *Silence and Power: A Reevaluation of Djuna Barnes,* edited by Mary Lynn Broe. Carbondale: Southern Illinois University Press, 1991. 370–73.

———. "Gertrice/Altrude: Stein, Toklas, and the Paradox of the Happy Marriage." In *Mothering the Mind: Twelve Studies of Writers and their Silent Partners,* edited by Ruth Perry and Martine Watson Brownley. New York: Holmes and Meier, 1984. 123–39.

———. "Gertrude Stein and the Lesbian Lie." In *American Women's Autobiography: Fea(s)ts of Memory,* edited by Margo Culley. Madison: University of Wisconsin Press, 1992. 152–66.

———. "Gertrude Stein and the Transposition of Gender." In *The Poetics of Gender,* edited by Nancy K. Miller. New York: Columbia University Press, 1986. 1–18.

———. "Reading for Love: Canons, Paracanons, and Whistling Jo March." *New Literary History* 21 (1990): 957–76.

Stowe, Harriet Beecher [Christopher Crowfield, pseud.]. *House and Home Papers.* Boston: Fields and Osgood, 1864.

———. *Oldtown Folks.* 1869. New Brunswick: Rutgers University Press, 1987.

———. *Uncle Tom's Cabin.* 1851. New York: Norton, 1994.

―――. *The Writings of Harriet Beecher Stowe.* Vol. 14. Boston: Houghton, Mifflin and Co., New York: The Riverside Press, 1896.

Strickland, Charles E. "Juliette Low, the Girl Scouts, and the Role of American Women." In *Woman's Being, Woman's Place: Female Identity and Vocation in American History,* edited by Mary Kelley. Boston: G. K. Hall, 1979. 252–64.

―――. *Victorian Domesticity: Families in the Life and Art of Louisa May Alcott.* Tuscaloosa: University of Alabama Press, 1985.

Suleri, Sara. *The Rhetoric of English India.* Chicago: University of Chicago Press, 1992.

Sundquist, Eric, ed. *New Essays on "Uncle Tom's Cabin."* Cambridge: Cambridge University Press, 1986.

Sutherland, Donald. *Gertrude Stein: A Biography of Her Work.* New Haven: Yale University Press, 1951.

Tate, Claudia. "Allegories of Black Female Desire; or, Rereading Nineteenth-Century Sentimental Narratives of Black Female Authority." In *Changing Our Own Words: Essays on Criticism, Theory, and Writing by Black Women,* edited by Cheryl A. Wall. New Brunswick: Rutgers University Press, 1989. 98–126.

―――. *Domestic Allegories of Political Desire: The Black Heroine's Text at the Turn of the Century.* New York: Oxford University Press, 1992.

―――. *Psychoanalysis and Black Novels: Desire and the Protocols of Race.* New York: Oxford University Press, 1998.

Tebbel, John William. *Between Covers: The Rise and Transformation of Book Publishing in America.* New York: Oxford University Press, 1987.

―――. *A History of Book Publishing in the United States.* New York: Bowker, 1972.

Tedesco, Laureen. "Making a Girl into a Scout: Americanizing Scouting for Girls." In *Delinquents and Debutantes: Twentieth-Century American Girls' Cultures,* edited by Sherrie A. Inness. New York: New York University Press, 1998. 19–39.

Terry, Jennifer. "Theorizing Deviant Historiography." *differences: A Journal of Feminist Cultural Studies* 3 (1991): 55–74.

Toklas, Alice B. *The Alice B. Toklas Cookbook.* 1954. Garden City, N.Y.: Anchor Books, 1960.

―――. *What Is Remembered.* San Francisco: North Point Press, 1985.

Tompkins, Jane. Afterword to *The Wide, Wide World,* by Susan Warner. 1850. New York: The Feminist Press, 1987. 584–608.

―――. *Sensational Designs: The Cultural Work of American Fiction, 1790–1860.* New York: Oxford University Press, 1985.

Toth, Emily, ed. *Regionalism and the Female Imagination: A Collection of Essays.* New York: Human Sciences Press, 1985.

Trachtenberg, Alan. *The Incorporation of America.* New York: Hill and Wang, 1982.

Traub, Valerie. "The (In)Significance of 'Lesbian' Desire in Early Modern England." In *Queering the Renaissance,* edited by Jonathan Goldberg. Durham: Duke University Press, 1993. 62–83.

Turner, Kay. *Baby Precious Always Shines: Selected Love Notes between Gertrude Stein and Alice B. Toklas.* New York: St. Martin's Press, 1999.

Van Dusen, Wanda. "Portrait of a National Fetish: Gertrude Stein's 'Introduction to the Speeches of Maréchal Pétain." *Modernism/Modernity* 3.3 (1996): 69–92.

Van Why, Joseph S. Introduction to *The American Woman's Home,* by Catharine Beecher and Harriet Beecher Stowe. 1869. Hartford: The Stowe-Day Foundation, 1991. n.p.

Veeser, H. Aram, ed. *The New Historicism.* New York: Routledge, 1989.

Vendler, Helen. "Elizabeth Bishop: Domestication, Domesticity, and the Otherworldly." In *Part of Nature, Part of Us.* Cambridge: Harvard University Press, 1980. 97–220.

Vicinus, Martha. *Independent Women: Work and Community for Single Women, 1850–1920.* Chicago: University of Chicago Press, 1985.

———. "'They Wonder to Which Sex I Belong': The Historical Roots of the Modern Lesbian Identity." *Feminist Studies* 18.3 (1992): 467–97.

———. "What Makes a Heroine? Nineteenth-Century Girls' Biographies." *Genre* 20 (summer 1987): 171–88.

Vincent, John. *Queer Lyrics: Difficulty and Closure in American Poetry.* New York: Palgrave, forthcoming.

Wagner-Martin, Linda. *"Favored Strangers": Gertrude Stein and Her Family.* New Brunswick: Rutgers University Press, 1995.

Walker, Jayne L. *The Making of a Modernist: Gertrude Stein from "Three Lives" to "Tender Buttons."* Amherst: University of Massachusetts Press, 1976.

Wallace, James D. "Where the Absent Father Went: Alcott's *Work.*" In *Refiguring the Father: New Feminist Readings of Patriarchy,* edited by Patricia Yaeger and Beth Kowaleski-Wallace. Carbondale: Southern Illinois University Press, 1989. 259–74.

Wardley, Lynn. "Bachelors in Paradise: The State of a Theme." In *The Return of Thematic Criticism,* edited by Werner Sollors. Cambridge: Harvard University Press, 1993. 217–41.

Ware, Vron. *Beyond the Pale: White Women, Racism and History.* London: Verso, 1992.

Warner, Michael, ed. *Fear of a Queer Planet: Queer Politics and Social Theory.* Minneapolis: University of Minnesota Press, 1993.

———. "Homo-Narcissism; or, Heterosexuality." In *Engendering Men: The*

Question of Male Feminist Criticism, edited by Joseph A. Boone and Michael Cadden. New York: Routledge, 1990. 190–206.

———. *The Letters of the Repubic: Publication and the Public Sphere in Eighteenth-Century America.* Cambridge: Harvard University Press, 1990.

———. "The Mass Public and the Mass Subject." In *The Phantom Public Sphere,* edited by Bruce Robbins. Minneapolis: University of Minnesota Press, 1993. 234–56.

Warner, Susan. *The Wide, Wide World.* 1850. New York: Feminist Press, 1987.

Watkins, John Elfreth. Introduction to *How to Win and Hold a Husband,* by Dorothy Dix. 1939. New York: Arno Press, 1974. i-xv.

Welter, Barbara, "The Cult of True Womanhood: 1820–1860." *American Quarterly* 18 (1966): 151–74.

———. *Dimity Conventions: The American Woman in the Nineteenth Century.* Columbus: Ohio University Press, 1976.

West, Elliott, and Paula Petrik, eds. *Small Worlds: Children and Adolescents in America, 1850–1950.* Lawrence: University Press of Kansas, 1992.

Weston, Kath. "Do Clothes Make the Woman? Gender, Performance Theory, and Lesbian Eroticism." *Genders* 17 (fall 1993): 1–21.

Wexler, Laura. *Tender Violence: Domestic Visions in an Age of U.S. Imperialism.* Chapel Hill: University of North Carolina Press, 2000.

Wiegman, Robyn. *American Anatomies: Theorizing Race and Gender.* Durham: Duke University Press, 1995.

Willis, Patricia C. *Marianne Moore: Vision into Verse.* Philadelphia: Rosenbach Museum and Library, 1987.

———. "The Owl and the Lantern: Marianne Moore at Bryn Mawr." *Poesis* 6.3–4 (1985): 84–97.

———. "The Road to Paradise: First Notes on Marianne Moore's 'An Octopus.'" *Twentieth-Century Literature* 30.2–3 (summer/fall 1984): 242–66.

Wilson, Christopher. *The Labor of Words: Literary Professionalism in the Progressive Era.* Athens: University of Georgia Press, 1985.

Wilson, Ellen. *They Named Me Gertrude Stein.* New York: Farrar, Straus and Giroux, 1973.

Wilson, Harriet. *Our Nig; or, Sketches from the Life of a Free Black.* New York: Vintage, 1983.

Wishy, Bernard. *The Child and the Republic: The Dawn of Modern American Child Nurture.* Philadelphia: University of Pennsylvania Press, 1968.

Wood, Mary E. "'With Ready Eye': Margaret Fuller and Lesbianism in Nineteenth-Century American Culture." *American Literature* 65.1 (March 1993): 1–18.

Woody, Thomas. *A History of Women's Education in the United States.* New York: Science Press, 1929.

Yellin, Jean Fagan. "From Success to Experience: Louisa May Alcott's *Work*." *The Massachusetts Review* (fall 1980): 527–39.

Young, Elizabeth. *Disarming the Nation: Women's Writing and the American Civil War*. Chicago: University of Chicago Press, 1999.

Zboray, Ronald. "Antebellum Reading and the Ironies of Technological Innovation." In *Reading in America: Literature and Social History*, edited by Cathy N. Davidson. Baltimore: Johns Hopkins University Press, 1989. 180–200.

Zehr, Janet S. "The Response of Nineteenth-Century Audiences to Louisa May Alcott's Fiction." *American Transcendental Quarterly* 1.4 (December 1987): 323–42.

Zwinger, Linda. *Daughters, Fathers, and the Novel: The Sentimental Romance of Heterosexuality*. Madison: University of Wisconsin Press, 1991.

INDEX

‹✿›

163–65, 235–37. *See also* Capitalism

Contending Forces, 103, 270 n.150

Costello, Bonnie, 211, 217, 289 n.6, 304 n.8

Counterpublic, 44; definition of, 15–16; and semipublic/semiprivate space, 15–16

Country of the Pointed Firs, The, 23

Coverture laws, 251 n.14

Crane, Hart, 174, 233

Crane, Louise, 202, 229–32

Damon, Maria, 152, 282 n.45, 286 n.75

Davidson, Cathy, 128, 250 n.11

Davis, Pheobe Stein, 286 n.75

de Certeau, Michel, 164

de Lauretis, Teresa, 9, 172, 245 n.33, 277 n.77, 291 n.13

Derrida, Jacques, 285 n.67

Desire: and identification, 7–12, 44–46, 49, 51, 95–96, 103–4, 137, 238–39; in oedipal model, 7–9; queer theories of, 9–11; and semipublic/semiprivate space, 15. *See also* Identification; Identificatory erotics

Dickie, Margaret, 279 n.12

Diehl, Joanne Feit, 221, 229, 289 n.6, 293 n.28, 294 n.34, 296 n.47, 304 nn.5, 15, 306 n.18

Diggs, Marylynne, 3

Disciplinary intimacy: Brodhead's theories of, 2, 5, 7, 12, 19–20, 35, 45; critique of, in Marianne Moore's poetry, 230–31; as cultural imperialism, 17, 85–87, 99–100; feminist interpretations of, 45–46; the Girl Scouts and, 17, 113–25; and ideologies of individualism, 46–47; in

Little Women, 42–53; in *Megda,* 17, 47, 91–104, 269 n.135; New Historicist theories of, 11–12; in *Oldtown Folks,* 39–41; psychoanalysis and, 7–12; and race, 17, 47, 85–86, 88, 91–104; reading as form of, 47, 75–88, 112–23; self-making and, 46–47; slavery and, 20; in *Uncle Tom's Cabin,* 19–20, 47, 86–87; in *The Wide, Wide World,* 12–14; in *Work,* 62–65, 120. *See also* Identificatory erotics

Disidentification, theories of, 100–01, 206, 238. *See also* Identification

Dix, Dorothy, 199–201

Doan, Laura, 217 n.5, 272 n.20

Domestic ideology: the cult of true womanhood and, 48; the Girl Scouts and, 105–6, 115–16, 125; in *Ladies Almanack,* 131; in *Little Women,* 1, 4, 43–52, 62–65; Marianne Moore and, 196–201; Mary Moore and, 196–98; in *Megda,* 89–93, 98–99, 102–4; in *Tender Buttons,* 141, 143, 144, 147–50, 159–60, 163–65; and theories of lesbian identity, 197–201; role of the mother in, 1, 5–7, 13–14, 26–27, 29–34, 36–37, 43–52, 62–65; view of the market, 29–32, 36. *See also* Domesticity

Domesticity: female-female forms of, 62–65, 83–85, 97–98, 188–201; male-male forms of, 62. *See also* Domestic ideology

du Maurier, Daphne, 81

duCille, Ann, 88–89, 103, 270 n.152

Duggan, Lisa, 1, 243 n.19, 260 n.32, 272 n.20

Dworkin, Andrea, 82–83

Bishop's relationship as example of, 17–18, 167–209, 227–32; mother-daughter relationships as model of, 169–78

Lorde, Audre, 100

Love that dare not speak its name, the, 168

Low, Juliette Gordon, 108, 110, 131

Lyon, Mary, 50

Machines: female subject-formation and, 28, 30, 32, 131, 222–23; queer bodies and, 28, 129–131, 150–51

Mailloux, Stephen, 259 n.22

Mapplethorpe, Robert, 82

Marriage: in *Diana and Persis,* 68–70; in girls' series novels, 124–25; in *Little Women,* 52, 54–56, 80, 124; in *Megda,* 88–91, 97–98, 102–3; racial differences in approaches toward, 21–22, 88–90, 102–3; significance of, for African Americans, 21–22, 88–90, 102–3, 249 n.4

Marx, Karl: *The German Ideology,* 154

Marxism, views of production/reproduction in, 14–15, 153–55, 163–65, 235–36

Masculinity, female: in *Little Women,* 52, 54–59; in *Oldtown Folks,* 37–38; queer theories, 294 n.39

Mass production, and ideologies of (queer) subject-formation, 30, 107, 109–110, 117, 126, 129–32, 235–36

Masturbation: and crying in *The Wide, Wide World,* 13; prohibitions against, in Boy Scout Handbook, 121–22; prohibitions against, in

Girl Scout Handbook, 121–22; reading and, 76; and work in *Oldtown Folks,* 34–35

Matthei, Julie A., 252 n.24

McAlmon, Robert, 212

McCabe, Susan, 293 n.29, 30, 310 n.55

McCarthy, Mary, 202

McCullough, Colleen, 80–81

Meigs, Mary, 182–83

Merish, Lori, 244 n.24

Merrin, Jeredith, 289 n.6

Mighty Fortress Is Our God, A, 231

Miller, Cristanne, 186, 290 n.9, 294 nn.32, 37, 298 nn.62, 64, 306 n.25

Mimetic reversibility, 113, 122–23, 125, 210. *See also* Imitation

Mitrano, Mena, 285 n.69

Modernization: African Americans and, 142–43; lesbian identity and, 16–17, 41–42, 129–32, 142–65, 236; women and, 28, 142–43, 236. *See also* Capitalism

Molesworth, Charles, 210, 292 n.19, 294 n.37

Moon, Michael, 12, 62

Moore, John Warner, 184–85, 210

Moore, Lisa, 2, 4, 242 n.8

Moore, Marianne: attitude of, toward male homosexuality, 173–75, 292 n.19; attitude of, toward marriage, 181–82; and Auden, 174–75, 292 n.19; *The Cock,* 195–98; and Hart Crane, 174, 233; and Louise Crane, 202, 229–32; and domestic ideology, 196–201; *Efforts of Affection,* 203; gender identity of, 179–81, 186–89, 211–24, 294 n.37; and H.D. and Bryher, 184, 212–15, 292 n.20; *In the Days of*

Moore, Marianne (*continued*)
  Prismatic Color, 217; and Peggy
  James, 183–84, 296 n.51; *Letters,*
  183–185, 195, 214, 296 n.51, 299
  n.67; *Marriage,* 181–82, 210–11;
  To Military Progress, 195; and
  John Warner Moore, 184–85; and
  Mary Moore, 170, 184–89, 195–
  201, 232; motherhood in poetry of,
  227–32; nationalism and, 181,
  209, 222–24; *Notebooks,* 185; *An
  Octopus,* 14, 207, 209–224, 229;
  The Paper Nautilus, 207, 210,
  227–33; role of art in, 198–99,
  211–24, 227–32; sexual identity
  of, 183–89, 211–24, 234, 294
  n.37, 296–97 n.51, 298 n.64, 299
  n.26; significance of clothing to,
  179–81, 186–87, 205–6, 223–24;
  single women and, 212–23; as
  spinster figure, 181, 212–23, 294
  n.37; *The Steeple-Jack,* 198–99;
  and Whitman, 173–75, 212, 233.
  See also Moore, Marianne, and
  Elizabeth Bishop
Moore, Marianne, and Elizabeth
  Bishop: accounts of first meeting,
  178–80; feminist interpretations
  of, 169–78; identificatory erotics
  between, 169–207, 227–34; importance of the unspoken to,
  174–75; oedipal model of mother/
  daughter relationship as applied
  to, 169–78, 227–34; relationship of, as example of literary influence, 17–18, 167–209, 227–
  32; as represented in *Exchanging
  Hats,* 201–06; *Roosters* incident,
  189–201, 229, 233; significance
  of gift-giving to, 228–29. *See
  also* Bishop, Elizabeth; Moore,
  Marianne

Moore, Mary: and domestic ideology,
  196–98; and John Warner Moore,
  184–85; and Marianne Moore,
  170, 184–89, 195–201, 232; and
  Norcross, 186, 298–99 n.65; role
  in *Roosters* incident, 195–201
Mother/daughter relationships: in
  The American Woman's Home,
  26–27, 29; attitudes toward, in the
  Girl Scouts, 112, 116, 120–23; as
  imitated in schools, 50–51; in
  Little Women, 1, 4, 43–45, 47–52,
  57–59, 71; oedipal model of, 7–8,
  169–78, 227–34, 262 n.44; and
  theories of literary influence, 17–
  18, 169–78; in work of Smith-
  Rosenberg, 5. *See also* Mothering
Mothering: in domestic ideology, 1,
  5–7, 13–14, 26–27, 29–34, 36–
  37, 43–52, 62–65; in *Oldtown
  Folks,* 25–42; professionalization
  of, 26–27, 131; as queer practice,
  1, 3–5, 13–14, 57–59, 129–31,
  227–34; as sexual identity, 6. *See
  also* Mother/daughter relationships
Mt. Holyoke College, 50
Mt. Rainier National Park, 210–11
Mulvey, Laura, 80
Muñoz, José, 100–01, 134, 136–37,
  238
Murphy, Ann, 49, 262 n.44

National parks, establishment of,
  219–20
Neruda, Pablo, 187
New Historicism, 11–12, 102
New Woman, 108, 111, 186, 255
  n.47
Norcross, Mary, 186, 298–99 n 65

O'Brien, Sharon, 260 n.32
Ohmann, Richard, 146–47

Kathryn R. Kent is Assistant
Professor of English at Williams College.

⧉

Library of Congress Cataloging-in-Publication Data
Kent, Kathryn R.
Making girls into women : American women's writing and
the rise of lesbian identity / Kathryn R. Kent.
p. cm. — (Series Q)
Includes bibliographical references and index.
ISBN 0-8223-3030-X (alk. paper)
ISBN 0-8223-3016-4 (pbk. : alk. paper)
1. American literature—20th century—History and criticism.
2. Lesbians in literature. 3. Alcott, Louisa May, 1832–1888—Views on
sexual orientation. 4. Stein, Gertrude, 1874–1946—Views on sexual
orientation. 5. Moore, Marianne, 1887–1972—Views on sexual orientation. 6. Bishop, Elizabeth, 1911–1979—Views on sexual orientation.
7. American literature—Women authors—History and criticism.
8. Lesbians' writings, American—History and criticism.
9. Homosexuality and literature—United States.
10. Women and literature—United States.
11. Sexual orientation in literature.
12. Women in literature.
13. Girls in literature.
I. Title. II. Series.
PS228.L47 K46 2002
813'.50935206643—dc21 2002008828